KILLING FOR THE REPUBLIC

Black Sea

Mutina
Sentinum
Philippi
Pydna
New Carthage

Mediterranean
Sea

0   300 Miles

0   300 Kilometers

Italy in the
First Millennium

Patavium
Placentia Cremona Po
Trebia
Mutina
Rubicon →
Metaurus →
Sentinum

Trasimene →
Ilva
Clusium
Tarquinii Nepet
Caere Veii
Rome Praeneste
Ostia Tusculum
Velitrai
Antium Satricum
Circeii Tarracina
Cumae

Tiber

Ausculum

Adriatic
Sea

Corfinium

Arpinum
Bovianum
Asculum
Beneventum/Maleventum
Capua Venusia
Pompeii
Paestum

Cannae

Brundisium
Tarentum

Corsica

Sardinia

Neapolis

Carales

Tyrrhenian
Sea

Thurii

Croton

Ionian
Sea

0   80 Miles

0   80 Kilometers

Locri
Rhegium

Sicily

AFRICA

Killing for the Republic

CITIZEN-SOLDIERS AND THE ROMAN WAY OF WAR

Steele Brand

Johns Hopkins University Press BALTIMORE

© 2019 Johns Hopkins University Press
All rights reserved. Published 2019
Printed in the United States of America on acid-free paper

2 4 6 8 9 7 5 3 1

Johns Hopkins University Press
2715 North Charles Street
Baltimore, Maryland 21218-4363
www.press.jhu.edu

Library of Congress Cataloging-in-Publication Data

Names: Brand, Steele, author.
Title: Killing for the republic : citizen-soldiers and the Roman
way of war / Steele Brand.
Description: Baltimore : Johns Hopkins University Press, 2019. |
Includes bibliographical references and index.
Identifiers: LCCN 2018048626 | ISBN 9781421429861 (hardcover :
alk. paper) | ISBN 1421429861 (hardcover : alk. paper) |
ISBN 9781421429878 (electronic) | ISBN 142142987X (electronic)
Subjects: LCSH: Rome—Army. | Rome—History, Military. |
Military art and science—Rome.
Classification: LCC U35 .B69 2019 | DDC 355.00937—dc23
LC record available at https://lccn.loc.gov/2018048626

A catalog record for this book is available from the British Library.

Maps and diagrams courtesy of Lucidity Information Design, LLC.

*Special discounts are available for bulk purchases of this book. For more
information, please contact Special Sales at 410-516-6936 or
specialsales@press.jhu.edu.*

Johns Hopkins University Press uses environmentally friendly book
materials, including recycled text paper that is composed of at least
30 percent post-consumer waste, whenever possible.

To Will, for giving it a chance
To Matt, for believing in it
To Megan, for putting up with it

Contents

Why Care about Long-Dead Fighting Farmers?

In 146 BC, armies of the Roman Republic concluded their 118-year struggle for the western Mediterranean when they breached the walls of their inveterate foe Carthage. Roman troops slaughtered many of the citizens in brutal street fighting, enslaved those that remained, and leveled the city. The Roman commander Scipio Aemilianus watched Carthage as it was being destroyed and pondered its seven-hundred-year existence. Overcome with the magnitude of the moment, he wept. Scipio then turned to his friend, the historian Polybius, and remarked, "A glorious moment, Polybius; but I have a dread foreboding that some day the same doom will be pronounced on my own country" (Polybius, 38.21; Appian, *Punica*, 132).[1] Later that year across the Mediterranean near Corinth, another Roman army defeated the Achaean League. In the preceding half a century, Rome had repeatedly humiliated Alexander's successor kingdoms in Macedonia and Syria, and this battle terminated what freedom remained for those Greek states caught in the middle. When the Romans entered Corinth, they enslaved its population and plundered its treasures. Uncouth soldiers supposedly played games atop famous works of art (Polybius, 39.2). In this fateful year, Rome became the master of the Mediterranean world. Even more remarkable was that they had done so with citizen-soldiers. How did such a thing happen? What had made Rome so powerful? And, if Scipio was right about the rise and fall of republics, does this have any meaning today?

This book answers these questions by describing how Roman farmers were transformed into ambitious killers. Like many expansionist states throughout history, Rome instilled something violent and vicious in its soldiers, making them more effective than their opponents. But unlike the Assyrians, Persians, Macedonians, and other imperial peoples of history, the Romans did so with part-timers. They perfected civic militarism in a way no other civilization ever has.

The Roman Republic was born in a chaotic world where competing city-states, kingdoms, and empires sought to dominate or annihilate their neighbors. By the end of the fourth century BC it had outstripped its neighboring Italian city-states and leagues by creating the best constitution with the deadliest citizen-soldiers. In the third century, Rome defeated the multitalented mercenaries of monarchic adventurers like Pyrrhus and commercial republics like Carthage. In the second century, Rome looked east and distinguished itself from the Hellenistic kingdoms that flourished in the wake of Alexander's death. In the Roman mind these monarchies had done away with the republicanism of city-states such as Athens and Sparta, and the Macedonian war machine now threatened liberty and justice in the West. Rome shocked the Mediterranean world by defeating the heirs of Alexander one by one and then taking over their domains. This is the story of how they did it and why it still matters.

Rome's capacity for winning wars in this struggle to survive is well known, but the legacy of how it won its wars through republican virtues is disappearing. Today, intellectuals often describe the Roman Republic as an undemocratic, militaristic precursor to the more important empire that would follow. Postmodernists decry the colonialism, imperialism, and patriarchy of ancient Rome. And younger generations often sympathize with the titanic personalities that orchestrated the republic's collapse; characters like Pompey, Caesar, and Antony are often seen as victims of their circumstances who were just trying to get ahead in an amoral world. Each of these critiques has a point, but they undervalue the circumstances of Rome's uniqueness as the finest ancient republic. They also miss the singular genius of Rome's republican spirit, which earned it the right to dominate the Mediterranean in the last centuries before Christ. This same spirit eventually inspired the rebirth of republicanism for future generations in places like Florence, Venice, Britain, and the United States.

With the limited sources remaining, we do not know all the qualities of Rome's neighbors, but we do know what ancient authors said made Rome distinctive. Historians like Polybius, Livy, and Dionysius argue that the Romans created the best republican system in the most capable federation of the ancient world. Roman political ingenuity was matched by capable military institutions, which marshaled vast numbers of men, absorbed defeats in the field, adapted technologies from neighbors, and allowed the best commanders and troops to achieve victory in the long run. Yet Roman institutions were imperfect and would have achieved little had they not rested on a resilient culture that inculcated civic virtues like honor, piety, loyalty to patrons and family, hard work, and the rugged independence inherent in small-holding farmers. Rome survived by unifying disparate political elements under constitutional orders that relied on average citizens with agricultural lifestyles. Farming may have been ubiquitous in the ancient world but politically empowered farmer-citizens were not, and militarily proficient farmer-citizen-soldiers were rarer still. These citizens took ownership of their republic to such lengths that they heartily sacrificed themselves and their enemies on the altar of republican glory. This was the Roman way of war.

The history of Rome's citizen-soldiers has implications for the United States in the twenty-first century. Rome was maintained by different values and defended by different strengths than modern republics. The Roman republican embodied physical interaction with the soil, resistance to tyranny, and personal sacrifice for the public good. This civic mode of being is increasingly foreign today. Roman citizens were more aware of the land and the climate. They were more self-reliant and leery of concentrated power. They were more in tune with the sacrifices of war. In a modern world beset by environmental challenges; military conflicts waged by technocrats, professionals, and drones; and large, bureaucratic nation-states where average citizens offer little participation in politics, especially in the ways they autho-

rize and fight wars, the story of the ancient republican is more important than ever before.

ROMAN CIVIC MILITARISM

As a military history of Roman citizen armies, this book examines the
relationship between the republican spirit and the citizen-soldier, ana-
lyzes how this spirit motivated men on the battlefield and explains why
those concerned about the trajectory of their own republicanism should
care about Roman warfare. I weave cultural ideologies into a broader
tapestry of the military culture that includes practical considerations
such as Mediterranean "geopolitics," strategic goals, and technological and tactical innovations. I outline the general history but then
pause for a deeper examination of specific battles, explaining how the
constitutional and cultural evolution of Rome affected battlefield tactics at the battles of Sentinum (295), New Carthage (209), Pydna (168),
Mutina (43), and Philippi (42).

As a political and cultural history, this book also engages the recent
debates on the nature of Roman militarism, republicanism, and federalism. During its republican era Rome manifested three overarching
themes conducive to citizen armies: liberty, divided sovereignty, and
participatory citizenship. These terms had different meanings than
they do now and can be briefly defined here. Liberty was the absence
of slavery and foreign domination. Divided sovereignty was the constitutional commitment to a degree of balancing between the three
pure forms of government as well as the incorporation of federated
levels of sovereignty at the familial and local level. Participatory citizenship was the moral foundation of society that demanded personal
character, loyalty to class and family, piety, and civic-mindedness.
When Rome sought to defend and extend its power, it applied these
republican tenets in its martial institutions. Political leadership used
oratory in public spaces to condemn enemies as threats to liberty. Citizens then mustered to defend the state from domestic or external
foes. Political norms and institutions created an environment where
councils managed diplomacy, statesmen became commanders, trea-

ties furnished allies, and citizens authorized warfare. The foundational element was civic virtue. Religious rituals, civic monuments, an agrarian lifestyle, family honor, and communal glory habituated citizens to the idea of fulfilling their duty. When troops finally faced their enemy on the field of battle, their values, institutions, and upbringing had suitably prepared them for the rigors and horrors of war.

Civic militarism was self-defense writ large for the state, with each citizen waging war on behalf of the community.[2] It cultivated all the necessary martial virtues so that ordinary citizens could be prepared for war. From birth, a citizen's peers, family members, religious leaders, and magistrates actively instilled martial virtues such as initiative, strength, discipline, persistence, courage, and loyalty. By the time he had grown into a man, the Roman citizen was expected to appreciate and defend agrarian values, civic participation, family honor, and the glory that could be achieved in defending the community. I am prone to agree with John Keegan that "war embraces much more than politics: that it is always an expression of culture, often a determinant of cultural forms, in some societies the culture itself."[3] The sword of the state can force a man to march onto the battlefield, but when fleeing that same battlefield will save his life, something deeper often obliges him to stay.

My choice of Rome is not intended to deny the importance of Hellenic novelties in constitutionalism and citizen-soldiering. However, it is important to note that most ancient authors, such as Plato, Aristotle, Polybius, and Plutarch, critiqued the political institutions of the Hellenic states. Athens was too democratic. Sparta was too restrictive. Thebes was too ephemeral. As I explain in the prologue, early Americans believed the best insights stemmed from Rome, and this is an important factor in why the historical lessons from the Roman Republic are incredibly valuable for the United States and other modern republics of the Western Hemisphere.

In the mid-fourth century, Rome expanded beyond city-states into a federation of Italian states. This federation was substantially stronger than the Greek leagues and more heavy handed than most modern federations. Nonetheless, Rome's federal arrangement was the best alternative to other masters. It was organic, meaning it relied on preexisting institutions and political structures. This sort of republicanism—both within the citizen's republic and the broader federation—stood in opposition to the Spartan model and even, to a certain extent, the Athenian, where local and family structures were unnaturally rearranged so that they could not challenge the polis. Rome placed a greater emphasis on mixed government (a mixture of monarchic, aristocratic, and democratic institutions). It slowly developed a complex version of mixed government that divided political sovereignty during the floruit of its citizen armies. This mixed government tended to favor the aristocracy, but it still distributed sovereignty to monarchic and democratic elements. Athens, on the other hand, traded its mid-fifth-century model of mixed government for a meteoric democracy.

Constitutionalism and participatory government in the Hellenic world achieved marvelous feats in philosophy and the arts, and their citizen armies guaranteed a Greece free from Persian rule. However, Hellenic political and military culture also caused the disastrous century from the beginnings of the Peloponnesian war to the conquest by Philip. What Hellenic culture had accomplished the century before, it sacrificed in internecine wars that led to the eventual domination of Macedon. Rome, on the other hand, achieved enough unity to gradually build an empire. The political and military machinery of Rome was later synthesized with Greek intellectual culture and Christian philosophy to breathe life into what became the West. This breath of life spawned important religious, institutional, and legal contributions to human civilization. It should never be forgotten that this was only the case because Roman citizen-soldiers fought for the dominance of Rome.

CIVIC MILITARISM'S MEANING TODAY

In this volume, I reconstruct the story of the citizen-soldier on the field of battle. There is no shortage of books explaining Rome's rise and Rome's republicanism, but as of yet, no one has told the story of how Rome created the best citizen-soldiers in history and how these citizen-soldiers then conquered the world.[4] My own interest in this phenomenon is practical as well as scholarly: I served in the United States Army as an intelligence officer from 2009 to 2013, which included a 2012 combat tour to Afghanistan. I wanted to understand military history from the perspective of the common soldier, so I joined the army after defending my dissertation. As a soldier I examined my army experiences with the lens of an academic, and after I was discharged, I approached Roman military history with the lens of a practitioner.

One thing I discovered was that modern republics often misidentify their troops as citizen-soldiers. Active-duty soldiers are constantly referred to by this term, but they are nothing like the citizen-soldier of the Roman Republic. They also do not resemble the American minutemen or the militias of the early United States a mere two centuries ago. Instead, they are much closer to the Spartan soldier-citizen or even the warrior classes of the Persian Empire or the Hellenistic kingdoms.

I clarify what the citizen-soldier is by defining him and describing his historical origins. The latter half of the book reconstructs some of the most important battles fought by Rome, providing momentary glimpses of the norms and beliefs for which citizen-soldiers fought. I identify what drove them forward at the crucial moment, the moment, as much as any moment can, when cultural dominance was on the tipping point. The battles have been chosen because of their exceptional character in portraying the ethos of the combatants. I explain the heritage of the citizen-soldier for a culture that has forgotten who he is and why he fights.

I also reflect on the modern analogies to Rome. The best ancient historians are conversant in the latest research of their subdisciplines, but they also explain why their research is relevant. Eric Cline recently described the Bronze Age collapse in light of today's global wars and climate crisis. Josiah Ober offers the latest research on Athens' democracy to provide insights for modern democracies promoting their values abroad. Arthur Eckstein describes Rome's rise in terms of modern international relations theories. Other recent works apply the insights of ancient history to modern strategy, politics, civil-military relations, and leadership.[5]

Historical analogies are a tricky business, but modern nation-states such as the United States have already demonstrated a penchant for them. The presence of Gaius and Papinian in the US House Chamber, neoclassical architecture such as the Capitol, the text and iconography on currency, and geographical sites named Tiber Creek in Washington, DC, are merely the tip of the iceberg when it comes to how the United States created its own allusions to Rome. The analogies are already there, but they deserve more reflection. This is especially important for the United States, which was itself conceived as a Roman-style agrarian republic with a mixed government and militias.

America is in the midst of a transition that is filled with temptations toward political virtue and vice. Citizens would do well to remember Polybius' cycles of government, which are indebted to the political treatises of Plato and Aristotle. I do not follow them precisely, but I do accept the classical notion that all republics are born, mature, decline, and then perish. This historical guarantee is as certain as the human biological cycle. It was true with Rome, and it is true of modern republics. At the center of this life cycle are civil-military relations because the soul of any state is most clearly defined when it decides what it is willing to kill and die for.

There is a great deal of discontinuity between the civil-military relations of an ancient and a modern republic. Barbarian invasions, systems collapses, renaissances, reformations, scientific revolutions, industrial revolutions, nuclear bombs, and the age of the computer all separate America from its model. Yet people still fight for resources, land, and prestige. They still dream of the ideal political society and then kill each other in their attempts to achieve it. Liberty is still a goal and tyranny decried. Peace is still sought; yet war is as prevalent as ever. This work examines the successes and failures of individual citizens, both exceptional and average, who demonstrated great character or great folly. It gives modern republicans much to contemplate by explaining how their ancient counterparts dreamed, how they achieved their dreams, and how they destroyed their achievements with their own hands.

The prologue explains the special favor Rome and its citizen-soldiers have enjoyed in modern republics, especially the United States. Clas-

sical city-states and empires from throughout the Mediterranean—
including Sparta, Athens, Persia, Alexander and his heirs, Carthage,
and the Greek leagues—have been referenced by generations of Americans, but the Roman preference for agrarian republicanism and
citizen-soldiering made it the most revered and the most emulated.
This fact makes knowledge of Rome's republican warfare a modern
necessity.

Part 1 describes the ancient, republican citizen. Chapter 1 intro-
duces the life and priorities of the citizen-soldier. Life as a hardworking, independent farmer may have made him a sturdier soldier,
but it also complicated his function as a soldier. Citizen armies balanced a tension between the peaceful activities of citizens and the
martial nature of soldiering. Chapter 2 describes the citizen-soldier's
republic. "Republic" is a term that means many things to many people,
so I clarify how the Roman Republic evolved and how it was unique.
Roman republicanism was managed by an elite nobility of commanders, but it was defended by the loyalty of smallholding farmer-citizen-
soldiers with a stake in the state. The farmer understood the earth that
gave him his home and his living and provided for his family. The citizen created and existed in the society of his fellows. The soldier was
willing to kill for these things.

Parts 2 through 4 tell the history of Rome's republican wars. Each
chapter opens by referencing how the stages in Rome's republican
life cycle are relevant today. Part 2 describes the formation of Rome's
citizen-soldier ethos. Chapter 3 explores the stories associated with
Rome's birth as a city-state governed by kings and how Roman militarism evolved into a revolutionary culture. Rome's citizen-soldiers
emerged in a distant and murky past that was later idealized in order to
define the character of the virtuous commander and citizen-soldier.
Chapter 4 describes the first two centuries after the expulsion of the
kings as the new republic attempted to survive in a multipolar anarchy.
It explores the meaning of Rome's revolution and how Rome distinguished itself by using civic militarism to build a federation in central
Italy. Rome nearly succumbed to internal autocrats attempting to resurrect the monarchy at the same time that external foes were set on

obliterating Roman citizens and seizing their lands. Marauding Gauls from the north, tribal peoples from the Apennines, and neighboring city-states all threatened Rome. It survived by finding political solutions that increased its manpower base and by adapting tactics and weapons suited to each of its foes.

Part 3 describes the triumph of Roman armies as they conquered the Mediterranean world. Chapters 5, 6, and 7 describe Rome's incredible expansion in the third and second centuries. Each chapter focuses on a particular battle that highlights the political convictions, military ethos, and innovative tactics of Roman commanders and common soldiers. Chapter 5 describes the breakout years of the republic. Rome's decisive victory at Sentinum in the Third Samnite War paved the way for Rome's control of Italy. Sentinum was a close-run battle that displayed the capabilities of Rome's nascent manipular legions in the hands of two dissimilar commanders intent on outshining the other. Chapter 6 narrates Rome's greatest trial. In the third century, Rome faced off against its greatest nemesis, Carthage, and the tactical genius Hannibal. The republic seemed on the brink of disaster after several devastating defeats in the Second Punic War, but it was able to triumph through loyal allies, an unending supply of soldiers and commanders, and the equally great tactician Scipio Africanus. The end result was Roman dominance in the western Mediterranean. Chapter 7 explains how unprecedented success tested the legendary flexibility of Roman republicanism. Rome achieved more incredible victories when it defeated Alexander's successor kingdoms in the East in the second century. The Battle of Pydna in 168 showcased the tactical independence and superiority of Rome's citizen-soldiers against Macedonian phalangites.

Part 4 covers the last, chaotic century of the republic. Chapter 8 explains how Rome's expansion raised the political stakes at home. The republic's final century was punctuated by chaos and civil war as it tried to adjust its constitution to meet growing needs. Rome achieved the high point of military success, was able to defeat the toughest armies in battle, and reached its farthest territorial limits. However, Rome itself was becoming a literal battleground. Several decades of colorful personalities from the Gracchi brothers to Marius and Sulla and from Pompey to Julius Caesar were using the changing world of the empire to further their own agendas at the expense of the republic. Mob violence, assassinations, and mutinies proliferated, and rogue commanders vied for legitimacy as the republic veered out of control. But despite what many moderns think, the end was not inevitable. The greatest articulator of Roman republicanism—indeed, the triumphal culmination of all classical republican thought—was Cicero, who flourished in these years. In the wake of Caesar's assassination, Cicero united the republic into one final coalition to crush Marc Antony. Cicero's last great political triumph resulted in a military victory at Mutina, but the battle demonstrated how Rome's citizen-soldiers were now a dangerous asset that was already wrecking the republic. Chapter 9 explores the sudden and simultaneous end of Rome's republicanism and Roman citizen-soldiers. In an unpredictable flurry of events over eighteen months the republic descended from near victory to total defeat. Up until the final moments in the Battle of Philippi, Rome's fate hung in the balance, as it teetered between victory for the autocratic heirs of Caesar and for his republican assassins. Both sides relied on the massive and indomitable manpower of citizen-soldiers, but only a republican victory would have kept them and their constitution in existence. In the end, Rome's citizen-soldiers committed mass fratricide, the republicans lost, and the way was cleared for the professional armies of an emperor.

The epilogue explains how the republic's ideal of citizen-soldiers perished shortly after its greatest exponent. It closes the work with a comparison of Horace and Livy, two republicans who were co-opted into the new imperial regime. Both kept alive the shadows of republicanism and citizen armies, one by gazing nostalgically backward and the other by appropriating its themes. Their insights simultaneously buttressed and challenged Augustus' new world order, and they raise some interesting questions for republicans then and now.

Unless otherwise noted, all translations from classical sources in the text come from the editions that make up the Loeb Classical Library.

KILLING FOR THE REPUBLIC

The Roman and American Republics

The American revolutionaries and framers studied Roman history for insights on law, statesmanship, military command, and constitutional institutions.[1] They seemed to have heeded the challenge of the Greek historian Polybius in his *Histories* about Rome's unprecedented rise as the first republic to rule the world: "For who is so worthless or indolent as not to wish to know by what means and under what system of polity the Romans . . . succeeded in subjecting nearly the whole inhabited world to their sole government—a thing unique in history?" (1.1). Early Americans would not allow Polybius' ghost to accuse them of either worthlessness or indolence.

Take the US Capitol, for example, which was begun at the end of the eighteenth century. The building is replete with references to the classical world, from its architecture to its numerous portraits, paintings, busts, statues, reliefs, frescoes, murals, and sculptures. Some of the features, like the Pantheon-inspired dome, Corinthian columns, numerous eagles and fasces (the bundle of rods symbolizing power), and mythical figures like the *Justice* relief in the Old Supreme Court Chamber, the *Liberty and the Eagle* statue in Statuary Hall, and the *Peace* and *War* statues in the niches outside the east entrance specifically channel ancient Rome. *War* is simply Mars dressed as a gladius- and scutum-toting Roman soldier. The references to Rome were both in vogue and intentional. Neoclassical art and architecture were the rage across Europe and the Americas in the eighteenth and nineteenth centuries.

The Capitol's most famous painter and fresco worker, Constantino Brumidi, was born in Rome and trained amid the ancient glories of the city. Other artists used Roman models or completed their works in Rome. The figures from the *Progress of Civilization* pediment, for example, were modeled in Rome in 1854. The title of one book on the Capitol, *American Pantheon*, even makes the case.[2]

The American founders were also educated in the classical tradition and wanted to pay homage to Greek and Roman ideals such as republicanism, the rule of law, democracy, free speech, citizen-soldiering, and civic virtue.[3] They first conceived the Capitol in the 1790s, and its current footprint was completed by the 1860s. During those eight decades it underwent substantial changes, and it remains an evolving building to the current day. Its ongoing alterations reflect the shifting civic sentiments of the American people. The Capitol's design and decoration were intended to capture the civic—and the civil religious—idealization of what Americans believed their growing republic embodied. American republicanism would have a different meaning and a different majesty from its European progenitors.[4] Here we explore how Rome was adopted as the most important classical model for Americans and then conclude with the US Capitol's most enduring reminder of the Roman Republic, its fighting farmers.

CLASSICAL MODELS AND ANTIMODELS

A classical education was in fashion on the continent in the seventeenth and eighteenth centuries, but a number of early Americans questioned whether it was worthwhile. William Penn, for example, believed an education should focus on more practical skills. They also feared, in the words of John Wilson, the "Ignorance, Lewdness, & Profanity," that would stem from studying those ancient heathens. Benjamin Rush, a signer of the Declaration and Philadelphia physician, campaigned against classical education for these reasons, and he also believed it was inherently elitist. Even the polymaths Thomas Jefferson and Benjamin Franklin had their doubts. Franklin asserted that Americans should look within themselves to find the virtue and knowledge that would enable them to carve out a new republic unfettered by the faults of Europe's past.[5]

By the early nineteenth century this view was increasingly prevalent, as captured by Tocqueville. Political architects in the new world, he suggests in *Democracy in America*, should not be too keen on applying ancient models:

> When I compare the Greek and Roman republics to these republics of America, the manuscript library of the first and their coarse populace, to the thousand newspapers that crisscross the second and to the enlightened people that inhabit the republics of America; when I then think of all the efforts that are still made to judge the one with the aid of the others and to foresee what will happen today by what happened two thousand years ago, I am tempted to burn my books, in order to apply only new ideas to a social state so new.[6]

Despite Jefferson and Franklin's reservations and Tocqueville's blustering, no one actually burned their books. Most still believed a classical education would help the best men create the best sort of republic. Critics such as Rush still remarked that the classics contained "much useful knowledge," and Franklin and Jefferson saw the sense of civics, aesthetics, and virtue that a classical education could inspire.[7] Even Tocqueville was not yet comfortable jettisoning a classical education. He saw a great deal of discontinuity between ancient and modern republics, but he still thought that reading Greek and Latin would foster freedom and democracy in modern republics. The ancient republics, he notes, "have special qualities that can serve marvelously to counterbalance our particular defects."[8]

The classically educated American founders quote liberally from the histories of Greece and Rome, but they give preference to Rome for two reasons. First, Roman republicanism was seen as the culmination of that which was best from the classical world. Second, Rome was believed to have outdone the Hellenes in its republicanism. Although oligarchic—or, as John Adams styles early Rome, an "aristocratical republic"—Rome's virtues as a pastoral, mixed government republic were unsurpassed in the classical world.[9] Two ancient authors in particular lent credence to these views: Polybius and Plutarch.

Polybius surveys the best constitutions of the Mediterranean in book 6 of his *Histories*. He finds much to praise in Carthage, Sparta, and Rome, and Rome was the best of these. Democracies like Athens and Thebes, on the other hand, modeled failure better than success. The primary obstacle to Athenian and Carthaginian virtue was their nature as commercial, seafaring republics. Polybius treats the Roman Republic's mixed constitution at length, but he believed its agricultural economic system was just as important. Roman farmers were insulated from the corrupting effects of trade, and their simplicity made them pious citizens who valued virtue over profit. They also made sturdier soldiers. Polybius argues that Rome's victories over Carthage were due in no small measure to its pastoralism (6.51–56).

From the field of Greek and Roman history, Plutarch would pluck out the best and worst statesmen as character studies for his *Parallel Lives*. His biographies were famous in the ancient world and had become useful in the early modern period. English versions of his *Lives*, especially John Dryden's seventeenth-century translation, were widely used by the eighteenth-century founders. Plutarch compares Greek and Roman statesmen, with Romans usually earning more of his favor. Roman republicans are the best models of patriotism, virtue, and leadership. Rome's leaders during the republic, such as Camillus, Fabius Maximus, Aemilius Paullus, Marcellus, Cato the Elder, Flamininus, and Cato the Younger, are the heroes of Plutarch. Greek republicans win the same praise from Plutarch, but there are fewer here: Pericles, for example, is finer in certain respects than Fabius Maximus, and Philopoemen is more noble than his Roman counterpart Flamininus. The tragic Athenian statesman Phocion is one of Plutarch's favorites. However, Hellenic statesmen like Alcibiades and Nicias and Hellenistic autocrats like Pyrrhus are complex examples of both virtuous and vicious traits; Coriolanus is the only Roman in this mold until Plutarch's biographies about the fall of the Republic. The Athenian democracy itself is often a villain in his biographies. The worst villains are those men responsible for the destruction of republicanism, like Marius, Sulla, and Marc Antony.[10]

The founders essentially adopted the thinking of Polybius and Plutarch: Sparta was to be preferred to Athens, which was exceedingly problematic, but Rome was even better than Sparta. Whether or not Polybius' estimation of the ancient republics was right, the founders still found his articulation of Roman mixed government convincing. John Adams thought Polybius' wisdom was indispensable for modern republics, especially America's. In his *Defence* he explains: "I wish to assemble together the opinions and reasonings of philosophers, politicians, and historians, who have taken the most extensive views of men and societies, whose characters are deservedly revered, and whose writings were in the contemplation of those who framed the American constitutions. It will not be contested that all these characters are united in Polybius." As a civic republican, advocate of checks and balances, and Federalist, Adams could find no better model for America's own mixed government than the one outlined by Polybius for Rome. He concludes his chapter titled "Ancient Democratical Republics" with a history of the Roman Republic through the time of Polybius, declaring that "this commonwealth, by the splendor of its actions, the extent of its empire, the wisdom of its councils, the talents, integrity, and courage of a multitude of characters, exhibits the fairest prospect of our species, and is the most signal example, excepting England, of the wisdom and utility of a mixture of the three powers in a commonwealth."[11]

Thomas Jefferson may have been Adams' political rival and philosophical opposite in American political thought, but he still found much to admire about Rome. His affinity for the Roman Republic grew out of his love of farming and the virtues of agricultural life. Jefferson led those Americans, particularly the Democratic-Republicans, who believed the United States was uniquely blessed with abundant land and that this land would provide the setting for America's "citizenry of Virgilian farmers."[12] Incidentally, this was one of the key motivators for Jefferson's uncharacteristically unconstitutional move to secure the Louisiana Purchase, which guaranteed more farmland for America's pastoral republic.

Like the Greek city-states in the fifth century, Rome relied on farmers to fight its wars. This started to change in the second century, and

Plutarch pins the blame for the republic's demise on Marius' reforms
that professionalized the army around 100 BC, although this process
was actually more complicated than he allows (*Gaius Marius*, 9). Benjamin Rush agrees with Plutarch and other founders who cite Marius
and Sulla as the two principal villains who used corruption and money
to end the virtue and austerity of the Roman Republic.[13]

Rome's republican history was seen as a golden age ruined by
Plutarch's villains. All that was best of the classical world was found in
the history of preimperial Rome. For the founding generation, the
"Roman republic was virtuous; the later Roman Empire was decadent,
aggressive, and evil."[14] Common antimodels from the classical world
were the Roman emperors, Roman militarism, and the statesmen that
caused the collapse of the Roman Republic. Philip and Alexander were
comparable antimodels from Greek history. Greek democracy as a
whole was just as problematic—Athens was the easiest target when it
came to historical examples of ambitious demagogues and reckless
assemblies.[15]

Rome may have been the best of the ancient world, but it was not
flawless in the eyes of the founders. Even during the republic, Rome's
hamartia was its overbearing federalism and militarism, twin evils that
colonial Americans believed themselves to be chafing under in the
modern equivalent of the overbearing colonial mistress, Britain. The
Rome that expanded and acquired colonies became more and more of
the tyrannical mistress that Americans saw in Britain.[16]

Fisher Ames, a leading Federalist and member of the first United
States Congress, articulated some of these problems. He used both
Greek and Roman statesmen for pen names, from Lucius Junius Brutus and Camillus to Phocion. It is telling, however, that Brutus and Camillus come from the virtuous beginnings of Rome, whereas Phocion
is from Athens' declining days in the fourth century. Although Ames
admired Rome, its militarism troubled him: "There was scarcely one
of the twelve hundred years that Rome subsisted, that her dominion
was not odious and dangerous to her neighbors." Postcolonial scholars
should appreciate Ames' portrayal of Rome as a voracious conqueror,
a polity for whom "there was but one trade, and that was war; all were

soldiers." Ames critiques postrevolutionary France as modeling the militaristic Romans, but he clarifies that they more closely resembled "the Romans after they were corrupted and had lost their liberty." Like most of the founding generation, Ames believed that the Roman Republic was a model of virtue, mixed government, and liberty (if only for themselves) but that this was ultimately destroyed by a combination of corruption and militarism. Rome's conquests were its idol, and Ames feared that America would be tempted by the equally destructive vice of avarice.[17]

Sparta was another favorite model of a mixed constitution, but its tyrannical rule over its neighbors was even worse than Rome's. Ames follows Alcibiades and quips that the oppressive and tyrannical nature of the Spartan constitution made them welcome death in battle. He also found Sparta problematic as a constitutional model because in his view it was only a military aristocracy propped up by slave labor.[18]

Greek confederations were seen as less tyrannical than Rome's federation. However, their decentralized nature was cited as a culprit in the tumultuous history of the Greek city-states. The Amphictyonic, Achaean, and Lycian leagues were discussed at length in the constitutional debates of the late 1780s.[19] In *Federalist* 4, John Jay uses the failure of the Greek confederacies as an example of what would happen should America fail to unite under a stronger constitution.[20] Madison (or possibly Hamilton) agrees in *Federalist* 18, which reads like a history treatise on the confederations of ancient Greece. The Greek city-states may have eked out successes against the Persians in the fifth century, but their confederations could not keep the Greek city-states from destroying one another in the Peloponnesian War and its aftermath. Nor did they withstand the Macedonian menace. The ineffectual leagues were put out of their misery by Rome. The Hellenes' "ancient liberty, was torn into pieces; and such imbecility and distraction introduced, that the arms of Rome found little difficulty in completing the ruin."[21] Madison concludes by stating that this history offered a warning that the new constitution must be accepted, lest America suffer a similar fate.

A number of American thinkers followed ancient authors like Plato,

Aristotle, Polybius, and Plutarch and critiqued the political history of the Hellenic states. At the Federal Convention of 1787, members added force to their arguments by citing this history. Madison, Hamilton, and Georgia delegate William Pierce used Athens as a historical example to argue against democracy.[22] In *Federalist* 14, Madison critiques "the turbulent democracies of ancient Greece and modern Italy." He quips in *Federalist* 55 that "had every Athenian citizen been a Socrates, every Athenian assembly would still have been a mob." Hamilton concurs in *Federalist* 9: "It is impossible to read the history of the petty republics of Greece and [modern] Italy without feeling sensations of horror and disgust at the distractions with which they were continually agitated, and at the rapid success of revolution by which they were kept perpetually vibrating between the extremes of tyranny and anarchy."[23]

In *Federalist* 63, Madison (or Hamilton possibly) uses Athens as the whipping boy again, citing it as an example of the popular government that was devoid of "so provident a safeguard against the tyranny of their own passions." He found better examples in Sparta, Carthage, and Rome, which all contained senates.[24]

Jennifer Tolbert Roberts investigates Athens' historical reputation in *Athens on Trial* and concludes that "for the framers of the American constitution the story of Athens was the story of failure." Modern Americans may look at the ancient model of democracy to derive some valuable lessons, but the idea that it has insights to offer "contrasts strikingly with the conviction of America's founders that what little Athens had to teach was entirely of the negative variety." Even the Anti-Federalists with their democratic tendencies were reluctant to use Athens as a model. The same could not be said of Rome, Roberts concludes:

> The Romans fared somewhat better, most obviously in the shaping—and naming—of the Senate and in the adoption of Roman mottos and catchwords such as *E pluribus unum* and *Novus Ordo Saeclorum*. . . . Despite the rejection of Athenian-style democracy, the classical ideal of republican government served as an important legitimizing tool for American constitutionalists seeking to demonstrate the ancient pedigree of accountable and nonmonarchic governments.[25]

Roman patriotism, courage, and pastoralism were lauded as the best virtues of the classical world. Rome's constitutional features were also the most praiseworthy. The constitutions of Athens, Sparta, Carthage, Thebes, Crete, and Rome provided source material for the founders when they were discussing the American constitution and early American lawmaking, but the Roman constitution was the most influential. A bicameral legislature, the senate and its "advise and consent" role, property qualifications, congressional war authorization, Rome's more robust federalism, age requirements for officeholders, term limits, and, of course, the vast corpus of Roman law and Latin legal terminology made Rome the uncontested classical favorite for the art and science of American republicanism.[26]

REPUBLICS OF THE FIGHTING FARMER

The founders' use of their classical education was not always a sophisticated affair. Like adolescent boys adulating one another as superheroes, the founders likened one another to classical heroes. Thomas Jefferson compared John Adams to Themistocles, although Adams preferred Cicero for himself. James Wilson adored Cicero as well. Abigail Adams compared Madison's future vice president, Elbridge Gerry, to Cato. And George Washington was often compared to Fabius Maximus.[27]

An even more popular parallel for Washington was Cincinnatus. Cincinnatus was given special attention in the US Capitol when Brumidi painted his first mural, the *Calling of Cincinnatus from the Plow*, in the House Agricultural Committee Room. The subject was the exiled Roman commander Cincinnatus who was farming his small plot of land when he was summoned by the Roman people to rescue the state from invaders. Instead of maintaining his power, however, he surrendered it and returned to his farm. Cincinnatus did all this in sixteen days. It took Brumidi much longer to recreate the scene in paint from January to March 1855.[28] The Cincinnatus anecdote was a powerful one during the American Revolution, and Brumidi acknowledged Cincinnatus' exemplarity by painting the *Calling of Putnam from the Plow to the Revolution* across from him in the same room.

The comparison of generals such as Washington and Putnam to Cincinnatus represented one of the most important analogies to ancient Rome. Preserved for future generations in the Capitol building, stories like this were meant to instruct lawgivers and citizens with regard to their civic ideals. In the traditional history of early Rome, Cincinnatus was part of the second generation of leaders that emerged after the Romans ejected their kings. His accomplishments in securing domestic peace were as important as his valor in war. Another anecdote that looks suspiciously like a doublet has him once again summoned to take command of the Roman state, put down a monarchic conspiracy, and restore domestic peace (Livy, 4.13–16). Washington, like Cincinnatus, was the master of both war and peace. This ancient narrative was invaluable to American revolutionaries. They cast their cause as noble as that of the self-denying Cincinnatus. Americans, like their idealized Romans, envisioned themselves as innocent, hardworking farmers forced to offer their lives by taking up arms in defense of liberty.

Eighteenth-century Americans were justified in their praise of Cincinnatus because they believed that the best polity was a republic based on pastoral virtues. They also believed that citizens should be willing to fight for it. America's economy will never again be as agricultural as it was during the founding, and even at that time the amount of industry and trade in America surpassed that of Athens and Carthage. Nonetheless, the US Capitol once again captures how America perceived itself as the new Rome. The rotunda's *Frieze of American History*, painted by Brumidi and Filippo Costaggini, valorizes the pastoral virtues of early Americans. The fresco begins with Spanish colonization in all its monarchic grandeur. Columbus dazzles the natives, and Cortés and Pizarro conquer them. DeSoto is buried ceremoniously. The painting portrays them as the dashing conquistadors in search of riches and glory, with Catholic missionaries in tow. The Spaniards are followed by the fantastic romantic tale of John Smith and Pocahontas, which was probably just too saucy to ignore.

The next scenes portray what English colonization was supposed to embody. The Pilgrims piously land at Plymouth in 1620. Next, Penn treats with the Indians in 1682. New England is colonized in the next panel, and the final colonial scene is of Governor Oglethorpe treating with the Indians in 1732. The frescoes are magnificent, but the people in them are not. Compared to those portrayed in the Spanish frescoes, they are positively prosaic. The pilgrims are simply clothed, lacking the armor and mounts of the Spanish. They are praying or working with chests and bundles of sticks and tools. The colonization of New England panel shows the colonists hard at work, chopping wood, installing beams, and erecting buildings. The point is simple here: the English colonists that settled the thirteen colonies came to farm, work, and build a new life. The colonists in the Penn and Oglethorpe panels are also clothed plainly when they treat with the Indians. Unlike the Spanish panels, these two panels show the colonists on equal terms with the Indians. They did not come as conquerors, but as peacemakers.

The contrasts may be overstated, but they nonetheless represent the peaceful pastoralism Americans wanted to remember about their history. Hard work, frugality, and austerity characterized the colonists as they had characterized the ancient republicans millennia ago. The rotunda painting is only one of the many pastoral scenes throughout the Capitol. Others include the *Apotheosis of Democracy* sculpture in the House Pediment, the *Calling of Putnam from the Plow to the Revolution*, the bottom scenes of the Senate bronze doors, the Senate's east entry, the *Progress of Civilization* sculpture in the Senate Pediment, the *Embarkation of the Pilgrims at Delft Haven* hanging in the rotunda, and *Agriculture*, the top scene of the right valve in the Amateis bronze doors.

Another republican principle on display was the colonists' civic militarism. If pastoral republics are to remain republics, they must also be defended by farmers willing to set aside the plow. Civic virtue for the pastoral republic must translate on the battlefield to civic militarism because citizens were afforded liberty only as long as they were willing to fight for it. These themes are prevalent in many of the pastoral scenes throughout the Capitol, like the Cincinnatus painting, and in other artworks. The Senate's bronze doors include the image of another American farmer-soldier fighting a Hessian mercenary. The Senate Chamber's east entry sports an engraving of a citizen-soldier with

one arm brandishing a sword and one hand leaning on his plow. Cincinnatus thus represented the spirit of the American citizen-soldier,
from commanders such as Washington and Putnam to the ideal of the
nameless, average militiaman.

The rotunda painting emphasizes the martial values necessary to
defend the hard work of the colonists. Following Oglethorpe's peace
the next scenes are the Battle of Lexington, the reading of the Declaration of Independence, and the surrender of Cornwallis at Yorktown.
The citizen-soldiers fight the professional British armies at Lexington
and win the victory over them at Yorktown six years later. The Declaration scene is telling from another perspective. It does not show the writing or approval of the Declaration in private chambers but the reading
of it in the public square. Adams, Jefferson, and Franklin are thus positioned amid the Philadelphia commoners, who receive the document
with jubilation. The scene testifies to every republic's two essentials:
the leadership of good men and the consent of a devoted, industrious
citizenry.

These two essentials were symbiotic. Sacrificial leaders like Putnam,
Franklin, Jefferson, and Adams were supposed to have Cincinnatus'
prowess and also his disdain for power. Unlike Washington in the pre-
posterously divine and monarchic *Apotheosis of Washington* in the top
of the rotunda, these men are attired like and positioned among their
fellow republicans. They lead by the power of their own arguments
and examples. Their fellow, average republicans consent to their leadership. Republics need wise and sacrificial leaders, but they also need
a broad base of virtuous citizens. The soldier with the plow and sword
above the Senate's east entry and the soldier-farmer fighting the Hessian mercenary in the Senate's bronze doors represent this common
citizen. He communes with the earth as a farmer during peacetime,
but serves his republic as a citizen-soldier during war. He is a man worthy of the leadership of Putnam, Adams, Jefferson, and Franklin.

If Americans wish to take their country's history seriously, they must
also take seriously the ancient republics that educated their framers.
The Capitol is a complex structure that appropriately identifies the

many historical strands that explain how the United States has gotten where it is. Some of these reflect the currents of the founding, and some of them indicate later tendencies that sailed against this current. Unless they wish to dismiss historical models entirely, modern Americans must choose from which models they will learn. Rome left the legacy of a republic that was imperfect but also instructive and inspiring. Its pastoral culture cultivated virtue. Its constitution was well balanced, enabling it to counter corruption. Its citizens were willing to defend and expand the liberties and laws of the republic. If America seeks a future inspired by the virtues of its past, then it must not merely derive inspiration from the founders. It must look to the Roman Republic that inspired them.

PART 1

Farmers, Citizens, and Soldiers

1 · The Soldier's Farm

On 11 May 1778, a seemingly bizarre event concluded the harrowing winter at Valley Forge. George Washington and his soldiers watched a play. Due to logistical maladministration that prevented much-needed materiel from reaching the troops, the winter of 1777–78 had given the Continental Army a test greater than any battlefield defeat—a fact evidenced by the atrocious casualty rates that far exceeded those incurred in any of the engagements throughout the war. Starvation, extreme weather, and disease had reduced fighting strength and morale. The play was designed to lift soldiers' spirits and remind them what they were fighting for. The selection was Joseph Addison's tragedy *Cato*, which told the heroic stand of Cato the Younger against Julius Caesar. The play cast the first-century Roman republican as a liberty-loving icon of virtue and duty against Julius Caesar and his tyrannical bid to destroy the republic. Cato represented the disappearing virtues of the republican citizen-soldier that were giving way to the opportunism and avarice of Caesar and his professional soldiers more loyal to him than the dying republic. Washington, the avid theatergoer, either chose or approved the play with the obvious intention of inspiring his own weary troops to fight the British tyrant and his professional armies currently occupying Philadelphia.[1]

Regardless of the historical veracity of the play, the story of a die-hard republican sacrificing himself for republican principles would have inspired the Continentals. The recruits at Valley Forge would have understood the sacrifices of Cato with his modest vision of a republic. The Continentals under Washington's command filled a vital role the militia did not by simply staying constituted regardless of the situation. However, these were still citizen-soldiers. They had only recently enlisted, and the Continental Army's enlistments were notoriously ineffective. Originally, Congress had intended enlistments to last for the duration of the war, but this effort had largely failed by the winter of 1777. The soldiers in the militia always prioritized their farms and families first, and this same sentiment kept the Continental regulars from extended enlistments. None of these soldiers saw themselves as professionals, and all of them expected to return to their real work at their homes when the conflict concluded.

It is difficult to determine whether American soldiers would find Cato's story inspiring today.[2] On the one hand they see themselves as defenders of a great republic. On the other hand they would probably prefer the professionalism and martial prowess of a Julius Caesar. As members of a standing army themselves, they would also be more familiar with the discipline and training of Britain's standing army. Even National Guard and Reserve units today look less like citizen-soldiers and more like professionals given the number of deployments in recent years. The predominance of the citizen-soldier in America is a thing of the past.

SOLDIER-CITIZENS OR CITIZEN-SOLDIERS?

When army recruits in the United States begin basic training, it doesn't take long for them to understand they are being separated from society. Removed from their families, friends, mobile phones, video games, and fast-food chains, they begin an intense indoctrination that goes far beyond communing in mess halls, drilling at firing ranges, and engaging in tactical maneuvers. Drill sergeants and other trainers are primarily concerned with creating and maintaining a distinct army culture. They consistently explain that their task is to "break down" the civilian so they can "build" the soldier. On behalf of the young recruits, they create a new family and a new moral order, complete with a warrior ethos, a code of honor, and long doctrinal lists of dos and don'ts. This is why soldiers often refer to their squads, platoons, and companies as families, and why many describe their military branch in ways others might describe their church.

This kind of indoctrination extends to the downright silly. Common exercises like jumping jacks are renamed "side-straddle hops." Haircuts from the 1950s like the flattop and the high and tight are ubiquitous. Soldiers also become experts at the singular workout regimen of running around in circles of varying sizes until each individual becomes his own emaciated, marathon-running, doppelgänger. None of these quiddities has much to do with efficient military training. Soldiers do not shave their heads and faces for hygiene, run five miles a day for physical fitness, or speak the military dialect for superior tactical communication. Medical technology is now capable of managing beard-related bacteria. Physical training programs for athletes have proven that a predominantly running-based workout is ineffective for most activities. And the side-straddle hop still involves jumping like fitness expert Jack LaLanne. Antiquated haircuts, peculiar dialects, and communal running perform the same function as church liturgies, national pledges of allegiance, fraternity hazing rituals, and the secret handshake. They create a culture that separates adherents from nonadherents.

This cultural separation between civilians and soldiers has created a chasm in civil-military relations that widens year by year. In 2010, when the country was heavily involved in the war on terror, only 3 percent of Americans polled cited the war in Afghanistan as an important issue, compared to 60 percent who cited the economy. Of those polled, 43 percent claimed they were following the economy closely, yet only 23 percent said they were doing the same with Afghanistan. Those perplexed by the growing gap between civilians and their armed forces should not be surprised. Why would most Americans care? No one will get drafted, the battles are far away, and deficit spending seems to preclude any economic consequences. Aren't most people safe in thinking "Just leave it to the professionals"?[3]

American military personnel complain that their civilian counterparts do not identify with their sacrifices, but do they have cause to complain? For professional soldiers, war is simply a job for which they often enjoy better pay and benefits than their counterparts of equal qualifications and education. They experience the horrors of war, but like trauma doctors, explosives handlers, and ice truckers, they are compensated for their time and risks. Soldiers are also worshipped in ways that would have been unthinkable in the 1960s and '70s. Most businesses offer military discounts, and nearly any soldier who strays outside the base in uniform will receive a "thank you for your service" at the checkout line or have his or her meal comped at a local restaurant. National holidays revere veterans and the fallen as national heroes in ways that are comparable to how Roman Catholics venerate saints.

For the civilians, on the other hand, war is not something you experience, it is something you watch in a movie or read about in a book. They may oppose the war, feel mildly guilty that they didn't serve, idealize war stories, or just be glad they didn't have to do it themselves. Most praise the soldier for defending our freedom, which counts for nearly anything these days—including vaporizing those ever-threatening mule herders of the Hindu Kush with $65,000 automated missiles. An overwhelming majority of Americans have never served; indeed, military participation rates have reached all-time lows in spite of the fact that America was recently locked in two wars and numerous minor engagements for over a decade. The American preference for specialization of labor has resulted in war being specialized.

In 1953 Arthur A. Ekirch predicted that the American conception of a citizen army would become obsolete because the new Cold War military looked more like the standing armies that earned so much loathing in past centuries. Military historians were quick to adapt, however, hailing the "soldier-citizen" as the new minuteman. Soldier-citizens make up a much smaller percentage of the population. They have spent decades in the military and supposedly exemplify virtues such as honor, courage, and loyalty. However, unlike the citizen-soldier, they are defined by their commitment to military culture. As the title swapping indicates, the soldier comes first, and the citizen is second.[4]

The question naturally raised by all this is whether citizen armies as conceived by the ancients will ever be possible again. Americans may produce films about the Greek city-states' stand against Persia, but long gone is the minuteman who shared features with his Athenian counterpart. News of a Persian invasion in 490 BC prompted a mustering of farmers who marched to Marathon, fought a battle, and then returned home to farm some more. In the decades following Marathon, Athens recruited higher percentages of its citizens to fight, which was a tendency bolstered by its naval activities. Even poor Athenian citizens could serve on a trireme. Sparta, on the other hand, represented the opposite end of the recruitment spectrum. Approximately nine out of every ten men in Spartan society were either free, noncitizen locals or state-owned slaves called helots whose chief function was to maintain the agricultural economy of the Spartan citizens. With the farming left to the second class or the subjugated, full citizens were free to participate in a unique military culture that made Sparta the most formidable polis in Hellas. Spartiates were the "soldier-citizens" of the ancient world, who knew comparatively little about economics, farming, and civilian life. In this way, American soldiering increasingly looks more like the Spartan "soldier-citizen" than the Athenian "citizen-soldier."

WHO WILL DO THE KILLING?

Since war doesn't seem to be going away anytime soon, cultures must still find an institutional arrangement that allocates warfighting. Which is better, to play the role of Athens and partially dehumanize more of the population by making them part-time citizen-soldiers or to play the role of Sparta and completely dehumanize a small portion by creating a warrior class of professional soldiers? Ultimately, all polities must decide which they prefer. The decision is informed by a matrix of cultural ideals. Is soldiering better than vocations such as farming? Is courage in battle superior to hard work on the farm? Should politics and war involve as many citizens as possible or as few as possible? How warlike should a population be? One of the reasons I focus on Rome here is that it answered these questions by forging a "middle way" between the Athenian and Spartan preferences. It made its amateurs incredibly proficient.

Regardless of how cultures sort out these ideals, war is a nasty business. In the ancient world, successful soldiers became proficient at slashing metal implements into the skulls, bones, and joints of their enemies so that they could crush or hack off arms, legs, and heads. They used arrows, spears, javelins, and swords as thrusting tools that would cause blood to gush, internal organs to burst out of the body, and the internal anatomy to shut down. After destroying human life in these gruesome ways, soldiers ending a siege would often loot property, rape defenseless women, and kill their children. If a commander could halt the rapaciousness of his soldiers, the remaining population would be enslaved. In the course of more comprehensive rampages, valuable property would be removed wholesale, beautiful architectural feats would be leveled, and settlements would be burned to the ground. Surrounding croplands that had not been damaged by raids would have been used to supply the armies, whether en route or encamped for a siege.

Killing, destroying, and enslaving strip out every ounce of humanity from both subject and object. The dehumanizing may only last for the moment of the death blow, the instant of the fire lighting, or the transaction of the slave sale, but most of the time its effects linger. Such dehumanizing acts were the norm in the ancient world, and it is not altogether different in war zones today.

William Tecumseh Sherman was right in 1880 when he declared to American Civil War veterans and rosy-cheeked academy cadets that "there is many a boy here to-day who looks on war as all glory, but, boys, it is all hell."[5] Sherman's tactics in the war made him uniquely suited to understand the inhumanity soldiers inflict on humans in warfare. The century following Sherman's pronouncement demonstrated the hellish nature of humans and hindered claims to moral progress. If the twentieth century showed anything about the human propensity for destruction, it was that what took the ancients days, weeks, and sometimes years to accomplish could be achieved by the moderns in seconds. Take the World War II atomic attacks as an example.

At 8:15 am on 6 August 1945, Hiroshima was full of life and industry. At 8:16 am, most of it was gone. It took less than a minute for the bomb named Little Boy to reach its detonation point after being dropped from the *Enola Gay* and less than a second to obliterate everything in downtown Hiroshima.

Hiroshima and Nagasaki inaugurated a new era in warfare. Teams of scientists, highly placed politicians, military administrators, and twelve aircraft crewmen achieved their tactical goals at Hiroshima in moments. Seventy thousand were killed. A strategic city was incapacitated. A vital military-industrial center was neutralized. Compare Hiroshima with events in the Second Punic War between Rome and Carthage. It took Hannibal's soldiers the entire day to hack up to seventy thousand legionaries to death at the Battle of Cannae. It took Marcellus two years to break through the defenses of Syracuse and capture the town. And it took Scipio Africanus five years to neutralize the industrial and military capabilities of Carthaginian Iberia.

The contrasts between Hiroshima and the Second Punic War also highlight differences in civic participation. Hannibal, Marcellus, and Scipio required tens of thousands of soldiers capable of slashing, stabbing, and killing other human beings. The postatomic age only requires a handful of scientists, administrators, and military specialists. Soldier-citizens may eventually be replaced by military technocrats— teams of technological specialists that manipulate the course of wars by a series of button pushes.[6]

These trends toward specialization must be confronted, and one way to do that is by reflecting on the history of civil-military relations. A good starting point for this is an examination of the republican ethos in the Roman world. The average family in Roman Italy sent multiple military-aged males to fight in the war against Carthage, and even the mercenary-hiring Carthaginians were required to arm themselves when the war reached Africa. Killing is much easier and more specialized today, with average citizens in developed countries spectating war on the sidelines, if they even watch it at all.

This modern trend may be viewed by many as more just, more efficient, and more "free." However, it is historically less republican. In the ancient republican ethos, the act of taking up arms for the public good made a citizen virtuous. That citizen was willing to sacrifice his own humanity—in killing, and possibly even in dying.[7] "The citizen who is patriotic, brave, and worthy of a leading place in the state," Cicero writes, "will dedicate himself unreservedly to his country. . . . [H]e will surely cleave to justice and honour so closely that he will submit to any loss, however heavy, rather than be untrue to them, and will face death itself rather than renounce them" (*On Duties*, 1.25).

Livy believed that the Roman Republic earned its liberty because the citizenry as a whole learned to manifest this sort of virtue. They had been tempered by "the pledges of wife and children and love of the very place and soil," which "had firmly united their aspirations," at the same time that their leaders rejected a king in favor of magistrates whose terms and scope of power were limited (2.1–2). This love united them to oust a tyrant and erect a republic. Romans were convinced that republican government could only maintain its cohesion if each citizen actively defended this object of his love. The virtuous life must not merely be personal and private but public, and one of the clearest manifestations of public virtue was when citizens united into a citizen army.

So what is a "citizen army"? A citizen army, whether ancient or modern, is a marshaling of soldiers designed to defend a polity that is somehow subject to them and represents their interests. This is most readily seen in the citizen-soldier's role in authorizing campaigns as part of a legitimate political process. Citizens fight not merely for a governing elite and its interests but for their own lives, profits, and well-being. Soldiers' loyalty belongs to the public good rather than commanders (which could lead to client or private armies) or themselves (which could lead to mercenary armies). Most importantly, while they exercise allegiance to the state, they nurture prior obligations to their communities, farms, and families. A citizen-soldier is to be distinguished from a professional soldier. The former fights by exception to protect his profession, which is something else. The latter, having no productive or creative profession, fights as his vocation.

The professional soldier, including the soldier-citizen, finds vocational fulfillment in warfare. Peace interrupts his work. The citizen-soldier, on the other hand, requires peace in order to achieve his vo-cational worth. War interrupts his work. The citizen-soldier, who authorizes war, requires a justification for fighting it. The professional has little need for a just cause. He needs war because he needs pay. "He fights because he is trained and paid to obey orders; death is an occupational hazard." The citizen-soldier, however, sees death in bat-tle as "the price he may be called upon to pay for the cause."[8]

FARMERS, THE CHOSEN PEOPLE OF GOD

The farmlands of Rome's citizen-soldiers served as the foundation for Roman notions of civic militarism. As noted in the Prologue, Thomas Jefferson made the same link between farming and republicanism. In his only published book, Jefferson waxes lyrical:

> Those who labour in the earth are the chosen people of God, if ever he had a chosen people, whose breasts he has made his peculiar deposit for substantial and genuine virtue. It is the focus in which he keeps alive that sacred fire, which otherwise might escape from the face of the earth. Corruption of morals in the mass of cultivators is a phae-nomenon of which no age nor nation has furnished an example.[9]

Jefferson's phraseology reads like the Beatitudes from Christ's Sermon on the Mount in Matthew 5. Jefferson had little liking for the estab-lished churches of his day, so his reference envisioned a new church, that of the American farmer. They would be independent yet public minded and rugged yet virtuous. In his civil-religious thinking, they would make the most devout citizens.[10] Jefferson's vision of American republicanism depended on a self-reliant body of citizens with earthy wisdom and natural virtue. He opposed what he saw as Hamilton's cor-rupt, centralized sham that placed real power in the hands of bankers and merchants with paper money, credit, and stocks. Real wealth was found in farmland, and America's status as an agricultural society would inculcate virtue more than its political institutions or its religions.[11]

Jefferson's language may have been biblical, but his sentiments were clearly classical. He reveled in the agricultural musings of the classical authors, particularly the Romans Virgil, Horace, and Columella. Jefferson intended to erect a small temple at his burial ground that would house an inscription he recorded in his commonplace book. The passage was taken from Horace's *Epodes*, and it described the simple morality of the farmer. Jefferson copied out phrases like "Happy the man who, free from business worries, like the men of the old days, tills with his oxen his ancestral fields." He even tweaked Horace's description of a Roman farm setting to that of eighteenth-century Virginia.[12]

Horace was an excellent source for Jefferson's agricultural visions. Horace extolled the value of Rome's agricultural economy for a virtuous citizenry. He followed republican writers like Ennius who commonly lauded frugality and surplus while denouncing luxury, gluttony, and waste.[13] According to Horace, fickle Fortune could never grant a man virtue, but a simple life on the farm could foster both virtue and contentment (*Odes*, 3.29):

> The more a person denies himself, the more he will receive from the gods. Destitute myself, I want to join the camp of those who desire nothing; a deserter, I am eager to abandon the side of the rich, and thus acquire more credit for being master of the wealth I reject. . . . A stream of clear water, a few acres of woodland, a harvest that never lets me down—this is a more fortunate lot. . . . All is well for the man to whom God with a frugal hand has given enough. (*Odes*, 3.16)

And perhaps his most famous writing on country life begins:

> This is what I prayed for!—a piece of land not so very large, where there would be a garden, and near the house a spring of ever-flowing water, and up above these a bit of woodland. More and better than this have the gods done for me. I am content. Nothing more do I ask, O son of Maia, save that thou make these blessings last my life long. (*Satires*, 2.6.1–5)

He continues by describing how this modest life is the more appropriate setting among the educated for fundamental questions about

humanity and virtue. As he and his friends conclude the day in the re-
laxed setting of a country dinner, the conversation naturally tends to
these things:

> And so begins a chat, not about other men's homes and estates, nor
> whether Lepos dances well or ill; but we discuss matters which con-
> cern us more, and of which it is harmful to be in ignorance—whether
> wealth or virtue makes men happy, whether self-interest or upright-
> ness leads us to friendship, what is the nature of the good and what is
> its highest form. (2.6.70–76)

Horace's older contemporary Marcus Terentius Varro describes
Roman farm life in his famous book, *On Agriculture*. Varro opens book 1
by invoking the "twelve councillor-gods," but he dismisses the "urban
gods, whose images stand around the forum, bedecked with gold." Instead, he calls on "those twelve gods who are the special patrons of
husbandmen" (1.1).

The gods had blessed Romans with a singularly bountiful land.
Varro has Agrasius rhetorically ask, "You have all travelled through
many lands; have you seen any land more fully cultivated than Italy?"
(1.2). Agrasius' companions remark that there are no parallels. Funda-
nius responds, "What useful product is there which not only does not
grow in Italy, but even grow to perfection?" He then goes on to list the
trees, vines, and crops that flourish throughout Rome's Saturnian land
(1.2).[14] Varro's penchant for calendars and organization no doubt
prompted him to include several chapters in book 1 on the Roman cycles of farming. Starting in chapter 27 he breaks down the agricultural
tasks month by month and explains the varying seasons farmers could
use as categories, from four to six to eight. Farming was more than a
job; it was a mode of living that kept farmers in tune with the world
throughout the year.

Varro's life spanned the anarchy of the republic's last decades, and
he sets his narrative during a troubled time when the smallholder farm
and family had been irrevocably altered by societal, territorial, and
economic shifts. His book 1 abruptly concludes with a shocking tale.

His speakers are interrupted by a panicked freedman reporting the murder of his master. The hapless man had been to the city and stabbed in the midst of a crowd. No one could even identify the killer. The violent urban anecdote contrasts with the peaceful life on the farm Varro's speakers had just been describing.

As Romans were trying to return to normalcy after the chaos and civil wars of the first century, Virgil recommended a return to agricultural life. As book 2 of his *Georgics* explains, the farm was hardly free of strife. Citizens labored daily on their farms, forcing nature to bend to their will. He describes the hard work of viticulture and tree tending, saying, "On all, be sure, must labour be spent; all must be marshaled into trenches, and tamed with much trouble" (2.61–62). But the work was rewarding:

> O farmers, happy beyond measure, could they but know their blessings! For them, far from the clash of arms, most righteous Earth, unbidden, pours forth from her soil an easy sustenance. . . . [T]hey have sleep free from anxiety, a life that is innocent of guilt and rich with untold treasures. The peace of broad domains, caverns, and natural lakes, and cool vales, the lowing of oxen, and soft slumbers beneath the trees—all are theirs. They have woodland glades and the haunts of game; a youth hardened to toil and inured to scanty fare; worship of gods and reverence for age; among them, as she departed from the earth, Justice left the last imprint of her feet. (2.458–60, 467–74)

Within the bosom of the farmer justice and virtue found a fitting home.

In taming nature, humans also learned to tame their own nature. It taught them how to avoid vice and fear: "Blessed is he who had succeeded in learning the laws of nature's working, has cast beneath his feet all fear and fate's implacable decree, and the howl of insatiable Death." The farmer was unmoved by the temptations of vanity, men's praise, and greed (*Georgics*, 2.490–99). Virgil concludes book 2 with nostalgic musings on the lost days of ancient Italy before the civil wars. Justice and virtue last resided in the farmers, and it was from them that the Roman people would recover it.

Varro, Virgil, and Horace wrote for a readership that was becoming urbanized. Many of their readers, especially the urban aristocrats, had forgotten what life on the farm was actually like; even if they owned estates, they rarely labored on them. These authors were perpetuating an older ideal of the virtuous citizen-soldier. Roman citizens during the republic, however, were the genuine article. They were no doubt much more crude, raucous, and discontented than their depictions by Augustan-age authors, but they did embody the earthy republican spirit that had enabled Rome to defeat each of its rivals in the arts of war, peace, and politics.

TRAINING THE FARMER-CITIZEN-SOLDIER

Several centuries before Varro and Virgil, Italy was part of an unstable world that constantly witnessed armed bands and invading armies traversing the land. As they cut paths through the countryside, settlers would be killed, homes would be burned, crops would be taken or destroyed, and the already delicate balance of agricultural life would be overturned. The existence of Virgil's farm "far from the clash of arms" was suddenly threatened by that very thing. Farms needed protecting. And the Romans discovered how to make their farmers the best at doing it.

The smallholder's farm was the incubator for Roman moral, physical, and practical education. The home held the family's hearth, before which they worshipped the ancestral gods. Piety and family devotion served as the basis for loyalty to the broader political community. This family-based civic upbringing was important because education in the Roman Republic was a simple affair until the introduction of Greek traditions in the third and second centuries. Prior to that time the boys that would become citizen-soldiers learned what they could from their parents. Until their mid- to late teens, when boys adorned the *toga virilis* as a sign of their manhood and responsibilities as a citizen, boys learned their family histories, acquired the literacy and mathematics necessary to conduct business transactions and the practical skills needed for fighting and campaigning, and absorbed the cultural mores of Roman society such as respect for authority, honesty, duty, and honor. Roman fathers were expected to instill discipline, frugality, industriousness, and self-reliance in their children.[15]

Self-reliance was a valuable Roman character trait. Varro remarks that "nothing should be bought which can be raised on the place or made by the men on the farm" (*On Agriculture*, 1.22). Part of this independence involved the ability to defend oneself and fight in the army. Cato the Elder taught his son to read, and trained him in the martial skills of hurling javelins, fighting in armor, riding horses, boxing, enduring extreme temperatures, and swimming. All of this constituted his "moulding and fashioning his son to virtue" (*Cato Major*, 20). There may have been schools in some settlements that supplemented this family-centered education, although Livy, Cicero, and Plutarch disagree as to whether this was the case.[16]

Horace's famous ode on military virtues describes the sort of man Roman fathers like Cato produced. "A youngster should be toughened by the rigours of a soldiers life and learn how to put up with the constraints of poverty cheerfully." His physical stamina and ability to kill should terrify his enemies (especially the enemies' wives and daughters) into seeing him as a "lion that is savage to the touch and whose rage for blood sends him rampaging through the thick of the carnage." Horace's rhetoric aside, the point was that military training began for the young in their homes. The father especially would guide his son's initial training, introduce him to physical hardship, and demand discipline and responsibility from him. Only the attentive parent could produce a youth that would believe "it is sweet and fitting to die for one's country" (*Odes*, 3.2).

Roman families were not uniform. Some resembled the nuclear families of today, but many included several generations and branches of families from brothers and sisters. Adoption was also quite common. The amount of education and military training was also limited by the capabilities of the parents. Aristocratic families that produced commanders and tribunes would have differed from the poorer families that supplied skirmishers, but these differences were incorporated into Roman constitutional and military institutions because the army needed both cavalry commanders and skirmishers.

Beyond the farm soldiers would also receive some training in the field. Fathers and farms could produce discipline, hardiness, individual martial skills, and a familiarity with hunting and killing animals, but training as a unit would have to occur in communal settings. Within the environs of Rome, the Campus Martius would have provided an excellent training ground, and similar open areas existed in other settlements. Communal training on public grounds would have included the use of specific weapons such as swords, shields, and javelins. Training was still rudimentary beyond the community. Commanders expected their soldiers to know how to erect and protect the camp, and drilling was primarily in the form of marches, where men would learn "to follow the standards and to know their ranks in the battle-line" (Livy, 10.25, 23.35.6). Working within the camp, digging trenches, and other forms of labor would maintain their discipline and physical stamina while in the field.[17]

This basic level of training at the unit level is to be expected for an army of part-timers. In the phalanx men would primarily need to maintain formation, hold shields, and thrust the spear. The manipular system required a little more training with its back-and-forth and sideways movements, hence Livy's description of knowing and following the ranks. Still, as individual soldiers, men were trained in sword fighting and javelin throwing, as Cato reports, by their fathers. This entire system was heavily dependent on the family. Levied men would need to have already been disciplined and trained as much as possible by the paterfamilias. Training a son as a soldier made the son virtuous and reflected the virtue of the father (Plutarch, *Cato Major*, 20). Not doing so would bring shame to both, and in a culture obsessed with honor, this was unacceptable.

Roman authors certainly idealized the Roman family and farm, but this should not discount the fundamental role it played in Roman society.[18] The family was the first level of government, meaning that Roman boys and girls were taught the value of community within that context. The family was also the primary institution that habituated children to the civic necessity of fighting wars. Contrast this natural setting with the Spartan system that removed young children from their families for their indoctrination and training in military messes.

The Roman farm and family negated the need for messes. Varro makes the same point about Greek gymnasiums (*On Agriculture*, 2.1). The Romans required neither messes nor gymnasiums because education and training naturally took place in the family and on the farm.

The effusions of Horace, Virgil, and other late, upper-class writers are confirmed by the hard-nosed practitioners Cato and Polybius, who had led men in combat and personally witnessed Roman soldiers on the battlefield. Fathers did not merely teach their sons the basics of how to fight, as Cato describes, but also why to fight. Polybius mentions how Roman homes were shrines to republican warfighting. Their walls were decorated with the awards for valor won by fathers and grandfathers. Cupboards near the hearth held the busts of illustrious ancestors. Cato describes how, for centuries, dinners in Roman homes were accompanied by songs and poems that celebrated the virtues and great deeds of famous men. This is what made Roman citizen-soldiers—indeed, entire legions—capable of eagerly marching to certain death. They knew their fathers had done so, and they wished to equal or surpass that legacy.[19]

Sacrifice for the republic was a noble undertaking because the republic was both an extension and a culmination of the local community. Cicero, who had also commanded armies, argues that it was appropriate for an Italian-born man in his time to see himself as being a citizen of both his local community and the republic. These two citizenships were not opposed, however, but bound together by justice and a common cause. Cicero believed that because the Roman Republic was the most just state, fighting for it often meant fighting for world order. Serving the republic reflected piety and courage (*On Duties*, 2.2; *On the Republic*, 6.24–27). It also protected the freedom of those farms and hearths, which were bound together in a republic of citizens who shaped their communal political destiny. The average citizen-soldier, of course, could not articulate such thoughts in the manner of a Cicero. Nonetheless, Polybius argues that what made Roman citizen-soldiers different from their enemies was each man's deep belief that if the republic fell, their farms and hearths would no longer be free and their unique form of government would cease to exist (6.39, 52–53).

By the time Rome faced the other great armies of the Mediterranean in the third century, the republic had created a different recruiting base and basic training system from their opponents. Its procedure was not militarized or "bureaucratized" like that of classical Sparta or Thebes. It was not based on brilliant generals commanding mercenaries like Carthage. Nor was it centered on a strict, hierarchical monarchy and its warrior class, like the Macedonian kingdoms.

Roman citizen-soldiers might be defeated in battle by Carthaginian armies, for example, but they were much less likely, as Cato explains, to behave like stateless mercenaries, who "kill each other in great numbers in the camp, . . . desert all at once to the enemy," or "attack their general."[20] And what about those famous Hellenistic conquerors of the East? Cassius Dio has a Roman commander on the eve of battle with the "heir of Alexander," Pyrrhus of Epirus, give a speech to his men. Despite the Macedonians' reputation, Roman armies are better, the commander claims. Hellenistic armies are led by very capable generals, but their autocratic nature often makes them tyrants and neutralizes their talents. Roman commanders, on the other hand, fight alongside fellow citizens and with the love of their troops, not their fear. Only Roman citizen armies have true comradeship and cooperation on the battlefield (9.14-16).

Rome's military system was sometimes inadequate in specific moments. Too often Carthaginian or Macedonian armies proved better at killing in individual battles. But Roman farms—and the farms of their allies, which increasingly resembled Roman farms as the centuries passed—never failed to produce more citizen-soldiers. Every citizen and allied home was a training space and a recruiting ground. Rome's republicanism and civic militarism thus created an enormous manpower base, allowing Rome to absorb blows, adapt to varying challenges, and eventually defeat every opponent. It must be remembered, however, that this quantity in manpower was the result of the quality of its republican idea of soldiering.

Centuries later a fourth-century compiler of ancient Roman military manuals, Vegetius, bemoans this loss of manpower. In his time the citizen-soldier idea had even ceased to be a memory for most. Roman armies were a meticulously managed extension of the imperial office. He describes the need for the same kind of basic training Cato and Polybius recommend, including swimming, jumping, marching, handling weapons, and so forth. In his day the emperor needed to enforce a top-down regimen, which contrasted with the way of the ancient Romans, who grew up in a dangerous world where less formal but more effective training based out of the villages and homes of citizens made excellent recruits continually available. This, Vegetius exclaims, is how those ancient Romans conquered the world (*The Military Institutions of the Romans*, 1.preface, 9–10).[21]

BALANCING PEACE AND WAR IN ROME

Until the military reforms in the late second and early first century, Rome relied on this cultural framework to fight its wars. In the fifth and fourth centuries, soldiering most often took place in seasons. By the third and second centuries, it increasingly relied on men in their late teens, twenties, and early thirties to devote longer periods to ongoing campaigns. During this "life cycle," young Roman men could be drawn away for years, but it was always expected that the survivors would return to their lives on the farm on a full-time basis by their mid-thirties at the latest.[22] Unlike in Sparta, which devoted its male citizenry to war and left the farming to noncitizen and half citizen subjects of the Spartan state, citizen-soldiers in the republic were expected to function as productive farmers at certain stages of their lives.

Farming and fighting were mutually beneficial. Cato writes that "when they would praise a worthy man their praise took this form: 'good husbandman,' 'good farmer'; one so praised was thought to have received the greatest commendation" (*On Agriculture*, preface). Such prosaic themes rarely surfaced as the focus of the historian's pen, but they served as the foundation of every story about the Roman Republic. Any military history of citizen armies tends to neglect this most important dimension of its subjects' lives. This tendency is unavoidable because citizen-soldiers are not primarily warriors. The state expected citizens to fight its wars, but there would be no state and no wars to fight if the citizens did not farm first. This situation naturally created a tension in every citizen between wishing for peace and bracing for the inevitability of war. This tension was not as persistent as the ancient historians indicate. Their passion for writing about war overshadowed the fact that "most of the time, even if war was occurring in some society, it was not in most other societies. . . . At any particular time, if somewhere a boundary was being violated, tens or hundreds of others were being respected."[23]

Nonetheless, war affected the daily lives of citizens in the ancient world more than citizens in twenty-first-century liberal democracies. The ancient system of politics was often very chaotic, producing what international relations theorists would term a multipolar anarchy. Before Rome's ascendancy there was no superpower that could successfully arbitrate peace, so states were left to fend for themselves. Mediating third parties, religious observances, and part-time diplomats sometimes mitigated conflicts, but disputes usually morphed into warfare.[24] Plato's Clinias argues for the inevitability of war during this period as he describes the preparations citizens must make on behalf of the state: "If, then, these practices are necessary in war . . . they must be carried out equally in time of peace. For . . . 'peace,' as the term is commonly employed, is nothing more than a name, the truth being that every State is, by a law of nature, engaged perpetually in an informal war with every other State" (626A). The Athenian Stranger has Clinias tease out this view until he arrives at its natural conclusion, a Hobbesian style anarchy where "all men are both publicly and privately the enemies of all, and individually also each man is his own enemy" (626D). Clinias certainly represented a common outlook, which was bolstered by the human fascination by war. This morbid tendency still exists today. War is active, exciting, heroic, and dramatic. Heraclitus concisely romanticizes it: "War is both king of all and father of all, and it has revealed some as gods, others as men; some it has made slaves, others free."[25]

Given that military conflict appeared inevitable, republics saw the need to habituate their citizens to both peace and war. A subsistence, agrarian lifestyle made peace-habituation automatic. War required more effort, so the ethos of civic participation demanded civic milita-rism. Ironically, civic participation still prioritized peace over war in the long run. This apparent contradiction has a simple explanation. Part-time soldiers were only successful citizens if their creative acts outweighed their destructive acts. A Roman citizen had to function first as a farmer, son or father, and citizen before he was allowed to serve as a soldier. There were practical aspects to this—property re-quirements, the ability to own a panoply, and having a legal status in a community that enabled one to be recruited and function in public life—but there were also ideological underpinnings to the prioritiza-tion of peace.

The philosophical argument for this was first articulated by Plato. In book 1 of his *Laws*, the Athenian Stranger explains that courage is only one of the principle virtues. The battlefield "courage" of the Spartans and Cretans may be worthy of praise, but it is subject to the same crit-icisms the Athenian levels at these polities in Plato's day—warriors by trade are rarely positioned to advocate the more important virtues of wisdom, temperance, and justice. Civic virtue did not begin with mar-tial courage.

Early Romans would have been unfamiliar with Plato, but they voiced similar sentiments. Roman republicanism demanded wars justified by peace. One need look no further than how Roman authors characterized their founders to understand this idea. King Romulus' character as a warrior required the balance of King Numa's pious peace. Cincinnatus was first a farmer and a citizen, and these facts help us appreciate his story as a commander. The great statesman Ca-millus' wartime destructions in the early fourth century necessitated his peacetime dedication of the Temple of Concord. The foundation of republican culture rested not on warrior-leaders with a sufficient talent at administration but on politically talented artisans who could martially defend their laws, religion, and farmlands.

A desire for peace was not always obvious, yet it was a driving force behind conflict. Roman law demanded that just conflicts find a just conclusion. Wars deemed to be unjust—such as the Campanian mutiny that treacherously captured Rhegium instead of protecting it during the Pyrrhic War—were seen as aberrations requiring counteractive efforts. The Romans also institutionalized ritual cleansing related to warfare. Lustrations would be performed to purify armies. Reintegrating back into society after campaigning required ceremonies that cleansed the soldier of his inhumane acts and restored his human nature. This probably happened annually after the campaign season when the October horse was sacrificed. The sacrifice of the October horse was a debated issue even in the ancient world, but it seems most likely that the sacrifice was both a war ritual and an agricultural ritual. That it could be both seems reasonable because Rome's citizen-soldiers were farmers and warriors. War and agriculture were linked, especially in October when the citizen traditionally ceased being a soldier that killed the enemy and returned to being a farmer that planted next year's crops.[26]

Rome was at war as much as any other ancient polity, yet peace remained in the background. The citizen could never escape it. Whenever he marched to war he knew that it would dog his every step and overpower him should he tarry too long. It was the bride awaiting his return. It was the children that needed fathering. It was the earth that needed tilling, the hearth that needed maintaining, the grain that needed harvesting. Without the citizen, the soldier could become as violent and rapacious as his captain required. But the soldier could not fight forever because life would always beckon the citizen home. Peace always demanded the citizen's recall.

The precarious balance between war and peace that defined the citizen-soldier's life meant that war always threatened domination. Every campaign involved the dehumanization of death. Citizen-soldiers were not merely willing to die, they were willing to kill. In taking enemy lives and destroying their homes, crops, and temples, every citizen-soldier returned home less a human than he had left. So, when speaking of Rome, even during the height of the republic, how can one speak of peace? Is it possible that Rome, the city that only twice shut the doors of Janus, which symbolized the cessation of hostilities, ever countenanced a peaceful world?

The answer lies in the tension between peace and war that pro-

pelled Rome. As indefensible as it may seem today, Rome not inac-
curately saw itself beset on all sides by enemies ready to plunder and
destroy. The only means of peace appeared to be a determined defense and sometimes a preemptive offense. If the expansion of Rome
was earned by the Roman as a soldier, cultural goods were extended
abroad by the same man as a farmer, father, and citizen.

Machiavelli, an ardent admirer of Roman culture, argues that only
a citizen can truly seek peace. The Renaissance philosopher most responsible for renewing the spirit of republicanism, he devoted several
of his works to an intense study of the Roman Republic, especially as
portrayed by Livy. His *Discourses on Livy* reminded his contemporaries that the former greatness of the West lay not in monarchy but in
republicanism.

Using Rome as the paradigm, his later work *The Art of War* aptly
sums up the military power behind any republic. Republics, unlike
monarchies dependent on the favor of individuals, relied on their citizens to bear the cost of war. To be a good citizen, a man must first devote himself to a trade such as farming, craftsmanship, or trading. War
for Machiavelli is a profession ill-suited for commonwealths. Instead it
is the business of tyrants and those seeking tyranny. Moreover, tyrants
expected their professional soldiers to devote themselves to the baser
instincts elicited by war. He who by profession is a soldier must by his
very nature seek war to maintain his living. In the opening pages of *The
Art of War* Machiavelli opines that "since war is not an occupation by
which a man can at all times make an honorable living, it ought not
to be followed as a business by anyone but a prince or a governor of a
commonwealth; and if he is a wise man, he will not allow any of his
subjects or citizens to make that his only profession—indeed, no good
man ever did."[27] Machiavelli goes on to explain that good men cannot
make war their profession because war is inherently devoted to violence, deceit, and destruction; therefore, those who devote themselves
to the profession of soldiering abandon the possibility of peace.

Regarding Roman citizen-soldiers, Machiavelli exhorts that "there
was never any soldier who made war his only occupation; and so it
happened that few of them were dissolute or licentious—and those

few were severely punished." What drove Rome to greatness was a devotion to the creative act of hard labor. In Rome's time, toil on the family farm fostered the civic virtue that made Roman men good soldiers and better citizens. In Machiavelli's day the field of occupations had expanded, and today it has grown further still, but the guiding principle for citizen-soldiers of any day is that their vocational purpose is devoted to productivity. A man who does not have such a trade does not know the value of peace and therefore struggles to find the proper motivation for defending it in times of necessity.[28]

For these reasons Montesquieu emphasizes the importance of equalized landholdings under the republic in his *Considerations on the Causes of the Greatness of the Romans and Their Decline*. Roman law attempted to ensure that the majority of inhabitants had farmland and that no one person could accumulate excessive wealth. Relative economic equality among a citizenry that constituted the bulk of its territorial inhabitants was essential to ancient republicanism. Montesquieu understood how large numbers of farm-holding citizens make for large, capable armies.[29]

Rome's republicanism differed from the notable but ultimately unsuccessful versions of Sparta, Athens, and Carthage. Sparta's citizenry fielded an excellent army, but the Spartan state enslaved most of its population and thus paralyzed its military in the event of defeats. Athens' and Carthage's empires were based more on shipping and trade, which produced citizen-sailors and thalassocratic empires, but ancient commentators were right that this arrangement was no match for Rome's citizen-soldiers and their agricultural republic. Athens' democratic citizenry proved fickle and brittle, and the members of its empire quickly came to chafe at Athens' lack of wise management.

THE PRIORITIES OF THE CITIZEN-SOLDIER

Booty and social promotion always motivate soldiers, but the spoils of war for the Roman citizen-soldier did not obviate the need to continue the mundane work of fathering children and cultivating the land. When war did arrive on the doorstep of Rome, it was judged a defensive necessity (however unrealistic this assessment may be in modern eyes). Roman territory needed defending, and a large citizenry properly trained and armed was up to the task. Polybius distinguishes the antagonists of the Punic Wars by pointing out that Carthage sundered its liberties from its soldiers—hiring mercenaries and foreigners from its extensive thalassocracy—while Rome soldiered "natives of the soil and citizens" who fought "for their country and their children" (6.52). This marriage between the familial-economic center of the farm and the defensive institution of the state gave Rome the edge.

Rome's historical context precluded it from embracing a concept of peace with which the modern mind can justifiably find comfort. This may have placed it in a state of constant war, but war was fought by men who were not constantly soldiers. It did not rely on a warrior class until the republic had been terminated—a correlation that was not coincidental. Warrior classes comprised of full-time soldiers or mercenaries were deemed antithetical to republican virtue because a man's primary occupation should be farming, not fighting.

Rome certainly saw a glory in war, conquest, and empire. Yet this was only one dimension of a complicated international milieu. In the Roman mind the only alternative to war was subjugation. Whether this perspective was a valid justification or a flimsy excuse depends in some ways on the epoch of the observer. War before 146 BC was an ongoing life-and-death struggle that created habits of militarism which needed constant checking. Success had to be more than the warriors' code. It also had to involve more farms, citizens, and allies. Ferociousness on the battlefield must match peacetime ideals like law, order, and stability.

For the enemies of Rome, the qualities of Roman soldiers were less admirable or fearsome than the qualities of their citizens. As soldiers Romans were often tactically and technologically inferior to their opponents. Rome suffered countless defeats at the hands of neighboring city-states, Gauls, Samnite tribes, Hellenistic conquerors, and Carthaginians. During the opening years of the Second Punic War, for example, Rome was soundly beaten with an overwhelming and embarrassing consistency. Despite these soldiering shortcomings, Rome endured and eventually triumphed over every one of these enemies. The reason for this was that its citizens were more than mere soldiers. The Roman state could absorb such military setbacks again and again until the right opportunity surfaced to win. When Roman armies took the field of battle, what counted most was not the soldier who happened to be a citizen, but the citizen who understood why he fought as a soldier. This is why refusals to fight in Rome were so significant. When the citizen-soldiers seceded at home or mutinied in the field, they were exercising political sovereignty. For these ancient citizens, political protections and legal equality preceded military service, with the result that the republic had to function before the army could. There was no army until the republic was in order, and virtue was not derived from martial service but displayed in it.

2 · The Citizen's Republic

The ancient authors describe political associations and institutions that have modern parallels. One has to be careful though. The modern mind assumes statehood, constitutions, and interstate relations in a way that was unfamiliar to the ancients. In *States, Nations, and Nationalism*, Hagen Schulze opens his history of the political development of nation-states with the fall of the Roman Empire and the growth of its successors in the West, arguing that the twin concepts of state and nation emerged from the Middle Ages and subsequently became intertwined. Schulze is quick to concede that his analysis does not preclude the idea that there were states before this time. He stipulates from the beginning the existence of "the traditional concept of the state obtaining in the ancient world," although he finds this ancient concept wanting.[1]

States are formed by political actions, and politics is simply "the way in which people decide to live together and to understand the legitimacy of their social relations." The political act moves beyond brute force and becomes legitimate when other segments of society recognize a dominant force and allow it to exercise power and authority.[2] Ancient peoples understood that their common values, interests, and territory produced a sovereign state. This catalyzed a drive to protect the community of their state against domination by another state. Using these definitions, we can say that not only states but complicated international state systems would have existed as far back as 1400 BC.

Statehood, politics, and international law should not be understood as a "unique product of the modern, rational mind." According to David Bederman, at a minimum, the ancient Near Eastern kingdoms from 1400–1150 and 960–700, the Greek city-states from 500–338, and the Roman period from 358–168 provide ample data to construct an analysis of ancient state relations. This is not a novel assessment; it can be traced back through the writings of political theorists, including Machiavelli, Hobbes, Vico, Rousseau, Locke, Engels, and Marx.[3]

We can approach constitutionalism in the ancient world using the same logic. In the broadest sense, a constitution determines the "nature," "make," or "composition" of an entity. The essence of the term from a political stance can be applied to ancient polities as follows:

> Constitutionalism has one essential quality: it is a legal limitation on government; it is the antithesis of arbitrary rule; its opposite is despotic government, the government of will instead of law. . . . [T]he most ancient, the most persistent, and the most lasting of the essentials of true constitutionalism still remains what it has been almost from the beginning, the limitation of government by law. A constitution then is not limited to modern states or only those nations acquainted with the term.[4]

Constitutionalism binds a nation's rulers through some form of political or legal contract via custom, accumulated laws, or written documents. Its essential qualities are the rule of law as opposed to capriciousness and a constraint on the government as opposed to unlimited governmental power. Essentially, there are only two real forms of social organization—hierarchical forms that emphasize a singularly placed sovereignty and countervailance forms that emphasize a distribution of sovereignty.[5] The Roman Republic was the best ancient form of the latter.[6]

REPUBLICANISM

Cicero ensconced the term "republic" with his use of the Latin term "res publica." He lauds the Roman government during the republic as

the best polity, the historical embodiment of what political philosophers such as Plato had only hypothesized. Early in his *On the Republic*
Cicero has Scipio define the term:

> Well, then, a commonwealth [*res publica*] is the property of a people
> [*res populi*]. But a people is not any collection of human beings brought
> together in any sort of way, but an assemblage of people in large num-
> bers associated in an agreement with respect to justice and a partner-
> ship for the common good. The first cause of such an association is
> not so much the weakness of the individual as a certain social spirit
> which nature has implanted in man. (1.25)

Cicero understood republics (*res publica*, literally meaning "public
thing") as participatory associations designed for the good of their
citizens. They did not merely punish evil and prevent tyranny but also
shared public goods. Subsequent political philosophers paid tribute to
this view by using the term "republic" to describe constitutions dedicated to the common good of its citizenry.

In the thousands of years since Cicero used the term, "republic" has
come to mean many things to many people. Republicanism usually
denotes something akin to popular sovereignty, antimonarchism, participatory democracy, or representative government. More nuanced
explanations tease out the matter further. The rule of law is discussed
in relation to concepts such as consent of the governed, isonomy (legal
equality), public laws and procedures, and the like. Sometimes divided
sovereignty is referenced in light of mixed government, checks and
balances, the separation of powers, and limited government. Freedom,
liberty, noninterference, and nondomination play a part as well, and
civic virtue usually does too. The definition of republicanism becomes
even more complicated when taking into account the discontinuity
between the ancient, medieval, and modern worlds. Decisive breaks
in Western history separate political thinkers like Plato, Aristotle, and
Cicero from Augustine and Aquinas, and then from Machiavelli, Rousseau, and James Madison.

Republicanism is certainly an ancient concept, however. Daniel
Fleming, for example, argues that a "primitive democracy" existed in

Middle Bronze Age Mari. Others insist that strains of democracy are traceable to the first Sumerian polities of the Early Bronze Age and perhaps even before that. These arguments have provided a point of departure for a number of biblical scholars who see Old Testament Israel as a forebearer of Western republican mores.[7] As these examples demonstrate, republicanism and democracy are concepts that scholars are willing to locate centuries and even millennia before the Roman Revolution in 509.

The historical development of constitutional terms and ideas is an important project, but it would be a distraction to follow that winding path too much further here. History has furnished no shortage of historians, philosophers, statesmen, and educators willing to define the term "republic," and since my goal is to explain how republics successfully fielded citizen armies, I only briefly address a republic's qualities.[8] These qualities are definable if one can narrow down its definition by considering how it was used in specific places and times. John Adams recognizes as much when he writes to his cousin about how European governments abuse the term:

> There is not in lexicography a more fraudulent word. Whenever I used the word *republic* with approbation, I mean a government in which the people have collectively, or by representation, an essential share in the sovereignty. . . . Are we not, my friend, in danger of rendering the word *republican* unpopular in this country by an indiscreet, indeterminate, and equivocal use of it? The people of England have been obliged to wean themselves from the use of it, by making it unpopular and unfashionable. . . . They have succeeded to such a degree, that . . . a republican is as unamiable as a witch, a blasphemer, a rebel, or a tyrant.[9]

Adams identifies the same tendency in his day that exists in our own. Terms such as "democracy," "constitutionalism," and "republic" are ubiquitous to the point of becoming meaningless. The Soviet Union may have been called a collection of "republics." Egypt and Iran may have "constitutions." The Congolese may live in the Democratic Republic of the Congo. That hardly means they deserve the titles.

In seeking to redeem the term, the verbose Adams is not reticent to proffer his own definition. He continues by telling Samuel Adams that "if, in this country, the word *republic* should be generally understood, as it is by some, to mean a form of government inconsistent with a mixture of three powers, forming a mutual balance, we may depend upon it that such mischievous effects will be produced by the use of it as will compel the people of America to renounce, detest, and execrate it as the English do."[10] Adams was right to say that any study on republicanism must automatically begin by narrowing the term or clarifying how it applies at different times in different places. His solution was to write a multivolume tome that describes all the types of republics that had existed in European history, especially as they related to his cherished principle of mixed government. He classifies, defines, and details their features one by one. The work, *A Defence of the Constitutions of Government of the United States of America, against the Attack of M. Turgot, in His Letter to Dr. Price, Dated the Twenty-second Day of March, 1778*, has a length worthy of its title.

Unlike Adams, I focus on Roman republicanism. Several recent works agree on the basic characteristics of a republic. It is a combination of mixed government, antimonarchism, freedom that is legally guaranteed, and sovereign citizens that exercise civic virtue through political and military participation. This kind of citizenship is contingent on a relatively equal body of property-owning citizens that observe the same moral and religious values.[11] I narrow the definition even further. Rome had a constitutionally structured polity that was characterized by liberty, divided sovereignty, and participatory virtue. These characteristics originated in and were maintained by structures I reference throughout, such as a civic-based family education, an agrarian economy, public spaces and monuments, the distribution of civic honors, and communal religious rituals. This brief definition should adequately introduce the political foundation on which the Roman polity created its citizen armies.

Liberty: Nondomination

Liberty was understood by the ancients as the quality of living without a master—of not being a slave. From a civic standpoint, freedom was the avoidance of domestic tyranny, on the one hand, and foreign domination, on the other. Liberty was linked to morality in ancient republics, and its defense was a necessary duty for every citizen. Liberty was more than the modern preference for "noninterference." It was "nondomination." Just as masters may choose not to interfere, so states might not. But states also may decide to claim sovereignty, perhaps even in the name of the people, over the lives of their citizens. The goal of ancient republicanism was not freedom from a master's interference but the nonexistence of a master.[12]

The Roman Republic's concept of liberty differed from that of today, as evidenced by its unique assemblies and voting procedures. Liberty in Rome was defined by one's legal status, and voting was not based on the one-voter-one-vote principle. Voting was based on blocks, and a voter's status determined the block that person belonged to. The Tribal Assembly divided voters into tribes, and the Centuriate Assembly divided them into centuries. The Centuriate Assembly was based on the Roman army, with its tactical units of the centuries. It actually convened on the Field of Mars, the military parade ground, but it was not organizationally identical to the Roman army, even in its early stages. Voting according to centuries gave more voting power to the wealthy, who were spread across more centuries that contained smaller numbers of voters. Those who fought in the cavalry or in the first property class, for example, had more wealth and would have enjoyed more political pull. The poorest voters were lumped into fewer centuries, giving individual voters very little political power. In the archaic Servian constitution, all citizens who could not afford military equipment were placed into one century, meaning they had no real influence. Voting also gave preference to older citizens because centuries were divided between *juniores* and *seniores*. Voting ended when the necessary majority was reached, meaning some centuries—the ones made up of the poorest citizens—never even got a chance to vote.[13]

Legal and political status in the Roman block voting system prioritized wealth and age in ways that moderns might find unattractive, although it would be naive to presume that these factors are unable to unduly influence elections and policies today. The preference for wealth and age was part of the Roman ethos, which revered age, ancestry, and social and political status. Precise equality in voting power was less important to the Roman citizen than his actual participation in the process and in the decisions that followed, especially in decisions about warfare. Citizens in the United States experience the reverse. They feel that their vote makes a difference because of the one-voter-one-vote principle, but they also know that on any decision regarding war, they will not have to live out their decision by actually fighting. In the Roman world living without a master meant more than participating in voting; it also meant literally fighting off any potential masters.

The principle of nondomination also highlights the dichotomy between modern soldier-citizens and ancient citizen-soldiers. Modern soldier-citizens are expected to forfeit the civil liberties so valued in their liberal democracies. Their freedom of speech and their freedom of movement is limited or completely denied, and their war authorization is always assumed. Soldier-citizens are expected to fight wars whether or not they approve of them, move their family and household at the government's bidding, and refrain from opposing officials or its policies in any official capacity (even unofficial opposition can have deleterious effects on soldier-citizens). Soldier-citizens are on call 365 days a year. They cannot oppose superiors. They must keep working even if a bureaucratic error or a budgetary crisis cuts off their pay. Should they desert or mutiny, this same bureaucratic machinery will meticulously hunt them down. Soldier-citizens may "volunteer" to join, but once they do, they look more like slaves than free persons. In America they have been aptly deemed GI—like a piece of national property, they are just "government issued."

Ancient citizen-soldiers would have balked at being such a "volunteer." They avoided wars they didn't authorize, engaged in duels for personal glory, mutinied when denied pay, stayed in their camps when they had no confidence in their captains, put their commanders on trial, and executed failed generals. Most importantly, unlike modern soldier-citizens, who lead a nomadic life, citizen-soldiers had farmland that tied them to a community and gave their family and future a permanent stake in the creative and stabilizing act of farming and fathering. Ancient citizen-soldiers participated in their local community more and followed their general less.

Divided Sovereignty: Combined and Federated Government

Rome did not vest political sovereignty in any one institution. It was divided horizontally and vertically, that is to say, through mixed government and federalism. The theory behind mixed government was articulated by Plato and Aristotle, who overviewed the forms of government and recommended a mixture of the pure forms of democracy, aristocracy, and monarchy. Mixed government was the limitation and distribution of power into competing offices. Plato, in his *Laws*, and Aristotle, in his *Politics*, conclude that a mixed government, ambiguously called *politeia*, is the most just and the most stable over the longest period of time. In a *politeia* the pure forms are distributed in institutions alongside one another. The two forms Plato and Aristotle emphasize in this mixture are aristocracy and democracy (756a–757e). Aristotle further divides the forms of government into three functions, the deliberative, the executive, and the judicial, which anticipates the modern "separation of powers" (3.7, 4.7–10).

Plato and Aristotle were followed by Polybius and Cicero. They applied the descriptions of mixed government to the real-world example they saw in Rome, adding a twist that the forms were not "mixed" in harmony but were "combined" in balance. Writing two centuries after Aristotle, Polybius expanded on the *politeia* of Aristotle, explaining that the genius of the Roman *politeia* was its combination of all three forms of government—monarchic, aristocratic, and democratic. Polybius was the first political theorist to emphasize a balanced government with institutions designed to check one another. He and Cicero elaborated on what they saw was the applied genius of balanced government, the Roman Republic, which distributed power into opposing autocratic, aristocratic, and democratic institutions (Polybius, 6.11; Cicero, *Republic*, 1.35–71).

Federalism further distributed sovereignty to family, local, and national authorities. Fathers often had the power of life and death over

their own children. Local towns enjoyed autonomy so long as they provided troops and refrained from squabbling. And the Romans managed diplomatic and military affairs. Federalism is committed to levels
of sovereignty and is based on the principle of subsidiarity, wherein
political matters are managed at the lowest possible level, which in the
case of Rome would have been the family. The heads of families and
towns were sovereign in family and local affairs. For practical reasons,
this was prevalent in many ancient political systems, but in Rome it
was consciously institutionalized.[14]

   The Roman constitution was an evolving republican arrangement,
and as with all human institutions, it fell short of what Polybius and
Cicero claimed for it. It did not perfectly balance the three forms but
gave the aristocracy a somewhat larger share of power. Its federation
also became increasingly overbearing. Nonetheless, the Roman combination of the pure forms has rightly earned a place in history as the
oldest and best model of divided sovereignty. The Roman constitution depended on social distinctions, expected its aristocracy to carry
much of the state's burdens and make a larger share of the decisions,
and handed complete authority to autocrats in times of emergency.
Divided sovereignty as seen in Rome looks nothing like the popular
sovereignty and liberal democracy of today, which is what much of the
recent debate regarding Rome's republicanism has focused on.[15]

   Rome was not a republic in the modern sense of the word. Women,
slaves, and the very poor were excluded from the political process. Its
divided sovereignty enshrined a flexible class system. Not only were
there autocrats, aristocrats, and the masses, but there were also patriarchs, senior kinsmen, patrons, clients, priests, *seniores, juniores*, smallholders, "largeholders," wealthy, and poor. Plato argues throughout
book 4 of his *Politeia* that the political community is best served when
each acts according to how he has been gifted in the virtues of bravery,
temperance, and wisdom. What each man and each part of society
does must serve not only himself but the state as well.[16] This environment of natural but limited hierarchies was conducive to citizen-
soldiering. Patriarchs and patrons naturally commanded the respect
of *juniores* and clients, but capricious commanders would always have

to fear the legal power of the lower orders that could prosecute reckless or domineering behavior.

The wholesale participation of members within this hierarchy points to another difference between ancient citizen-soldiers and modern professional soldiers. It is unthinkable that a CEO, professor, doctor, or politician would don body armor and rush to the front lines. Neither they nor their sons and daughters would ever be forced to fight, which is why so few of them volunteer to do so these days. The result is that the "volunteer" military culture decreasingly represents the rest of the population. In the Roman Republic, by contrast, all citizens except for the extremely poor were expected to bear the burden of war, meaning that although citizens might be stratified economically, socially, and militarily, on the battlefield those hierarchies were leveled. Here every citizen was vulnerable to the same weapons. Each would have to muster the same courage to counter those weapons and would have to personally participate in the brutality of killing other human beings.

Participatory Citizenship: Civic Virtue and Civic Militarism

Rome's combined government rested securely on a citizen base that was morally inclined to participate politically and militarily. Civic virtue manifests itself through frugality, courage on the battlefield, temperance and moderation in politics, and fidelity to the divine. It creates a basic moral community that places the historical values, prescriptions, and customs of the community above private well-being. Families inculcated personal habits that served and, if necessary, sacrificed for the community and the public good. Yet civic virtue was not characterized as sacrifice per se; if it worked toward the good of the republic, it was merely a good and proper action, for good and proper *personal* actions should also be good and proper *public* actions.

For Aristotle, a mixed constitution was buttressed by the civic virtue inherent in its citizenry (4.9.6–9). A polity should be "one in which there naturally grows up a military populace" (3.11.11). The smallholder citizenry gains power in part with a change in military organization, tactics, and strategy. Aristotle explains that city-states commonly identified their citizenry with their soldiery, meaning that the development of democracies and mixed governments gave a state more soldiers and consequently more citizens. The larger numbers of citizen-soldiers serving as heavy infantry could often overpower smaller aristocratic cavalries. They were also formidable opponents against even larger numbers of combined light infantry and cavalry, as seen in the Persian wars.[17]

With this increase in freedom came a necessary increase in duties. The most important duty of the citizen was to don the heavy armor of the infantryman and defend the state. This duty was understood as virtue (4.10.10-11). Aristotle refers to the "many elements of virtue" in the military life of cultures such as Sparta (2.7.8). It was not merely the obedience and discipline of training in the martial lifestyle that promoted virtue but war itself:

> Therefore it is proper for the state to be temperate, brave, and enduring; since, as the proverb goes, there is no leisure for slaves, but people unable to face danger bravely are the slaves of their assailants. Therefore courage and fortitude are needed for business, love of wisdom for leisure, temperance and justice for both seasons, and more especially when men are at peace and have leisure; for war compels men to be just and temperate, whereas the enjoyment of prosperity and peaceful leisure tend to make them insolent. (7.13.17-19)

Herodotus traces the historical development of Sparta's martial virtues, reaching the same conclusion. Sparta, "the worst governed of well nigh all the Greeks," began its rise to greatness after "they changed their laws for the better," most significantly by changing "bad laws for good ones" in "all that related to war, the sworn companies, and the bands of thirty, and the common meals" (1.65-66). Thucydides has Pericles acknowledge similar martial virtues in Athens' rise to empire (2.35-39). Civic virtue, argued the ancient political theorists, must translate on the battlefield to civic militarism.

Roman thinkers, as we have seen, found the relationship between farming and fighting a natural one for characterizing civic virtue. Civic militarism among farmers could not take the form of a life dedicated to the destructiveness and death of war. On the contrary, hard work and the productivity involved in farming the land were fundamental to instilling virtue. Cato's *On Agriculture* is a fitting testament to his belief in frugality and hard work. He opens his work with an explanation of why the honest and hard work of a farmer is superior to that of a trader, who must engage in too much risk taking, or a money lender, who is dishonorable. Yet Cato also praises the other virtues of the farmer, his martial qualities: "It is from the farming class that the bravest men and the sturdiest soldiers come, their calling is most highly respected, their livelihood is most assured and is looked on with the least hostility, and those who are engaged in that pursuit are least inclined to be disaffected" (preface).

Varro echoes Cato's praise of the farmer. Roman citizens had no need for the gymnasiums that littered Greek cities because they were accustomed to the hardships and natural training found on the farm. This resilience was ingrained in Rome's early citizens. He explains that "it was not without reason that those great men, our ancestors, put the Romans who lived in the country ahead of those who lived in the city." The qualities of soldiers did not emerge from the city because "those who live in the villa are lazier than those who are engaged in carrying out work on the land." This was something to decry in Varro's own day, when "all the heads of families have sneaked within the walls, abandoning the sickle and the plough, and would rather busy their hands in the theatre and in the circus than in the grain fields and the vineyards." Athleticism and industriousness had been abandoned, but even worse was the loss of independence. Rome increasingly relied on imported grain in Varro's lifetime, which was brought in to feed the urbanites. In better times, the smallholder fed himself and his family from his own fields (2.1).

Civic militarism in republics did not promote conquest through any means. This is how the "barbarians" fought—an appellation the Romans applied to Gauls and Iberians—in their destructive campaigns that left the conquered areas bereft of civilization. Nor did Rome build its empire on swift and systematic conquest as Alexander had. The Roman Empire was arduously cultivated by hard work and the slow expansion of Roman farmers and the Roman farming ideal. The citizen-soldier of Rome knew that his way of life could be maintained and compensated through booty during his service in the republic's wars; more importantly, he understood that if he did not defend the republic, his freedom, political power, and farmland could be lost.

Civic virtue demanded much from its citizens during wartime, and wars were very frequent. Between 197 and 168 BC, for example, an average of 47,500 out of 250,000 adult male citizens fought every year in Rome's wars. Compare this 19 percent to the less than 1 percent of Americans in the military now.[18] Even if we take into account the non-fighting population not counted in the Roman census, such as women and children, the ratio is still significantly higher at around 5 percent. And when you consider that many modern "soldiers" sit behind computer screens, administer paperwork, drive trucks, repair equipment, and manage supply routes, the percentage of military personnel who actually fulfill the role of the average legionary—killing the enemy—is even lower.

Modern societies tend to uphold their soldiers as the best of their citizens because they are the ones who "serve." They are the ones willing to die for their country. They are the ones willing to make "the ultimate sacrifice." According to ancient republics, this is backward thinking. The soldier-citizen isn't the best citizen simply because he serves. Instead, citizens make the best soldiers because they are free. Free citizens make the most virtuous citizens, and the most virtuous citizens make the best soldiers. Montesquieu later took this concept even further, asserting that where republics rely on citizen-soldiers, monarchies require professional armies (*Spirit of the Laws*, 5.19).[19]

Livy makes the same claim in his "alternate history" that imagines a war between Alexander and Rome. He labors to explain that Alexander would have been defeated because he would not face another great captain like himself but a multitude of great leaders and citizens instead. Monarchies could muster one outstanding general, but republics had a larger pool from which to choose. Livy cites the possible commanders that could have been summoned from their farms: "Marcus Valerius Corvus, Gaius Marcius Rutulus, Gaius Sulpicius, Titus Manlius Torquatus, Quintus Publilius Philo, Lucius Papirius Cursor,

Quintus Fabius Maximus, the two Decii, Lucius Volumnius, Manius Curius. . . . Any one of these was as highly endowed with courage and talents as was Alexander" (9.17). Yet by his own time, Livy had seen the tragedy wrought by great generals who began to dominate fellow aristocrats and the great sea of citizen-soldiers. These "great men" pursued their own greatness at the expense of the republic, hastening the demise of their fellow statesmen and the republic in the process.

Citizen armies make war's incentives more complex. The commencement of hostilities is often complicated enough, but it becomes more complicated when the armies fighting them have so many competing motivations and so much personal liberty. Factors such as personal glory, impious or pious acts, the collection of booty, family honor, social status, the violation of diplomats, infringements on security and boundaries, imperial ambition, and aristocratic competition weave together the religious, the moral, the economic, and the political. Republics must court such interests and channel them into a concentrated civic energy directed at the enemy.[20] For example, Romans acquired grants of land in the Italian colonies that were a boon to them personally, but this also meant that Roman culture and values were spread beyond the gates of Rome. Members of the nobility, on the other hand, could gain social prestige, more economic clients, and political power through great deeds in war, provided that these deeds were in line with Rome's security and strategic goals. The wise state connects virtue in the pursuit of self-interest with benefits to the republic. Self interest is not problematic, but personal gains are most valuable when they yield benefits to the public as well. Republicanism created and relied on a massive base of manpower that was motivated to protect the governing apparatus because it relied on its citizens and embodied those values and interests for which each soldier was willing to kill and die. When there was a disconnect between the values of the state and the interests of the citizen-soldier, Rome experienced the soldiers' check on the state—a refusal to march to war.

Do republics and citizen armies always go together? History answers in the negative. Sparta had its soldier-citizens, Carthage and Venice their mercenaries, and Britain its standing armies. More often than not, however, Montesquieu hits the mark in drawing a link between republics and citizen-soldiering. Rome emphasized part-time, non-vocational soldiers as essential to its republican political systems, and this relationship was so close that it transitioned to permanent armies and away from republicanism at the same time.

SEARCHING FOR THE EARLY REPUBLIC

We are fortunate to have the works of the classical historians, which provide details, insights, and commentary about the Roman Republic; other polities in the ancient world were not so lucky. Nonetheless, the purposes and methods of the ancients were very different from modern writers, and they have created three challenges for any study of historical Rome. The first is the historians' chronological separation from the events about which they wrote. Historians were contemporaries of certain ancient events. Thucydides, for example was a participant of the Peloponnesian War, and Polybius was a well-placed Greek that witnessed Rome's ascendancy in the mid-second century. More often than not, however, the first accounts of historical events have been lost. This situation is then further complicated by the availability of the earliest manuscripts for these historians. The transmission process from event to manuscript can be rendered using the following formula: historical events → first accounts → historical literature → available manuscripts. This route of transmission from event to available historical manuscript must be kept in mind. Days, years, decades, and centuries can separate these four stages, with historiographical complications increasing in due measure.

The second challenge lies in the aims of the ancient historian, who approached his craft with a different task in mind than his modern counterpart. T. P. Wiseman describes the work of ancient history with the metaphor of Clio's cosmetics.[21] Clio, the muse of history, is supposed to reveal "the bare truth with no artificial colour in her style," but this ideal was not always realized in practice. Historians instead applied cosmetics to a countenance that enhanced, misdirected, or betrayed what truly lay beneath. Roman historians wrote treatises to teach lessons to political leaders, make a patriotic defense of events, and/or entertain their readers. Most of them lived in a world where Rome was the unquestioned, dominating power, and this situation could have increased historians' anachronisms as they reconstructed domestic politics and international relations.

The third challenge is the sometimes stormy relationship between material data, epigraphic documents, and literary texts. Archaeology can be very helpful in those cases in which the textual transmission process has left gaps or uncertainties. Unfortunately, it can also lead to greater uncertainty. Archaeological evidence requires interpretation as well, and it can be even harder to decipher than texts. This study primarily relies on the literary accounts because texts are far more helpful for understanding cultural ideals, political theories, and battlefield tactics. As Arnaldo Momigliano explains, "We have also learned that archeology and epigraphy cannot take the place of the living tradition of a nation as transmitted by its literary texts."[22] With these limitations in mind, however, I endeavor to keep textual interpretations "grounded" as closely as possible with the archaeological data available to us.

These limitations are especially apparent in the context of the early history of the republic. Most agree that at sometime near the turn of the sixth century the monarchy that had existed in Rome ceased to exist. Rome's regal period was influenced by the Etruscans, although the extent of this influence is debated. During the monarchy Rome became an established city-state capable of defeating enemies and forging alliances with powerful neighbors. The shadowy figure Lars Porsena of Clusium played some sort of role in the expulsion of the kings, and the cast of early Roman characters such as Brutus, Publicola, and Cincinnatus, who may or may not be historical, are reported to have participated in activities that speak to some of the important themes during the early years of the republic. In the mid-fifth century a legal revolution of sorts occurred, possibly involving the publication of laws called the Twelve Tables.

Rome continued to develop as a city-state not unlike other Italian city-states in the fourth century. At the beginning of this century, two events dramatically altered Rome's situation. Rome first conquered a nearby rival, Veii, and then was itself sacked by an invasion of plundering Gauls in 390. During Rome's recovery in the first half of the fourth century, it increasingly dominated an alliance with its neighbors, most notably the Latins. The constitutional structure of Rome underwent several experiments and changes after 449, and most of the major magistracies had taken shape by the middle of the fourth century. After restructuring its federation with the Latins in 338, Rome became the greatest power in central Italy and by 300 was poised to dominate most of the Italian peninsula. After 300 the skeleton of Roman history begins to acquire flesh and blood. The year 300 also marks the resolution of a slight snafu in the Roman dating system that put it at odds with itself and the Greek records, so dates can be fixed with greater certainty.[23]

The first stage of the literary transmission process (historical events → first accounts) is completed around this time with the development of the Roman genre of history writing. Aside from the available material data, which did not generally interest ancient historians, documentary resources were available in the form of yearly chronicles. The most famous of these were the *annales maximi,* which stretched back into the fourth century. They were maintained by the *pontifex maximus* and listed the annual magistrates and documented other public affairs. Different kinds of *fasti* (calendars) recorded sacred, legal, and political information in other lists. Historians could also make use of earlier Greek historians, family records, oral traditions, and, for recent events, eyewitness accounts. Like all historical sources, each of these offered unique challenges for classical historians. The first of the Roman historians were Q. Fabius Pictor and L. Cincius Alimentus, who wrote in Greek. They were followed by Cato's Latin *Origines*. Others, such as Calpurnius Piso Frugi, began the annalist tradition in the middle of the second century, with even more following in the first century. Piso and those that followed are called annalists because of their tendency to record entries year by year. There were also the *Carmen belli Poenici* of Naevius and the *Annales* of Quintus Ennius, which narrate the history of Rome in epic form.[24]

Unfortunately, only fragments remain from these early historians of Rome. We must content ourselves with the historians that used these initial accounts as sources when they wrote their own histories (first accounts → historical literature). Polybius remedies the problem somewhat. He was taken captive by Rome but soon found his way into the inner circles of Roman politics. He believed that the true historian is something akin to a dashing Homeric hero and wrote a history that accounted for Rome's rise and served as a moral commentary on state-craft. Polybius has earned modern praise for his dedication to present-ing factual accounts; one recent commentator on his histories, F. W. Walbank, surveys his flaws: "They amount in total to very little, and leave the overwhelming impression of a reliable and conscientious writer, with a serious theme and a determination that at all costs his readers shall comprehend and profit by it."[25]

Diodorus of Sicily and Dionysius of Halicarnassus were two other Greek historians who included Rome in their works. Diodorus dedi-cated thirty years to writing his religiously conscious and moralistic *Library of History*. He often used different sources from Livy and had reasons as a native of Sicily to dislike Octavian, and so his history has a different coloring than that of Livy, who was patronized by Octavian. Diodorus has been ridiculed by scholars, but his status has been reha-bilitated recently.[26] Dionysius wrote *The History of Archaic Rome*, which employs a great deal of embellishment to enhance the early history of Rome. He has been rightly hailed as the "typical example of rhetorical historiography," but by comparing his account to Livy's, we can make strides in reconstructing the history of early Rome.[27]

There were Latin histories of Rome written during the first half of the first century. Unfortunately, with the exception of the work of Sal-lust, who wrote about late second- and early first-century events, no substantial portions of these histories remain. By the end of the first century, the craft of the Roman historian had reached maturity with Titus Livy. Livy wrote during Augustus' reign, but he still managed to compose his history with deference to republican mores. Livy ex-pressed more anxiety about the republican transition to Augustus than other luminaries at the emperor's court or the historians that would follow him. He was no "subtle salesman for the regime" but instead was pessimistic about Rome's future and saw his *From the Founding of the City* as a skeptical summons to "spiritual and moral awakening."[28]

Like Cicero before him, Livy believed history must preserve the past and instruct the present. It is like a monument that reminds those who gaze on it to remember the values that made Rome great. History ought to check the laxness and luxury of the current age with reminders of the past's frugality and simplicity.[29] With his unwavering moral conviction and subtle challenges to the new regime, it is likely that Livy influenced Octavian far more than the potentate influenced the historian.[30]

Later biographers and historians such as Plutarch, Appian, and Cassius Dio assist the reconstruction of early Roman history, sometimes providing slightly different accounts drawn from different sources and filling in the gaps where portions of Polybius, Diodorus, Dionysius, and Livy are lost. The earliest available manuscripts (historical literature → available manuscripts) for Polybius, Diodorus, and Dionysius all date to between the tenth and eleventh centuries. Manuscripts for Livy date back to the ninth century and are traceable to a fourth-century manuscript, of which fragments remain.[31]

Events before 300 are thus difficult to detail with certainty. The historical outline is probably correct in the available accounts, but the fanciful details are almost certainly embellishments. These embellishments are not useless, for they tell a story of what Rome was supposed to represent. They may be cosmetics, but they tell us what later audiences believed the Roman spirit ought to have been. After 300, a traceable historical record exists that begins to grant certainty to the details—a feature noticeable in Livy, who increasingly fills more pages with shorter periods of history. The situation is still imperfect. Historians like Polybius and Livy were often patronized, and patrons invite bias. Audiences also enjoyed a good story, and the historians were willing to add flourish. They might, for example, take an entry in the *fasti* or an annalist's sparse description and then fill in more details or reframe the story according to contemporary concerns and debates.[32]

EVOLUTION OF THE ROMAN REPUBLIC

By taking into account the lineage of Roman historiography and by keeping in mind the applications of cosmetics, a modern reader can approach Roman history and the Roman constitution with restrained confidence. But how did the republic evolve? Like all constitutions in history, it was not static, I conclude this chapter with one final note on the frameworks that contextualize the Roman state's emergence, the constitutional principles it embodied, and the shifting ethos of the Roman citizen-soldier (table 2.1).

The traditional framework represents how classical scholars typically categorize the development of the Roman Republic. Between the regal period and the principate, Rome's status as a republic is divided into early, middle, and late periods, not unlike the way scholars have characterized the historical phases of Egypt, Babylonia, or the Hittites. Different scholars will mark the transitions at different times (table 2.1). These transitions are usually seen as continuous shifts as opposed to discontinuous breaks. Any number of dates could serve as the date the republic fell, but from 49 to 45, when the Pompeian-Caesarian civil war took place, 43, when the second triumvirate was formed, and 27, when the special powers and titles were granted to Octavian, are the usual choices.[33]

The traditional framework adequately serves most projects and isn't likely to disappear anytime soon. However, it lacks precision and implies too much continuity. Harriet Flower has offered the most recent and persuasive challenge. She presents her model as a republics framework.[34] She differs in three respects from the traditional view. She sees more breaks, more discontinuity, and a narrower time frame for the republic as a whole. Her argument weighs in heaviest regarding the final decades of the republic in the late second and early first centuries, where she marks Sulla as an equally if not more important figure than Caesar or Augustus in the republic's collapse. The remarkably stable republic of the *nobiles* was ended in 88, and the republics after that were very different creatures from what had come before. This break was the "decisive watershed," as Flower puts it, and the cast of characters that followed played the political game by different rules. Flower's view is that after Sulla, there is no longer a functioning republic to maintain or save from collapse.[35]

In the constitutional framework, Flower's scheme is given a twist (table 2.1). Perhaps it is best to think of the differences between the two

Table 2.1. Roman statehood frameworks

	Traditional framework			Republics framework	Constitutional framework
	Version 1	Version 2	Version 3		
754–509: Traditional seven kings	Regal period				Monarchic constitution
509: First consuls				Prerepublic	Transitional oligarchic constitution
494: First army secession		Early republic		Protorepublic	
451–449: Decemviri, Twelve Tables, Valerio-Horatian Laws	Early republic			Republic 1	Republican constitution: era of the patrician city-state
390: Gauls sack Rome			Early republic		
367/366: Licinio-Sextian Laws				Republic 2	
338: Dissolution of Latin League					
300: Priesthoods open to plebs				Republic 3 (*nobiles* republic 1)	
287: Hortensian Law					
264–241: First Punic War		Middle republic	Middle republic	Republic 4 (*nobiles* republic 2)	Republican constitution: era of the *nobiles'* federal empire
180: Cursus honorum fixed	Middle republic				
146: Carthage, Corinth destroyed					
139: Secret ballot introduced				Republic 5 (*nobiles* republic 3)	
133: Tiberius Gracchus' tribunate					
107: Marius reforms army					
91–88: Social War					
88: Sulla's march on Rome	Late republic	Late republic		Transitional	
81: Sulla's dictatorship				Republic 6	
60–53: Crassus-Pompey-Caesar alliance			Late republic	Oligarchy of three	Republican constitution: era of the "Sullan" constitution
49: Caesar crosses Rubicon				Transitional	
49–44: Civil war and Caesar's domination		Late republic		Protoprincipate	
44–43: Caesar's death; Battle of Mutina					
43–33: Triumvirate; Battle of Philippi				Oligarchy of three	Transitional autocratic experiments
31: Battle of Actium				Transitional	
27: Augustus' principate begins	Principate			Principate	Principate

Note: Multiple dates indicate doublets, reiterations, or disputed years for events. Many of these are debated, although the basic outline is accepted by most scholars. Solid lines represent discontinuous breaks in republican history, while dotted lines represent continuous breaks.

frameworks in terms of France's republics and Britain's unwritten constitution. France's five republics, which resemble Flower's republics, are characterized by all those messy breaks and rewritten constitutions, but the British system's flexibility seems to absorb change and adapt itself to whatever circumstances require. This analogy cannot be carried too far, but it aptly illustrates the constitutional framework's preference for continuous shifts and better describes the unwritten constitution of the Roman Republic.

Roman constitutionalism began under the monarchy, when political features emerged that would dominate in later times. We cannot make too much out of the descriptions in Dionysius and Livy, but it does seem like the monarchy had some constitutional elements compared to the two other autocratic forms common in the Mediterranean during the archaic period—hereditary kingship and tyranny. A decisive break in 509 and an important shift in 449 bookend a transitional stage. Both involved crucial steps toward the republic, and perhaps a republic indeed existed between 509 and 449, although this is a much-debated matter. Following Flower's republics framework, we can see this period as an experimental phase that involved monarchs desperately trying to regain power, powerful aristocrats with client armies, military strikes by farmer-soldiers, and a resulting decline in Rome's power. At the end of these six decades, however, Rome had expelled its kings, posted public laws, and recognized a degree of political sovereignty for the citizen-soldiers in its armies.

The constitutional framework follows Flower's breakdown of the early republics and the republic of the *nobiles*, except that it simplifies things. Flower's brilliant argument notwithstanding, the traditional schematic of early, middle, and late is here to stay, so the constitutional framework of the republic follows the same chronological markers of the early (oligarchic and patrician eras), middle (*nobiles*), and late (Sullan and transitional experiments) republic. There is one republic from 509 to the middle of the first century. Its constitution was most republican from the time of the Twelve Tables to the end of Sulla's reformed constitution, when the last great republicans—especially Cicero—died trying to maintain the old order. Transitionary periods insulate it from the monarchic epoch that preceded it and the imperial epoch that followed it.

As opposed to six republics, with the third, fourth, and fifth republics representing the first, second, and third *nobiles* republics, this study assumes one republic with three constitutional eras and continuous shifts around the year 338 and in the 80s. Even Flower refers to her framework as "a pre-republican" period, "a proto-republic," and "two full-fledged republics." Flower ultimately recasts this framework again, referring to a single "functional republican system" and "traditional republican politics" that were effectively finished by 60 BC.[36] In the constitutional framework, two moments indicate the vital shift in the fourth century. The first, occurring in 367–66, was an internal reorganization of the republic. The second, occurring in 338, was an external reorganization of the relationship between Rome and its allies. And Sulla represents a second shift that attempted to adjust the constitution to accommodate Rome's growing empire. It could have succeeded, but—in one of history's greatest tragedies—it didn't. This book sees the republic as ending in 43 with the assassination of Cicero, although the following year's defeat at the Battle of Philippi would be another appropriate choice.

This framework outlines the historical context in which Roman citizen-soldiers lived. Constitutional shifts reflected alterations in political goals, civic habits, and military requirements on the part of the citizen-soldiers. Nonetheless, their basic character as farmers and citizens exhibited constants. When this character was intentionally or accidentally assailed by geopolitical circumstances, leaders' ambitions, or a decline in the republican ethos, the republic was equally endangered. It may be difficult to determine what was the cause and what was the effect, but history indicates that the Roman citizen-soldier ceased to exist about the same time as his republic. With many modern republics making similar shifts, it is a relevant time to explore how the first republican citizens functioned as soldiers. I have defined the semantic categories, explained the historiographical concerns, and outlined the constitutional framework for Rome. Now it is time to tell the citizen-soldier's story.

PART 2

The Making of Rome's Citizen-Soldiers

3 · Origins

KINGLY ARMIES OF
THE ROMAN HILLS

FACT AND FICTION IN ROYAL ROME

In his *Defence of the Constitutions of Government*, John Adams argues that Roman republicanism began under their kings, who ruled from 753, when Rome was founded, until 509, when the last one was ousted. Adams follows the Roman tradition that assigned republican characteristics to most of the kings. They were modest and just, established the first political institutions, governed with degrees of cooperation from aristocrats and the lower orders, and expanded the Roman state through the successful prosecution of wars. Adams concludes that regal Rome never could have maintained a balance between the three orders, but that this would be remedied by the republic that followed. He thus draws on Roman traditions about the kings to remind Americans about the necessity of checks and balances in a republican constitution.[1]

His treatment of regal Rome is flawed with respect to a few essentials and many of the details, but he was doing a noble thing by using insights from the monarchy of Rome to explain how America was creating a new republic after separating from the monarchy of Britain. Adams appreciated Polybius' belief that Rome, "more than any other, has been formed, and has grown naturally, and will undergo a natural decline and change to its contrary" (6.9). As he defended the origins of the United States, he found it fitting to look to the origins of America's favorite ancient model as well.

As Adams' chapter on regal Rome demonstrates, Roman tradition asserted that law and warfare emerged together long before the republic, with the *leges regiae* (royal laws) supposedly being codified by a man named Papirius.[2] Sallust also references the Roman penchant for lawgiving from the beginning, stating that even under the kings "they had a constitution founded upon law" (*The War with Catiline*, 6). According to Dionysius, the first Roman assembly deferred to the rule of elected kings because this was the best way to achieve domestic liberty and foreign conquest (2.4). And Cicero remarks that the first king, Romulus, founded more than a city (*urbs*); he also founded a republic (*res publica*) (*On the Republic*, 2.3). It is difficult to sift through claims such as these and discover what is anachronism and what is archaic, but two things are certain. First, the kings existed. Second, they served as types for the origins of Roman law, custom, and warmaking.

Although the identities and details of the kings' reigns may be suspect (they are given impossibly long consecutive reigns from 753–509, and the names of the first four could be complete fiction), historical kings certainly existed by the late seventh or early sixth centuries. The Regia, a building associated with the kings, dates back to this time, and the ancient shrine known as the Lapis Niger contains one of the first Roman inscriptions with the word "rex" ("recei"). There are several bits of evidence that help us identify roughly when the Romulus and Remus legend was established. These royal twins destined to found Rome were supposedly sentenced to death by exposure, but they survived through the intervention of a wolf that nursed them as one of her own pups. The famous bronze statue of a she-wolf now in the Capitoline Museum alludes to their wolf surrogate and is possibly from the sixth century. The Bolsena mirror features twins like Romulus and Remus being suckled and dates from the mid-fourth century. Silver coins from 269 fix the she-wolf tradition no later than the early third century. In addition, ancient writers such as Pliny and Dionysius referenced statues of the kings that went back to the sixth century.[3]

Data such as this strongly suggests that some of the regal stories must have begun circulating during the fourth century, if not sooner. Regal Rome was the setting for the development of historical institutions and traditions that were becoming encoded in Rome's societal DNA. The basic events and actors in the story of regal Rome provide an outline for the real environment in which the republic was born. There are very few reliable details, but the basic structure helps us understand the precursors to Rome's republicanism and citizen armies.

This real environment was later filled out with fictionalized details. The first annalists and historians began to fix these tales in the historical imagination. As these legends were circulated, they increasingly shaped a picture of the ideal Roman. Stories were embellished; details were invented; and an elaborate narrative was created around the historical characters. The legends about Rome's earliest kings provided exemplars that Roman citizens could imitate. Whether these stories were read by Roman aristocrats, told by doting fathers and grandfathers, or brought to mind by the statues and public buildings one might see during a walk through the streets of Rome, they taught civics to the Romans. After the demise of the monarchy and the birth of the republic, didactic "historical" tales likewise developed around republican exemplars. I describe this murky period here by introducing Rome's competitors, providing the traditional account of the kingly commanders that opposed them, and then reconstructing how the archaic Roman regime actually took the field of battle against its neighbors in history.

THE WARRIOR BANDS OF ARCHAIC ITALY (NINTH TO SEVENTH CENTURIES)

Cicero uttered the first version of the cliché "Rome wasn't built in a day:"

> Cato used to say that our constitution was superior to those of other States on account of the fact that almost every one of these other commonwealths had been established by one man, the author of their laws and institutions. . . . [O]ur own commonwealth was based upon the genius, not of one man, but of many; it was founded, not in one generation, but in a long period of several centuries and many ages of men. (*On the Republic*, 2.1)

Cicero appreciated Cato's belief that an ongoing, civic culture in Rome consistently allowed the best men to guide its republic of farming citizens. Rome was slowly etched into existence through a long series of innovations, compromises, and deliberations, like a canyon that is created by a river's slowly wearing down stone and earth.

Cicero and Cato, like so many others between the third and first centuries, were attempting to explain why Rome had defeated everyone else and mastered the Mediterranean. Rome enjoyed a strategic position, but geography alone could not explain how it had managed to assimilate its Italian neighbors, Carthage and the western Mediterranean, and then Alexander's successors in the East. Polybius dedicated the whole of his historical acumen to answering that question—five complete books and numerous fragments remain with us today out of the forty he penned. He answered the question by focusing on Rome's third and second century wars. Cicero, like the Augustan writers Dionysius, Livy, and Virgil, attempted to answer the question by looking to the very founding of Rome. Even in the ancient world, a superpower's beginnings fascinated historians, just as the origins of superheroes engross comic book geeks.

Cicero was right that Rome's slow rise to dominance was a centuries-long evolution that relied on generations of good citizens, but Rome was equally revolutionary. Not only did it experience a literal revolution at the turn of the sixth century, but its people consistently used revolutionary methods to manage old challenges. Rome evolved much like other nascent Italian communities up to the seventh century, but between the mid-sixth to the fourth centuries, the Romans began exercising a genius for political and military affairs through a combination of conservatism and innovation. Virgil writes that Rome was fated for such genius, saying, "Roman, be sure to rule the world (be these your arts), to crown peace with justice, to spare the vanquished and to crush the proud" (*Aeneid*, 6.850). Virgil prophesies with the advantage of hindsight, but no one was making prophecies like this when Rome surfaced in archaic Italy. By the time Roman kings mustered the first armies, the small city-state consolidating control of the Roman hills had no small number of neighbors determined to keep it at bay or even destroy it.

Hierarchy and Hoplites in Greek and Etruscan Italy

Rome was surrounded by four different types of inhabitants. The Italiote Greeks were dotted here and there along the southern coastline; the Etruscans lay to the north; various Italic mountain peoples lay along the Apennine spine of Italy to the east; and the Latins occupied lands to the south. The first of these, the Greeks, had begun colonizing the ports of the Mediterranean with the Phoenicians in the eighth century. Greek city-states were concentrated in the north and Phoenicians in the south. Both founded colonies that became famous enemies of Rome during a series of epic conflicts starting in the third century. In the beginning, however, the few Greek and Punic interactions with Rome were more pacific.[4] Sophisticated wares, architectural innovations, and artistic styles were among the goods Greece offered. From a political and military perspective, the most important influence was the Hellenic combination of polis, hoplite, and phalanx. This combination reached its high point during the Persian wars of the early fifth century, when the Greeks successfully fended off Persia's imperial invasions.

Etruscan city-states shared a common culture but preferred political independence from one another. Bounded by the Arno and Tiber rivers to the north and south and by the Apennines and Tyrrhenian Sea to the east and west, Etruscan territory was divided into three geographical regions: a northern area rich in metal resources, an inland region along the Apennines, and a southern coastal plain which was the leader in cultural sophistication and trade. Territorial expansion in the middle of the first millennium pushed the influence of the Etruscans north into the Po Valley and south into coastal Campania. This expansion was not part of an orchestrated effort. Instead, it occurred through an infiltration of aristocratic chieftains. Wealthy and influential families seem to have been able to move around central Italy with ease during this time, and the most successful among them secured control of settlements in the areas to which they migrated.[5]

The Etruscan polity was shaped by kinship and socioeconomic distinctions. Eighth-century tombs indicate a wealthy aristocracy that rose to unprecedented preeminence. Society became stratified, and the leaders took positions at the head of Etruscan gentes, which approximated tribal clans. The aristocracy became entrenched as they accumulated landholdings and traded goods over a mass of kinfolk, clients, and slaves. An Etruscan middling class does not seem to have existed. About a century later, the *oikos* (household) became the prominent form of social grouping, when wealth, status, and relationships became concentrated in individuals. A parallel institution known as the paterfamilias (head of the household) developed in Latium.[6]

Monarchies in Etruria emerged simultaneously with cities, but as the aristocracy gained power in the sixth and fifth centuries, Etruscan kings were increasingly threatened by local oligarchies.[7] The Etruscans took part in a religious league, but it never worked to their military advantage. As in the Greek city-states, religious, linguistic, and other cultural similarities rarely effected political and military unity.[8]

Military cooperation would have been helpful for the Etruscans. They lived in a "militarized anarchy" that was bolstered by the bardic tradition of their aristocracies and warlord-kings. They were constantly at war on land and sea. The Greeks and Carthaginians contested the coastline and coastal plains, and the Apennine peoples and Gauls became an even greater threat by the fourth century before Rome permanently ended Etruscan independence in the third. The famous naval battle at Alalia around 540 featured an Etruscan-Carthaginian alliance against the Greeks. The battle was technically won by the Greeks, although it led to the strategic expansion of the losers. A defeat at Cumae in 474 led to Etruscan retrenchment in the south. The Etruscans were just as content to squabble among themselves. When Rome besieged and captured Veii in 396, it had received little help from its kinsfolk. Some Etruscan city-states like Caere even supported Rome.[9]

The Etruscan cities were strategically situated in easily defendable positions located atop hills and flanked by river valleys, cliffs, and ravines.[10] The cities were defended by armies that are best described as warrior bands, which should not be confused with the hoplite phalanxes developing among the Greek city-states. By the sixth century Greece was in the midst of its polis-hoplite-phalanx revolution. In many city-states, political power slipped from monarchs, tyrants, and oligarchies into a middling group of citizens. One of the most important political functions of citizens was armed conflict. Citizen armies from poleis were equipped with body armor, the thrusting spear, and the round shield (*hoplon*). They fought in a densely packed formation that relied on every man playing his part. The Etruscans developed (or adopted) aspects of this military culture, but they never fielded a full-fledged citizen phalanx like the Greeks.

Extant pictorial representations and panoplies from grave sites prove that Etruscan aristocrats proudly donned the hoplite armor, but the civic ethos was notably absent from a society still dependent on the gentilicial structure (which was somehow derived from families and clans). Etruria transitioned from raising Homeric-type armies with dueling aristocrats into forming armed bands of clients under the authority of aristocratic condottieri. Rome's Servian reforms would later undermine the power of the gentes there, but the Etruscan city-states never comprehensively overhauled their social institutions in a like manner. This inhibited political evolution. In contrast to Greek hoplites, Etruscan soldiers exercised little political sovereignty and were dependent on the martial authority of their patrons.[11]

Warfare among the Apennine Peoples

The Apennines harbored a very different sort of warrior. Mountain peoples inhabited the Apennine spine from northwest Italy all the way down to the Italian toe. From the perspective of early Rome, the Sabines, Aequi, Volsci, and Samnites were the most important. The Aequi and Volsci presented a proximate threat to the Latins, while the Sabines alternated between peaceful and bellicose exchanges with Rome. Most of them seem to have mixed pastoralism with small-scale farming. Politically, they were organized in a "cantonal arrangement with village headmen and perhaps tribal assemblies."[12] Evidence from Samnite sites suggest that they constructed chains of hill forts that were used as outposts, refuges, and bases during the summer months when the pastures and farm lands of the mountains were accessible.[13]

The city-state did not exist among the mountain peoples. The Samnites, about whom we have more archaeological and literary information, were organized around the *touto*, which was roughly equivalent to the Latin *populus*, or people. The *touto* was divided into the obscure *pagi*, which were administrative districts comprised of settlements such as *vici* (villages) in the flatlands and oppida (towns) and *castella* (forts) in the mountains. According to Strabo and Livy, Samnite tribes such as the Caraceni, Caudini, Hirpini, and Pentri could each constitute a Samnite *touto*. Important settlements such as Aufidena, Caudium, Malventum, and Bovianum served as respective capitals. The Samnites were among a growing number of Italic peoples who had republican, mixed governments from the sixth to the fourth centuries. The *toutos* were not kingdoms, but a government comprised of magistrates, council, and assembly. By the fourth century the Samnites had formed a formidable religious and military federation, the Samnite League, and it would present Rome's greatest challenge to the hegemony of Italy.[14]

One of the more fascinating aspects of Apennine culture was the rite called the sacred spring, wherein all those born in the spring were devoted to the god of war. When the children reached adulthood, they would be sent off as a sort of population control to inhabit the lowlands. From the perspective of the lowland communities, this constituted an ongoing stream of small-scale invasions and raids. In the fifth century these erupted into a large-scale migration that dramatically increased warfare in the Tyrrhenian plains.[15]

Not much is known about early mountain warrior tactics. The Samnites and other Apennine peoples wore a variety of helmets, from Greek and Gallic imports to local hybrids. The earliest chest protector other than cloth or hide was the *kardiophylax* (a bronze disk over the heart) strapped to back plates. The Samnites were well known for their linen tunics, which were worn underneath the triple-disked breastplate, an advanced *kardiophylax* that had developed by the mid-fourth century. If they carried shields, they were constructed of wood or hide. The scutum, an oblong shield, was common throughout much of Italy, especially among the mountain peoples. Weapons included thrusting spears, light javelins, heavy javelins (pila), and two-edged short swords.

There were variations in weapons and protective gear used by the soldiers in every army. Formations were probably flexible, ad hoc, and intended for raiding and other small-scale engagements. Pastoral and agricultural cycles, rites such as the sacred spring, and the restricted geographical exchanges of archaic Italy habituated the Apennine peoples to a life of constant but limited warfare.[16]

The military prowess of Italy's mountain peoples had already become well known as far away as the Greek mainland by the late fifth century. Thucydides mentions how the "Opicans" (Oscans) aggressively expelled the Sicels from Italy (6.2). Oscan-speaking peoples continued to pressure the lowlands of south Italy, overrunning parts of Campania, colliding with the Italiote city-states along the coast, and taking part in conflicts with powerful Greek tyrants such as Dionysius I of Syracuse and Alexander the Molossian. When the Roman-Samnite Wars erupted in the mid-fourth century, the Samnites had already proved to be just as expansionary, imperialistic, and violent as the Romans and other powers in central Italy.[17]

The Latin Plain

The Romans became enamored with Greek culture between the third and first centuries and envied the rich tales of their past. To sate their jealousy, the Romans sought a baptism in Greek legend. With a little literary license, poets and historians alike managed to associate Rome and Latium with the ill-fated Trojans. As Troy lay burning around him, Aeneas was said to have fled the city at the head of a small band of Trojans who eventually landed in Italy and settled Lavinium. Aeneas' son Ascanias then founded the important Latin settlement of Alba Longa. The earlier legend about the founding of Rome by Romulus and Remus was merged with the Aeneas legend, and the twins were made Aeneas' descendants as well. Romulus and Remus, like Sargon the Great and Moses, were set adrift in a basket in a river. Whereas Moses had been so placed by humble peasants and discovered by royalty, the twins were abandoned by royalty and discovered by the humble peasant Faustulus.

These fanciful tales correctly hint at the geographical unity and cultural exchanges between archaic Romans, Latins, and other nearby peoples such as the Sabines, but not much else about them can be trusted. The archaeological evidence shows that Latium and its environs had settlements at least as far back as the fourteenth century. By the tenth century Latium had developed a distinctive identity, and increasing surplus levels suggest the ability to concentrate wealth. Eighth-century grave sites reveal a growing economic disparity. Multi-chambered tombs were constructed for generations of family members, indicating that a local aristocracy was developing similar to that in Etruria. By the seventh century, when the wealthy began dedicating their resources to public projects instead of private tombs, the major centers had public buildings. An increase in settlements meant that land was becoming scarce. Wars for the best territory loomed on the horizon.[18]

Like in Etruria, politics in Latium was transformed from simple relationships in clans and villages into systems based on the gens and clientage. Both of these are obscure and complex to us today, and attempting to explain them comprehensively here is not possible. What is important is that gentilicial and patron-client relationships created a sociopolitical environment well suited to warrior bands. Leaders of clients and "clansmen" were responsible for sacred, political, and military leadership. When it came to armed conflict, these leaders commanded units of their supporters in raids against other bands from nearby settlements. Capable strongmen could occasionally unify these bands, as early kings and tyrants did in archaic Italy, but this was a primitive system that inhibited the growth of strong states with capable militaries.[19]

Geography eventually brought unity to the settlements of Latium in ways not afforded to the Etruscans, whose lands were cut into their threefold division by rivers and mountains, or the Greeks, who resided in small, isolated valleys or on islands. Instead, the open plain of Latium called for a unified defense or an isolated defenselessness. The Latin settlements began as village communities with cult centers; as the population increased these centers gained political value. Religious leagues emerged as in other Italic communities, but these leagues had more utility among the Latins. Shared sacred sites such as the Alban Mount, Lake Nemi, Aricia, and Lanuvium became popular at the same time that shared legal and social rights like the ability to intermarry, engage in commerce, and negotiate contracts increased. Skirmishes no doubt continued among the Latins, but a common identity began forming as well.[20] Alba Longa may have exercised some sort of early hegemony. However, leadership eventually fell to that settlement that occupied the most strategic location between the Sabines to the east, the coast to the west, and the Etruscans to the north and that was the natural gateway along the Tiber: Rome.

THE FIRST ROMAN ARMIES (C. 750–C. 550)

Romulus and the Roman Condottieri

The first king of Rome was Romulus, a morally complex person who killed his brother Remus, raided the Sabines to kidnap wives for his warriors, and made war on all his neighbors. The point of such legends, including the bad ones, was that Romulus always acted for the good of Rome.[21] He may have been a Machiavellian warlord, but he was a Machiavellian warlord for Rome. The Romulus of tradition was able to expand his nascent polity because he commanded a particularly capable warrior band. He attracted brigands that Livy describes as "an obscure and lowly multitude" and "a miscellaneous rabble" (1.8). Such a description accords well with the armies of the period— warrior bands of clients that were attached to a king or chieftain with charisma and influence. Consistent with other Mediterranean tyrants, Romulus supposedly handpicked a standing bodyguard of three hundred soldiers, was "more liked by the commons than by the senate, and was preeminently dear to the hearts of the soldiers" (Livy, 1.15).

Rome's unique political institutions originated with Romulus. According to tradition, he divided the Roman people into thirty curiae and created three centuries of knights (Livy, 1.13). The curiae were derived from three tribes and supposedly supplied a thousand men each in Rome's first army. The Curiate Assembly, which granted imperium (military authority) to commanders, undoubtedly originated during Rome's regal period, as it was one of the earliest assemblies known to the city. Tradition also credits Romulus with the creation of a council of a hundred that later grew into the senate (Livy, 1.8). These early noblemen were surely warrior chiefs within the gentilicial structure who had their own client-soldiers like the Etruscan condottieri. The emergence of institutions such as the Curiate Assembly and the senate parallel Latin and Hellenic transitions from primitive monarchies to aristocratic bodies with the power to make or break kings. The people, organized into the curiae, theoretically formed a third power, giving the republic its basis for a division between magistrates, senate, and assemblies.[22]

The archaic Roman army resembled its Etruscan and Greek neighbors. The material data suggests that offensive weapons included javelins and swords and that the spear predominated. Typical armor included a bronze helmet, a pectoral protector, and a wooden shield with a central handgrip and possibly a metal rim. Armies probably fought small engagements in tight formations led by condottieri. Equipment ranged widely among the troops, with the wealthiest and most experienced being better equipped. The condottieri themselves were patrons and familial chiefs who could command impressive numbers for the day. Attius Clausus supposedly emigrated from Sabine country to Rome with five thousand warriors; Gaius Marcius Coriolanus had a similar band of armed clients; and the Fabii clan waged its own war on behalf of Rome against Veii in the early fifth century. The Lapis Satricanus, an inscribed block from the early fifth century, references the "companions" devoted to Poplios Valesios, who may have been the famous Roman consul Publius Valerius. The inscription implies that Valesios acted as "an independent warlord." These and other examples easily fit within the seventh- to fifth-century paradigm of independent armies attached to powerful chiefs who exercised political and social authority over their men at the same time that they fought in small-scale, independent skirmishes in central Italy.[23]

Numa and the Sacral Nature of War

The religious reforms of Rome's second king, Numa Pompilius, rounded out the warlike attributes personified by Romulus and Numa's successor, Tullus Hostilius. The complementary legends of Romulus and Numa were necessary for later writers. Numa's kingship, devoted to the religious mores of Rome, added piety as a Roman virtue. Dionysius and Livy credit him with the priestly colleges and detail his meticulous respect for the augurs. Numa gave Rome "a new foundation in law, statutes, and observances," which further strengthened it by ensuring that it would henceforth be "well organized in the arts both of war and of peace" (Livy, 1.19-21; Dionysius, 2.56-76). For Cicero, Numa's reforms brought "kindness," "benevolence," sophistication, and stabilization to the Roman people (*Republic*, 2.14). Regardless of the historical role Numa played in Rome's early religion, the narrative of his kingship stressed the value the historians placed on the origins of Roman piety. A nice touch in the tradition has Numa build the temple to the mysterious, two-faced god Janus. If its doors were opened, war was unleashed, and if closed, peace reigned. Numa, of course, had them shut (Livy, 1.19).[24]

In light of this, it seems reasonable for Polybius to include his analysis of Roman religion in a discussion of the Roman constitution. Roman conceptions of the national pantheon and personal *pietas* could serve as reproofs to state actors or guides to their future courses of action (6.56). Religious observances occasionally provided a soft check on the activities of the magistrates. The ancient authors record that this is first seen when the augur Attus Navius prevented King Tarquinius Priscus from doubling the number of equestrian centuries (Livy, 1.36). The power of religious officials such as Navius had been entrenched by Numa's formal institutionalization of them. Religious positions and powers rarely functioned independently. Roman priesthoods were held by most of the same men who held magistracies. In fact, a distinction of Roman religion was how little it interfered with the state. Unlike ancient Near Eastern states, or even Greek polities for that matter, dreams, prophets, auspices, and omens rarely impacted Roman politics or warmaking negatively. Instead, Roman religion exhibited a degree of flexibility lacking in other ancient nations, affording Roman imperial ambitions a greater latitude for success.[25]

One of Numa's most important innovations was the institution of the fetiales, a body of priests who ensured that Rome's foreign policy and political dealings abroad were conducted properly—especially official declarations of war (Dionysius, 2.72). Cicero mentions the fetiales as one of the most important reasons Rome was able to expand beyond its village into all of Italy and eventually the Mediterranean. The fetiales ensured that war was "never undertaken by the ideal State, except in defense of its honor or its safety" (*Republic*, 3.23). In the moral mindset of the Romans, this devotion to a code of "just" wars granted Rome the legitimate authority to acquire an empire. Cicero believed that because Rome's wars were meticulously pious, the gods granted them success. His reasoning gave birth to the mantra of Roman defensive imperialism: "But our people by defending their allies have gained dominion over the whole world" (*Republic*, 3.24). Numa, as the creator of the fetiales, represented Rome's early efforts to instill piety in warfare. Throughout Rome's conquests, piety "underwrote Roman power."[26] All of Rome's battles, whether against petty neighbors in the sixth century or against colossal Mediterranean kingdoms in the third and second centuries, were justified by a painstakingly legalistic understanding of the gods that emerged under the kings.

Tarquinius and Rome's First Public Spaces

Numa was followed by three more regal stock characters. Tullus Hostilius was the warrior king. If Numa had closed the doors of Janus, Hostilius reopened them. He hosted the famous Horatii-Curiatii duel between two sets of triplets, conquered and then destroyed Alba Longa, and made war against Rome's chief enemies, the Veientines and Sabines. Ancus Marcius was the consolidator. He codified some of Numa's reforms, incorporated neighboring territory, and founded the Roman port Ostia. Tarquinius Priscus was the great builder whose works supposedly included no less than the Capitoline temple to Jupiter Optimus Maximus and the Circus Maximus. Archaeologists have verified that Rome indeed underwent expansive building in the sixth century. Connections with earlier kings are dubious, but Tarquinius Priscus was probably a historical figure responsible for some of the improvements.

The regal building programs physically unified the early hill settlements. The marshy terrain of Rome's low-lying areas was drained and filled with gravel, creating a public space where rituals could be exercised, honors conveyed, and meetings held. The Cloaca Maxima, a drainage system constructed at the end of the sixth century, might have enabled this. Pavements were created across the landfill and structures such as the Regia, the Sant'Omobono temple complex, and the buildings related to the Vestal Virgins began to appear.

Elites in Etruria and Latium were using their resources and relationships to construct physical testaments to the civic communities that were emerging, and Rome was keeping pace. The area of the Circus Maximus, which had been drained and demarcated like the forum, provided a focal point for elite patronage and vehicles such as the chariot. The new public space also enabled rituals such as the triumph (a kind of military parade and one of the most important honors for Roman aristocrats). The first Roman assemblies could now meet in the drained and paved area near the Regia, and the early senate could convene in the Curia Hostilia, supposedly built by Tullus Hostilius. Atop the Capitoline the massive, Etruscan-modeled temple to Jupiter loomed as a sacred unifier of the Romans. Its construction was surely begun during this time, although its completion may have been delayed in the tumult of the late sixth century.[27]

THE ROMAN "PHALANX" (C. 550–509)

Rome in the mid-sixth century occupied a space of about 285 hectares, which ranked it larger than most settlements in central Italy but somewhat smaller than Italiote sites in the south such as Metapontum and Gela. Rome's comparative size afforded it ample manpower, which became an asset for local and foreign condottieri who sought to secure election as king or to seize Rome by force. In the open structure of archaic Italy's aristocracies, any distinguished and powerful man could come to power. Numa Pompilius was a Sabine, and his successors Tullus Hostilius and Ancus Marcius were descendants of Sabines. Tarquin Priscus and Tarquin Superbus were Etruscans, and possibly Servius Tullius too. Lars Porsena, who may have briefly ruled Rome after the revolution, was also Etruscan. These men would have been attracted by Rome's size and its strategic position as a hub for Etruscan, Latin, Greek, Apennine, and Phoenician trade.[28]

Tradition has it that Rome's sixth king, Servius Tullius, fully exploited Rome's manpower through a set of comprehensive reforms that transformed the nature of Roman citizenship and military service. Rome was probably under pressure from the Etruscan and Greek city-states to modify its armor and tactics. Kaeso, a later author, would claim as much: "the Etruscans used to wage war against us armed with bronze shields and arrayed in a phalanx, not arranged in maniples. We changed our equipment and adopted theirs, and arraying ourselves in battle against them overcame them, though they had long experience of fighting in a phalanx formation."[29] Kaeso is off on the details—the Etruscans did not field a pure hoplite phalanx—but he captures the spirit of Rome's first series of military adaptations in the sixth and fifth centuries. Grave sites and contemporary depictions make it clear that the Etruscan city-states, along with the Italiote Greeks and Latins, were shifting to state-based militaries that favored close-ordered infantry armed with hoplite equipment. By the fourth century, many of Rome's neighbors along the Tyrrhenian plains were regularly fielding these kinds of armies.[30] The reforms of Servius constituted Rome's response to these developments.

The Servian reforms stabilized the aristocracy, regularized the army, and incorporated more citizens as troops. Like Kleisthenes did in Athens, Servius rearranged and increased the old tribal structure, turning the three tribes into a territorial system of twenty-one tribes that reflected Rome's recent conquests. However, the foremost change was the creation of the Centuriate Assembly, which arranged the Roman army into five classes based on the male citizenry's property ratings. Livy and Dionysius disagree on some of the details, but at least the first three property classes of the Servian constitution carried a helmet, shield (round *clipeus* for the first class, scutum for the second and third), spear, and sword similar to the weapons carried by hoplites. The fifth class served as skirmishers and carried javelins and slings. The fourth class fought in the formation if Dionysius was correct and with the skirmishers if Livy was correct. The poorest were exempt from military service—and also therefore denied political power (Livy, 1.42–44; Dionysius, 4.16–18). Classes were further divided between senior and junior centuries, which separated the older and younger men. Supplemental to this was the equestrian class, drawn from the largest property owners, who served as the cavalry. At first, the new levy (from "legio") formed one legion from the Roman centuries; this was subsequently augmented to two legions. If scholars are correct in estimating that the population of Roman territory was forty thousand, this would produce a manpower base of nine thousand, making it reasonable to assume a formation of about five thousand to six thousand men.[31]

The reforms surely did not all occur during this time. They may not even have been military reforms but instead political reforms that later authors interpreted in a military light. It is even possible that a shift in the curiate organization gave rise to Servius' "centuriate" organization, which combined the responsibilities of the Curiate Assembly and the later Centuriate Assembly. The new assembly bestowed imperium, elected magistrates, authorized war, and constituted the army. The army was still dependent on aristocratic cavalry and warrior bands, which is corroborated in the literary depiction of the first half of the fifth century. However, the stage was set for another shift.[32] Roman citizenship, property ownership, and military participation were becoming linked. This is confirmed archaeologically with a downward shift of resources as evidenced in graves and building projects and with the record of new military equipment. It is thus reasonable to assume an evolution in military institutions that paralleled a revolution in political ideals.

Over the course of the sixth and fifth centuries, this new system, whether Servian or not, transformed Rome's warrior bands into a phalanx-like state army. Citizens equipped themselves according to their ability to afford specific arms and armor. The poorest clients could only afford javelins or slings; the wealthiest patrons could afford greaves, ornate helmets, and superior chest protection such as a muscled cuirass. In between these extremes were men who bore chest plates, a range of helmets, and wooden shields that differed in size, shape, and quality. The first three or four classes would have constituted the heavy infantry and the last one or two the light infantry. Equipment variations were unavoidable and would not have necessarily affected the tactical requirements of Rome's small-scale warfare. Rather, what was crucial was the communal army of citizens organized by the new system that cut across gentilicial and clientage structures.

Romans did not suddenly view themselves differently, dismiss their patrons, and shake off the gentilicial structure, but over time the fixed, legal nature of the reforms would counterbalance these older systems, which is an innovation the Etruscans never adopted. This empowered Rome as a state and strengthened the sense of a Roman community and not just communities of Fabii or Junii or Valerii that resided in Rome. The ideology behind the changes sought to establish a common set of values for as many citizens as possible. It shaped a civic ethos for warmaking at the same time that it enlarged and empowered Rome's martial capabilities. By the end of the fifth century, these changes had been completed, and Rome was in a position to reap the rewards.

The inauguration of these reforms under the monarchy may have played a role in Rome's competition with the Latin settlements. Rome had enjoyed successes against the Latins earlier, but it definitely gained the upper hand by the late sixth century if a treaty preserved in Polybius that has Rome claim hegemony in 509 is valid. Servius and his successor Tarquin Superbus were both associated with Rome's ascendancy over the Latins in the late sixth century.[33] When the latter seized power, he commanded a capable city-state and a formidable army that was slowly carving up its opponents. The nearby Etruscan city-states were cooperative or conquered. The Apennine peoples were kept at bay. Latium was slowly falling under the power of Rome and its kings. What could possibly threaten this? The answer was revolution.

4 · Proving Ground

SURVIVING IN CENTRAL ITALY

In 1783 the American War of Independence had been won, but many wondered precisely what it had achieved. What constitution and what moral character would define the new republic as domestic crises and foreign foes threatened it in the 1780s? Fisher Ames answered this question by referencing the two most important early Roman republicans. In a series of pamphlets between October 1786 and March 1787, Ames defends Massachusetts' republicanism, which was reeling from the chaos of Shays' Rebellion. His pamphlets also argue for a broader, national republicanism for the new American republic. The Shays' rebels were farmers, and a looming debt crisis that echoed themes in early Roman history was prompting former patriot soldiers to march against the state. Ames argues that Massachusetts' republican constitution must remain intact, the government must respond strongly, and this democratic uprising must be crushed. Republican governments should not give in to the pleas of democratic revolutionaries, especially when they destabilize constitutional balance and political order. Ames' pamphlets were received well, paving the way for his emergence as a key defender of the constitution in the next years. The pseudonyms Ames used for the pamphlets were "Lucius Junius Brutus" and "Marcus Furius Camillus." Brutus was the founder of Rome's republic, and Camillus was a late fifth- and early fourth-century statesman often called the "second founder of Rome." These two figures flourished at moments when the Roman Republic was teetering between greatness and oblivion.

At the time Ames used the classical pseudonyms, the fledgling American governments were entering their own proving ground after the revolution. All republics, especially those based on mixed governments and militias, must constantly demonstrate the will to survive. The Anti-Federalists and their successors, the Democratic-Republicans, had a point when they attacked the Federalists' praise of mixed governments. History "proved that the balance between orders was constantly in jeopardy, if not wholly impossible to maintain." Some Anti-Federalists, like "Centinel," preferred a simple democracy tempered by the practical necessity of representatives. "Centinel" did not openly claim it, but he was essentially embracing the democratic model of Athens. He argued, much like the "seventeenth-century monarchists, that mixed government was a mirage."[1] In challenging these sentiments, Ames references the best possible examples, early Roman republicans like Brutus, Cincinnatus, and Camillus who were capable republican statesman and talented commanders of citizen-soldiers. As with the regal period, not all of the stories and details recorded by later historians were accurate, but they represented how Roman citizens tread the path between democracy and monarchy and then defended it on the battlefield. So what were the historical circumstances in which republicanism developed, and how did Rome survive the centuries after its revolution in the proving ground of central Italy?

THE EVOLUTION OF EXEMPLARITY

The stories surrounding Rome's last king, Lucius Tarquinius Superbus include all the literary ingredients in a perfect recipe for revolution. Tarquinius plotted with the old king's daughter to murder him and usurp the throne. He used treachery to expand his territory. He was a brutally capable commander but as vicious to his people as to his enemies. His son raped a noblewoman, Lucretia, who then committed suicide out of shame, prompting the nobles to seek justice and liberty for the people. Meanwhile, a hero waited in the wings that had been feigning stupidity at the king's court.

This hero, Brutus, had already demonstrated both piety and insight when he correctly interpreted a Delphic oracle that he would one day rule Rome. After witnessing Lucretia's tragic end, Brutus rallied the nobles and gave a stirring speech to the assembly, which flocked to his cause. Brutus enrolled his own army from the assembly, outwitted and expelled the king, and then guided the Romans as they formed their own new republic led by annual magistrates, a senate, and popular assemblies. But the story of Brutus did not stop there. In his first year as one of the annual magistrates, he adjudicated a conspiracy against the republic involving his own sons and dutifully had them executed, after which he died in battle on behalf of the nascent republic while locked in a personal duel with the expelled king's son.

The story is tantalizing, but it tells us more about Roman notions of republican exemplarity than the revolution itself. Brutus was the paradigmatic Roman magistrate. He was crafty, honorable, inspiring, capable on the field of battle, and, most importantly, willing to sacrifice his own sons and his own life for the good of the republic. Other early magistrates such as Cincinnatus, who was consul in 460 and dictator in 458, were crafted from the same mold. Cincinnatus followed his first legendary dictatorship with a second one just as epic, when in 439 he rescued the state from the attempted tyrant Spurius Maelius.

Traditions like these developed for every level of society. The slave who uncovered the coup of Brutus' sons, Vindicius, showed how good deeds for the republic can yield rewards, liberty, and citizenship (Livy, 2.5). Women such as Lucretia, Cloelia, Veturia, and Verginia demonstrated the productivity, tenacity, loyalty, and purity of Roman maids and matrons. Daring men like Horatius Cocles, who single-handedly protected a bridge from invading forces, and Mucius Scaevola, who burned his own hand in a flame to prove Roman resolve, showed how the citizen-soldier must be willing to risk life and limb.[2] These characters belonged to the entire *populus Romanus* and not simply the elite. They illustrate how Roman exemplarity in the literary tradition was transferred from virtuous kings to average citizens possessing civic virtue.

Given the evidence from earlier sources like Polybius, monuments, and other artifacts, we know that many of these stories were definitely

circulating as early as the third century. While the fanciful details cannot be confidently traced back to the beginning of the republic, it is
probable that the legendary status of certain citizens had been promul-
gated from the beginning. Etruscan-style statues of Attus Navius (the
augur who opposed Tarquinius) and Brutus were supposedly erected
soon after the actions ascribed to them.[3]

The real history of Rome's early days as a republic demonstrated
the need for civic exemplarity. Italy was still a violent and perilous
world, and the situation was made worse by new unrest and migra-
tions, just at the time that Rome had weakened itself with a revolution.
The period was characterized by ongoing battles for survival, both in
domestic politics and foreign wars. These events form the backdrop to
the story of Rome's slow transformation from beleaguered city-state
to imperial republic (table 4.1).[4]

LIVES OF FARMING AND FIGHTING (509–390)

Republican Revolution

The physical space of the republican community had already been
marked out during the regal period, but it took on a new importance
with the demise of the kingship. The magistrates retained the accou-
trements of imperium, but now senate and assembly were elevated.
The senate would have met in the Curia Hostilia, if it had indeed been
built by that time. Opposite to the Curia was the speaker's platform,
called the rostra after 338 when it was decorated with captured ships'
prows. In between these two was the space known as the Comitium,
which was the primary location for the assembly until the end of the
second century, when it began meeting in the Forum owing to the
need for more space. This area became one of the most important civic
spaces, rivaled perhaps only by the Field of Mars, where the Centuriate Assembly met as an army for elections.[5]

The revolution did not sweep in a full-fledged republic in one magnificent stroke. In fact there is a great deal of discussion over whether
a republic was created at this time. Others have skillfully addressed

this question, as I have noted in chapters 1 and 2; still, it is useful to consider a few relevant points on the early constitution.[6]

Polybius later extolled the Roman constitution of his time, remarking that "such fairness and propriety in all respects" characterized the way aristocratic, democratic, and monarchical principles were used in "drawing up the constitution . . . that it was impossible even for a native to pronounce with certainty whether the whole system was aristocratic, democratic, or monarchical" (6.11). Polybius has come under scrutiny for the accuracy of his analysis, but he was on to something with this statement.[7] That scholars continue to quibble over which governmental form—magistrates, senate, or assemblies—dominated at Rome, proves Polybius' point. Rome was clearly a stratified society. There were divisions between patricians and nonpatricians, citizens and noncitizens, free men and slaves, and patrons and clients, but such divisions provided the makings of a good ancient republic. Mixed government republics are neither egalitarian nor strictly hierarchical but instead occupy a middle ground that incorporates the various strata of society. Societal divisions in a republic become problematic only if the entirety of a state's sovereignty is concentrated into one political body. Roman culture maintained its cohesion by alternately uplifting the virtues of each respective branch, just as the imperial Roman historian Florus notes: "At one time it championed liberty, at another chastity, at another the dignity of birth, at another the right to distinctions and insignia of office" (1.17.26).

The first two centuries of Rome's republican existence demonstrated the flexible and evolutionary nature of political sovereignty. New magistracies with new powers were constantly developing under the pressures of conflict, consensus, and compromise (table 4.1). One of the most unique was the Roman dictator—an office that vested absolute, temporary power in one man during a crisis. This would have bumfuzzled the constitutional sensibilities of Hellenic assemblies.[8] The dictatorship was that much more remarkable given the way the aristocracy dealt with figures that aimed at the autocratic power of a classical Greek tyrant. Spurius Cassius in 485, Spurius Maelius in 439, and Marcus Manlius in 385 discovered the fatal consequences. In Rome

Table 4.1. Rome's fifth- to fourth-century battles

	The external wars		The internal struggle
509	Lars Porsena besieges or captures Rome, possibly expelling Tarquinius Superbus	509	Roman Revolution: the kings are replaced by dual magistrates in a violent upheaval
509	First Carthage Treaty: Rome claims dominant position in Latium	509/449/300	*Provocatio*: right to appeal a magistrates' corporal or capital punishment is granted
508/504	Battle of Aricia: Porsena is defeated by a Latin-Italiote alliance	494	First secession of the plebs: the Roman army mutinies over debt bondage
505–449	Sabines continually raid Roman territory	494/471	Plebeian magistrates: creation of plebeian tribunes, aediles, and an assembly
490s	Aequi and Volsci begin incursions into Latium, taking half its territory	485	Spurius Cassius executed for proposing agrarian laws in attempt to secure kingship
499/496/493	Battle of Lake Regillus: Romans victorious over Latins	457	Plebeian tribunes increased from five to ten
494–455	Annual fighting with Volsci and Aequi, including Cincinnatus' victory in 458	451	Decemviri: ten-man board appointed to codify laws
493	Treaty of Cassius: defensive and social alliance with Latins	449	Second secession: the army secedes again to oust a second tyrannical board of decemviri
490–488	Volscians overrun most of Latium and threaten Rome	449	Twelve Tables: after the decemviri and secession, a code of private law is published
486	Latin and Roman alliance with Hernici	449	Valerio-Horatian Laws: made plebiscites binding, possibly on entire state
483–474	First Veientine War: Roman defeat, including disastrous Battle of Cremera	446	Quaestors: lowest-level magistracy created
473–400	Iapygian, Lucanian, Bruttian invasions begin overwhelming Italiote Greeks	445	Canuleian Law: law forbidding patrician-plebeian intermarriage overturned
437–426	Second Veientine War: over Fidenae; twenty-one-year truce with Veii follows	444–367	Consular military tribunes: new chief magistrates available to plebs are appointed
431	Battle of Mons Algidus: major defeat of Aequi; eight-year truce follows	443	Censors: new magistracy created that will become the most distinguished
423	Etruscan ruling class expelled from Capua by Samnites	439	Spurius Maelius executed for supplying wheat in attempt to secure kingship

The external wars		The internal struggle	
406–396	Siege and capture of Veii; military pay introduced; possibly tributum as well	430/501	Dictatorship: most powerful magistracy created by this date, if not earlier
395–394	Treaties with Veii's former allies Capena and Falerii	385	Marcus Manlius executed for proposing debt laws in attempt to secure kingship
390/387	Gauls defeat Romans at Battle of the Allia and then capture Rome temporarily	367–366	Licinio-Sextian Laws: plebeians attain consulship; public landholdings limited; praetorship created; debt alleviated
380	Rome defeats Praeneste's coalition	367	Curule aediles: made official magistracy of the state; soon after available to plebeians
366–345	Numerous battles with Hernici, Etruscans, Latins, Volsci, and Auruni	362	Romans elect six military tribunes as subordinates to consuls
354	Treaty with Samnites: probably as equal powers for simple security concerns	356	Plebeians attain dictatorship
348	Second Carthage Treaty: a non-aggression pact that favored Carthage	351	Plebeians attain censorship
343–341	First Samnite War	342	Genucian Law: plebeians guaranteed a consulship; mandated consulship interval
340–338	Latin War, including Campani, Sidicini, Aurunci	339	Publilian Laws: plebiscites made binding on state; plebeians guaranteed one censor
340–326	Numerous battles with Aurunci, Sidicini, Acerrae, Fundi, Privernum, and Neapolis	336	Plebeians attain praetorship
326–304	Second Samnite War, including disastrous defeat at Caudine Forks in 321	326/313	Poetelian-Papirian Law: dissolution of debt bondage
312–292	Numerous battles with Marsi, Etrsucans, Hernici, Aequi, and Umbrians	300	Ogulnian Law: plebeians attain priestly colleges of pontiffs and augurs
298–290	Third Samnite War	287	Hortensian Law: plebiscites again made binding on the entire state

Note: Multiple dates indicate doublets, reiterations, or disputed years for events. Many of these are debated, although the basic outline is accepted by most scholars.

the charisma of tyrants was avoided through the constitutionalism of dictators.

The two most important years in Rome's fifth century were 494 and 449. Both saw secessions of the army when citizen-soldiers used their value as soldiers to demand political power as citizens. In 494 the famed first secession led to the creation of a plebeian "state within the state," which included the Plebeian Assembly and the Tribunes of the Plebs. The events of that year foreshadowed those in the crucial years 451–449, which concluded the republic's first dramatic six decades by making Rome's constitution more than a tool of elites. The secession in 449 expelled another tyrannical body, this time the decemviri. The political fruits were the publication of laws and another step toward making plebiscites, laws passed by the Plebeian Assembly, binding on the entire state.[9]

The end result of Rome's political wrangling in the fifth and fourth centuries was that a new chapter was written in the history of politics. Rome was not a pure monarchy, and it was not a pure democracy or a pure aristocracy either. It wasn't even a polis.[10] It was something else. It was politics that promoted ancient liberty and virtue by managing, albeit imperfectly, to keep sovereignty divided. This is why magistrates had the absolute and terrifying power of kings when they exercised their imperium abroad, why the senators exercised so much clout in the everyday politics of citizens and patrons, and why the assemblies could bring the entire state to the brink of collapse, which it ultimately did in the first century when it conferred powers on individuals that became permanent dictators, and then emperors, and then gods.

Republican Rhythms

The century after the revolution was a bad one for Rome. The sixth century had seen a boom in building and expansion under strong kings who were productive in peace and formidable in war, but the fifth century saw a steep decline in such endeavors. The sources fail to report temple foundations after 484, and grave goods become noticeably cheaper. The revolution weakened the new republic on the Tiber. And there were other problems—Italy at this time was beset by economic recession and famine, and the infiltration of mountain tribes and other peoples exacerbated the situation. Things began to look better when Rome decisively won its back and forth contest with Veii. Unfortunately, within a decade of the republic's greatest success, the Gauls swooped down into central Italy, raided Etruria, vanquished a Roman army at the River Allia, and captured all but the citadel of Rome. The city had undergone a century of economic stagnation, internal upheavals, and indecisive campaigns, making one wonder whether it had indeed been better off under the kings.[11]

In its first sixty years, Rome fought all of its neighbors, including erstwhile allies like the Latins and future allies like the Hernici. Annual campaigns against the Sabines, Volsci, and Etruscans are recorded by the sources. Rome did not always acquit itself well. During the late third and second centuries, triumphs averaged two out of every three years. By contrast the entire fifth century saw only twenty-two triumphs and ovations (lesser triumphs). There were several Roman defeats, but worse was the dearth of victories.[12] The new republic found itself striving for something more basic than dominance. It was trying to survive.

The string of inconclusive efforts was mitigated somewhat in the second half of the fifth century, when Rome secured truces with some of its enemies. Still, war was ubiquitous. Between 440 and 416, fifteen years have recorded campaigns. Between 415 and 367, only 412, 411, 387, and 384 do not have recorded campaigns. And the pattern continues throughout the republic. Between 415 and 265, there is a lack of recorded campaigns for less than 10 percent of the years.[13]

It was a time of ongoing, small-scale, indecisive engagements, and not just for the Romans but for most of Italy as well. Multipolar anarchy reigned. With no dominant power, each city-state, federation, or tribal entity acted violently in its own best interest to achieve anything it could at the expense of everyone else.[14] Everyone was trying to plunder, enslave, and kill their neighbors. For Rome, this meant that its republican citizens were habituated to the destruction of fighting almost as much as they were to the creativity of farming. They expected to see war every spring, and the nascent state was constantly preparing commanders and soldiers for the next inevitable campaign.

The unrefined armies of the time adapted warfare to agricultural life. The Roman citizen prepared his land in early September, and his principal crops would have been sown between late September and December. The crops would be harvested between June and August, depending on the temperature zone. Some minor backup crops might have been sown during winter or other times, but this was the crucial cereal grain cycle. This made crops most vulnerable precisely when campaigning began, which is no coincidence. In late spring and early summer the crops were too mature to replant and not quite ready for harvest. An invading army could thus threaten the crops and force a battle. If the invaders lingered or timed it perfectly, they could supply themselves with the ripe but unharvested grain of the invaded.[15]

During these engagements, the part-time armies relied on formations that required little training or discipline. Citizens would have received rudimentary training in weapons and other martial skills at home, and this would have been supplemented by some basic drilling by their commanders. Daily life on the farm accustomed the men to animal carnage and the responsibilities and physical exertions of farm management. This still would have left many of them unprepared for the gore of killing fellow human beings, so formations guaranteed combat for the uninitiated. The front ranks were manned by the less experienced, and veterans were posted in the rear to inspire courage and stave off any desire to retreat.

Close-ranked, phalanx-like armies and ad hoc marauding bands were the preferred tactical units. Armies would seek a quick decision in battle so that they could return to their agricultural duties. Eradicating crops is difficult and time consuming, so invading armies destroyed crops more to incite a fight than to effect a food shortage. Campaigns were probably restricted to a few weeks. Armies could clash in the summer months after the harvest, but most engagements would be cut short from a lack of supplies and the invading armies' need to return to the plow. Campaigns were ended by winter rains that inhibited movement, necessitated additional cold-weather supplies, and low-ered morale.[16]

Every year saw new campaigns led by new magistrates who levied new armies. The regularity of conscription and battle was interwoven into the life of the fighting farmers. Spring and autumn rituals book-ended campaigns, just as sowing or harvesting did in the agricultural cycle.[17] Rome was governed by a "sacral rhythm of war" that constituted a state of perpetual conflict. Yvon Garlan details how the Roman cal-endar that originated in early Rome geared the populace for conquest:

> The seasonal rhythm of the consecration and deconsecration of mili-tary activity involved the following ceremonies. In the spring, during the months of February and March, the Salians started off by perform-ing sacred dances to arouse the supernatural forces, striking their staves against the sacred shields (*ancilia*) one of which was said to have fallen from the heavens. Next, the military equipment was puri-fied, in particular the horses, by holding races at the feast of the *Equir-ria*, and the trumpets on the day of the *tubilustrium*. In the autumn, there was the purification of arms (*armilustrium*), and the "October horse" was put to death. . . . Before leaving the city, the army under-went another lustration rite, while its leader brandished the lance of Mars and shook the sacred Salian shields. Simultaneously, the doors of the temple of Janus were opened.[18]

The *tubilustrium* was a spring ceremony that purified the war trum-pets and consecrated their use for a new season of declaring and mak-ing war. The *armilustrium*, on the other hand, took place in autumn and purified the weapons that would be stored for the winter (Varro, *On the Latin Language*, 5.153, 6.22). These ceremonies are somewhat obscure, especially for early Rome, but it is logical to assume that the arms purification had a cleansing function. The ceremonial items rep-resented the troops' own blood-stained weapons, which would be pu-rified and set aside as men were returning to their homes. The ritual was probably more important for the communal sense of cleansing. The individual soldier would have "reintegrated" by returning to the creative tasks of the farm. The timing of the ceremonies was crucial. The *armilustrium* was held on 19 October, which was an ideal time to begin sowing winter wheat.

Religious rituals and agricultural rhythms thus fostered the martial spirit of these early citizen-soldiers. Opening the doors to the temple of Janus meant that Rome had opened communications with its armies within the city itself and with its allies and enemies abroad. Only twice did republican Rome shut the doors, after the First Punic War in 241 and after the Battle of Actium in 31—meaning that Rome always found it necessary to communicate with its legions and allies for the next campaign. In light of this, Garlan astutely asks, "Was it war, or was it peace that was shut up in the temple?"[19]

Republican Strategy

Rudimentary Roman strategy operated on interior lines, an approach that was followed throughout the republic's history. Reliance on this strategy stemmed more from instinct than conscious effort. Rome built alliances outward from central Italy, constructing a solid military infrastructure through a network of roads that connected the colonies and allies of Rome. The Latins were an obvious first ally. A second, with the Hernici in 486, forged a triple alliance that kept the three one step ahead of their enemies. Rome was responsible for the northern approach threatened by the Etruscans, and the Latins and Hernici provided Rome a buffer against the Aequi and Volsci. Effective diplomacy was rare, but Rome was also able to establish a friendship with the Etruscan city-state Caere, for example, which helped it recover from the Gallic invasion in 390.[20]

Rome's alliance with the Latins stretched back to the monarchy, when the two worked in concert to push the boundaries of their territory outward and reclaim those parts of Latium that had been occupied by the Apennine peoples. For reasons that are obscure in the tradition, Rome's relationship with the Latins became strained at the end of the sixth century. One attractive possibility is that Lars Porsena occupied Rome and enabled the overthrow of the Roman kings. When his invasion of Latium failed at Aricia, a conflict between the new republic and its old allies was inevitable. It could even be that the Latin League transitioned from a religious league to a political coalition precisely to oppose Rome at Aricia and then again at Lake Regillus. Under the leadership of Tusculum, the Latin League attempted to permanently end Roman claims of leadership, but the sources report that the Battle of Lake Regillus ended in a Roman victory. A treaty was made soon after, the Treaty of Cassius. The nature of the relationship has been debated—especially with regard to who dominated—but the treaty worked to the advantage of both.[21]

A vital asset for the alliance was the founding of colonial outposts. Some conquered territories, like Veii and Labici, were incorporated into the Roman state, and their occupants immediately became citizens. Others, however, became colonies. When a town or territory was conquered, Roman and Latin settlers transplanted culture and security burdens to strategic sites. Settlers and their families received farmland and then began to build a civic community of their own. The most valuable resource—farmer-citizen-soldiers—became the new frontier and the first line of defense. Most of the colonies were not adjoined to Roman territory. Latin colonies founded before the Latin League's dissolution in 338 became known as Priscae latinae coloniae (ancient Latin colonies). The term "Latin" here denotes a legal status, as opposed to ethnic. Latin colonists were not Roman citizens, but they did enjoy the rights of commercium (property ownership and trade), conubium (intermarriage), and *ius migrandi* (migration with citizen rights). These formed the legal and social basis for the future expansion of Roman citizenship, territory, and alliances in centuries to come (table 4.2).[22]

Colonies were dangerous enterprises, especially given that colonists might be settled as a minority in the midst of the conquered. In locations where settlers already existed, the Roman emigrants were expected to help the surviving inhabitants adjust to their new status as enrolled colonists. A number of colonies would be founded, fall into enemy hands, and need to be recaptured. They were all settled in formidable locations:

All these sites were skillfully chosen, and defence considerations were uppermost in their selection. All of them were militarily useful and

Table 4.2. Priscae latinae coloniae

Year founded	Colony	Strategic location	Targeted enemy
		Monarchic colonies	
Eighth or seventh century (Romulus' reign) / 498	Fidenae	On a "hill that controls the last Tiber-crossing above Rome"	Etruscans
Sixth century (Tarquinius Superbus' reign) / 501	Cora	On a "slope that dominates NW route around the Volscian Mountains"	Aequi, Volsci
Sixth century (Tarquinius Superbus' reign) / 501	Pometia	Precise location unknown	Aurunci, Volsci
Sixth century (Tarquinius Superbus' reign) / 495	Signia	On "the powerful site that overlooks the valley" of the Volscian Mountains	Aequi, Volsci
Sixth century (Tarquinius Superbus' reign) / 393	Circeii	On a mountain promontory that overlooked "the southern limit of Latium" and the coast	Aurunci, Volsci
		Republican colonies before the league's dissolution	
494 / 401	Velitrae	On the "southern rim of the Alban hills," it controlled the gap to the Volscian Mountains	Volsci
492	Norba	On a "well-nigh inaccessible bluff" that overlooked the Pomptine marshes	Volsci
467	Antium	Anchorage on Latin coast that overlooked the coast and the Volsci	Volsci
442	Ardea	On high ground, it "straddled the southern approaches to Rome"	Volsci
418	Labici	On high ground, it controlled the Algidus Pass	Aequi
395	Vitellia	On a hill, it controlled the corridor between the Alban Hills and the Volscian Mountains with Velitrae	Volsci
385	Satri-cum	Occupied the prominent position between Antium and the Alban Hills	Volsci
383	Setia	On the "southern underfalls of the Volscian Mountains" that formed the entrance to Latium with Circeii	Volsci
382	Sutrium	Twin fortress with Nepet that overlooked the route to Volsinii	Etruscans, Gauls
382	Nepet	Twin fortress with Sutrium that overlooked the route to Falerii	Etruscans, Umbrians, Gauls

Note: Multiple dates indicate doublets, reiterations, or disputed years for events. Many of these are debated, although the basic outline is accepted by most scholars.

most of them naturally strong. Almost every one was perched on a hilltop; some were flanked by ravines; streams protected others and forests camouflaged yet others. Ostensibly settled by peasant-farmers, they were in fact powerful bastions, and their strategic contribution was notable. They formed a network of fortresses, controlling river crossings, mountain passes, roads and tracks.[23]

Like everything with Rome, transformation was not immediate. Early colonization is a hotly debated topic, and the current consensus leans against anything close to a swift Romanization as Rome expanded over the centuries. Italic peoples demonstrated resilience long after battlefield defeats.[24] Nevertheless, Roman alliances, citizenship, laws, and mores slowly infiltrated every territory where Roman citizen-soldiers fought in Italy and the Mediterranean. Colonies were yet another way that Rome used its citizen-soldiers to great advantage. As outposts on the frontier, their value as farmers would become more important than their security presence. They would not simply protect the frontier but transform it—making the farmlands of former enemies the farms, homes, and hearths of Romans and Latins.

Colonization tapered off between 382 and 338, probably as a result of successes against enemies and rising tensions between Rome and its allies. These tensions would not be resolved until Rome defeated its allies in the Latin War and forced a new settlement. Colonization was then begun anew with Rome as the unquestioned superior in the arrangement.[25]

THE DECISIVE CENTURY (390–298)

In 396 Rome captured its longtime nemesis Veii and added 562 square kilometers to the 822 square kilometers it reportedly possessed when the kings were expelled. To enable Veii's capture, Rome expanded its strategic repertoire. It introduced pay for troops to maintain the siege of Veii over the winter, and it may have also introduced *tributum*, a military tax.[26] Veii's fall was a vital boon for Rome, but the success was quickly reversed by the Gallic sack. Even after the Romans bribed the

Gallic commander Brennus to leave Rome, the raids continued. The returning invaders even intermittently occupied parts of Latium in the decades following an invasion in 367. Another sack was narrowly averted in 360.

The sack of 390 was a disaster that drove the Romans to increase their militarism and expand their frontiers, most noticeably with the founding of Sutrium and Nepet. It also probably provided the impetus for the early fourth-century walls encircling the city. Memories of the sack haunted Romans for centuries, a fear that became reality every time the Gauls invaded again. The date of the Allia defeat, 18 July, was forever marked as a day of ill omen.[27]

Aristocratic Leadership

The sources tried to erase the disgrace of the sack with a tale of how the famous conqueror of Veii, Marcus Furius Camillus, recovered Roman honor, refounded the city, reformed the military, and led Rome to new heights of success. Whatever historical role Camillus played in Rome's recovery, his real contribution emanated from his legacy as princeps—the leading citizen of Rome. Deemed the republican equal of Brutus and Cincinnatus, he was the fourth-century embodiment of Romulus.

In the mist of Rome's early history, Camillus' status as a legendary general was clear. He successfully captured Veii when other commanders had failed; he celebrated the greatest Roman triumph to date; and he recovered Roman dignity after Allia and the sack. Dionysius, Livy, and Plutarch all attribute these successes to him (though in varying degrees) and also record other feats after these famous accomplishments. Yet there was more to Camillus' life than martial success. At the very least, there was more to his story for the Roman historians. After describing his death from pestilence in 365, Livy summarizes his significance to Rome by describing him as "foremost in peace and in war" (7.1). The accuracy of the phrase has been questioned, for although Camillus more than proved his mettle in war, his designation as "foremost in peace" seems inflated. Or is it?

The historians went to great lengths to establish his record as an arbiter of domestic harmony. Like Cincinnatus, he accepted a wrongful exile with reserve and dignity, and when Rome needed him after the Gallic invasion, he did not hesitate to redon the commander's mantle. He led the restoration of Rome following the Gallic invasion—a role that would have demanded more than martial talents. He incorporated the Faliscian city of Falerii into the Roman alliance by refusing to hold children hostage that had been brought by a potential betrayer of the city. The citizens' gratitude prompted a grateful surrender with good terms for the Falisci that Camillus accepted (Livy, 5.27). Camillus exercised a similar restraint regarding reconciliation with Tusculum in 381 (Livy, 6.25–26). He was also instrumental in the reconciliation that occurred during his dictatorship in 367 (Livy, 6.42; Dionysius, 14.8–10). The passage of the Licinio-Sextian rogations in that year was one of the most significant political milestones of the republic.

Camillus the war hero was simply not enough for the literary tradition. To be a true princeps, a man must also have been a hero of peace. Much has been made of Rome's tradition of war, but equally important was the Roman tradition of the peaceful arts such as diplomacy, justice, law, administration, and clemency. Roman wars were fought with the intention of creating peace and order in a world riven by chaos and violence. For any Roman general to be successful, he must also have valued peace. He could not merely reflect Romulus but must also exhibit the talents of Numa. If Plutarch is to be believed, this truth was architecturally noted in Camillus' lifetime with his two temple dedications— one to Juno following the destruction of Veii, and the other to Concordia after the reconciliation (*Camillus*, 42).[28]

The model of Camillus was used by historians to frame superior leadership in the final years of the republic and during the empire.[29] As a historical figure at the beginning of Rome's rise to dominance, Camillus helps modern readers understand what constituted the patriotic and prominent aristocrat. He may not have achieved all that is accorded to him, but he embodied everything that was important for the developing *nobiles*.

By the end of the fourth century the early republic had developed a system wherein a nobility of officeholders used a competitive war-and-politics tradition to acquire honor for themselves and Rome. They were not a class but a group defined by the status of office. They included older patrician families and new plebeian officeholders. By granting imperium and honor, the assemblies of citizen-soldiers formally created the senatorial order, and in the fourth century this aristocratic branch of the Roman government coalesced into a political body. Senators filled the ranks of Rome's generals, priests, diplomats, and councilors, but they did not cast themselves as magnificent individuals that deserved to be kings or oligarchs. Instead, they created an ideology of service, dedication, and leadership. They portrayed themselves as sacrificial servants of the state who, like Romulus, Brutus, and Camillus, would stop at nothing to bring Rome glory.[30]

The aristocratic order that had emerged by 300 was forged through political compromise, foreign conquest, and a communal identity as statesmen. Over the course of the fifth and fourth centuries, laws and customs emerged that mitigated the patrician-plebeian tension, made new offices more available, regulated reelection, extended commands through prorogation, and granted exceptional power in times of necessity. These rules allowed enough men enough opportunities for individual glory at the same time that they kept any one man from acquiring too much power.[31]

Public spaces and religious rituals were increasingly dominated by and civic honors were increasingly accorded to the *nobiles*. Like Camillus, they dedicated temples, celebrated triumphs, distributed spoils, oversaw the passage of just laws, and were memorialized in reverent funerals. Portrait shields had supposedly already originated with Appius Claudius in 495 (Pliny, *Natural History*, 35.12), and these expanded in the following centuries into portrait statuary, especially of "triumphators on horseback or in a chariot."[32] The Forum was redesigned in 310 to accommodate lavish displays of Roman spoils, and streets started to be adorned with portraits and statues of successful commanders. Temple dedications also increased immediately following this period; the fifth and fourth centuries saw seven apiece; the third century saw over forty. The dedication of a manubial temple for wartime feats guaranteed a commander immortality in stone.[33]

The spoils of victory were enjoyed by all. When a magistrate acquired military command or was given a civic honor, the entire elite was implicitly recognized. To everyday Roman citizens partaking in the expansion of Rome between the fourth and second centuries, it must have seemed that the nobles deserved praise and adoration for the benefits they brought to the entire state. It is no coincidence that as Rome began to conquer more territory in the latter half of the fourth century domestic tensions eased. Citizen-soldiers acquired booty on campaigns, but the real benefits were the elimination of debt bondage in 326 or 313 and the acquisition of more land. By 290 Roman territory had expanded to five thousand square kilometers. New tribes were added, plebeian citizens were settled on the new lands, and a great economic crisis had been alleviated. Conquest and statecraft had led to the creation of more land that more citizens could farm when they were not fighting in war.[34]

Pragmatic Federation

Rome's war with its old allies in Latium erupted in 340, was hotly but briefly contested in favor of Rome, and concluded with an overhaul of the current alliance. The immediate spark was the First Samnite War, which ended with Rome and the Samnite League dividing west central Italy into two spheres. However, the Latin-Roman tension had been building while Rome accumulated more and more territory in the first half of the fourth century. Rome used its victory in 338 to manage this territory with itself as the unquestioned head of a federation.[35]

The Roman federation was not truly "federal" according to most definitions. While the language of Roman law birthed the terminology of federalism, the spirit of Roman rule left little room for federal liberty.[36] Rome allowed, and expected, its allies to manage their internal affairs, but foreign policy, war authorization, and the supplying of troops were left to Rome. Only full citizens could formally influence these decisions, and that was only true of those near enough to participate in politics within the city itself. Still, when compared to other empires and polities of the day, Rome's federation promoted a great deal of local autonomy and was closer to the mark on the ancient understanding of liberty. A principal difference between Greek and Roman notions of freedom, as exemplified by Aristotle and Cicero, is that the Greek model emphasized political status as equal participants whereas the Roman model emphasized legal status. For Aristotle and the Greek model, one is free if one participates in politics as an equal. For Cicero and the Roman model, one is free if one is granted the legal status of *libertas*.[37] Roman thinking, of course, was inflexible regarding military participation, which was demanded of all under their rule.

From the beginning Rome was exceptionally inclusive of outsiders entering the Roman system. Romulus incorporated ruffians and indigents from the surrounding areas. There is little hint here of the cultural and ethnic snobbery exhibited by the ancient Near Eastern empires or even among the Greeks. In fact, Rome's original population was so uncivilized and literally "manly" (too heavily populated by males) that it raised a stench in the nostrils of its neighbors, as exhibited by their refusal to offer brides to Roman men. This catalyzed the infamous "rape of the Sabine women," when the Roman bachelors kidnapped Sabine maidens in order to produce another generation (Livy, 1.9–10). The legend itself hints at the early incorporation of the Sabines into the Roman populace. Rome continued this inclusive practice on a larger scale as it expanded its federation of Italic states in the fourth century.[38]

Roman civic affiliation after 338 was a complicated affair that varied based on who was being included and the reasons for their inclusion. It should be noted that affiliation with Rome after 338 established a political and military relationship, usually with Rome in the dominant position, but it did not immediately lead to the "Romanization" of all citizen or allied communities. Most Italian towns maintained their own local traditions, languages, religions, and civic ceremonies. Being a Roman ally or even a Roman citizen hardly obliterated deep-seated, native traditions. Over the course of centuries, these older traditions might be supplanted or fused with Roman ones, but this was not something that occurred in 338, or even comprehensively during the republic for that matter.[39]

Roman legal recognition was extended to two groups, incorporated communities and allied communities. Both were required to furnish troops. Incorporated peoples included full citizens and half citizens, the latter being termed "cives sine suffragio" ("citizens without the vote"). Full citizens included those born in Rome, those settled in Roman colonies on public land, and neighboring communities absorbed by Roman territory, such as Tusculum, Lanuvium, and Aricia. Full citizens enjoyed complete political rights, including suffrage. Half citizens, on the other hand, enjoyed local autonomy as well as the rights of *provocatio*, commercium, and conubium, but they could neither stand for office nor vote. Capua was the famous example here. Half citizenship was not necessarily advantageous, except to Rome, which was able to directly control the troops of half citizens.[40]

Rome's allies were theoretically independent states. Each was bound by a separate treaty uniquely situated to the manner and circumstances of their inclusion. Roman allies were also of two kinds. First were the allied Latins, which included the original colonies, colonies formed from 338 to 268, and colonies created after 268. Latin colonies served as security outposts at vital locations along Roman roads. Second were the other socii (allies) that had concluded treaties as equals (often made under peaceful conditions) or unilateral treaties (often made after wartime defeats). They also enjoyed independence, except in the matter of furnishing troops.[41]

The two new types of colonies served different purposes. Latin colonies were established on favorable sites where a new community could flourish, sometimes next to the preexisting, conquered community. A settler would expect to receive and develop an adequate plot of land that could support his family and his position as an allied infantryman. Seven *iugera* seem to have been the minimum allotment that could support an infantryman's (*assiduus*) family in the fifth class. Roman colonies on the other hand, were settled by *proletarii*, or the poorest citizens, who were not expected to fight as infantrymen (although they could serve in the navy). They were granted two *iugera* of land and were expected to eke out a living by using the town's communal land. Roman citizen colonies were located in less than optimal terrain, but they all held strategic value, hence the need to colonize them with the poorest citizens if necessary. Ports such as Antium, Alsium, and Tarracina are all good examples. Viritane distributions—plots allocated to individual families for farming—were another form of settlement. These were usually granted to veterans, as in the case of settlers sent to Sabinum during the Third Samnite War.[42] All of these methods were standard strategies for Romanizing conquered land through the explicit use of farming citizen-soldiers.

The Roman federation demonstrated two notable strengths: flexibility and military cohesiveness. Flexibility avoided a narrowing uniformity that would have given too little autonomy to Rome's allies, and unity provided Rome with a continuous supply of citizen and allied contingents for its ongoing wars. The system of alliances was undoubtedly of a military nature, but it functioned with unparalleled success. By 264 "Rome had concluded permanent treaties with over 150 nominally independent Italian communities, which had either been defeated in war or had voluntarily agreed to become allies."[43] War provided a common enemy and a common set of benefits, not all of which can be viewed positively—including land seizures, booty, and a lucrative slave market. The entire Roman system was based on the citizen-farmer and his ability to immediately and efficiently transform into a citizen-soldier when necessary. War also formed an important part of what bound Rome to its allies. Romans and their allied counterparts all fought on the same field and faced the same risks.[44]

The consolidation of the peninsula was constant, slow, and laborious. Like tasks on the farm, control of the Italian soil required one to have a patient work ethic and to put in a lot of hours. Rome slowly gained the upper hand over its neighbors with a delicate combination of martial brutality, political practicality, diplomatic savvy, legal consistency, and a steady stream of civic militarism. The people of most conquered cities in the ancient world would expect to be killed or sold off into slavery and their homes to be destroyed or pillaged. Rome, like everyone else, was not above engaging in such acts in the face of recalcitrant foes, but it could also be merciful and generous, offering a degree of independence, a share in the spoils of war, Roman law and culture, and the possibility of citizenship.

Rome's dominion was achieved within the same chaotic Mediterranean milieu as that of the Hellenic city-states and their ephemeral empires. Athens' dazzling political successes were buried in the sea like all those triremes lost in the Peloponnesian War. By the middle of the fourth century, its naval power was as valuable as sunken treasure in preventing Macedon from taking possession of Greece. Sparta and Thebes were the only other polities that could have opposed Macedon, but they had destroyed one another as thoroughly as Athens had destroyed itself half a century before. Macedon established its domination of Greece the same fateful year that Rome defeated the Latins and became a master of its own. The two would test their hegemonic strengths in battle 125 years later.

Legionary Maniples

The Roman army underwent as many beneficial changes as the constitution and the federation. Fourth-century Rome ended the previous century's cycle of annual, indecisive campaigns and started collecting victories. Terror from devastating invasions like those undertaken by the Gauls, shame from never finishing off enemies like the Volsci, and the fear of new enemies like the Samnites motivated reconciliation in domestic politics. Civil strife had crippled Rome's military strength, so reconciliation became necessary. While this made some Roman citizens mourn the loss of their old exclusive powers and others yearn for still more, everyone became stronger in the end. Political accommodation led to partially unsatisfied parties but a satisfactory state of affairs overall. This balanced mindset worked just as well with Rome's allies. Some were dissatisfied with their loss of independence, but overall, most believed Rome's status quo was better than anything else another hegemon could offer. Rome was mighty in victory, but it could also be beneficent, so siding with it was often a rational choice. The republican federation always mustered enough military strength to fend off the best armies cast its direction.[45]

Political and social change accelerated military reform. The Licinio-Sextian Laws, the Genucian Law, and the Poetelian-Papirian Law helped unify all aspects of the Roman citizen-soldiery, from aristocratic cavalry, wealthier heavy infantrymen, poorer light infantrymen, and the poorest colonists and citizen-sailors. The first election of military tribunes in 362 afforded these mid-level officers a greater opportunity to mix with the common soldier in the ranks. It is no coincidence that it became possible at the same time to double the legions from one to two. More reforms and more successes in the field led to another doubling by 311. Concurrent with these developments was the increase in *ager Romanus*, and as land was dealt out to rich and poor alike, this also brought peace at home. Much has been made of the Roman need to fight wars in order to settle domestic problems, but it is equally valuable to consider the possibility that the settling of domestic problems led to an increased ability to fight wars.[46]

Citizen-soldiers also started thinking of warfare in terms of life cycles as opposed to annual cycles. The Second Samnite War took Roman soldiers outside Latium, and later wars continued to expand geographically. This meant that campaigns lasted through the winter. As Rome became involved in distant places like Sicily, Spain, Africa, and Greece in the third century, citizen-soldiers would be expected to leave the farm for years. The Samnite Wars laid the foundation for how they could leave without devastating their families. Young men began to expect that there would be periods of their lives, especially between their late teens and early thirties, when they might be conscripted to serve for years at a time. They became accustomed to the idea that they would farm during their adolescence, leave to fight for stretches of time in their twenties, and then return to marry and manage their own farms in their thirties. Rome and its allies enjoyed a large enough manpower base so that many sons and young fathers could stay home, and exceptions could always be made for farms in dire straits, but most families learned to absorb the absence of one or two military-aged males for long stretches of time.[47]

Adaptation

Ancient historians praised the Roman penchant for martial adaptation. Diodorus and an anonymous historian in the *Ineditum Vaticanum* tell a famous story filled with historical examples. On the eve of the Punic Wars, the Roman envoy Kaeso taunts a Carthaginian with a history of Roman resilience, explaining that the Romans took the hoplite armor and phalanx from the Etruscans, cavalry and the scutum-pilum-maniple combination from the Samnites, siegecraft from the Greeks, and would learn naval tactics from the Carthaginians. Other historians and tacticians offer similar remarks.[48] These tales err in the details. The Romans had just as likely taken the phalanx from the Greeks, they developed the scutum-pilum-maniple combination on their own or from several Italic neighbors, and they were quite capable at siegecraft long before they fought the Greeks.

Still, the story has some merit. Adaptation is indispensable for any military, and the Romans particularly relished it. Their ability to withstand numerous defeats, learn from these defeats, and then use what they learned against their foes stemmed from an obsession with communal achievement, and the *nobiles* were exceptional in their quest for glory. Such openness to adaptation made their military institutions uncharacteristically progressive, which, as Polybius remarks, was "one of their virtues." "No people," he adds, "are so ready to adopt new fashions and imitate what they see is better in others" (6.25). So how did Roman adaptation give it the edge in the fourth century? The answer to this question has been the subject of much scholarly wrangling, but the following is one plausible interpretation of the military revolution that set the stage for Rome's breakout in the early third century.

The Polybian Army (c. 260–c. 150)

In the middle of the second century, Polybius offered the first contemporary analysis of Roman warfare. Polybius was the son of a leading Megalopolitan aristocrat and was a Greek commander himself until he was taken hostage by the Romans. He later traveled with Roman elites on numerous campaigns throughout the Mediterranean. His description of the army's conscription, formation, tactics, officers, cavalry, and encampments fills chapters 19–42 of his *Histories'* sixth book. The work begins with the Second Punic War (218–201), but its long introduction includes the First Punic War (264–241) and a few references to earlier events such as the Gallic sack. His details regarding the Roman army, although not perfect, can thus be regarded as reliable at least back to the Second Punic War.

According to Polybius, the army of the late third century had long since given up its phalanx tactics and hoplite equipment. Instead, it fought in tactical formations called maniples. The principal arms were pila (heavy javelins that replaced the typical spear of the hoplite), the scutum (a larger oblong shield that replaced the *clipeus*), and the gladius (a cut-and-thrust sword longer than those carried by hoplites). Soldiers had some form of body armor, which ranged from the expensive chain mail and cuirass to the cheaper pectoral plate; they also wore a helmet (most often of the Montefortino variety) and, if affordable, greaves. The new legion separated into three horizontal lines organized into thirty vertical maniples of one hundred twenty men (or sixty centuries of sixty men, as each maniple was composed of two centuries). The first line of ten maniples was composed of twelve hundred *hastati*, the front line of youngest troops. The second line held twelve hundred principes, the middle line of seasoned troops. The final line of half maniples was composed of six hundred *triarii*, the oldest, veteran troops. The *triarii* armed themselves with spears or used pila as thrusting weapons like hoplites; they served as a last line of defense. These three lines of heavy infantry were arrayed in a checkerboard pattern with gaps between the ranks and files. Twelve hundred *velites*, light infantry armed with javelins, and three hundred cavalry accompanied the heavy infantry, bringing the standard legion size to around forty-five hundred soldiers. Legions could range as high as six thousand.

By 311 a consul's army included two Roman legions that usually occupied the center and two complementary allied units that usually fought on the wings (alae), making a consular army approximately twenty thousand strong. Alae were commanded by local captains and resembled the legion in form and size. The strength of Rome's cavalry was supplied by its allies, who fielded nine hundred cavalry, three times the strength of the citizen cavalry. Cavalry occupied the flanks outside the alae. Within Rome, the legions were marshaled at the command of the consuls.[49] They would muster the army after an announcement in the popular assembly. Messengers were likewise sent to the allied cities to conscript their troops at the same time. Because this for-mation is described by Polybius, it is often called the "Polybian" army (6.20–23, 26; see also Livy, 8.8).

As with the phalanx, unity in battle was necessary. This was espe-cially important because of the nature of manipular tactics. The legion was designed to shift the horizontal rows of the checkerboard pattern sideways as well as backward and forward during battle to replenish weary or defeated ranks if necessary. There is dispute over whether the checkerboard gaps were closed or left open when hand-to-hand combat was commenced. If the first line, the *hastati*, were exhausted from combat, the principes would shift into their positions. If the prin-cipes were then exhausted in turn, the last line, the *triarii* would use its fresh men to decide the battle, defend a retreat, or allow the first two ranks to reform. Roman battles typically involved two aspects: mid-range, missile fighting with javelins and pila and close-range, sword-and-scutum fighting (Livy, 8.8).[50]

The Army in the Latin War (c. 400–c. 326)

Polybius' description is helpful for third and second century battles but is wanting when it comes to events between the Gallic sack and the Punic Wars. So how did the Roman army transition from close-ordered formations and warrior bands to Polybius' manipular legions?

It is probable that by the beginning of the fourth century, with the capture of Veii and the Battle of the Allia, Rome was most closely ap-proximating the hoplite phalanx, as indicated by Servius' centuriate reforms. Some authorities claim that immediately following these two events, Rome began the shift to maniples. The introduction of sol-diers' pay and *tributum* during the siege of Veii enabled the change, and the Gallic defeat provided the motivation. Plutarch and Livy sup-port the association of Camillus with this reform. Plutarch claims Ca-millus changed Roman helmets and shield rims. It is unlikely that such changes were made, and even if they had been, they would have been tactically irrelevant for the maniples, but they may reference some genuine reforms Camillus inaugurated (*Camillus*, 40).

Evidence in Livy is more substantial. He describes armies that fought in the Latin War in similar terms as Polybius. According to Livy, both Latins and Romans fought with the developed manipular legion, although it is unclear whether Livy describes heavy infantrymen in the first two rows armed with the thrusting spear (*hasta*) or with heavy javelins (8.8).[51] He also may simply be using the manipular army anachronistically for rhetorical effect here. He closes his description of the battle dramatically by emphasizing the escalating repetition of two manipular armies clashing, saying "not only must section meet in battle with section, *hastati* with *hastati*, *principes* with *principes* . . . centurion with centurion," before he describes a duel fought between two centurions.

It has been argued that Livy and Plutarch are wrong because passages from *Ineditum Vaticanum* and Diodorus say the pilum-scutum-maniple formation was borrowed from the Samnites. But archaeological evidence does not bear this out. Early forms of the scutum date to as early as the eighth century, and Rome could have adopted it from a number of its neighbors. Rome may have even used the scutum before it borrowed the *clipeus* from the Greeks and Etruscans for its phalanx-type formation (Diodorus, 14.116; Dionysius, 4.16, 13.8; Livy, 1.43; Plutarch, *Romulus*, 21). As for the pilum, its origins are shadowy, but it could also have originated elsewhere or perhaps been adapted by the Romans themselves from standard javelins.[52] Since the pilum, scutum, and maniple were interrelated, armies probably attempted to incorporate each at the same time. In the end, it is safest to assume that the Romans had begun experimenting with the maniples, but that this transition was still developmental during the First Samnite and Latin Wars. This could account for some of the obscurities in Livy's account and explain his differences from Polybius.

The Army in the Pyrrhic War (c. 326–c. 260)

By the end of the fourth century, the Roman army could not be confused with the phalanx. The Polybian army was not fully developed—the Spanish gladius, for example, would not appear until the Punic Wars—but Rome had introduced its checkerboard maniples armed with pila or similar heavy javelins, the scutum, and a sword longer than the old hoplite *xiphos*.[53] Plutarch describes a battle with Pyrrhus that makes these changes apparent. When Pyrrhus fought Rome from 280 to 275, he used the common infantry formation of the Hellenistic age: a combined arms force that featured effective cavalry, elephants, and an advanced phalanx of pikemen. Plutarch stresses Pyrrhus' need to fight on unbroken, level terrain, which the earlier hoplite phalanx like-wise required. Pyrrhus had intended to prevent the Romans from using their preferred tactics, whereby they would take advantage of some-what uneven terrain to give their flexible maniples an "opportunity for sidelong shifts and counter-movements." Pyrrhus feared that the legionary "swords" would overcome his phalangites' "spears" unless he maintained formation and prevented the Roman army's manipular movements (*Pyrrhus*, 21).

Dionysius also describes the Roman army at war with Pyrrhus. He references the fatigue Pyrrhus' phalangites suffered while they were "advancing against hilly positions by . . . goat paths through woods and crags" with their heavy armor and unwieldy weapons. They were not accustomed to the Italian terrain as a Samnite or Roman would have been. Like Plutarch, Dionysius also mentions that Pyrrhus' army had trouble maintaining ranks.

Dionysius' most interesting observation regards the Roman army. He makes the seemingly odd statement that "those who fight in close combat with cavalry spears grasped by the middle with both hands and who usually save the day in battles are called *principes* by the Romans" (20.11). It is possible that Dionysius confused the *triarii* with the prin-cipes. However, another intriguing solution has recently been offered by David Potter, who suggests that Dionysius is in fact describing the early third-century purpose of the maniple's second line. Although the principes carried a sheathed sword and a shield, they still fought with the old thrusting spear. The *hastati* would be armed with the scutum, pila, and sword, as Plutarch describes. The *hastati* would unleash their pila into the enemy ranks until a break in the enemy's formation devel-oped. This process could take hours, but once a vulnerability was de-tected, the principes would surge in and decide the battle. Their name, meaning "first men" or "important men" describes their position as the most important rank in the manipular legion—they are the ones who force a decision.[54]

This interpretation makes much sense if we view the fourth-century army as one in transition. The memory of the phalanx kept the spearman important throughout the fourth century, but he had been relegated to the second rank by its end. As the effectiveness of the pila-and-sword wielding *hastati* was demonstrated again and again throughout the third century, the principes kept their name but took on the weapons of the *hastati,* and the principes' weapons in turn became those of the *triarii,* creating the Polybian legion as we know it. The spearman was reduced to the third rank by the end of the third century and was obsolete by the first. This reconstruction might be inaccurate in some of the details, but it aptly illustrates the idea that the army was undergoing the changes that gave it a battlefield edge.

A change that is much clearer during this time was the elevation of the javelin. Alexander Zhmodikov's study of Roman heavy infantry-men explains the role of missile fighting in the complex maneuvers of the legion. He defends the account of Livy, who emphasizes a predominance of missile fighting in his battle descriptions (against Polybius, who sees sword fighting as predominant). Long battles are more common than short battles for Rome's citizen-soldiers, a conclusion we are able to infer from Livy's many references to pila. Both sword fighting and missile fighting are a regular feature, and in some battles sword fighting prevailed; however, a long battle of missile exchanges was the norm.[55]

This study's analysis of Sentinum and Pydna bears out Zhmodikov's hypothesis. Sentinum hints at repeated shock actions, with Livy mentioning multiple "assaults" by the Samnites, but the narrative also describes "the missiles they discharged," and Livy does not mention the use of swords (10.29). Assaults were part of the rhythm in Roman battles, but armies could secure lulls through renewed attacks with missiles after assaults had not achieved the desired effect. If the two centuries of the maniple were side by side, all six ranks of men could simultaneously hurl their pila, which had a range of thirty yards. If the centuries were front to back, one century could throw and then the next and so on. Prolonged missile exchanges resulted in the lengthy battles that Livy describes—and Sentinum was one of these long, missile battles. By contrast, battles such as Pydna, lasting less than an hour (Plutarch, *Aemilius Paulus*, 22), exemplified the phalanx's tendency to force a decision as quickly as possible. This makes sense given that Rome's enemies here were Macedonians, who specialized in phalangite shock tactics. If the Battle of Sentinum prioritized javelin exchanges, the Battle of Pydna showcased Rome's heavy infantry, as the manipular legions clashed with the Macedonian phalanx.

The Romans were afforded the opportunity to refine their tactics continually through the fire of battle. At the end of the fourth century, Rome's greatest military challenge was the mountainous Samnite League. The Samnites fielded armies that tactically functioned between heavy and light infantry. They were experts at flexible tactics that could be adjusted depending on the terrain and circumstances.[56] In true form, Rome learned to deal with Samnite flexibility and their use of mountain terrain. The Samnites did not yield their freedom easily, however. Between 326 and 304 the two were locked in a struggle to determine the fate of central Italy, and by the beginning of the third century, Rome appeared as the first possible hegemon of the entire peninsula, if it could finally finish off and assimilate the Samnites. During a grueling contest in the Third Samnite War (298–290), Rome was on the brink of total victory. To avoid defeat, the Samnites joined forces with Rome's other enemies. The war crescendoed into a final, desperate, pan-Italic effort against Roman control of the peninsula. The decision would be made at Sentinum.

PART 3

The Triumph of Rome's Citizen-Soldiers

5 · Breakout

COMPETITION AND
DISCIPLINE AT SENTINUM

From 1853 to 1856 Thomas Crawford sculpted the *Dying Indian Chief, Contemplating the Progress of Civilization*, which was part of the new US Senate Pediment. The Capitol was nearing completion, and the *Progress of Civilization* pediment conveyed the confidence and self-assured superiority of a nation on the rise. The *Dying Indian Chief* was inspired by several classical works, but the clearest parallels are the *Fallen Warrior* and the *Dying Gaul*. Like the *Dying Indian Chief*, the *Fallen Warrior* adorned a pediment—atop the Temple of Aphaia in Aegina—and depicted a vanquished foe. The *Dying Gaul* was first created for Attalus of Pergamon and then later copied by Roman artists. The Gauls struck terror into their victims with their devastating raids and barbarity, and Crawford no doubt had a parallel between the Gauls and Native Americans in mind. Crawford could not have selected a more perfect muse for the peoples that were slowly facing extinction as the American juggernaut crept across the continent. He foresaw that America's own barbarians, the "noble savages" on their doorstep, would suffer the Gallic fate. America was perched on the edge of greatness, and by the early twentieth century, it would break out and join the world stage, subjugating any civilization that stood in its way.

As the *Fallen Warrior* and the *Dying Gaul* exemplify, the "fallen" figures of classical artists ennobled their subjects. The Gaul is a magnificent depiction of tragic heroism, with the naked warrior's perfect physique marred by injury and the body in physical pain. The countenance of the Gaul is still serene, even if anguished. He represents a race that was austere, brave, warlike, and formidable. Yet his way of life is fading, just like his own existence. His culture will be defeated and absorbed by the rising power of Rome.[1]

Copies of the *Dying Gaul* were created at a time when the Gauls no longer threatened the existence of Rome, but at the opening of the third century, that day had not yet come. It had been a century since the Gauls sacked the city, and they had been a perennial peril that would periodically burst out of northern Italy and wreak havoc. This was bad enough, but in 296 the unthinkable happened. Rome's enemies forged an alliance with the Gauls. Once the common enemy of all, some Gauls now joined forces to attack Rome, making it the common enemy.

Rome was ready, however. The developments of the fourth century were the first steps in establishing Rome's martial reputation. In the wars of the early third century, Rome reaped the dividends of its century-long revolution in military organization, tactics, and technology. Polybius acknowledges this by dedicating a paragraph to the events between the Gallic sack to the beginning of the First Punic War. He pledges to begin his history with the latter, but he still has to acknowledge what made Rome's control of Italy possible. He also notes the importance of the Battle of Sentinum in a summary of the campaign in book 2 (2.19). Rome's "struggle with the Samnites and Celts had made them veritable masters in the art of war" (1.6).[2] In the republican life cycle, Rome was emerging from the Italian proving ground as a mature and powerful state worthy of taking on the Mediterranean's greatest powers. This was Rome's breakout moment.

THE COMPETITION OF NOBLES

The Third Samnite War reached its dramatic climax when the Samnites' alliance coalesced into the most serious challenge Rome had yet seen. "Four races . . . were uniting in arms, the Etruscans, Samnites, Umbrians, and Gauls," forbodes Livy (10.21). Their forces were so vast that it was necessary to divide their camps in two; no space of land could suitably contain the enemy host. This convergence of enemies resulted from a combination of events: Rome had been annually campaigning against the Etruscans and Umbrians since 302; a new Gallic invasion descended against Roman allies in the north in 299; and the Samnite truce broke down in 298. Livy tells us dramatically that the Samnite leader, Gellius Egnatius, cobbled together an Italic alliance for "a mighty war . . . on the part of many nations" (10.18).

The severity of the alliance was noted in the consular elections for the year 295. The consul Volumnius was recalled to Rome to hold the elections, where Livy has him inform the assembly of the dire circumstances confronting them, adjuring them to select the most competent commanders (10.21). According to Livy, the assemblies dutifully heeded the counsel of their leaders and elected two prestigious consuls, Q. Fabius Maximus Rullianus and P. Decius Mus. Tranquility was tested by a possible debate between Decius and Fabius as to who would be assigned the northern theater against the coalition, but, in the end, Decius deferred to the age and authority of Fabius, advising "that all be left to the free and unhampered judgment of Quintus Fabius." Always the thorough storyteller, Livy has Fabius later sentimentalize about Decius: "There was no one living with whom he would sooner share his commission; he should have troops enough, if Decius were with him, and his enemies would never be too numerous" (10.25–26).

The citizen-soldiers in the assembly were so charged by the danger of the circumstances, the greatness of the consuls, and the glory to be gained that "nearly all the younger men now flocked about the consul, and each gave in his name, so eager were they to serve under such a captain." In deference to the material incentives of the men, Fabius promised "to bring all my men back with their purses filled" (Livy, 10.25). This did not hinder Fabius' sense of discipline, however, for when he entered his field of operations in Etruria, he bid the soldiers strip down the ramparts of the camp. Under the former consul, Appius, the soldiers had built up a double rampart and a trench because they were "in mortal fear" of the enemy's strength. When Fabius saw Romans gathering wood for yet a third rampart, he was determined to put their timidity to an end. Thenceforth, he told them that the Romans would have no rampart; instead he would march the army out in the open to keep them "more mobile and more healthy." Cowardice was not a vice Fabius would tolerate (10.25).

Can we trust the details recorded by Livy? It is difficult to say with certainty. On the one hand, the first Roman historians, Q. Fabius Pictor and L. Cincius Alimentus were born in the middle of the third century and would have had access to eyewitness accounts when they were younger. There still would have been a reliable oral tradition at the end of their lives when the next generation of historians such as Cato were beginning to write. Livy's sources are now reaching a point when historical details can be trusted, so it is possible that such details are genuine. However, it is difficult to ascertain what Livy knew about the specific deliberations of early third-century politics from his position as a bookish first-century writer surrounded by his available sources. Surely Livy's reconstruction of specific debates and conversations are fabricated, but he is probably drawing on a genuine, traceable tradition for his account of many of the campaign events.[3]

Livy's reconstruction of the selection of Fabius and Decius stresses the strength of Rome's constitution, which was foregrounded by the severity of the military crisis at hand. Livy captures all the classical republican mores: courage, deference, the pursuit of glory, the sharing of benefits, and concord. He weaves a harmonious tapestry of the republican ethos, where the good of the state necessitates deference to leadership and a slight alteration in constitutional norms. The Sentinum campaign is paradigmatic of how he depicts Rome as a "moral community" bound together by the "goodwill rooted in trust and friendship." There was "conflict and consensus," but ultimately, the leading nobility worked harmoniously with the rest of the citizenry through negotiation and an acknowledged mutual dependence. Virtue bound together those who were socially unequal in a legal equality that was beneficial for all.[4]

Livy's account, although filled with flourish, captures the exceptional nature of the circumstances. The enemy coalition was extraordinary, and the Roman response was outstanding in turn. A remarkably high number of eight men held imperium that year: the two consuls, the praetor, and five promagistrates. All of them actively campaigned against the coalition. The consuls themselves had shared office three times already. The pair had proven especially capable in their consulships in 308, when Fabius fended off Rome's southern enemies and Decius the northern ones, and in 297, when Decius won a victory at Maleventum and Fabius captured Cimetra. They had also shared the distinction of the censorship in 304.[5]

The selection of Fabius and Decius highlighted the Roman talent for constitutional flexibility in two ways. First, their election to the consulship would normally have been prevented by the Genucian Law, which prevented a consul from holding office twice within ten years (assuming the law did indeed date to this time). This also would have been discouraged by the conservative *mos* (custom) of Rome's governing elite, who would have frowned on such iterations because they had the effect of limiting the consulship to just a few. Fabius and Decius already had had their commands extended as proconsuls in 296. Second was the choice of the assembly to forgo the normal process of assigning campaigns by lot. Instead, they assigned the dangerous Etruscan theater directly to the senior commander, Fabius (10.24).[6]

Even if this specific debate was a later annalistic elaboration, a dispute like the one Livy mentions between Fabius and Decius accords with what one would expect from a culture of competing aristocrats. This is archaeologically attested in tombs related to the commanders of 295. Aristocrats' tombs and houses "were clustered together, expressing their rivalry in death as well as in life." Mid-republican tombs were modest memorials that did not approach the extravagance of kings, but they expressed the dignity, exceptionalism, and authority the *nobiles* believed they deserved.[7]

The first tomb is an early third century Esquiline grave with a fresco that depicts the Oscan "M. Fannius, son of Staius" and another man named Q. Fabius, which may mean this is the actual tomb of Q. Fabius Maximus. The tomb indicates the "aristocratic male culture" of the period, memorialized even in death by these men who could afford elaborate tombs decorated with accounts of their achievements.[8] Another, more famous, tomb is that of L. Cornelius Scipio Barbatus, one of the year's promagistrates. The Tomb of the Scipios complex included Barbatus and a number of his descendants. Their sarcophagi bear inscriptions that boast of their service to the state, especially their martial leadership. The inscription describes Barbatus as "strong and cunning" ("fortis vir sapiensque"), and his outward presence conformed to his inward virtue ("quoius forma virtutei parisuma fuit"). The epitaphs for Barbatus and his son mention their status as consuls, censors, and curule aediles, using the second-person plural pronouns "with you" or "among you" ("apud vos"), which refer to the common citizens on behalf of whom they served. A Persian monarch or a Hellenistic king was not expected to reference his achievements on behalf of those that placed him in power and gave him civic honor, but it was important for the Roman aristocrat to do so.[9]

Another epitaph for a magistrate of 295 is an imperial inscription possibly recorded from the family records about Appius Claudius Caecus, the consul for 296 and the praetor for 295. The inscription lists his accomplishments:

> Appius Claudius Caecus, son of Gaius, censor, twice consul, dictator, thrice interrex, twice praetor, twice curule aedile, quaestor, thrice military tribune. He captured several towns from the Samnites, routed an army of Etruscans and Sabines, prevented peace being made with King Pyrrhus, paved the Via Appia in his censorship, conducted water into the city, and built a temple to Bellona.[10]

The epitaph relays all that ought to be known about him. These are the martial and monumental achievements of a timocrat.

The Roman aristocracy was dependent on magisterial status and not simply familial lineage, so every new generation felt the pressure to maintain their families' legacies. Maintaining status in the inner circles of the *nobiles* was even more trying. Each family needed to produce one effective male that lived long enough to climb the cursus honorum—the magisterial ladder of power that started with the quaestor and concluded with the consul and, for the very few, the censorship.[11] A man could only attain rank and status by achieving conquest or concord on behalf of the republic, and the former was the surer thing. Birth into such a family provided an advantage, but only glory on behalf of the republic secured status among the elite. This kind of harmonious rivalry on behalf of the republic was present in the jockeying of Fabius and Decius, and it would be acted out in full in the coming battle.

Magistrates like Claudius, Fabius, Decius, and Scipio were supposed to represent their family heritage and honor. This became such a necessity in Rome that family histories began to develop types of those qualities a leading member of the family would represent. A Claudius would be self-confident, ambitious, and overbearing. A Fabius would be principled, dogged, and unshakeable. A Scipio would be crafty and charismatic. A Decius would be pious and self-sacrificing. Roman republican history is therefore sometimes redundant about members of families in implausible ways. Such family records created problems for historians trying to determine what was true and what was merely a type, but the memories of past glories surely stimulated descendants of great ancestors. Even when the accounts are merely ahistorical doublets, they still emphasize the fact that in Rome, family history and honor mattered more to the functioning of the state than in most other places of the ancient world.

THE SANCTION OF GODS

As the consuls were marching to their respective theaters, an enemy force crossed the Apennines, engaged and defeated the smaller army of the propraetor Scipio Barbatus near Clusium, and then camped in the vicinity of Sentinum. Fabius quickly realized the enemy's strength far outmatched his own and requested that Decius speed north with his army (or, perhaps, the two had already joined forces). Livy tells us that the Samnites and Gauls were intending to confront the Romans in battle, leaving the Etruscans and Umbrians to assault the Roman camp. Through a combination of luck and strategic sagacity, this initial plan was thwarted. Three Clusinian deserters reported the enemy strategy to Fabius, and he sent the promagistrates Fulvius and Postumius to ravage Etruria. With their homes threatened the Etruscans and Umbrians departed in pursuit of the raiding promagistrates, leaving the Samnites and Gauls to attack alone (10.27).[12] Even so, when the enemies finally faced each other, the two largest armies in Italy's history were assembled. The Romans fielded around forty thousand and the enemy an even larger force.[13]

Before each side engaged, a deer was seen running onto the field of battle, followed by a wolf. The deer frolicked into the Gallic lines and was struck down; the wolf, on the other hand, was allowed passage through a gap in the Roman lines. Livy has one of the soldiers call out to the enemy: "That way flight and slaughter have shaped their course, where you see the beast lie slain that is sacred to Diana; on this side the wolf of Mars, unhurt and sound, has reminded us of the Martian race and of our Founder" (10.27). The historians tacked on this episode to illustrate the piety of the Romans; nonetheless, it also genuinely reflected the superstitious spirit of the Roman soldiers arrayed for battle. This was as true in 295 as it was in Livy's day and even down to our own. Soldiers still place value in symbols that represent that for which they fight, be they mascots, crosses, crescents, flags, trinkets, or other sacred articles of war.

The year had already seen "many portents, to avert which the senate decreed supplications for two days" (10.23). Some speculate that at the very least, sometime around the battle, whether on the march, in the camp, or perhaps even afterward, a wolf had been seen that caused the revelation.[14] In Roman religion, it was not the portent that mattered, but the interpretation, which in this case was used with good effect—either by the soldiers in battle or by Livy in framing how the Romans achieved the victory. Both deer and wolf symbolized divine sanction of the Roman cause. This was especially so with the wolf, the legendary beast that had suckled Romulus and Remus until they were found by the peasant Faustulus.

It is also important to note Livy's emphasis here on the omen's meaning to the common soldier. Just as Fabius had brought a renewed courage to the legions and alae when he entered the camp of Appius, now the wolf drew insight from a soldier serving in the front ranks. Rome's citizen-soldiers were perfectly capable of understanding (and publicly interpreting) the importance of a religious portent. The next phase of the battle would demonstrate how leaders exemplified its importance, to the point of death.

THE DEVOTION OF DECIUS

The Glory of Decius

At the clash of the two armies, the Roman left, led by Decius, was pitted against the Gallic forces. The Roman right, led by Fabius, took on the Samnites.[15] Decius intended to achieve an immediate success against the Gauls. Following his first unsuccessful charge, he called on the other young nobles serving as the Roman cavalry and renewed a second one. Livy has Decius hearken to their manly spirits, lauding their capture of a "double share of glory" should his left wing defeat the Gallic enemy before Fabius' right defeated the Samnites (10.28). Livy is again recounting details impossible to trace or verify, but he has surely captured the competitive spirit that prevailed.

Unfortunately for the eager Decius, the nobles' charge against the Gallic cavalry was unsuccessful owing to the sudden appearance of "chariots and wagons" that scattered the Roman cavalry to such an extent that the Roman infantry also began to flee.[16] Celtic chariotry was a lingering holdover from Bronze Age warfare, but it could still prove dangerous, as it did on this occasion. The chariotry was used as a sort of quick reaction force (as Diodorus describes in 5.29 and Caesar in *Gallic War*, 4.33), or on the wings (as the Gauls did at Telamon in 225), or in front of the infantry as a screen, where it would disrupt the enemy lines prior to an infantry charge (as the Persians did at Gaugamela in 331 and as did Caesar's British opponents). Decius thus crashed into it behind the cavalry or broke into the flanks where the chariots counterattacked. The former seems to be the case given the surprise Livy conveys in 28.8–10.

Decius was immediately repulsed, and the Gallic chariots pursued them up to the Roman infantry, where they routed the front ranks of *hastati*. Seeing the confusion in the Roman lines, the Gallic infantry

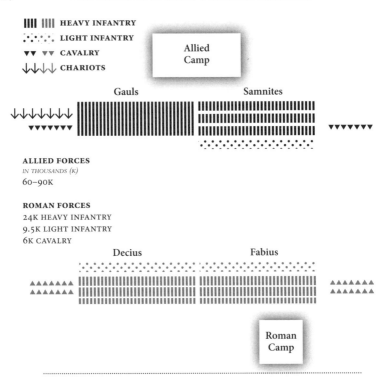

Battle of Sentinum, 295 BC, phase 1: opening dispositions

pressed the advantage and charged into the melee. It looked like the Gauls would inflict a quick defeat on Decius and then make themselves available to finish off Fabius. At this point, Decius must have realized that he had not only lost the opportunity to outshine Fabius but was about to secure their mutual annihilation.

In desperation, Decius cried out the name of his father, turned to the pontifex Marcus Livius who had accompanied him to the battle, and bid Livius "devote himself and the enemy's legions." When the pontifex complied, Decius rushed into the enemy lines by himself (10.28). Livy describes his end vividly:

Having added to the usual prayers that he was driving before him fear and panic, blood and carnage, and the wrath of gods celestial and gods infernal, and should blight with a curse the standards, weapons and armour of the enemy, and that one and the same place should wit-

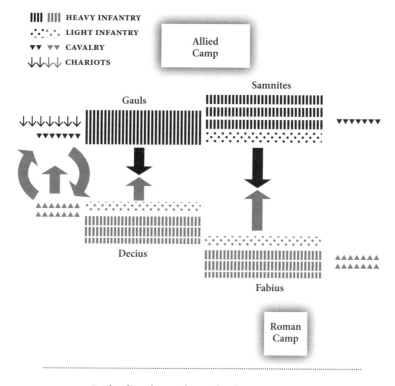

Battle of Sentinum, phase 2: battle commences

ness his own destruction and that of the Gauls and Samnites,—having uttered, I say, these imprecations upon himself and the enemy, he spurred his charger against the Gallic lines, where he saw that they were thickest, and hurling himself against the weapons of the enemy met his death. (10.28)

To the outsider, Decius' behavior seems incredible. With context, however, his rationale becomes apparent, and the entire scenario becomes more plausible. First of all, Decius' actions were made possible by the rhythms of the battle itself. A missile battle allowed for a long exchange with multiple charges and shifts in tactics. It also provided opportunities for leadership to confer, and we have good reason to believe Sentinum was a missile battle given that accounts prioritize missiles over other weapons.

The battle was also said to have lasted several hours, with Fabius

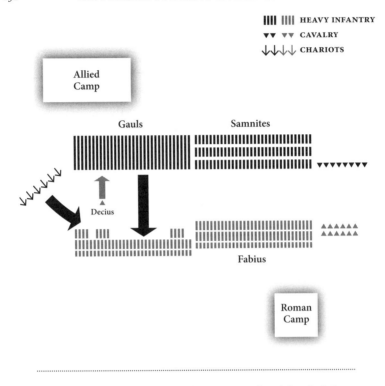

Battle of Sentinum, phase 3: Gallic counterattack and *devotio deciana*

prolonging it as long as possible. Part of the indecision on Decius' wing could have been that the chariots were arrayed in the front and proved unable to break the Roman lines with their javelins until the chariots sent Decius' cavalry crashing back into the infantry. Livy additionally remarks that near the end of the battle, a large supply of missiles had been exchanged, leaving enough for the Roman soldiers to collect (10.28–29).[17] Decius would thus have had time to alter his tactics several times while executing manipular maneuvers. He attempted an infantry assault, several cavalry charges, and, when all hope had failed for a swift decision on the left wing, his own *devotio*.

Devotio Deciana

Numerous theories offer explanations for Decius' behavior. Some argue he was motivated by his father's identical sacrifice in the Latin

War in 340; some see him competing for the greater glory with Fabius; others claim he was rash and overly dramatic; still others see him attempting to achieve recognition for the plebeians.[18] We cannot know for certain about any of these, but all of them could have played a role. Given that his father died in 340 and that he himself had been consul in 312, he was probably in his late forties at least. He cannot therefore be characterized as an impetuous youth. His career thus far had been illustrious; nonetheless, he was still constantly overshadowed by his friend and rival Fabius, who was probably ten years his senior. Fabius and Decius were both capable commanders, and their concurrent successes spurred each to try to outdo the other in the best traditions of the republic's aristocratic code. The patrician Fabius had already celebrated two triumphs, one in 322 and another in 309. The plebeian Decius and his father had never done so, and this surely must have gnawed at him, regardless of how much he may have admired or cooperated with Fabius.

There are fascinating religious aspects to Decius' act as well. The *devotio* was a sacred martial undertaking with a history in Rome's conquest of Italy. When the Gauls sacked Rome in 390, most fled the city. However, some of the elder statesmen stayed behind in their homes to perform *devotiones* of their own. As the Gauls infiltrated the city, these former magistrates donned the insignia that marked the highest offices they had held, seated themselves in ritual positions, and recited incantations against their enemies. The Gauls entered their homes at first believing them to be statue-like representations of gods. When a Gaul touched one of the senators, he replied by striking him with his staff, after which the Gauls commenced a wholesale slaughter of the old men. Their devotions were thus completed (Livy, 5.41). This Roman obsession with glory was part of their republican DNA, from the sacrificial Brutus and the aged senators of the early republic down to its final days. Even the decidedly unwarlike Cicero found himself bewitched by the lure of a glorious death instead of a peaceful retirement.

The *devotio* of Decius' father had been no less dramatic. The elder Decius devoted himself in order to achieve victory in battle against the Romans' erstwhile allies several decades previously (Livy, 8.9–10). Before his actions at Sentinum, Livy has the younger Decius proclaim: "Why

... do I seek any longer to postpone the doom of our house? It is the privilege of our family that we should be sacrificed to avert the nation's perils. Now I will offer up the legions of the enemy, to be slain with myself as victims to Earth and the Manes." The familial angle of the story was credible for Roman historians who intimately understood the pressures of family piety and glory. Spurred on by his own father's noble end, Decius called on the gods to accept his sacrifice so that the enemy might perish.

Fabius already held the edge in the eye of the public, who insisted on granting him the Etruscan theater. After the theaters were assigned, Decius must have glumly resigned himself to the fact that he must outshine him in battle. This would be the year to outpace Fabius. First he would attempt glory through courage; if that failed, he would opt for the *devotio*. The lingering legacy of his father was probably in his mind during every campaign he fought. He did not grow up with a father in flesh and blood, but a father of legend must have towered over his entire career. Like the pontifex he kept alongside him, Decius' plan to engage in the *devotio* accompanied him into his theater of operations. When his rash attempts at a quick victory on the left did not materialize, he fell back on his father's example.

The tradition of the Decii has been appropriately named the *devotio deciana*. The republican tragedian Accius even wrote a play about it in the second century.[19] The *devotio deciana* emerged from the *devotio hostium*, which offered a pledge or sacrifice in exchange for a nearly identical gift—the destruction of the enemies. The elder Decius offered a countercurse when his Latin enemies had made a similar imprecation. The caveat was that in order to effectively foil the curse, the petitioner had to sacrifice his own life first.[20]

From Livy's perspective, Decius' devotion also distanced Roman religion from the barbaric practices of their neighbors. The formation of the Samnite "linen legion" shortly after Sentinum is described in 10.38, and the juxtaposition is clear. The defeat at Sentinum depleted Samnite manpower. In order to recruit men in 293, the Samnites mustered any that were available and forced them to take strict religious oaths. Those who dared refuse "were beheaded before the altars, where they lay amongst the slaughtered victims—a warning to the rest not to refuse." Livy decried the religious ceremonies of the Samnite armies and cited the gods as eager in their wrath to wage war on behalf of Rome. In Decius' religious sacrifice, he offered himself and the enemy legions; in the Samnites' sacrifice, they pledged the death of their own troops.[21]

The magical element behind the entire episode bears strong similarities to the biblical concept of herem. The parallel has not escaped the notice of Roman scholars, who have made comparisons with Joshua's taking of Jericho, among other biblical incidents. Even in Rome, so often viewed as the ancient archetype of shackled religion, spiritual warfare played a part in battle. This spiritual dimension had discernible human effects as well. If the *devotio* itself was historical, there is no reason to doubt that those soldiers witnessing Decius' sacrifice were not also driven by their own superstitions and conceptions of honor on behalf of their plebeian commander. They would have been spurred to action. Livy captures the spirit: "From that moment the battle seemed scarce to depend on human efforts. The Romans, after losing their general—an occurrence that is wont to inspire terror—fled no longer, but sought to redeem the field. . . . [T]he pontifex Livius . . . cried aloud that the Romans had won the victory, being quit of all danger by the consul's doom" (10.29). Decius' final act won the support of the fleeing troops, who returned to pin down the Gallic right wing.[22]

Years later this inspirational power was feared by Pyrrhus when he faced a third Decius (grandson) in the Battle of Asculum (279). Pyrrhus mocked the magical aspects but was wary of its power over the minds of the troops. Before the battle, he investigated the ritual, ascertained the attire of the consul so that he might be recognized, and commanded his officers to ensure that Decius was not killed (Zonaras, 8.5).[23]

The Gauls facing Decius, however, had not the future wisdom of Pyrrhus, and like the consul, were devoted to destruction. Decius' actions in the battle, from the ferocity of his first charge, to his upbraiding his fellow nobles, to his final act of *devotio*, exemplify several manifestations of the Roman martial spirit. His sacrifice was the purest form of religious, familial, personal, and martial offering to the Roman state—one that had few, if any, parallels in the ancient world. The act was tactically unwise and wasteful of Roman energy and men, but it worked. Like so many foolhardy decisions in war, it appealed to the irrational aspects of humanity and was well received.

THE DISCIPLINE OF FABIUS

The action on the right wing under Fabius was the opposite of Decius' fortune on the left. Fabius and Decius may have enjoyed years of collegial success, but the tone and tactical patience of the consuls were quite dissimilar. Fabius had undertaken numerous campaigns and employed varied tactics against the Samnites and Etruscans during his consulships in 310, 308, and 297. His dogged strategy and tactics rounded out Decius'. The Roman art of war, if seen only through the lens of Decius, would too closely resemble the frenetic stereotypes of the Samnites and Gauls they confronted. Livy demeaned the Samnite and Etruscan transience in battle, commenting that

> their general was persuaded that both the Samnites and Gauls fought fiercely at the outset of an engagement, but only needed to be withstood; when a struggle was prolonged, little by little the spirits of the Samnites flagged, while the physical prowess of the Gauls, who could least of all men put up with heat and labour, ebbed away, and, whereas in the early stages of their battles they were more than men, they ended with being less than women. (Livy, 10.28)

The description is unfair to the tactical abilities of the Samnites but accurately represents how historians traditionally viewed the Gauls. It also says a great deal about Fabius and the Roman determination to doggedly wear down their opponents.[24]

Fabius disciplined his men to resist the initial onslaughts of the enemies by "defending themselves rather than attacking." His strategy was to wear out the Samnite left wing by encouraging his men "to prolong the struggle to as late an hour in the day as possible" (10.29). This meant a constant shifting of the maniples, and it also required maneuvers catered to the repeated exchange of missiles. Fabius' tactical superiority was so much greater than both the Samnites and his colleague that he was able to send the proconsul Scipio and lieutenant Marcius to support Decius.[25] The manner of Decius' death, Livy remarks, gave them "a great incentive to dare everything for the republic." Girded on by Decius, the lieutenants led their soldiers with their pila against the remaining Gallic troops, who had formed a testudo ("tortoise shell"—a defensive maneuver wherein soldiers packed together and raised their shields above their heads and all around themselves) (10.29).

While the Roman left was fighting the Gallic testudo, Fabius noted a decrease in the Samnite assaults and missile exchanges. His accurate assessment of the enemy's stamina now yielded the predicted result. Eager to press the advantage, he ordered his cavalry to attack the Samnite flank while his troops began a slow assault. When they met little resistance, Fabius ordered a full assault, and the Samnites fled past their Gallic allies, whose numbers were dwindling under a hail of pila. Fabius finished off those remaining by ordering a charge of Campanian cavalry and Roman infantrymen on the Gallic rear, now exposed by the flight of the Samnites (10.29). Livy's detail that Fabius used the principes to finish off the Gauls lends credence to the theory that the principes were designed as the decisive line of battle.

This final maneuver seems simple enough to the untrained eye, but it revealed the high level of discipline achieved by Fabius' command. Soldiers that have gained a victory would, in their great thirst for hard-earned spoils, usually race to take the enemy camp and the booty within it. Fabius' ability to withhold one of his contingents in pursuit of the enemy implies a great respect on behalf of the soldiers for their commander and a great mastery on behalf of the commander over his soldiers. Meanwhile, all discipline had evaporated from the Samnites, who fled with such haste to their camp that a great throng formed outside that could not enter through the narrow gates. After a brief resistance, the camp was won. The rabble-rousing Samnite commander Gellius Egnatius was found among the dead.

Fabius' measured tactics—from his initial distraction of the Etruscans and the Umbrians, through his battlefield patience, to the capture of the enemy camp—present a picture of Roman warfare that is markedly different from Decius'. Without Fabius there would have been no

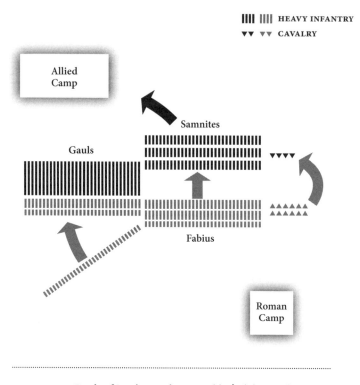

Battle of Sentinum, phase 4: Fabius' triple assault

opportunity for success, for it was his insight that cut the enemy forces in half before the battle. His operational aggression had divided the enemy forces from the start, and his tactical conservatism had secured victory in the end. Fabius' generalship was superior to that of his colleague. Decius achieved victory on the left wing, but at a much greater cost. Not only did the Roman right keep its consul, but it also suffered far fewer casualties. Decius' impetuous charges cost Rome seven thousand casualties, compared to the more palatable seventeen hundred casualties on the Roman right (10.29).[26]

FUNERALS, TRIUMPHS, AND TEMPLES

Fabius crowned his victory by vowing a temple to Jupiter Victor before he took possession of the enemy camp. When he found the body of

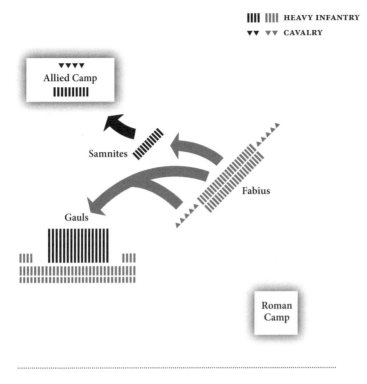

Battle of Sentinum, phase 5: destruction of the Gauls and capture of the camp

Decius among the dead after an extended search by his troops, he adopted a very different posture and immediately held a funeral for his colleague. In doing so, he memorialized a member of his own order alongside the community of citizens who had just fought with the deceased.

Polybius later reflected on the nature of Roman funerals, especially for those who had died in battle. Funerals are the "single instance" he cites to "indicate the pains taken by the state to turn out men who will be ready to endure everything in order to gain a reputation in their country for valour" (6.52). Polybius details the elaborate honors conferred on the death of illustrious men. Their sons delivered touching eulogies that affected the Roman people, an image of the deceased was brought before the people, his achievements and character were recounted, and the whole of Rome turned out for the ceremony.

He marvels at the impact such an event must have on the future generations:

> There could not easily be a more ennobling spectacle for a young man who aspires to fame and virtue. For who would not be inspired by the sight of the images of men renowned for their excellence, all together and as if alive and breathing? . . . By this means, by this constant renewal of the good report of brave men, the celebrity of those who performed noble deeds is rendered immortal, while at the same time the fame of those who did good service to their country becomes known to the people and a heritage for future generations. (6.53–54)

Polybius concludes with the final power of the ceremony—the people learn to set "a higher value on the interest of their country than on the ties of nature that bound them to their nearest and dearest" (6.54).

Cicero and Livy share Polybius' estimation. Cicero writes that centuries later Romans were still inspired by Decius' example to sacrifice everything for the republic (*On Old Age*, 20.75). In tribute to the character of both commanders at Sentinum, Livy described how he "postpon[ed] his concern for everything else" and "celebrated the funeral of his colleague with every show of honour and well-merited eulogiums" (10.29).[27] Both Fabius and Decius received the immortal glory they coveted, one through a magical sacrifice and posthumous recognition and the other through a vowed temple and a triumph.

The triumph Fabius received when he returned was well deserved. The period between the Second Samnite War and the Punic Wars saw the most triumphs in Roman history. From the years 312 to 293 and 282 to 264, at least forty were recorded in the triumphal *fasti*.[28] These years saw Rome transition from a regional power in central Italy to a Mediterranean power worthy of notice by other great states. Agricultural virtues had stabilized the Romans, politics had laid the foundation for success, but war won Rome international acclaim. The Romans themselves acknowledged this in the triumphal procession, which patriotically recognized citizen-commander and citizen-soldiers as exemplars of the republic before reintegrating them back into the civilian community.[29]

Staying true to the republican spirit of citizen armies, the celebrations of victory did not neglect the soldiers. Behind the triumphal procession, the soldiers of the consular armies chanted verses in praise
of Fabius' victory and Decius' "glorious death." They remembered the
family of Decius in their praises, "reviving by their praise of the son
the memory of the father, whose death (and its service to the commonwealth) had now been matched." If Livy is to be believed, following the triumph, each soldier was given spoils from the victory—"a
present of eighty-two *asses* of bronze, with a cloak and a tunic, a reward
for military service in those days far from contemptible" (10.30).

The temple to Jupiter Victor that Fabius vowed in the heat of battle
was indeed constructed, although the details as to site and year are unknown today. Fabius' specific choice of Jupiter Victor probably stemmed
from Rome's contact with Greece and its knowledge of Alexander's
interest in Nike (the Greek equivalent to Victoria). A statue of Hercules
had already been erected in 305, and in 294, a year after the battle, the
consul Postumius Megellus dedicated the temple of Victoria. Fabius
was aware of Sentinum's import for all of Italy, so he was consciously
adopting the same conquering mentality for Rome. Henceforth, Rome's
unstoppable imperial federation would be associated with the goddess
Victoria.[30]

PYRRHIC AND PUNIC PROBLEMS

The victory at Sentinum ensured Rome's role as the pacifier and protector of Italy. No longer would the Umbrians and Etruscans prove too
troublesome, and two years later at Aquilonia the Samnite opposition
in the third war was decisively dispatched. The Gauls would, of course,
continue to invade intermittently. Despite these setbacks, such as the
defeat at Arretium in 284, Rome would continue to overcome through
victories like the one at Lake Vadimo in 283.[31] The loss of Livy's books
11–20 leaves the picture incomplete, but by the opening of the Punic
Wars, the Italy Polybius describes was dominated by Rome.[32]

The Samnite Wars pitted the Roman federation against the Samnite
League, one collection of citizen armies against another, and the victor
of this contest emerged as iron sharpened by iron. Sentinum crowned

Rome as the master of Italy's destiny, and it made the victor stronger because it had to adopt the best techniques of its Italian brothers in order to defeat them. The tactics, equipment, and manpower of the Samnites, and all the other neighboring peoples, were thus assimilated by Rome. The result was that Rome would furnish the finest example of Italian citizen-soldiery as the peninsula became embroiled in the broader Mediterranean wars of the third century.

In the 290s and 280s, Rome followed up its successes in the north with colonies and alliances in the south. The Italiote enemies of the Samnites found a natural ally in Rome, and city-states such as Thurii, Locri, Rhegium, and Croton sought Roman military protection. This discomfited Tarentum, which had historically vacillated between strained relations and leadership over its Italiote brothers. This Greek city-state on the northern coast of Italy's southeastern bay, like every other polity in Italy, had a long tradition of warfare. Tarentum may have even been one of the city-states through which Rome learned of Victoria, given that Tarentine coinage from the fourth century often featured Nike. Spartan colonists founded the city in the late eighth century, and since that time they had constantly fought their Italic neighbors and other Italiote city-states.[33] They recruited Alexander I of Epirus (the Molossian) to beat back the aggressions of their Italic neighbors like the Samnites in the late 330s, so it was instinctive for them to invite aid again when confronted by Rome.

Assistance from across the Adriatic took the form of warrior classes and mercenary armies commanded by adventurers and kings. Pyrrhus of Epirus, the so-called heir of Alexander "in arms and action," was overeager to take on the barbarians to the west on behalf of Tarentum (Plutarch, *Pyrrhus*, 8). Because there were not many opportunities in Greece, he decided to try his hand at an Italian and Sicilian empire. His failure in spite of two brilliant victories at Heraclea (280) and Asculum (279) demonstrated that Rome's talents for federal cohesiveness and tactical adaptation could match every challenge.

Pyrrhus represented a new brand of military leadership in Greece. The Greek city-states had been beset by as many troubles as central Italy during the fourth century, but they developed along very different lines. Where Rome demanded more of its citizen-soldiers, the Greeks had begun demanding less. The old hoplite ethos was replaced by the elitism of adventuring generals and mercenary soldiers. The reasons for this transition were complex, but at the very least they were enabled by the disaster of the Peloponnesian War, ongoing internecine rivalries, the troubled fourth-century economy, and the rising demand for mercenaries from the western Persian empire, Sicilian tyrants, and other powers like Carthage. Throughout the fourth century, citizen levies were increasingly rivaled by mercenaries. In the wake of Alexander's conquests the elite warrior aristocracies or killers-for-hire of Hellenistic kings became standardized. The Macedonian military innovations of Philip and Alexander had resulted in "an era of mercenaries."[34]

Pyrrhus thus used a system with values diametrically opposed to Rome's. He still employed citizen levies—like those of Tarentum—but his core of phalangites enabled his adventurism and produced his victories. Rome, on the other hand, despised mercenaries or warrior elites that fought merely for pay, glory, or reward. It saw its federal armies of farming citizen-soldiers as virtuous men who fought for the good of the republic.

Rome was now the head of a considerable coalition of forces that looked to the republican head of the federation for unity and protection. This system of alliances proved hardier than Pyrrhus anticipated. After his initial victories, Pyrrhus searched in vain for allies to buttress his battlefield successes. When he marched north after his victory at Heraclea, he was disappointed to not win over allies disaffected with Rome. Even more discouraging was the reappearance of opposing legions. Recruited from the citizenry and socii, the army was now larger than the one he had previously defeated. Zonaras has him famously remark in despair that the legions, "when cut to pieces grew whole again, hydra-fashion" (8.4).

The loyalty on the part of Rome's allies was due to its keen rule. Even if they were not patriotic about Rome, they were practical. Rome was fierce in war, but fair enough in peace.[35] This became apparent in the difference between Roman and Pyrrhic governance. Pyrrhus' tactical and strategic brilliance enabled him to acquire empires. His lack of political sagacity, on the other hand, resulted in a tendency to lose these empires, as he had in Greece, southern Italy, and Sicily. Even the Tarentines regretted their having summoned him after he pressed them into service, forbade assemblies, unnecessarily rationed their food supplies, and discreetly assassinated discontents. Zonaras quipped that the Tarentines "found in Pyrrhus a master instead of an ally" (8.2).

By contrast, Rome's faithfulness to its allies was affirmed by examples such as the punishment of the Rhegium deserters in 271. When Rome was beset by the invasion of Pyrrhus, a garrison of Roman and allied deserters took over the city under the leadership of a Campanian named Decius. After the war's conclusion, Rome retook the city and slayed most of the deserting troops. Rome then immediately restored the city to its citizens. The three hundred soldiers from the garrison that had survived Rome's recapture of Rhegium were sent to the Roman Forum where they were scourged and beheaded. Polybius explains Rome's design in the punishment of its own soldiers: their object was "to recover as far as possible by this punishment their reputation for good faith with the allies" (1.7).

Rome's first encounter with a great Hellenistic general and his crack soldiery yielded a number of telling anecdotes that are recounted by the ancient historians. Pyrrhus' forces contrasted significantly with Rome's citizen-soldiers. He had a select expeditionary force of Macedonian-style warriors—the best soldiers of the day—that numbered around twenty-nine thousand, including the famous Macedonian phalangite and special forces such as cavalry, slingers, archers, and a small elephant corps. To this he added his Italian allies, which included the recently defeated Samnites and some of the Italiotes. As everyone would have expected, this highly proficient, well-led army defeated Roman armies on the battlefield. What surprised Pyrrhus—and this surprise is testified to by him in all the sources—is that he could not defeat the Roman political order that produced these armies. The republican federation continued to furnish new citizen-soldiers.

The classic ingredients of Rome's civic virtue are present in the accounts. On the verge of a treaty, old, blind commanders come to the senate and browbeat the senators not to accept peace while Pyrrhus remains in Italy. Statesmen that Pyrrhus tries to bribe profess they would rather enjoy the produce of their own simple farms than the riches he promises them. Men previously terrified by Pyrrhus' forces—particularly the previously unknown elephants—keep trying new tricks until they neutralize them in battle.

Again, the details of the authors here may be fanciful elaboration, but they all testify to the same thing: the Roman Republic created a unique idea of public service. Young men displaying weakness should be beaten back into line by old commanders. Leaders should be immune to bribes. Citizen-soldiers must be willing to face the most fearsome foes that have already defeated them. These same men must be able to adapt, learn from their enemies, and then discover how to defeat them. And finally, these republican ideals should inspire others in Italy to fight for the values of a republican federation rather than for the tyranny of a Hellenistic despot. That others in Italy were indeed inspired to fight for such values ensured that no matter how many battles Pyrrhus won, he could not afford to lose any of his highly proficient troops because potential recruits would prefer fighting for Rome than for him.[36]

Pyrrhus' defeat and withdrawal after his extremely costly and hard-fought battles earned Rome a treaty with another Hellenistic king, Ptolemy II Philadelphus in 273. It also brought Rome face-to-face with the naval empire of the West—Carthage. Undaunted, Rome continued to extend its control. Rome and Carthage's struggle for the Tyrrhenian islands in the First Punic War was one of the longest continuous conflicts in the ancient world, and yet its drama was outdone by the carnage that followed in the Second Punic War, when Hannibal brought Carthaginian arms to the very gates of Rome itself.[37]

Like the Hellenistic monarchs, Carthage earned Roman disdain because it preferred to hire out soldiers. This preference is all the more remarkable given that Carthage had a similar constitution as Rome. Aristotle was one of the more famous ancient authorities who lauded the Carthaginian *politeia* (2.8). Polybius agreed that Sparta, Crete, and

Carthage were among the best examples of the ancient mixed constitution (6.43–57). Carthage's principal difference from Rome was its nature as a thalassocratic and mercantilist republic, which, as a consequence, made it tend to see war too much in terms of cost. Carthage also preferred to use specialists and mercenaries instead of citizens to fight its wars, which prompted it to separate civil from military command.[38]

Polybius contrasts Rome's symbiosis of agriculture, civic virtue, and military strength with Carthage's reliance on a trading, maritime empire to fund its war coffers and supply its commanding officers mostly with paid troops from subject states. Where Carthaginians used mercenaries to protect their freedom, Polybius asserts that Romans "relied on their own valor and on the aid of their allies." This shaped a resilience in the Romans that was unmatched by other ancient polities. The Romans, "fighting as they are for their country and their children, never can abate their fury but continue to throw their whole hearts into the struggle until they get the better of their enemies" (Polybius, 6.52).

The Punic military was led by Carthaginians who had been trained in the elite minority of citizens groomed for command. They commanded a polyglot army composed of Balearics, Spanish, Libyan, Gallic, and Numidian subjects. Their tactical formations depended on the needs of the battle and the soldiers that were serving at that particular point in time. Balearics, for example, were known as slingers and light infantrymen. Numidians were known for their cavalry and skirmishers. Libyan mercenaries often formed the largest contingents, and they were known as multipurpose fighters who could serve as either light or heavy infantrymen. Spanish warriors were famed for their guerrilla tactics and for their pila-throwing and gladius-wielding swordsmanship. Greek subjects probably still relied on hoplite tactics, and Macedonian influences produced a familiarity with close-ranked phalangite warfare. When Gallic units were incorporated, they added their flair for half-naked, long-sword shock tactics. Carthaginians also sported an elephant corps, complete with mahouts who would drive a spike through the brains of rampaging elephants that turned on their masters. As this description illustrates, the Carthaginians suffered the disadvantage of variations in the nationality and training of their fighting forces. On the other hand, they also drew on a tactically vast manpower base that, when placed in the hands of a capable general, could counter an enemy's every move.[39]

When Rome faced Carthage it challenged the greatest naval power of the Mediterranean. As an established land power, Rome had always relied on its coastal allies to furnish any ships of war. Nonetheless, Rome would not follow the Spartans, who, when confronted with Athenian naval superiority, refused to innovate until Persia intervened. Instead, Rome, as Kaeso forewarned, *became* a naval power. Recall the prediction Kaeso was provided by the *Ineditum Vaticanum* and Diodorus. He warned the Carthaginians that although Rome did not have a fleet capable of mastering the Carthaginians, if forced to, they would learn to build one: "Do not force the Romans to engage in affairs of the sea; for if we have need of naval forces we shall, in a short time, equip more and better ships than you, and we shall prove more effective in naval battles than people who have long practiced seafaring."[40]

This "prediction" on the part of the ancient authors reflected historical reality in the First Punic War. Rome wisely decided against fighting the Carthaginian navy on its terms. Instead, it created an ingenious solution. It equipped each ship in its fleet of quinqueremes (a naval warship powered by groups of five rowers) with a novel device, the *corvus*. The *corvus* was a plank with an iron spike on the end that could grapple enemy ships and then allow a landing party of marines to board the faster but undermanned Carthaginian galleys (Polybius, 1.22). Rome also demonstrated resolve when it had to build three such fleets throughout the course of the war after storms and defeats destroyed them. The Carthaginians, lost in their own military conservatism, could not furnish a proper response, and the greatest naval power succumbed to a newcomer in naval tactics.

Rome also had to cope with new variables in land warfare, most notably Pyrrhus' and the Carthaginians' use of war elephants. When the Romans confronted Pyrrhus at Heraclea, Asculum, and Beneventum (275), they were forced to develop a means to conquer the intimidating beasts he brought with him as a rudimentary armored division, his elephant corps. It took eighty years of experimental tactics employed against the beasts for Rome to finally create a sufficient counter to them. Yet by the time of Scipio Africanus' battle with Hannibal at Zama (202) and his brother's battle at Magnesia (190), the Romans were adept at neutralizing them. Eventually Rome even incorporated the beasts, as the Battle of Pydna (168) attests.[41]

The Pyrrhic and Punic Wars were contests to see whose brand of militarism would triumph in the Mediterranean. Would mercantilist mercenaries led by brilliant tacticians and the specialist armies of kings win the day? Or would it be the Roman agrarian federation and its aristocrats with their code of statecraft and farmers with their civic duty of part-time soldiering? Pyrrhus' ephemeral efforts proved inconclusive, so the quest to humble Rome turned to a second Punic effort under the leadership of the most famous general of the ancient world, Hannibal Barca.

6 · The Greatest Trial

BEATING YOUR BETTERS
AT NEW CARTHAGE

Rome's life or death struggle with Carthage was arguably the most famous rivalry in the ancient world. The series of conflicts from 264–146
has provided fertile ground for references by Americans. As discussed
in the prologue, characters like Regulus, Fabius, Hannibal, and Scipio
were commonly identified with founding luminaries. Fisher Ames used
the ancient contest in his foreign politics essays, where he compares
France to Rome and Great Britain to Carthage.[1] A century later Calvin
Coolidge was reveling in the thrilling war stories he learned in school.
He vividly recalls their impressions in his autobiography: "I heard the
tramp of the invincible legions of Rome, I saw the victorious galleys of
the Eternal City carrying destruction to the Carthaginian shore."[2] It is
fitting that Coolidge was remembering his Roman studies in 1929. Like
Rome during the Punic Wars, America had recently broken onto the
world stage and would soon face its own greatest trial.

Nine years before Coolidge wrote those words, Italians were also
thinking about Carthage and Rome. In 1920 the Italians erected a monument that references their disastrous defeat at the Battle of Caporetto
in 1917. Oddly enough, Caporetto is a passing reference in the monument and not the subject being memorialized. The monument instead
commemorates the Second Punic War. It is located at the site of Rome's
disastrous defeat at Lake Trasimene in 217 and inscribed with the following words: "In this place, where Hannibal vented his unremitting
hatred of Rome, destiny resolved through one of the most important

battles of history, supremacy in the Mediterranean. The tragic outcome of this ancient Caporetto was later reversed at Zama, with sturdy faith and unshakeable valour."[3] Two thousand years after the Second Punic War, Italians still remembered that greatest of trials that nearly brought the Roman Republic to its knees.

FOR REVENGE

More than two millennia before the Italians erected the memorial, another man contemplated Rome. Hamilcar was the greatest commander in the First Punic War and the general most responsible for putting down the mercenary revolt (241–238) that followed. Tradition presents him as the inveterate foe of Rome, who never forgave his own government for quitting the fight in the First Punic War and never forgave Rome for stealing Sardinia and Corsica during the mercenary revolt. Hamilcar was also one of the principal architects of the reconstructed Carthaginian presence in the Mediterranean. He crossed into Spain, subjugated the Iberian tribes, and carved out an empire across half the Iberian peninsula. Legend has it that before crossing the Pillars of Hercules (Strait of Gibraltar) to reassert Carthaginian power, he made his nine-year-old son Hannibal swear an oath on the altar to Baal that he would never be a friend to the Romans (Livy, 21.1; Nepos, *Hannibal*, 1).

Many scholars tend to dismiss this fanciful story about Hannibal's origins, and legend indeed it may be. But can we entirely dismiss the notion that Hannibal did not seek revenge on Rome? This son of Hamilcar dedicated his entire military career to fighting Rome across the Mediterranean, from Iberia in the west, the Alps in the north, Africa in the south, and the Seleucid Empire in the east. If Italians could still muster vitriol for Hannibal more than two thousand years after Lake Trasimene, is it not reasonable to allow that Hannibal may have sworn an oath of enmity against Rome?[4]

Carthaginian Victories

Whether he was motivated by revenge, a violated treaty, fear of Roman power, or a simple misunderstanding, Hannibal was definitely the spark that set off the conflagration of the Second Punic War when he captured, sacked, and massacred the male population of Saguntum.[5] Hannibal had also ensured that his forces were at their maximum efficiency. When he mustered out of Spain, he had mobilized 122,600 infantry and cavalry alongside about two hundred war elephants. Many of these would remain in Spain and Africa, but it is a testament to Hannibal's operational genius and personal command abilities that he entered Italy with a force large enough to counter any consular army. The Romans, by comparison, had only approximately seventy thousand men in arms.[6]

Hannibal's plan was to strike Rome so hard and so fast that it would be isolated from its allies and their potential manpower. His consolidation of communication lines in northeastern Spain, a fighting march across southern France, and a winter crossing of the Alps reduced his expeditionary force to less than forty thousand, but he would be able to replace these numbers with newly won Italian allies such as the Gauls or defectors from the Roman federation.[7] In the short run, Hannibal had the advantage. If he could achieve enough quick and devastating victories, he could force Rome to terms.

Originally, the Romans intended to respond with coordinated offenses. The consul Publius Scipio and his brother Gnaeus were sent against the Carthaginian armies in Spain. While Hannibal was distracted, an African expeditionary force was to inflict enough damage to demoralize the Carthaginian heartland. P. Scipio moved quickly enough, and a skirmish occurred near the Rhone in southern France (Polybius, 3.45). The Roman skirmishers won a small victory, gained sight of Hannibal's camp, and returned to report. Then the unexpected occurred. When Scipio found Hannibal's camp near the Rhone, he discovered it was deserted (Polybius, 3.49). Not only had Hannibal crossed the Rhone, but he was racing toward the Alps to break through Rome's northern frontier.

Hannibal's swift crossing caught the Roman command of 218 off guard. When Publius learned that Hannibal was cutting off his own communications in order to directly strike Roman territory, he decided to follow through with the original imperative of the senate. He sent his brother Gnaeus with the consular army on to Spain. The passage of one Carthaginian army through southern France and down through the Italian Alps was troublesome enough, so Gnaeus would seek to prohibit the passage of another by carrying the war to that theater.

Publius himself crossed the sea and returned to Italian soil to face Hannibal. Livy writes that each commander marveled at the fleetness and determination of the other; yet it was Hannibal who proved the greater general (21.39). Hannibal defeated Publius, who nearly lost his life during the Battle of Ticinus. What saved the consul from being the first death of a Roman commander in the war was the audacity of his son, "who was just reaching manhood" (Polybius, 10.3; Livy, 21.46). The younger Scipio braved the Carthaginian onslaught to reach his father and bring him back to safety. This would not be the last the Carthaginians saw of the young man.[8]

After Hannibal's successful skirmish at Ticinus, he proved his tactical superiority with three more resounding victories. At the Trebia River in 218 he smashed two consular armies, and at Lake Trasimene in 217 he obliterated two legions. The worst disaster came the following year, when Hannibal annihilated up to seventy thousand legionaries and killed a consul at Cannae, essentially erasing eight legions from existence. Before the news had even sunk in at Rome, more devastating information flowed in: Lucania, Bruttium, and Capua had revolted, and two more legions had been shattered and another consul killed by the Gauls in northern Italy. Here were Hannibal's quick and devastating victories. Surely the Romans would follow the typical pattern in Hellenistic warfare and capitulate. After all, even the mighty Persian Empire had collapsed after Alexander's three stunning victories at Granicus (334), Issus (333), and Gaugamela (331).

Republican Response

Hannibal's strategy was to destroy the federation's cohesion by inflicting defeats on Italian soil. He assumed Rome's citizens would despair and that its allies would desert following so many consecutive losses. After enough defeats and defections, he could then secure a humiliating settlement. Cannae should have put him significantly closer to that goal. Instead, his first bargaining chip—the ransom of eight thousand Romans captured from the camp outside Cannae—was summarily rejected. After earnest deliberation in the senate, the Romans refused his demands on the grounds that doing so would only fill his coffers and display a weakening resolve.

In the eyes of any opponent, such a gesture was a terrifying testament of iron will. For this reason, Polybius pauses his history at this moment to write his long digression on the Roman constitution. Polybius goes to great lengths in his sixth book to describe the superiority of the Roman constitution over any that the world had yet produced. For Polybius, what provided victory for Rome, even in its darkest hour after Cannae, was the strength and moral clarity of its republican constitution. When Livy reaches the disaster of Cannae in his writing, he similarly remarks that "surely there was no other people that would not have been overwhelmed by a disaster of such vast proportions" (22.54).

The magistrates, senate, and people of Rome continued to function after this devastating series of events. At Canusium, the young Scipio united the scattered survivors, providing them leadership until they could return to the fight. Varro, the general who had rushed into disaster at Cannae, returned to Rome a wiser man and was welcomed by the people "because he had not despaired of the state." Unlike the Athenians, Carthaginians, and Persians—who often tried, executed, exiled, or disgraced such generals—the Romans still honorably welcomed his return. Meanwhile, the senate prevented chaos and regulated public mourning, calmly arranging for the continuation of the Roman state, the renewal of the legions, and the maintenance of the war. Wounded but determined, the republic plodded onward (22.53, 55, 61).[9]

Another problem for Hannibal was the network of Roman colonies, which tenaciously clung to Rome regardless of their location. The Latin colonies of Placentia and Cremona had been wisely stocked with six thousand colonists apiece. They were crucial in the north, aiding the consuls during Hannibal's invasion and possibly saving the Roman defensive in 208–207 when Hasdrubal wasted precious time in a failed siege of Placentia. In the south, Cales was in the divided Campanian heartland a few hours march north of Hannibal's new ally Capua. Venusia bordered the Samnite and Lucanian defectors. Beneventum lay deep within Samnium itself. Yet because these colonies remained loyal, they served as resupply points, safe havens, and staging grounds for Hannibal's foes.[10]

Rome's federation was bound by a belief that Roman dominance— embodied in its laws, institutions, and civic norms such as flexibility, inclusivity, fairness, and local autonomy—was far more formidable than Hannibal's brilliant battlefield tactics. The lesson of Cannae, and really of the Second Punic War and the entire Rome-Carthage conflict, is that there is more to warfare than strategy, tactics, and political ends and means. Culture was the deciding factor following Cannae, and this is the factor that Hannibal overlooked, as Victor Hanson explains:

> Students of war must never be content to learn merely how men fight a battle, but must always ask why soldiers fight as they do, and what ultimately their battle is for. The tragic paradox of warfare is that so often courage, audacity, and heroism on the battlefield—what brave warriors can do, see, hear, and feel in the heat of killing—are overshadowed by elements far larger, abstract, and often insidious.

Military dominance through superior militarism (even a civic one) does not necessarily mean cultural sophistication. In fact, it can sometimes imply the opposite. Military success for a republic, however, must be linked to the cultural values of its statesmen and citizens, whether sophisticated or not, and Rome had created a civic culture that Italian allies found more appealing than anything Carthage could offer.[11]

According to Polybius, even Hannibal recognized the ideals underlying Rome's unpredicted temerity with a sense of foreboding. "Hannibal's joy at his victory in the battles was not so great as his dejection, when he saw with amazement how steadfast and high-spirited were the Romans in their deliberations" (6.58.13). Polybius captures the mixture of respect and frustration Hannibal must have surely felt—respect at his opponents' unparalleled qualities and frustration that these qualities made them undefeatable. He was beginning to dread Rome's civic militarism.

Everything had gone according to Hannibal's invasion plans, but he had not planned for this. Like Alexander, he had won his three "decisive" battles, and unlike Pyrrhus, he had actually started winning over important Roman allies and rebels like Capua. Unfortunately, there were still far too many Roman *nobiles* who wanted the honor of popular reverence or the glory of a victory, too many citizens willing to serve Rome during the fighting stage of their life cycle, and too many allies who thought Rome was a better choice than Carthage.

New Strategy

The Romans adopted the strategy advised by one of their leading statesmen, Quintus Fabius Maximus (the great-grandson of the victor of Sentinum). According to Fabius, the way to fight the superior tactics of Hannibal was . . . to not fight him. That is, the way to defeat him was to only accept or offer Hannibal battle in extremely favorable conditions; in the meantime, the Romans would wage a war of attrition against an invader that would inevitably become increasingly weaker. Given that the civilian, electrum-coin-counting Carthaginian senate was traditionally stingy with support for their martial counterparts, the strategy was a sound one. For his plan, Fabius was surnamed "Cunctator," meaning "delayer," "procrastinator," or "cautious one," and to this day military strategists still refer to the "Fabian strategy of attrition."

The Romans also increased their strength in the field. Between 218 and 216, they had already raised their legionary strength from six to seventeen. By 211 they would be up to twenty-five, and the annual number of legions stayed between eighteen and twenty-five until the final year of the war.[12] Rome was stretching its available manpower to the furthest limits, even lowering the property qualification and conscripting slaves and proletariats for the navy. Despite their fighting strength, the years from 215 to 212 saw more maneuvering than action. Whenever one side gained a moderate victory, it soon saw an equal defeat. The next years marked the turning point, however, when Syracuse, which had defected after the death of its loyal king Hiero II, was captured in 212. The following year saw the fall of Capua. With the tide slowly turning in Italy, revenge now belonged to the Romans.

The capture of Capua provides one of the best examples of how a Roman commander used his imperium to exact personal vengeance on behalf of Rome. The leading citizens of Capua were reminded of this grim reality by the proconsul Fulvius Flaccus. When the fortunes of the war turned on Capua, their once defiant city became beleaguered by the Romans, who denied Hannibal every opportunity of raising the siege. In desperation, messengers were sent enjoining Hannibal to return, but Fulvius captured the messengers, scourged them with rods, cut off their hands, and then sent them back to Capua. This gesture "broke the spirit of the Capuans," who eventually turned on their leaders and betrayed the city (Livy, 26.12). Before the gates were opened, a number of the Capuan senators took poison to spare themselves the anticipated punishment.

Their fears were justified. The remaining leaders were divided into several groups, one of which was sent to Rome via Cales for referral to the senate because Fulvius' colleague Claudius recommended their pardon. Fulvius, an aged patrician and former censor who had battled the Gauls multiple times in the previous three decades, could countenance nothing but the severest punishment for the rebels. He promptly executed the leading citizens of Capua and raced to Cales where a letter awaited him from the senate. Fulvius accepted the letter but refrained from opening it, whereupon he had his lictors execute those Capuans in Cales. Following the execution, Fulvius broke the seal of the letter and read the decree of the senate that they should not be punished. Fulvius continued with his duties, inflicting the same punishment on the rebellious leaders of Atella and Calatia (Livy, 26.12–16). The Capuans later appealed to Rome regarding their plight, but the senate found his behavior in keeping with the office of a magistrate (Livy, 26.33–34).

The ruthless Fulvius was only one of Rome's assets. Throughout the war the ingenuity and toughness of Rome's institutions gave rise to a competitive system that eventually allowed the best solutions to take the field. Fabius' initially unpopular but eventually hallowed strategy of attrition held Hannibal at bay until, through repeated consular elections year after year, tactically sufficient generals like M. Claudius Marcellus and G. Claudius Nero could thwart Hannibal's movements and cut off his hopes of reinforcement. Meanwhile, the strength of the Roman bond engendered the desperately needed resolve of its citizens and the loyalty of enough allies, providing an unending supply of manpower.

It was only a matter of time until an equally brilliant tactician, the young Scipio, could take the offensive and defeat Hannibal himself. He had thrice battled Hannibal and learned enough to turn Hannibal's tactical genius against the Carthaginians. Polybius and Livy both use Scipio as a foil to Hannibal. The choice is fitting, given that both were the sons of tragic figures and that they were themselves exceptional tacticians, charismatic commanders, and capable diplomats. For our purposes, it is helpful to point out how Scipio's position as a commander of citizen-soldiers overcame the independent generalship of Carthaginian commanders like Hannibal and his mercenary armies.[13]

FOR THE FAMILY

The same year that Fulvius captured Capua brought disaster in Spain. Following the Roman defeats at Ticinus and the River Trebia, Publius had sailed for Spain to contest the Carthaginian armies in that theater. The Scipio brothers reaped several victories that brought hope to Rome in the wake of Hannibal's success in Italy. In 217 Gnaeus Scipio won a victory over Hasdrubal Barca, brother of Hannibal, at the mouth of the Ebro with a joint land and sea attack (Polybius, 3.95–96; Livy, 22.19–20). In 215 the Scipio brothers joined forces to defeat Hasdrubal again at Ibera (Livy, 23.28–29). Using their fortified base out of Tarraco in northeast Spain, they had successfully severed the Iberian theater of operations from any link with Hannibal in Italy and were slowly pushing southwest. However, the offensive in Spain was on the verge of collapse in 211 when Publius and Gnaeus were killed and their armies destroyed one after the other in less than a month (Livy, 25.32–36). Despite their defeats, the determination and efforts of the Scipio brothers became so legendary that the "Scipionis rogum," or the "funeral mound of Scipio," was remembered as late as the first century AD in Pliny's *Natural History* (3.1).[14]

Once the efforts of the Scipio brothers had been squelched, the situation began to seem beyond perilous again for Rome. With no Roman command structure in Spain and only the remnants of two destroyed armies, the Carthaginians had relinked their resources in the Iberian peninsula with Hannibal's tactically invincible army in Italy. Furthermore, the three Carthaginian armies roaming Spain—its largest force in any theater—provoked fear that these armies would finally launch attacks in Italy. Italy would then be overwhelmed by simultaneous attacks, thus making the inevitable capitulation of Rome only a matter of time. The fears of the Romans were not entirely justified given the Scipios' successful establishment of a diplomatic and military foothold in Spain; however, this would be lost if they did not act quickly. And Livy is probably not in error when he suggests that many in Rome perceived the situation to be extremely grim.[15]

Alarmed by the events in Spain, the assembly attempted to find a suitable replacement for the Scipio brothers. Livy records the dismal tone of the proceedings: "At first people had waited for those who thought themselves deserving of so important a command to hand in their names. When that hope was disappointed, grief for the disaster they had suffered was renewed" (26.18). In a spirit of mourning, the citizens descended to the Field of Mars where they despairingly looked about for one that could take the place of the Scipio brothers. Suddenly, the young Scipio emerged to take up his father and uncle's mantle. His boldness and family name renewed the assembly's spirit and provided a glimmer of hope (26.18).

As in the case of many Roman nobles of the time, Scipio's family legacy provided the impetus for his service. His suitability was further buttressed by his battlefield demonstration at Ticinus on behalf of his father—a deed made all the more legendary because it involved a son's daring loyalty to save his father from the clutches of death. Several generations later Sallust reflects on the morals exhibited by Roman nobles and on the two men who most embodied the quest to attain the virtue of their fathers and who were the heroes of the Second Punic War:

> I have often heard that Quintus [Fabius] Maximus, Publius Scipio, and other eminent men of our country, were in the habit of declaring that their hearts were set mightily aflame for the pursuit of virtue whenever they gazed upon the masks of their ancestors. Of course, they did not mean to imply that the wax or the effigy had any such power over them, but rather that it is the memory of great deeds that kindles in the breasts of noble men this flame that cannot be quelled until they by their own prowess have equaled the fame and glory of their forefathers. (*The War with Jugurtha*, 4)[16]

The lineage of a man's house was not merely personal or political. It was sacred. Livy's reconstruction of the election captures the mystical power his father and uncle held over the young Scipio and the Centuriate Assembly. Scipio probably already had the effigy of his father that stood "in the most conspicuous position in the house, enclosed in a wooden shrine" (Polybius, 6.53). Whenever he looked on it, as Sallust describes, the memory of his father's magnificent sacrifice must have taunted the young aristocrat to earn his own place of honor, both in men's memories and in his own home.

The Roman home, its hearth, and its atrium were intimately connected with the family's personal religious practices, whether the family was rich or poor. Aristocrats who could afford masks and their elaborate role in funerals stored them in a cupboard in the atrium. On holy days the cupboard would be opened and the masks decorated so that they could "participate" in the proceedings. The Roman family, as the fundamental level of government, was the foundation of Roman education, discipline, and politics, but it was equally important as the locus of religion, where even the dead could still worship.[17] Cicero acknowledges as much when he describes walking in the homeland of his fathers: "This is really my own fatherland, and that of my brother, for we are descended from a very ancient family of this district; here are our ancestral sacred rites and the origin of our race; here are many memorials of our forefathers. . . . For this reason a lingering attachment for the place abides in my mind and heart" (*On the Laws*, 2.1). Cicero's fatherland was the physical source of his lineage but it was equally important as the origin of his spiritual sense of being, which was centered on the physical space of his home.[18]

After his selection, Scipio turned to a broader dimension of ancient spirituality when the assembly regretted its haste in granting him the command of Spain. With a fickleness common to democratic institutions and probably encouraged by conservative senators displeased with his unprecedented appointment at such a young age and with such little experience, the Roman assembly began to question its own decision to vote Scipio proconsular authority for Spain. Ironically, the honor of his family's deaths in Spain worked to his disadvantage now, with some in the assembly superstitiously fretting over "the destiny of the house" and his theater of operations that held "the tombs of his father and uncle" (Livy, 26.18). In Roman culture, the legacy of a man's family shaped his virtue, his fortune, and even his doom.

Scipio was prepared to address such superstitions with a religious argument of his own. Both Polybius and Livy describe Scipio's particular talent for subtly displaying his command abilities in public "either as if they were prompted by visions in the night or inspired by the gods . . . as though emanating from an oracular response" (Livy, 26.19). Scipio took up the habit of passing secluded time in the temple, used religious beliefs to attain to the aedileship, and later claimed divine dreams regarding command decisions. It was even postulated that he "was a man of divine race" (Livy, 26.19). These tendencies had become well known and were circulated even more because he neither denied nor confirmed such rumors. This was rare behavior indeed for a Roman!

His pious proclivities did not prevent his using religion and rumors to his advantage when confronted with doubts about his youth and family's misfortunes. He overcame detractors in the assembly by acknowledging the exceptional favor of fate on his life. The gods had not abandoned his family, despite the recent tragedy. The proof of this was in the carefully calculated evidence his own life had subtly furnished for his fellow Romans. The gods had taken special care of him and would continue to do so in battle. When the assembly recalled these things and was convinced of his ability to curry favor with the divine, they reaffirmed their confidence in the younger Scipio's ability to carry on the work of his family in Spain (Polybius, 10.4–5; Livy, 26.19).[19]

FOR THE SOLDIERS

Resurrecting Old Generals

Scipio relied on his family legacy among the troops as well. On his arrival in Spain, he immediately began to build up the morale of the degraded Spanish armies by praising their communal valor and promoting those who had distinguished themselves in keeping up the spirits and discipline of their fellow soldiers (Livy, 26.20).[20] At the beginning of the fighting season in 209, Scipio gathered his troops and readied them for their campaign. He had personally served among the troops while learning the arts of Hannibal, was present at the Roman defeats at Ticinus, Trebia, and Cannae, and was familiar with Hannibal's other successes (Livy, 26.41). Scipio had shared the perils of battle alongside his fellow Romans, and he would continue to do so now as their commander.

Scipio did not outline the specific strategy the troops would undertake against the three Carthaginian armies, but he did remind them of the reasons for which they fought. The speech Livy and Polybius put into his mouth provided the historians with their own opportunity to weigh in on soldiers' incentives during the war. By all accounts, Scipio was a capable commander who would have been attuned to the importance of motivation, so there are likely some glimmers of authenticity in the speech the historians retrospectively provide. It is even possible that Polybius had access to a transcript of such a speech in family records.[21]

Livy and Polybius have Scipio reference the tragedies he had already shared with them, their personal courage in staying intact as an army, the favor of Fortune in giving him their command, and the favor of the gods in their future conquests. He tells them that he will now command in the stead of his family and honor "the one thing left standing, intact and immovable," namely, "the courage of the Roman people" (Polybius, 10.6; Livy, 26.41). Livy captures the spirit of the virtuous farmer-commander in the final words of Scipio's speech:

> Only do you, soldiers, look with favour upon the name of the Scipios, upon the scion of your generals, growing again, as it were, from stems that have been cut down. Come now, veterans, lead a new army and a new commander across the Ebro, lead them over into lands often traversed by you with many deeds of bravery. Just as now you note in me a resemblance to my father and uncle in face and countenance and recognized the lines of the figure, so I will soon take pains to reproduce for you an image of their minds, of their loyalty and courage, so that each man shall say that there has come back to life, or has been born again, his general Scipio. (26.41)

Scipio uses agricultural analogies as he references the effigy of his father, which was back in his home and still fixed in his mind. The young Scipio had not brought the effigy with him to Spain. There was no need to. He was the effigy. Now the republican commander would share this memory with the army the father once commanded. As the flesh and blood image of his father, he would inspire his veterans to avenge his death and embolden new soldiers to earn the honor of serving that memory. Together, they would resurrect his father and uncle by achieving victory.

Achieving New Objectives

When he could wait no longer, Scipio finally informed the army of his bold plan. He would avoid a direct confrontation with the three armies and instead attack the economic, political, and logistical headquarters of Iberia by assaulting New Carthage (modern-day Cartagena). The successful capture of the town would simultaneously weaken all the Carthaginian armies, and, as New Carthage was loaded with riches, it would be a source of immense booty and glory for the soldiers. When the troops reached the city and were preparing for its assault, Scipio assembled the soldiers again and proclaimed that the one that first mounted the wall would receive "gold crowns" in addition to "the usual rewards to such as displayed conspicuous courage" (Polybius, 10.11).

The portrait both historians paint of Scipio is of a commander who understood how to govern citizen-soldiers. Not only must the good commander possess the skills of any other general, but he must also exercise the skills of a statesman. Commanders of republics, unlike dictators or generals of monarchies, must have the deftness to lead fellow citizens. This picture is consistent with our knowledge of the Roman citizen-soldier. He was a man who governed his own home and farm, was a member of the assembly that put men such as Scipio in command, and was one who could reject that authority when it had been abused.

Much has been made of the Roman reputation for military discipline. However, a balanced reading of the ancient sources reveals an equally strong tradition of independence as well, hence the tendency toward draft resistance, single combat, mutiny, and desertion among the soldiers. Nearly every major conflict recorded by the historians features one or several of these displays of soldiers' independence. In addition to these traits, it is probable, according to Edward Best, that most Roman soldiers, unlike the soldiers of other ancient armies, possessed at least a rudimentary ability to read. From this emerges the picture of a Roman soldier torn between obedience to his authorities and the freedom to act according to his experience, knowledge, and conscience.[22]

Roman soldiers negotiated an ongoing tension between heeding monarchic hierarchy, deferring to the aristocracy, and upholding democratic individualism. They were not submissive drones driven by the orders of their superiors (like the Persians), but neither were they autonomous mavericks given to isolation or the fickleness of mob rule (like the Athenians). They were republican soldiers, who constantly had to deal with the frictions of republican government. They were aware of their martial duties to the state, but they were even more keenly aware of their duties to their farms and families. This middling class of citizens had much in common with the magistrates that commanded them. The army that Scipio led to avenge the Roman defeats in Spain was an army that had shared his grief and despair over the Carthaginian threat. The responsibility for winning the war lay in their hands, as it did for their commander, and should they win the day, to them, as to Scipio, would belong the spoils.

FOR THE GODS

New Carthage, on the southeast coast of Spain, was a suitable position for a fortress because natural impediments surrounded it on three sides. To the south was the port bay that emptied out into the Mediterranean, to the north lay a lagoon, and to the west was a waterway connecting the lagoon and the bay with a bridge joining it to the land on that side. A series of hills created a rim around the town, and the walls completed the highly defensible position. Only the east side was vulnerable to attack, which was beneficial for a defending force of only one thousand mercenaries and two thousand townspeople against an invasion force of twenty-five thousand infantry and twenty-five hundred cavalry.[23]

For any assault to succeed, the invading force would have to scale walls of considerable size—Polybius and Livy write that the walls were more of a hindrance than the defenders (Polybius, 10.13; Livy, 26.45). This situation was obviously well known to Mago, the commander of the citadel, and also to Scipio, who had properly reconnoitered the city. Mago's objective was simple: hold the impregnable fortress until one of the Carthaginian armies came to his relief. What seems to have been equally well known to the opponents was the tendency of the water in the lagoon to recede at specified times, prompted by unknown causes that the ancient historians described in terms of sea winds and tidal changes, which, incidentally, would have been an odd occurrence in the Mediterranean (Polybius, 10.10–12; Livy, 26.42, 45).

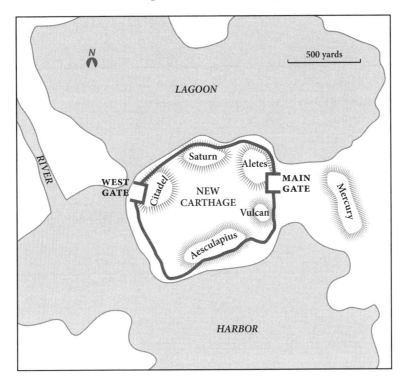

New Carthage (modern Cartagena, Spain), 209 BC

Various explanations on the scientific causes for the "low tide"—from salt flats, to sluice gates, to purely natural phenomena—have been put forth, which are not relevant here. What is important is how Scipio manipulated this information. Scipio's exceptional talent for employing Roman religion was once again put to good use in the siege. He explained to his soldiers that Neptune had appeared to him in a dream, told him what time the lagoon would recede, and instructed him on how to capture the city. By taking a small contingent of men in a stealthy approach through the lagoon, Scipio intended to capture the northern side of the city while the inhabitants were occupied with the defense of the eastern side (Polybius, 10.11; Livy, 26.45). He elucidated how Neptune had intervened on behalf of Rome. Livy writes: "What he had ascertained by painstaking and calculation, Scipio represented as a miracle and an act of the gods, who for the passage of the Romans were diverting the sea, he said, and draining lakes and opening up ways never before trodden by man's foot. And he bade them to follow Neptune as their guide on the march" (Livy, 26.45). Scipio once again played on the religious susceptibilities of his countrymen, which he himself may have even believed to an extent. What had worked so well on the Roman assembly was now working well with the army. Whether or not he used his knowledge of the receding lagoon level to invent the dream, it had the proper effect on his soldiers.[24]

That Scipio managed to correctly predict when the water would recede augmented their confidence in him. The incentive of spoils perhaps would have made them believe whatever was necessary to muster the courage to take the city. Polybius writes that "the combination . . . of accurate calculation, of the promise of gold crowns, and therewithal of confidence in the help of Providence created great enthusiasm and ardour among the lads" (Polybius, 10.11). Both Livy and Polybius doubted the sincerity of Scipio in the revelations of Neptune, but both equally believed in its power over the troops. Using his intelligence of the natural changes in the enemy terrain, he fully manipulated the situation in order to bolster his link to the divine and increase the favor of the gods in the eyes of his soldiers. Neptune was yet another arrow in the tactical quiver of Scipio.[25]

FOR TERROR

With the sanction of the gods and the hearty approval of his troops, Scipio opened his assault on the city. He attacked New Carthage by land while his confidant and second-in-command Gaius Laelius directed a missile assault from the sea. Mago countered by separating his Carthaginian forces, assigning half for distribution as needed from the citadel on the west and leaving half for the defense of the landward wall on the eastern side.[26] Mago also armed the citizens of New Carthage, placed some along the walls, and the rest at the eastern gate, perched for a counterattack on any forces that approached on that side (Polybius, 10.12).

When the bugle was sounded in the Roman camp, the city forces rushed out of the city, traversing the distance between the city and the

Roman camp. Mago was hoping to take advantage of the isthmus' bottleneck and immediately trounce any efforts by the Romans and thereby prove that the city was defended by more than just insurmountable walls. Scipio intentionally held his troops back closer to the camp, and a vigorous battle commenced on the eastern isthmus connecting the city with the surrounding land. However, when more Roman soldiers from the camp reinforced the battle, and it began to tip in the Romans' favor, the besieged found themselves too far from their own city walls. Many of them were cut down in a subsequent rout, and the Romans were in such hot pursuit that they almost entered the gates on their heels. In the panic, Roman soldiers were able to position their scaling ladders for the subsequent assault on the walls. Mago countered by fully manning the walls and distributing the city's large supply of missiles to the defenders (Polybius, 10.12; Livy, 26.44–45). With the external battle decided, New Carthage would await the inevitable assault.

During the battle, Scipio, observing from the hill of Mercury (where the Roman camp was), had noted that in their panic the defenders had abandoned certain portions of the wall. In light of this, he planned his next assault with the prearranged "aid" of Neptune who would lower the water level in the lagoon. He would assault the city from the east as anticipated by Mago, and when the citizens were again diverted to the point of assault, he would surreptitiously send the flanking force through the lagoon. Under normal circumstances attackers from the north would be easy targets for walls manned with missile-heaving defenders. In this case, however, with the defenders diverted to the assault in the east and the naval forces in the south, the soldiers approaching through the lagoon could enter the city unobserved.

Scipio launched an assault on the city, which was repulsed by the defenders with ease given the length of the wall and the stoutness of their defense. With Carthaginian confidence now bolstered, Scipio ordered another, more rigorous attack. He commanded the forces in person, and, as Polybius explains, "he contributed greatly to the success of the day; for he could both see what was going on and being seen by all his men he inspired the combatants with great spirit" (10.13). Livy similarly notes how it inspired the men toward an increasing rivalry with one another:

> He was there as witness and spectator of every man's courage or cowardice. And so men dashed on in the face of wounds and missiles, and neither walls nor armed men standing on them could restrain them from vying with each other in the attempt to climb. And at the same time from the ships an attack began upon that part of the city which is washed by the sea. . . . In making fast, in hastily landing ladders and men, in their impatience to get ashore, each the shortest way, they hindered one another by their very haste and rivalry. (26.44)

The soldiers' competition with one another, mimicking the rivalry of the Roman nobility, was so great that it was nearly unproductive. Yet eventually Roman success was guaranteed by the force sent through the lagoon, which easily traversed the northern walls and hacked through the gates from the inside while the defending forces were occupied with the assaults from the east and the south.

Once inside the city, the soldiers commenced their slaughter. Scipio maintained command amid the vicious din and sent his troops to take the citadel. Only after its surrender did he order the cessation of killing. Polybius writes that

> when Scipio thought that a sufficient number of troops had entered he sent most of them, as is the Roman custom, against the inhabitants of the city with orders to kill all they encountered, sparing none, and not to start pillaging until the signal was given. They do this, I think, to inspire terror, so that when towns are taken by the Romans one may often see not only the corpses of human beings, but dogs cut in half, and the dismembered limbs of other animals, and on this occasion such scenes were very many owing to the numbers of those in the place. (10.15)

It is a mark to Roman discipline that once "the signal was given," the slaughter terminated and the looting began. Even after this point, however, Scipio ordered the booty collected and placed in the marketplace. There, tribunes guarded it and later distributed it "among the legions on the usual system[,] . . . equally among all, including not only those who were left behind in the protecting force, but the men who are guarding the tents, the sick and those absent on any special service" (Polybius, 10.15–16). Equity in the distribution of spoils was important in a political system based on a relative equality among the citizenry. Polybius credits the Roman system of distributing booty in this manner for engendering a common sense of trust and confidence among the fellow soldiers and their commanders (10.16–17).

Adam Ziolkowski maintains that Polybius' description of the Roman sack might even be tamer than reality. Part of the sacking of a city involved leaving the legionary free to do as he pleased with the city and its citizens; wholesale theft, arson, murder, and possibly even rape were all on the table. Although Ziolkowski may make the Romans out to be worse than they were, it nonetheless is true that Roman assaults on cities, like those of every other ancient state, were a brutal business meant to strike terror into a populace that did not surrender. The assault on an enemy city, which in this case might have been more restrained than normal, was necessary in order to make the Roman war machine so viciously efficient.[27]

FOR THE CROWN

Another development after the city had been taken further enlightens the modern reader on the motivations of the Roman citizen-soldier. As Scipio had acknowledged in his injunctions to the soldiers, personal glory and the material rewards of courage were preeminent in the Roman mind. In fact, it would appear by the events that followed that glory in battle was just as important to the common soldier as it was to the commander. The citizen-soldiers were not to be outdone by their aristocratic captains.

When Scipio assembled the troops to reward them for their distinguished service and to award the mural crown to a conspicuous individual, two soldiers came forth and vehemently insisted that they had won the reward. One was a marine who had attacked the southern wall, and the other was a legionary who had attacked the eastern wall. Both claimed they had been the first to surmount their respective walls. The two claimants were so heated in their insistence that marines and legionaries on both sides began to join in the debate. Livy explains that "these men themselves were not so much hotly competing with one another, as already fanning the partisanship of the men of their respective arms of service." The contest reached such proportions that the army was on the verge of mutiny, and the growing crisis was not finally assuaged until Scipio bestowed a crown on them both (26.48).[28]

The episode captures the spirit of the Roman soldiers, who rivaled one another in displaying their manliness and devotion to the republic. The manipular system itself was designed so that these soldiers fought in concert with each other in the maniple at the same time that they rivaled each other in individual combat. The emphasis on martial distinction as an individual is also seen in the Roman tendency to settle issues by single combat. Some of the more prominent examples from Roman history are the Horatii and Curiatii, who engaged in a triple duel (Livy, 1.24–26), Siccius Dentatus, who claimed to have engaged in nine duels (Dionysius, 10.37), Manlius Torquatus, the slayer of a Gaul in a duel (Livy, 7.9–10), Valerius Corvus, who slew a Gaul with the assistance of a raven (Livy, 7.26), Manlius Torquatus, the son of the Gaul slayer, who killed a Latin (Livy, 8.7), and Marcellus, the famed Roman consul who achieved the highest award as commander for killing the opposing commander of the Gauls at Clastidium in 222 (Livy, *Periocha*, 20). Stephen Oakley maintains that "a coherent argument can be constructed to support the view that in the Middle Republic, at least, single combats occurred each year."[29] By the end of the third century, the dueling hero would have been a common exemplar in the mind of every citizen-soldier.

Roman discipline did not detract from the individual glory sought by soldiers. Perhaps the most significant example Polybius includes is this emphasis on dueling:

> But the most important result is that young men are thus inspired to endure every suffering for the public welfare in the hope of winning

the glory that attends on brave men. What I say is confirmed by facts. For many Romans have voluntarily engaged in single combat in order to decide a battle, not a few have faced certain death, some in war to save the lives of the rest, and others in peace to save the republic. (6.54)

In Polybius' mind, the seeking of individual glory was not to be discouraged; instead, Roman soldiers "should fight, both as individuals and collectively" (2.33). In fact, individual glory should be sought on behalf of the republic. There was tension between discipline and individual glory, but ultimately, it worked to the benefit of Rome's armies.

Roman soldiers also demonstrated a remarkable tendency to mutiny, as the events after the capture of New Carthage attest. Roman mutinies were part and parcel of the individualism and freedom afforded to the middling strata of citizen-soldiers. The Roman soldier grew up in a society that placed high value on "original thinking and acting" as a norm for political and military action. The *secessio*, as we have seen, was a check that the Roman soldiers and assembly could use against the consuls and senate. The tension between the furor, initiative, and personal drive for glory among the Roman soldiers was checked by the discipline, gravitas, and authority of their Roman commanders. And those imperatores with exceptional command over these assets, like the elder Fabius at Sentinum and Scipio at New Carthage, could channel the energy of these highly effective citizen-soldiers.[30]

This mindset of the soldiers was a characteristic shared with the people of Rome as a whole during the Second Punic War. It had, in fact, pushed Rome into its precarious position in the first half of the war. Fabius knew that engaging in a war of attrition was the proper strategic response to Hannibal almost from the beginning. The problem was that "from the Roman point of view it had two defects: it was inglorious, and guerrilla warfare is ill-suited to a heavy-armed soldier."[31] The backbone of the Roman political and military system, the legionary, stood opposed to such a cowardly enterprise. Fabius himself remarked that the true opponents in this strategy were the Romans themselves because such men could not countenance a strategy of delay (Livy, 22.39). It was only with the annihilation of the Roman armies at Cannae in 216—the greatest single Roman defeat up to that time—that Romans embraced the Fabian strategy in Italy, which then became firmly entrenched for the remainder of the war.

The honor inherent in the mural crown was also present in the commander. In his treatment of New Carthage, Scipio desired to present himself and the Roman people to the Spanish tribes as an honorable alternative to the Carthaginians. Several actions exemplified his intentions. First, his sack of the city was not as vicious as it could have been because he ceased the slaughter as soon as the Carthaginian garrison surrendered. Second, of the citizens remaining after the surrender, Scipio assembled them, bid the women and children return to their homes, and commanded the men to serve Rome throughout the war with their trades, after which they would return to their state of "freedom" as allies of the Roman people. Third, Scipio received the Spanish hostages that were being held by the Carthaginians in return for the loyalty of their respective tribes. After treating them kindly, he bid them write their families and tell them if they would ally themselves with Rome, they would be set free.

Polybius maintains that through his honorable behavior toward the citizens of New Carthage "he produced in the citizens great affection and loyalty to himself and to the common cause, while the workmen were most zealous owing to their hope of being free." And among the Iberian tribes, he not only earned the gratitude and friendship of those he had set free but was even able to press some of them to take up arms against their former masters (10.17–18; Livy, 26.40).

Scipio's wise leadership involved his ability to effectively use the incentives that drove his citizen-soldiers: memory of the dead, religious beliefs and superstitions, the spoils of battle, personal glory, and the defense of Roman liberty. His political insight as conqueror was equally sagacious and won him the loyalty of those who had been conquered to the good will of Rome. Like the soldiers who had been rewarded with their mural crown for bravery and daring, Scipio was now crowned with his own reward—the glory of conquering Spain for Rome.

Scipio used his new base at New Carthage to train his troops. Having faced Hannibal's armies in battle several times already, he knew the only way to beat the Carthaginians' tactical superiority was to train harder and fight smarter. Replenishing armies is never enough in warfare. Inferior strategies and tactics must be remedied. Polybius describes a strict, daily training regimen for both the army and the navy. Sword fighting, javelin hurling, running in armor, rowing, and land and naval maneuvers were practiced in specialized units, with Scipio carefully supervising the trainers. He also forged new weapons and made sure all the men took care of their equipment. The entire operation looked like "a workshop of war" (Polybius, 10.20). Scipio used this army to defeat each of the Carthaginian armies in Spain, including one led by Hannibal's brother Hasdrubal. Scipio would be forever remembered as the man who surpassed his family's legacy by conquering Spain and then eventually bringing Hannibal to his knees.

FOR A LEGACY

Scipio's victories in Spain demonstrated that in a relatively equal contest, replaceable citizen armies can defeat irreplaceable professionals in the long run. Spain had witnessed the destruction of two consuls and their armies, but the deaths of Publius and Gnaeus did not deter the younger Scipio; instead it made him even more determined to replace them in the Spanish theater. Scipio rallied the remaining troops to a stunning campaign in Spain that crippled Carthage's sustainment base.[32] Scipio was a brilliant commander, but more important was the fact that he and his soldiers were not so extraordinary that their destruction would imperil Rome. Moreover, Scipio's army in Spain achieved what they did only because Marcellus stalked Hannibal in southern Italy, Nero halted Hasdrubal at the Metaurus River when he finally came to the aid of his brother, and other Roman armies did what was necessary to defend the Roman federation. Scipio was one aspect of a concerted Roman effort against Hannibal and his subordinates.

Rome could endure the loss of armies like Scipio's in a disaster, but Carthaginian armies were too exceptional to lose. Wealthy Roman magistrates and cavalrymen died in such vast numbers that Mago supposedly took a container full of their golden rings to display to the senate after Cannae. Roman citizens and their allies were reduced by as much as a third, perhaps around a quarter of a million. Roman commanders, citizens, and allies could be annihilated, but the republic and its federation would plod on. The death of Hannibal at any stage of the war would have ended it. The defeat and death of Hannibal's brother Hasdrubal in 207 doomed Hannibal's hopes of winning in Italy. Scipio's handful of victories in Spain reduced that theater. And the final defeat of Hannibal himself brought an end to the war. Roman success against Carthage inaugurated a new trend in Mediterranean warfare. Alexander's spectacular victories gave him Darius' empire. Hannibal's had led to fifteen more years of a war that doomed Carthage.

The point about replaceability is not meant to downplay the genius of Scipio's generalship. After all, absorbing losses is one thing, but winning a war demanded inflicting defeats where Carthage would feel it the most. Scipio would be the man to achieve this. Despite protests from conservatives like Fabius and Flaccus, the assembly commissioned Scipio to take the war to Africa via his assignment in Sicily. However, cautious senior senators appear to have prohibited a normal levy in case Scipio foolishly led them into disaster. Scipio was thus forced to rely on those legionaries sent to Sicily as punishment for happening to survive the units crushed by Hannibal at places like Cannae and Herdonea (which was itself a powerful use of civic shame). He also levied seven thousand volunteers and built twenty quinqueremes and ten quadriremes from among his clients and those looking for plunder or adventure (Livy, 28.45–46).

His levying of volunteers has drawn much attention, but it should come as no surprise.[33] Rome's inherent social structure, as we have seen, enabled this kind of activity. Kings like Romulus and Tarquinius had bands of armed men, as did early republicans like Publicola (Poplios Valesios?) and the Fabii who carried on their ill-fated war against Veii. The late republic would see the fully actualized power that could be mustered by commanders using or creating client-type relationships with vast bodies of citizens. This tendency surely did not disappear in the middle republic, and it makes sense that a charismatic patrician such as Scipio was able to conscript volunteers for a campaign that many could reasonably conclude would end a horrific conflict. Scipio spent a year training this army, which had already been seasoned by some of the worst actions in the war, after which he took it to Africa. After two successful years of campaigning, he forced Hannibal's recall from Italy and faced off with the old general at Zama in 202.

The battle finally pitted the two against one another as commanders, with Hannibal enjoying an edge in overall numbers. Like champion chess players, the two generals alternately threw their forces at each other, reformed their lines, and tried new strategies. After hours of tough fighting, the armies had basically fought to a standstill and were poised for a last final push. What tipped the scales in the climactic moment is telling: the return of the Roman cavalry. Roman cavalry had been woefully outmatched throughout the war, which constantly placed Roman armies at a tactical disadvantage. This was finally remedied by three factors: new allies, bigger numbers, and better training. Scipio won over vital contingents of Carthage's best cavalry, the Numidian horse under Masinissa. The Roman horse at Zama also outnumbered Hannibal's, and he attempted to compensate by drawing them off the field with his own cavalry's retreat. However, the discipline of the Roman forces neutralized that ploy when the Roman horse returned to strike Hannibal in the rear. Scipio was victorious.

Once again Rome had won the crucial allies, adapted to meet new challenges, and proved that their discipline and their resolve could not be matched over the long haul. When the dust settled on the battlefield at Zama, it was not merely superior manpower that defeated Hannibal, it was superior soldiering as well. It may have taken fifteen years, but the Romans had just defeated him outright and showed the Mediterranean that Hannibal was no longer the best general and that the men under his command were not the best soldiers.

It is telling from a republican standpoint that Hannibal was not the only victim of Rome's civic mindset. Scipio proved that too much war and too much success as a republican can lead to an ignominious end. His successes against Hannibal, and later against Antiochus the Great of the Seleucid Empire (192–189) caused suspicion and envy at home. What followed were accusations and trials that pushed Scipio to the periphery of Roman politics. Scipio, however, chose the life of Cincinnatus and Camillus over Coriolanus and voluntarily exiled himself in Campania, where he died in peace. Whether his choice was one of virtue or despair will never be known for certain, but given his request to be buried far from Rome, the latter seems to be the case.

Scipio contrasts with the steady and cautious Fabius Maximus. Already an old codger when he saved Rome by refusing to fight Hannibal, Fabius trained his oratorical weapons on Scipio after Hannibal had been sequestered in southeast Italy. At nearly every opportunity, Fabius opposed his young political opponent and possibly prolonged the war in doing so. Yet the reader must look beyond normal politics when examining Fabius' motivations. Fabius feared the praise of Scipio because he had seen similar praise for generals such as Gaius Flaminius and Varro—men whose desire for glory at Trasimene and Cannae had caused devastating losses and brought Rome to the brink of destruction. He reminded his fellow citizens that "it was dangerous to entrust such vast interests to the fortune of a single man." Fabius died before Scipio wrested victory from Hannibal at the Battle of Zama, but Rome gave Fabius the noble end it refused Scipio. Although not a pauper at his death, Fabius was given a public burial; "each private citizen contributed the smallest coin in his possession . . . because the people felt that it was burying a father, whose death received honour and regard befitting his life" (Plutarch, *Fabius Maximus*, 27). In the republican tradition, Scipio may have been Hannibal's greatest rival, but Fabius was Rome's greatest hero.[34]

The *cunctator* died one year short of seeing victory. When Hannibal was finally dispatched, Rome was made the master of the western Mediterranean. Roman hatred for Hannibal hunted him down twenty years later to a small house in Libyssa where the Carthaginian, left with no options, ended his long-standing rivalry with Rome by suicide (Livy, 39.51). The only significant obstacle to Rome's domination of the entire sea was Alexander's successors in the East.

7 · Triumph

PHALANX KILLERS AT PYDNA

In 1989 Francis Fukuyama wrote a controversial article entitled "The End of History?" In what has now become the most famous early analysis of the end of the Cold War, Fukuyama boldly predicted that the world was moving toward "an unabashed victory of economic and political liberalism." This "triumph of the West" was nothing less than "the end point of mankind's ideological evolution and the universalization of Western liberal democracy as the final form of human government."[1]

Careful readers of the article would have discovered that Fukuyama's assertions were a little more nuanced than they seemed at first glance, and he even gave himself a backdoor because history could start all over again. But the bold assertions and the timing of the article in the midst of the 1989 revolutions and the collapse of the Soviet Union caused most to ignore this nuance. Many were even convinced that a real end of history was indeed possible. This was most pronounced in the United States, where triumphal visions of a world free from tyranny and political oppression captivated many an American. Few at the time seemed to consider the possibility that liberalism's day would come too, or that liberalism itself might be guilty of its own forms of tyranny and oppression.

If he had been afforded a glimpse into the world of 1989, Polybius would have seen the hope or prediction of an "end of history" as utter nonsense. He knew well that war, even of the "cold" variety, always offers its fair share of fortune and fate. And there is never an end to war. A native of Megalopolis and former cavalry commander in the Achaean League, he documented Rome's wars against Alexander's successors as a participant-observer. Polybius had experienced the vicissitudes of Fortune in his own life when he was taken captive by Rome and became an eyewitness insider as it conquered the world. Yet Polybius was also ever mindful of fate, which never allowed history to end. He believed it was pushing the republic toward its own dissolution. Unfortunately, only fragments remain from the later books of Polybius' *Histories*, but one interesting tidbit is a reflection that he puts in the mouth of Perseus, Rome's antagonist at Pydna. Sitting in the smoldering remains of the once great Macedonian Empire, Perseus asks if his predecessors could have possibly predicted its demise. He then thinks of how Alexander terminated the Persian Empire and wonders if the Persian kings predicted their demise even fifty years before it happened (29.21).

Before the war with Rome, Perseus had visited Delphi, among other cities, and had commissioned an impressive series of statues and monuments that would feature his likeness, demonstrating to all that he would be Greece's protector. After the war, the unfinished monuments remained but were repurposed by the Romans, who took over Macedon's role as the hegemon of Greece. Perseus' statue never made it into Delphi, but those of his conquerors did (Plutarch, *Aemilius Paulus*, 28; Livy, 45.27). He had pushed the boundaries and thrust himself into the hands of Fortune, only to lose everything.

Yet Rome would soon experience shocks that it also could not have predicted. In Polybius' mind Perseus was destroyed by Fortune, but Rome was driven forward by fate. Roman citizens were following the civic militaristic impulses that drove their every decision. The republican rhythms goaded aristocratic commanders and citizen-soldiers into instinctually responding to fear, glory, and conquest with resolve, eagerness, and prowess. Roman citizen-soldiers acted in accord with the martial virtues that had been instilled in them and showed how the famous soldiers of the Macedonian war machine were no match for them. But habitual expansion was straining the republic, its constitution, and its sense of civic virtue. Fate may take longer than fortune to play out, but the Roman Republic, like Macedonia, Persia, and every other great power before it, could not avoid the destruction that awaited. Rome's success at Pydna was one of the incredible conquests that was pushing the republic toward its own doom. According to Polybius, even in the midst of its triumph, Rome's day was nearing and it would offer warnings that every republic in every age should heed.

IMPERIAL ADVENTURES

When the Romans defeated Hannibal, the eastern Mediterranean was dominated by the three great powers remaining from Alexander's ephemeral empire: Antigonid Macedonia, Seleucid Asia, and Ptolemaic Egypt. Federations had also formed among the smaller Greek city-states, most notably the Aetolian and Achaean leagues. Other moderate powers like Rhodes, Pergamum, and Galatia filled in the jigsaw puzzle of Hellenistic geopolitics. At first, the most troublesome of these to Rome was Macedonia. Following the Second Punic War, Rome embarked on a punitive and preventative campaign against the ally of Hannibal, Philip V. The Second Macedonian War (200–197) finished with a relative state of peace established between the two states. A war in Greece and Anatolia with Antiochus (192–188) drew Roman attention farther east than it had ever been, and its conclusion redrew Anatolian boundaries in favor of Roman allies.[2]

Meanwhile, Rome steadily consolidated its control in the northern and western regions. The Gallic threat lingered after the end of the war with Hannibal, but after more campaigns, more colonies, and a strengthening of the colonies already established, northern Italy was pacified by the 170s. To Sicily, Corsica, and Sardinia, Rome also added the provinces of Hither and Further Spain. Fighting in Spain was especially violent throughout the second century as Rome pushed farther inland.

War broke out again in Macedonia with Philip's son Perseus. Perseus was attempting to reclaim Macedon's former greatness and had drawn a litany of complaints from Rome's allies in Greece. He had also supposedly prompted his father to execute his own brother, Demetrius, who had been held hostage at Rome (Livy, 40.20–25). Like Polybius, Demetrius developed good relations with Rome, and his death, whether from his own guilt or Perseus' intrigues, was not viewed with pleasure by the senate. When Eumenes II of Pergamum, an important ally of Rome in the region, complained to Rome of Perseus' warlike behavior and an attempted assassination of his person, Roman armies once again marched east. In all likelihood the protests of Rome's allies were merely an excuse for war. Rome was wary of Perseus' expansion of Macedonian power against their allies in the region and wished to put an end to his machinations before his strength increased to unwieldy proportions (41.19, 42.6, 25–31).

Rome's expansion after the Second Punic War has drawn much attention, especially how that expansion related to its imperial ambitions. Recent advocates of offensive imperialism, defensive imperialism, unipolarity, realism, and postcolonialism, to name a few, have been rehashing and enhancing the argument over why and how Rome took over the Mediterranean.[3] Overall, it is difficult to explain easily. As Eric Gruen explains:

> Worldwide supremacy appears first not as a goal but as an accomplishment. Roman behavior in the East seems too erratic, unsystematic, and unpredictable to apply any neat labels. And the process was anything but linear. Romans threw their weight around in certain places and at certain times. On occasion they exercised firm authority, barked commands, or carried off the wealth of a state. On other occasions and in other circumstances, they shunned involvement or decision, showed little interest in tangible gain, and shrank from anything that could be characterized as "empire."[4]

This study has tried to contextualize the growth of Roman republicanism in light of how other states and peoples were behaving. During the time frame in which Rome rose to power, international state systems were declining or totally absent, and anarchy and lawlessness were at their peak. Law, justice, order, and peace were impossible to maintain in a Hobbesian world where every state was as militaristic as the next.

What is important here is how the expansion of Rome's imperial republic began to affect the nature of Roman civic militarism and the character of the Roman citizen-soldier. When war erupted again with Perseus, the consuls' levy drew some controversy, and a centurion named Spurius Ligustinus was allowed to address the people. The entire speech is eminently fascinating for the details it affords about the career of a centurion. Ligustinus was apparently among the *proletarii*—he states he inherited a paltry one *iugerum* (about two-thirds of an acre)—but had been afforded the opportunity to start at the bottom ranks and work his way up over the course of a long and distinguished career. He was made chief centurion four times, rewarded for bravery by commanders thirty-four times, "received six civic crowns," and served a total of twenty-two years (Livy, 42.34). His military career began in 200, which means he had been hundreds of miles away in Spain, Macedonia, and Anatolia for twenty-two out of twenty-nine years. This kind of service was becoming increasingly common in the second century, and it was one of the new challenges facing Roman citizens as the second century wore on.

Rome's armies were still manned by citizens, but they were becoming increasingly professionalized. In many ways, this also meant they were more proficient. At the opening of the war with Perseus in 171, the manipular legion—the Polybian army—was fully developed and fighting at its best. It had been tested and improved through continued clashes with the Samnites, Pyrrhus, the Carthaginians, and the Iberians, to name only the most significant opponents. It had already fared well against the advanced phalanxes of Philip and Antiochus. In the Second Macedonian War, for example, the innovative tactics Scipio used so successfully in Spain and Africa were employed by men who might have been his subordinates in those theaters. At the Battle of Cynoscephalae (197), an unnamed military tribune removed a wing of the legion to take advantage of a Macedonian oversight, thereby outmaneuvering Philip and causing his defeat (Livy, 33.9, 28.26). This kind of initiative and flexibility exercised by a lower-ranking officer showcased the legion's tactical superiority in the hands of experienced men. The question as to whether phalanx or legion was superior would not be fully decided, however, until the Battle of Pydna.

In the thick of the combat that would come at Pydna, the natural hardiness of the Roman farmer and the tactical abilities of the increasingly proficient soldiers intersected perfectly. Agriculture had brought stability, a common set of values, and a common work ethic. It made the legionary's farming vocation the most conducive to "the pursuit of arms" (Cicero, *Republic*, 2.4). The extensive campaigning against so many enemies in such distant places brought a familiarity with every kind of tactic and brutality. But it was the competitiveness of the republican citizen that was the most important. This rivalry, in which, as Sallust puts it, "citizen vied with citizen only for the prize of merit" would be exercised on the field outside Pydna. He remarks: "To such men consequently no labor was unfamiliar, no region too rough or too steep, no armed foeman was terrible; valour was all in all. Nay, their hardest struggle for glory was with one another; each man strove to be first to strike down the foe, to scale a wall, to be seen of all while doing such a deed. This they considered riches, this fair fame and high nobility" (*The War with Catiline*, 7, 9).

ELECTED COMMANDERS

When the first Roman armies were sent to deal with Perseus, they achieved less than desirable results. At Callinicus in 171, the Romans were routed by Perseus, who sued for a peace that was rejected (Livy, 42.57–60; Plutarch, *Aemilius Paulus*, 9). Perseus was less successful at Phalanna in the same year, but he still inflicted damage on Roman morale (Livy, 42.65–66). Perseus' ally Gentius, king of the Illyrians, lured the Romans into an ambush at Uscana in 170 from which only half of the Roman contingent escaped (Livy, 43.10). Although the Illyrian victory was reversed at Scodra in 168, Perseus remained unfettered in Macedonia, and Rome was chafing from its lack of success (Livy, 44.31).[5]

In their consternation the assembly turned to Aemilius Paullus, a no-nonsense patrician with command experience fighting against Iberian tribesmen and Gauls. It was hoped that he would quickly and decisively resolve the war. Plutarch humorously remarks, "The Romans . . . decided that they would bid good-bye to the favours and promises of those who wanted to be generals, and themselves summon to the leadership a man of wisdom who understood how to manage great affairs" (*Aemilius Paulus*, 9). Once again, the Roman people exercised their prerogative to select commanders with the abilities and qualities they thought were best suited to manage the crisis at hand.

The historians cast Paullus as the reluctant but authoritative commander. He initially declined the requests of his fellow Romans; however, they continued insisting day after day with such fervor that he eventually consented. Without casting lots, the Romans gave him the command of the Macedonian theater, after which Paullus began his preparations for war.[6] Livy explains how in his decisive action he was unlike his predecessors: "It was at once obvious to everyone that Lucius Aemilius was going to prosecute this war in no sluggish fashion, not only because he was a warlike man, but also because without relaxing by day or night he turned over in his mind nothing but what concerned this war" (44.18). Paullus personified the preeminent virtue of a Roman statesman—his ability to command with audacity and resolve so that none questioned his leadership.

Rome invested great power in its leaders so that they could command without the hindrances of democracy. This power could be abused (and would be a century later), but when placed in the right commander, it would inspire the confidence of the troops and the hopes of fellow citizens. Republics rely on strong leadership that can guide the state in peace and in war. Paullus had become the classic exemplar of such leadership in Plutarch's day. He noted the relationship between the reverence of the citizens for him and his authority over the people. Having been elected by them despite his own protestations, Paullus now explained how he would carry out his command. Plutarch captures the tone:

> He was under no obligation to them; on the contrary, if they thought the war would be carried on better by another, he resigned the con-

duct of it; but if they had confidence in him they must not make themselves his colleagues in command, nor indulge in rhetoric about the war, but quietly furnish the necessary supplies for it, since, if they sought to command their commander, their campaigns would be still more ridiculous than they were already. (11)

This was not an unsuitable arrangement. The authority of Paullus and honor of the people reflected the civic sense of both according to how they had been gifted. Plutarch concludes by opining, "Thus was the Roman people, to the end that it might prevail and be greatest in the world, a servant of virtue and honour" (11).

Paullus' personal power of leadership was later contrasted with the deficient leadership of Perseus. Paullus himself led the first legion. He noted the pulse of the battle and was able to tactically respond, giving commands to his subordinates until victory was won. By contrast, Perseus fled the field with his cavalry, leaving his men to be destroyed in the rout after the battle was lost. An even more vital contrast between Paullus and Perseus was the origin and nature of their authority. Paullus' command originated from the Roman people, who were entrusted with the ability to confer or deny authority on those they deemed fit. Perseus, on the other hand, acquired his authority through lineage, intrigue, and monarchic majesty.

REPUBLICAN CAMPS

After careful preparations and a thorough reconnaissance, Paullus arrived in Macedon, a predator on the scent of his prey. Following several successful maneuvers at the Elpeus River and Pythium, Paullus outflanked the initial position of Perseus with a turning maneuver by his military tribune Scipio Nasica. Paullus achieved this by distracting Perseus, who was entrenched in a formidable position on the other side of the Elpeus River, with several attacks and an envelopment feint from the direction of the sea. While Perseus was thus engaged, Scipio marched up the Petra Pass and defeated the contingents sent by Perseus to guard it. With his position now compromised, Perseus moved to the fields near Pydna (Livy, 44.35; Plutarch, *Aemilius Paulus*, 15–16). Paullus then rejoined forces with Scipio on their way to confront the Macedonian king.[7]

When Paullus descended on Perseus' position on 21 June, the sight of the phalanx caught him by surprise, and he hesitated to give battle. Even for seasoned warriors such as Paullus, the sight of Perseus' phalanx, arrayed for battle on a plain perfectly suited for its tactical abilities, was intimidating. Plutarch writes, "When he saw how they were drawn up, and in what numbers, he was amazed, and came to a halt, considering with himself." Although Scipio urged him to give battle, Paullus put off the engagement, remarking that "many victories teach me the mistakes of the vanquished, and forbid me to join battle, immediately after a march, with a phalanx which is already drawn up and completely armed" (17).

Paullus was right to fear the Macedonians. Macedonian armies were not wholly comprised of subject levies or mercenaries; in fact, the most important units—although not always the most numerous— were native Macedonians, who enjoyed a distinguished status in the Macedonian state. Pausanias and Polybius, for example, refer respectively to the Romans as fighting against the "Macedonians and Perseus" (7.10) and "King Philip and the Macedonians" (18.46). Like Roman commanders and citizen-soldiers, these men were smallholders or landowners that managed farms. From the time of Philip and Alexander their political importance as an advisory assembly was linked to their military service to the king.[8]

Arrian credits Philip with turning the Macedonians into a communal fighting machine, but they seem to have always enjoyed a reputation for ferocity (Arrian, 7.9). Philip terminated the independence of the lowland poor that served as infantry and the noble dynasties that fielded elite units and the cavalry. Bending them to his royal will, he forged a formidable fighting machine that subdued Greece and, under Alexander, conquered Persia.[9] The Macedonians functioned as a warrior class in an autocratic regime, but these distinctions were not always as clear cut then as they are today. Nonetheless, the monarchy distinguished Macedon from the Greek city-states and the Roman Republic, for "the Macedonian *poleis* was subject to the will of the king as the executive arm of the Macedonian state." This restricted citizenship and political participation, however, and Macedon's inability to absorb defeats hardwired a weakness into the system.[10]

The Macedonians therefore needed to win, and they needed to win consistently. According to Livy and Polybius, their geographic position, hard lifestyles, and warrior ethos made this possible. Much like the Romans during their early years, they were bordered by barbarian tribes intent on their destruction. The western march in Philip's day, for example, was "cold, difficult to cultivate, and harsh," and they encountered "inhabitants of temperament like their land[,] . . . made fiercer by their barbarian neighbors," who gave them "training in warfare" (Livy, 45.30). Molded by this environment, the Macedonians were capable of any warlike endeavor, from "regular battles on land, . . . temporary service at sea, . . . digging trenches, erecting palisades, and all such hard work, just as Hesiod represents the sons of Aeacus to be 'joying in war as if it were a feast'" (Polybius, 5.2). When T. Quinctius Flamininus fought the Macedonians in 198 he initially found them so intimidating and their phalanx so impenetrable that he was "most reluctant to permit a comparison of men and weapons to be made" (Livy, 32.17–18).

So how would Paullus counter such inbred ferocity? He started by building a camp. Executing a delaying maneuver, Paullus arrayed his troops as if preparing for battle in the front, while the troops to the rear constructed a camp to the left of his position.[11] To the Greeks or Macedonians, a camp may have been moderately important, but to the Romans it was a reflection of their political system and manner of life. Polybius believed as much, inserting a very detailed description of the camp in book 6, right in the midst of his discussion of Roman constitutional superiority. The Roman camp, he maintains, was a "noble and excellent performance," "one of those things really worth studying and worth knowing" (6.26).

The camp was always located at a defensible site that afforded a standard construction, with "one simple plan of camp being adopted at all times and in all places" (6.26). It was surrounded by an entrenchment and a stockade. The commander's tent, the praetorium, was situated with the "best general view" in the center of the square camp so that the commander could easily issue orders. A forum for public business lay on one side of his tent and the army's supplies on the other. Crossroads met at the praetorium out to the four gates. Roman legions, broken down into their units, were always placed in the center to the front of the praetorium, with allied units on their wings, much like they were situated in battle. To the rear of the praetorium were the elite troops (*extraordinarii*) and other auxiliaries, skirmishers, and the cavalry. Smaller streets separated individual units and allowed for a consistent and quick muster. Two consular armies would simply place their camps back to back (6.27–32).

The camp's construction was only the beginning. Military tribunes oversaw everything in the camp, and in this way they practiced the rudiments of Roman politics and also encountered their fellow citizens face-to-face. Tribunes needed to diffuse tensions that arose between soldiers and commanders and also help maintain the needs of the men without slighting their subordinates. Roman soldiers—from the wealthiest cavalryman to the poorest skirmisher—would remember a tribune's command abilities and temperament when casting their votes if he subsequently ran for office.

The military tribunes administered an oath "to all in the camp, whether freemen or slaves." Men were forbidden from stealing or even tolerating the misplacement of equipment. The camp was to be immaculate, and specific units took turns guarding the walls, the horses, and the commander's tent. Regular roll calls ensured that all were accounted for and aware of the current watchwords. Guard duty was treated with appropriate seriousness: those found asleep or remiss in other duties were immediately court martialed by the tribunes. If found guilty, the offender would be touched by a tribune's cudgel, after which all the men of the camp would stone him to death right in the midst of the camp. Should any man somehow escape, Polybius says he would be denied entrance to the homes of his family and friends. Should any man desert his post or boast of false heroics, he would suffer the same fate. The citizen community, whether in the field or at home, ensured that he ended his life in shame (6.33–38).

In the same manner, rewards—from gear, to spears, cups, and gold crowns—would be dealt out to those who had demonstrated conspic-uous bravery. Polybius believed that these acts were "an admirable method of encouraging the young soldiers to face danger." The activ-ities of the camp were made complete when the soldiers returned home, where their spoils and rewards would be worn in processions and then adorn their houses. Young men had thus grown up in houses filled with such testaments of valor. In their first experience of a Roman camp, they gained the opportunity to live up to the honors of their fa-thers. Polybius concludes his weighty discussion of the camp simply: "Considering all this attention given to the matter of punishments and rewards in the army and the importance attached to both, no wonder that the wars in which the Romans engage end so successfully and bril-liantly" (6.40).

The camp's very nature demonstrated the doggedness, discipline, and consistency of the Romans, their laws, their constitution, and their soldiers. The camp transferred the republican community onto the battlefield and trained men to hate cowardice, love duty, and strive to rival one another on behalf of themselves and their republic. Rome's soldiers may have lacked an inherent, ferocious ethos, but their own disciplined, persistent civic militarism could be equally dangerous.

The Romans may have feared Macedonian ferocity, but the Mace-donians had now just witnessed a well-ordered delaying maneuver and the construction of one of the ancient world's engineering mar-vels. Perhaps the camp gave them pause about the sort of resolve and tenacity they faced. Paullus had successfully encamped his troops, but he knew the coming fight would not be an easy one. Being disciplined is one thing, but defeating Macedon's ferocious warriors would require more than that.

SUPERIOR SOLDIERS

Roman religion granted Paullus another reason for delaying the battle until the following morning. One of the tribunes of the soldiers, Gaius Sulpicius Gallus, possessed a knowledge of astronomy and was aware that an eclipse would occur that night. He forewarned his command

and the troops so that none would be alarmed. When the prediction was fulfilled, Sulpicius and Paullus were uplifted in the Roman camp as having semidivine knowledge. Such was not the case in the Macedonian camp, however, where the unexpected eclipse caused "uproar and wailing" among the soldiers, who believed that it might portend the eclipse of the Macedonian king (Livy, 44.37; Plutarch, *Aemilius Paulus*, 16).[12]

If Livy's version of Gallus' astronomical foreknowledge is correct, this once again supplies evidence of a Roman commander manipulating the superstitions of his men and the enemy. Religion, as at Sentinum and New Carthage, was interpreted in a manner most likely to spur on Roman victory. The following morning, Paullus employed religion again for the betterment of his troops, delaying the battle with sacrifices so that Perseus would end up attacking him on terrain more suitable to the legion and at a time when the sun would be in the eyes of the Macedonians (Livy, 44.37; Plutarch, *Aemilius Paulus*, 17).

When the two armies clashed in the afternoon of 22 June, it was "Fortune" that finally brought them together (Livy, 44.40; Plutarch, *Aemilius Paulus*, 18). A horse or baggage animal escaped from its grooms, and when it was pursued, Thracian infantry clashed with the Roman and allied cavalry. The accidental encounter began to engage more and more of each side until a full-scale battle was nearly at hand. At this point Paullus leapt into action, taking command of the first legion and riding out before his troops. In contrast to Paullus, Perseus fled the battle early in the fighting (Livy, 44.41–42; Plutarch, *Aemilius Paulus*, 19). Plutarch returns to the spiritual dimension of the battle, explaining that Perseus had fled to Pydna "under pretence of sacrificing to Heracles, a god who does not accept cowardly sacrifices from cowards, nor accomplish their unnatural prayers." The impious cowardice of Perseus is contrasted with the pious bravery of Aemilius. Although in his sixties, Paullus joined the battle with youthful vigor (Plutarch, *Aemilius Paulus*, 19).

Paullus formed his first and second legions in the center, with his elephant corps and the alae on the Roman right where the battle had begun. Perseus' phalanx faced the Roman legions, and his Thracians,

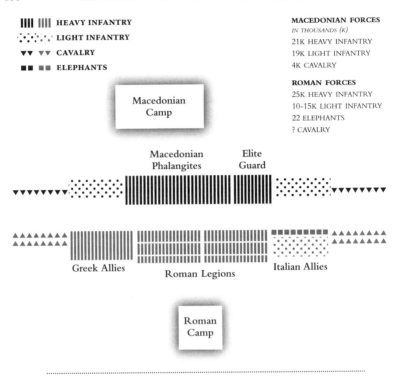

Battle of Pydna, 22 June 168 BC, phase 1: opening dispositions

mercenaries, and light infantrymen faced the elephants and alae. The performance of the elephant corps was yet another testament to Roman adaptability. Their well-trained elephants defeated the anti-elephant corps of the Macedonians, who were the first to flee the field. Ironically, it was a former contender for the Macedonian throne, Pyrrhus, who first taught the Romans the deadly uses of elephants; now, however, the old teachers could not master the beasts (Livy, 44.41).[13]

Perseus' flight did not make his phalanx any less dangerous. The Greek and Macedonian phalanx of pikemen, like the earlier hoplite phalanx of spearmen, was a tactical formation that relied on a compact and cohesive assembling of men that, when it held together, was quite formidable. To protect themselves while thrusting their pikes, the Macedonian pikemen carried a smaller shield than the old *hoplon*. The principal offensive weapon was the pike, a longer thrusting weapon (fifteen to twenty-one feet) designed for two-handed use. When the first ranks of the phalangites lowered their pikes, they produced a forbidding palisade of pike points in the tight, forward moving phalanx. The formation was designed for implementation in a group of men that could not be separated from one another but had to fight as a single unit (Livy, 44.41; Plutarch, *Aemilius Paulus*, 20).[14]

The Roman system, on the other hand, emphasized both group cohesion and individual achievement. The maniples allowed for a much higher degree of flexibility as a unit, and the use of the pilum, gladius, and scutum necessitated that each legionary be able to successfully wage hand-to-hand combat as an individual. In the Roman battle formation the first (*hastati*), second (principes), and third *(triarii)* lines were arrayed in a complicated checkerboard-type pattern and moved back and forth and to the right and left.

Following initial skirmishing, at medium range the legionaries hurled their pila in order to disorder the enemy, after which the *hastati* engaged. Unlike at Sentinum, shock tactics characterized the battle instead of missile exchanges. The legionary's panoply had different strengths and weaknesses than those of a phalangite. His shield, the scutum, was designed to cover most of his body alone, and his use of the Spanish gladius implied the necessity of the swordsman's free range of movement (the Greek phalangite, by contrast, would merely remain in formation and thrust with the spear or pike). The manipular formation granted twice the space as the phalanx for the swordsman to wield scutum and gladius against the enemy. As Polybius explains, "Every man must move separately, as he has to cover his person with his long shield, turning to meet each expected blow, and . . . he uses his sword both for cutting and thrusting" (18.30).[15] Because the phalanx guaranteed close-range combat, these differences were an asset if employed properly and disastrous if not. When phalanx finally clashed with legion at Pydna, disaster seemed imminent.

Perseus' wise choice of the plains to the south of Pydna tipped the battle in his favor from the beginning as the phalanx maintained its cohesion and forced the Roman center back closer to their camp. As phalangite confronted legionary, the legionaries were either pushed

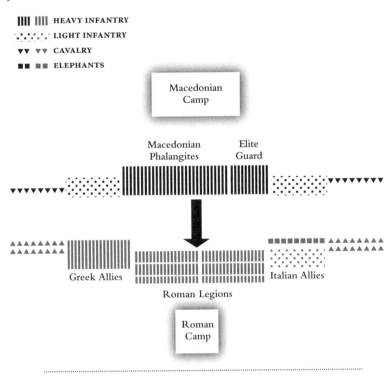

Battle of Pydna, phase 2: Macedonian phalanx pushes back Roman legions

back or speared by the robotic, forward-moving phalanx. The nature of the Macedonian formation meant that each individual Roman had to "stand opposite two men in the first rank of the phalanx," which meant he had "to face and encounter ten pikes" (Polybius, 18.30). The Pelignians had already fallen in a brave but foolish attempt to break through the wall of pikes during the skirmishing. Salius, their commander, had desperately thrown the Pelignian standard into the phalanx, and they rushed to retrieve it. Unable to get within range to use their swords, they were impaled in droves.[16] "Neither shield nor breastplate could resist the force of the Macedonian long spear" and those who stood firm against their advance met "a certain death." Even Paullus' faith was supposedly shaken. He tore his garments in consternation as he observed the slow but steady retreat of his men against a "dense barricade of long spears . . . everywhere unassailable" (Plutarch, *Aemilius Paulus*, 20).

However, terrain was about to test the phalanx, and an opportunity emerged if the legionaries could seize it. Paullus must have gained hope when he noticed a developing flaw in the Macedonian line. As the phalanx approached the Roman camp, it began to separate on the uneven ground past the plain. The phalangites, with their intimidating yet inflexible formation, did not counter this development and kept pushing forward. The Roman maniples then took the initiative and surged forward into the gaps, where the legionaries began taking on the phalangites one or two at a time. Once within range, the Roman gladius was more than a match for the isolated and unwieldy pike.

Plutarch, who emphasized the virtues of the commander, credits Paullus with the maneuver, whereas Livy attributes it to the soldiers (Livy, 44.41; Plutarch, *Aemilius Paulus*, 20). In light of the tactical ability Roman centurions and tribunes had demonstrated since the Second Punic War, it is more likely that the Roman soldiers themselves adapted to the situation on the field. The Macedonian soldier had been exposed by his unit's inflexibility, and he now fell prey to the maneuverability of the individual Roman. The Roman proved more than a match for his Macedonian counterpart, regardless of the latter's legendary ferocity: "For every Roman soldier, once he is armed and sets about his business, can adapt himself equally well to every place and time and can meet attack from every quarter. He is likewise equally prepared and equally in condition whether he has to fight together with the whole army or with a part of it or in maniples or singly" (Polybius, 18.32).

In that moment, the Roman citizens' independence and initiative at home was suddenly transported to the battlefield. When soldiers saw the gaps, they started rushing in on the breaks in the Macedonian line. The phalangites had been exposed and now fell prey to the Romans' longer swords and larger shields. Now the swordsman took over, vying against his fellows to draw more blood, hack more limbs, and sever more necks. The Romans quickly ended the battle within an hour and in the process killed twenty thousand men (Livy, 44.42). Roman elephants completed the rout by trampling those trying to escape.

The Battle of Pydna ended the question of whether the phalanx or the legion was superior, but tactics and technology were only part of

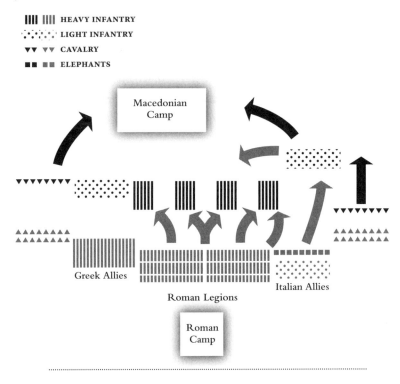

|||| |||| HEAVY INFANTRY

LIGHT INFANTRY

▼▼ ▼▼ CAVALRY

■■ ■■ ELEPHANTS

Battle of Pydna, phase 3: Romans break and rout the phalanx

what made the legionary win. Polybius dedicated several chapters to an extended discussion of this question. He judged that everything about Rome's war machine—its election of commanders and conscription, its camps and system of rewards, the household habituation of the paterfamilias and the elaborate funeral ceremonies, the centuries of technological and tactical adaptation, and the rivalry of individual citizen-soldiers on the field of battle—is why "the Romans have always had the upper hand and carried off the palm" (18.28). The king's men may have been ferocious fighters with a similar background on rugged farms, but Rome's citizen-soldiers were better killers and sacrificers for their republic.

The Roman farmer was tough enough and brave enough to withstand the onslaught of the phalanx. The legions were flexible, like the republic itself. They allowed for a retreat when necessary and an advance when advantageous. The tactical system harnessed the initiative, independence, and competitiveness of the individual as part of a corps that fought for the common good. The Roman who participated in the assembly and was eager to display his valor in single combat proved superior to the Macedonian. The phalanx taught the importance of unit cohesiveness but did not continually drill the necessity of single combat. Phalangites need only excel in the community; the legionary had to excel in the community and as an individual. Furthermore, the phalangite no longer served amid a corps of peers as had the classical Greeks but fought under the authority of a king, who would root out excessive initiative or dissent. At Pydna, the famous democracy of the phalanx, already degraded by the Macedonian monarchs, gave way to the republican legions.

GLORIFIED VICTORS

Paullus followed up his victory with the occupation and administration of Macedonia. The Roman army was warmly received by a number of Macedonians who had grown weary of Perseus' rule. Paullus stopped at Amphipolis, where "the pouring out of the entire populace to meet him showed to any one that Paullus had not robbed them of a just and good king" (Livy, 44.46). Later that year at Samothrace, Perseus and his children were captured, shackled, and carried off to Rome (Livy, 45.6). In 167, Paullus summoned representatives from throughout Macedonia and disseminated Rome's terms at Amphipolis, namely that Macedonia would keep its own laws, be divided into four, and be made directly subject to Rome (Livy, 45.29–32).[17] The historians claim that many Macedonian subjects were relieved and satisfied with the terms. This was due in no small part to Paullus' "occupying himself in ways alike honorable and humane" (Plutarch, *Aemilius Paulus*, 28–29). Paullus even celebrated a festival replete with games, sacrifices, banquets, and other entertainments (Plutarch, *Aemilius Paulus*, 29). "The man who knew how to conquer in war," Paullus quipped during the revelry, "could also arrange a banquet and organize games" (45.32).

Or so we are told. The beneficence the authors credit Paullus with and the cheerful resignation of the Macedonians at Amphipolis was hardly the whole truth. In Epirus, for example, Paullus' lieutenants sacked seventy communities, tore down their walls, enslaved 150,000 civilians, sold off the booty, and divvied up the proceeds between the cavalry and infantry. Incidentally, the infantrymen were not satisfied with their share and later complained of their treatment, precipitating a crisis that threatened his triumph (Livy, 45.34).

Paullus used some of the proceeds to modify the pillar at Delphi that Perseus had intended to top with a statue of himself. When Paullus saw it, he snidely remarked that "the conquered should make room for their conquerors" (Plutarch, *Aemilius Paulus*, 28; Livy, 45.27). Of all the Roman symbols to choose from, the question then was what should replace the dethroned king? A statue of Paullus himself of course!

Unfortunately, what remains to us today from Paullus' Delphic modifications is only a set of friezes. Not surprisingly, most of what survives is a depiction of the aristocratic cavalry at Pydna. Their distinguished role in the battle was to accidentally stumble into their opponents and launch the fighting, and yet these were the men Paullus made sure to glorify in stone. They were likely featured at the most prominent position at the monument's top, just beneath the imperator himself.[18] Overall, Paullus represented magisterial imperium to the full. He dealt out justice (and some injustice), distributed spoils, delighted crowds, delivered vengeance, and magnified the accomplishments of himself and his class.

TRIUMPHING FATHERS

Paullus uncharacteristically refrained from holding a victory celebration immediately after the battle had ended because he had received news that his son had disappeared. Paullus' son, one of four, had been adopted by Scipio Africanus' son (also named Publius Scipio), who was unable to produce an heir due to poor health (the son's adoptive name was Publius Cornelius Scipio Aemilianus). When Scipio Aemilianus could not be located, it was feared that he perished in battle. He had been carried away by his seventeen-year-old impetuousness in pursuit of the enemy and not returned. The men were dismayed at the loss, for

Aemilianus resembled his father and was loved by his fellow citizens. They rushed into the plain of battle, carrying torches, calling out his name, and searching the dead. To the relief of the entire army, Aemilianus finally returned with several other men, covered in the blood of those they had pursued and slain. Only then did the soldiers commence their revelry. Plutarch, who goes into much greater detail about the story, highlights the concern of the father for his lost son. The anecdote by Plutarch and Livy rounds out their portrait of Paullus as the devoted Roman patriarch who will stop at nothing to find his son, not unlike the shepherd of biblical lore that will stop at nothing to find his lost sheep (Livy, 45.44; Plutarch, *Aemilius Paulus*, 22).

The search for Aemilianus is also interesting in light of the triumph Paullus subsequently celebrated. A triumph was the crowning moment of any commander's career when he would celebrate his victory by displaying the captives and spoils of war while parading through the streets of Rome. Incredible artifacts could be exhibited during the process. Paullus, for example, displayed polished bronze and iron weapons, silver bowls and cups, an enormous, sacred gold offering bowl, a statue of Athena by the famous Pheidias, and paintings specially created for Paullus by another famous artist named Metrodorus.[19] Paullus himself did not appear until the last day. In front of the commander were 120 oxen for sacrifice, the chained Perseus and his children, and the most significant spoils from his campaign. The triumph was recorded in great detail by Livy and Plutarch, and it remains one of the finest recorded examples of the spectacle from the republican period. It was, in fact, so spectacular that the largest crowd in Rome's history gathered for the three days allotted for its activities (Livy, 45.40; Plutarch, *Aemilius Paulus*, 32–34).[20]

Normally an event of great joy and festivity, the triumph of Paullus was blighted by the death of his only two remaining heirs directly before and after the triumph (the younger two, Publius and Quintius were adopted by other noblemen). The deaths were in such proximity that the funerals for both sons were held before the acclaimed imperator delivered the customary speeches. Nonetheless, Paullus still spoke before the assembly.

The details of the speech, which can only dubiously be attributed to

Paullus, represent the historians' summaries of the statesman's life. In the speech, Paullus compares his pitiable state to that of Perseus, who had graced his triumph in chains. Perseus, the defeated victim of the triumph, still has his children while the victorious scion of the triumph has lost his own. While inveighing against the vicissitudes of his own fortune, however, Paullus cites his only comfort amid the tragedy: "But I am consoled in this disaster to my house by your happiness and the good fortune of the state" (Livy, 45.21; Plutarch, *Aemilius Paulus*, 36). Now at the end of his life with no sons to carry on his name, Paullus looks to the republic for comfort. In the gravitas of his rank and in his dignified approach to the changes of fortune, Paullus becomes the exemplar of stoic faith in the republic in the face of personal tragedy.[21]

After his death, Paullus' funeral was attended by the only heirs remaining to him, the Roman people. The funeral for an illustrious citizen was reminiscent of his triumph. Again there was a procession, speeches, and elaborate displays. The most incredible was a procession of actors who donned the ancestral masks, were escorted by lictors, and somberly took on the role of the deceased and his ancestors. When they reached the end of the procession, the actors took their seats in the magisterial chairs and functioned as a special, ghostly host for the eulogies.[22] In addition to hearing the eulogies, citizens took part in games, gladiatorial contests, and other events designed to showcase the dead man's accomplishments. Paullus' funeral procession, like his triumph, was magnificent, although in a different manner. As Plutarch explains, "His funeral procession called forth men's admiration, and showed a desire to adorn his virtue with the best and most enviable obsequies. This was manifest, not in gold or ivory or the other ambitious and expensive preparations for such rites, but in good will and honour and gratitude on the part, not only of his fellow citizens, but also of his enemies" (*Aemilius Paulus*, 39). Paullus—characterized as the imminent commander, brave warrior, and tragic father—at his end was now the honorable patriot. Livy and Plutarch tell us that the people of Rome loved their commander as much as he had loved his sons. Just as they had elected him to office in their time of need, they elected to remember him in adoration at his time of death.[23]

These final spectacles in Paullus' life earned him the position of a father to the Romans, but there is something insidious lurking in the background. Paullus had outpaced his fellows, and future rivals would respond competitively. Succeeding generations would endeavor to surpass the glory of Paullus not only through lavish displays and public entertainments but in taking over the role of the republic's father. The Roman paterfamilias was a powerful figure in his household who could even inflict death on his progeny when he deemed it necessary. The paterfamilias also had no rival. He was a monarch in his realm. What would happen if his realm was not his own family but the state instead?

In the coming years, the imperial republic offered commanders the opportunity to exercise greater independence in distant lands far from their colleagues in the senate. It was possible that one of them would accumulate a great deal of power and wealth and a great deal of control over his soldiers. He might then seek to return as the paterfamilias of the Roman people, not in a metaphorical sense but in a genuine, political sense. If he had accumulated enough wealth, enough military power, and enough popularity, perhaps no one could stop him from doing so.

PART 4

The Death of Rome's Citizen-Soldiers

8 · Questionable Legitimacy

THE IDEAL STATESMAN'S
BATTLE AT MUTINA

In an attack on his dreaded enemy, Thomas Jefferson said that Alexander Hamilton adored Julius Caesar. The story is that while the two were serving under Washington, Jefferson was hosting a dinner at his own home. Hamilton had noticed three busts, but, in his ignorance, he did not know who they were. Jefferson told him that they were Francis Bacon, Isaac Newton, and John Locke, which he considered his "trinity of the three greatest men the world has ever produced." Hamilton was said to have summarily dismissed such silly sentiments and responded that "the greatest man that ever lived was Julius Caesar."

Jefferson's recounting of the affair was damning indeed if it was true. It was a scurrilous charge in an age when every self-respecting American knew that Julius Caesar was the dreaded foe that had brought down the republic. No, the real heroes were Brutus, Camillus, Fabius, and Aemilianus. And the greatest hero, at least in the end, was Cicero. John Adams, James Wilson, and many others adored Cicero and gladly referred to themselves as modern day versions of the martyred republican. And Hamilton knew this too, which is why Hamilton scholars insist that Jefferson invented the story to smear his political opponent.[1]

Such an attack would hardly land any blows today. In fact, Caesar is often admired as an exemplar of courage, decisiveness, skill, genius, and good fortune. Caesar has been sympathetically portrayed in modern film and television by a broad range of actors from Claude Rains and Rex Harrison to Timothy Dalton and Ciarán Hinds. Modern audiences find much to like in his character, and many see his end as tragic and undeserved. This may merely be a change in taste, just as neoclassicism eventually gave way to other fads and forms of artistic expression, or it could represent a cooling in modern sentiment for devoted republicans relative to charismatic adventurers.

In the Roman Empire in the middle of March 44, the affection for Caesar was more widespread, more personal, and more virulent. Whether Caesar's life and achievements were intentional or accidental, or dangerous or beneficial to average Romans, he had nearly succeeded in bringing down the republic and ushering in a new manner of governing the empire. His death launched a new quest for legitimacy, and it would bring Cicero out of retirement. Regardless of the wisdom or reasonableness of Cicero's actions in 44 and 43, there cannot be any question that he was the final republican voice of the ancient world. For history's own reasons, Cicero's writings have been preserved more than any other Roman republican, and here I draw on them to explore the two years that witnessed the last triumph of Cicero's republican dream.

THE IDEAL OF AEMILIANUS

It should be no surprise that Cicero earned the adulation of early Americans. In their own minds the founders were opposed to the kind of violence perpetrated by the British Empire. They appreciated how Cicero criticized pointless militarism:

> Most people think that the achievements of war are more important than those of peace; but this opinion needs to be corrected. For many men have sought occasions for war from the mere ambition for fame. This is notably the case with men of great spirit and natural ability, and it is the more likely to happen, if they are adapted to a soldier's life and fond of warfare. But if we will face the facts, we shall find that there have been many instances of achievement in peace more important and no less renowned than in war. (*On Duties*, 1.22)

Over the course of his life, Cicero voiced many similar sentiments. For Cicero, wars should be legal, defensive, and justly waged. They must also keep the broader interests of humanity in mind, and peace must always be the ultimate goal. Through his writings Cicero shapes an ideal of Roman warfare, despite his having observed many instances when Rome fell short of that ideal. He thus deserves pride of place as the creator of just war theory.[2]

Cicero was no great military man. Over the course of his illustrious political life, he turned down most opportunities for military glory. Like all Roman statesmen, Cicero knew the basics of fighting and military command. He served in the Social War and even commanded a successful campaign against bandits in Cilicia, but there was nothing exceptional in his military experience (Plutarch, *Cicero*, 3; Cicero, *Philippics*, 12.27).

His temperament aside, however, Cicero did understand the importance of military glory. In one of his most famous philosophical treatises, *The Dream of Scipio*, he presents a trio of ideal statesmen and commanders who exhibit the perfect balance between ferocity and justice in warfare. In the dream Scipio Aemilianus is guided by his illustrious ancestors Aemilius Paullus and Scipio Africanus up to the heavens, where he is reminded of his duty to serve his country by serving virtue and justice. Only by seeing his own insignificance in the cosmos can Aemilianus come to understand that true glory comes by bringing justice to Rome and Rome's enemies.

Aemilianus was the natural grandson of Lucius Aemilius Paullus, the commander who valiantly died with his troops at Cannae. Yet he was also the adoptive grandson of Rome's greatest general in the third century, Scipio Africanus, who, readers will recall, fought at Cannae as well and then avenged that defeat by subduing Spain and defeating Hannibal. Aemilianus' biological father, Aemilius Paullus, had triumphed over Perseus in the Battle of Pydna, during which the seventeen-year-old Aemilianus had gone missing in his pursuit of the fleeing Macedonian army. This minor exploit was only the beginning of Aemilianus' career.

In the Third Punic War he had been a capable young officer in the lackluster siege of Carthage. Just as his father was seen as the best man for the job in Macedonia, he was seen as the best man to prosecute the war in Carthage, so he was elected consul for 147 to complete Carthage's destruction. Using the discipline and doggedness typical of the best Roman commanders in history, he captured and destroyed Carthage the next year. Twelve years later he repeated this performance at another frontier of the growing Roman Empire in Numantia. He was elected consul for 134, took up the command of the seemingly unending Numantine War in Spain, and captured the stronghold of Numantia the next year. The career of Aemilianus thus demonstrated how Rome was expanding in every direction. The same year that Aemilianus sacked Carthage saw Rome sack Corinth and permanently subdue Greece. The Mediterranean was now a Roman lake.

Yet Scipio Aemilianus was no mere brute with a sword and an army behind him. In his later years he collected around himself a band of cultural luminaries—artists, authors, and others—often today referred to as the Scipionic Circle.³ For his *Dream of Scipio*, Cicero had chosen a man who represented the best aspects of the Roman tradition. However, for Cicero, this was not manifested in his conquests, his education, or his association with cultural elites. Rather, Scipio and his ancestors are models of republican virtue. Aemilianus represented the ethos that made the Roman state and Roman armies unstoppable. Descended from the *nobiles*, he had been trained to outshine his colleagues in Roman virtues, and the citizen-soldiers, aware of his talents, naturally conferred rank and honor on him. He led these men to glory, they elevated him, and the Roman Republic won more territory as it "justly" acquired its empire.

The ideal statesman such as Aemilianus must also bring together the disparate factions of the republic against those forces wishing to tear the republic apart (*On the Republic*, 6.12). He will do this through wisely prioritizing harmony and concord. This quest for concord was one of the most important aspects of Cicero's political thought, and his own political life was dedicated to the idea of unifying the people under the leadership of the good men against the vicious who would put a tyranny in the republic's place. Cicero uses Aemilianus' own circumstances to highlight how the problem began at the end of Aemilianus' life. Aemilianus never had the opportunity to fulfill the role of the ideal statesman because he perished precisely when civil discord erupted in Rome. In 129 he was found dead under mysterious circumstances. Many suspected that his cousin Gaius Gracchus or a partisan of the Gracchi brothers was responsible for his death.[4] The republic's troubles had just begun, and the question was who would be the ideal statesmen to ensure that it remained intact.

Readers will recall that Polybius was one of the luminaries in Aemilianus' circle. Whereas Cicero looked back on Aemilianus as the potential savior that could have saved Rome, Polybius looked forward to a doom that could not be averted. Like all things human, the republican culture of Rome could not last forever. Polybius concludes his discussion of the Roman constitution by saying "that all existing things are subject to decay and change is a truth that scarcely needs proof; for the course of nature is sufficient to force this conviction on us." Foreign wars and the geopolitical environment are external factors—the "fortune"—that change a republic, and they are impossible to predict. "The growth of the state itself," however, "is a regular process" (6.57). It was fate. The Roman Republic had grown to great heights indeed, but Polybius somberly notes that its end was foreordained:

> When a state has weathered many great perils and subsequently attains to supremacy and uncontested sovereignty, it is evident that under the influence of long established prosperity, life will become more extravagant and the citizens more fierce in their rivalry regarding office and other objects than they ought to be. As these defects go on increasing, the beginning of the change for the worse will be due to love of office and the disgrace entailed by obscurity, as well as to extravagance and purse-proud display; and for this change the populace will be responsible when on the one hand they think they have a grievance against certain people who have shown themselves grasping, and when, on the other hand, they are puffed up by the flattery of others who aspire to office. (6.57)

Given this state of affairs, he believed the republic would quickly devolve into a democracy and then anarchy, relaunching the cycle that would begin again with autocracy. Polybius did not live to see the end of the republic, but he was not wrong that its demise was looming.

Or is this all merely coincidence? Was Polybius a learned prophet or just a lucky predictor? Hindsight is a deceptive thing. It is easy to interpret history the way we see it—looking backward. In some ways the generations after Aemilianus were challenged by all the things Polybius talks about: expansion, destructive rivalries, the prioritization of personal *dignitas* over communal honor and of greed over good faith, and the loss of civic virtue, especially among certain members of the ruling class. But some have persuasively argued that the republic expanded unaware of its impending doom because doom was not actually impending.[5]

At the opening of the second century, despite the squawking of orators like Cato the Elder, few were afraid that Rome was losing its soul, and this belief prevailed down to the first century. Magistrates would be elected, fellow statesmen and commanders would vie with one another, laws would be passed, troops would be conscripted, battles might be lost, but wars would be won. The constitution would endure. Throughout these years, Romans were right to expect that any changes in territory, conscription, or warfighting would of course be matched by changes in their constitution. This was the Roman model: adaptation and flexibility in the midst of expansion or geopolitical shifts. Rome would continue to expand in the first century as it had in previous centuries. The constitution would adapt and political culture would continue to habituate loyal citizen-soldiers and virtuous, patriotic commanders. But this isn't what happened.

THE SOLDIERS OF AEMILIANUS

Cicero may have crafted a fictional dream about who the ideal statesman was, but unlike his philosophical muse Plato, he did so for thoroughly practical reasons. He was looking for what qualities defined such a man, and he was seeing what statesman of his day could fit into that mold. When he wrote the dream in the 50s, he had been pushed out of politics and was watching Rome descend into another civil war.

Unlike his Greek predecessors, Cicero, in a thoroughly Roman way, was writing philosophy as part of a desperate search to identify a real statesman to command real citizen-soldiers.[6]

Cicero's three distinguished commanders embodied the republic's highest expectations of the *nobiles* as Rome consolidated its control of the Mediterranean world. But what about the men who served under them? What transitions shaped the soldier who left his farm, journeyed to the far reaches of the empire, marched through enemy terrain, dug trenches, fought battles, and then, if he survived, helped consolidate Roman victories? Was the world that he left when he mustered to war the same that he returned to in peace?

The predicament of the smallholding citizen-soldier in the middle of the second century is usually debated in light of the Gracchi brothers. The reformers Tiberius and Gaius Gracchus and their allies had noticed a decline in the number of smallholders that were available to serve as citizen-soldiers. The need for reform was first made apparent to Tiberius as he journeyed through Italy en route to service in Spain. Throughout Italy smallholder farms were being replaced by larger estates. At the same time, a slave revolt was breaking out in Sicily, and it was natural to suppose that the proliferating slave population laboring on larger estates was displacing smallholders.[7] Between 133 and 121 Tiberius and then Gaius attempted to legislate a way out of the perceived dilemma. Measures included removing public land (*ager publicus*) from the hands of wealthy citizens and distributing it to poorer citizens, increasing the judicial powers of the equestrian class, and elevating Latins to citizen status and allies to Latin status. In theory, all of these measures would increase the strength of Rome's citizen-soldiers.[8]

This need for land hints at the complex socioeconomic factors of the second century. It is fitting to return to the centurion Ligustinus who had given his stirring speech in 171. Despite his ongoing participation in various campaigns, Ligustinus was quite the family man. He had a wife, six sons, and two daughters. Although born at least four years before the Punic War, he never served in that war, presumably because his low property rating exempted him, even when Rome was making exceptions for these rules. Rome's wars in Greece and Spain finally gave him his big break—the opportunity to fight. He probably farmed his own land and any available *ager publicus* for subsistence when possible, but the more he campaigned, the more his living must have derived from pay and booty.

Ligustinus' speech may be an embellishment, but if so, it still seems to suggest that there were problems regarding war, death, and farms in second-century Italy.[9] Property qualifications for military service were falling, yet census records indicate that the population was rising. These trends may not indicate a decrease in middling smallholders as much as they indicate a rise in poorer Romans. One theory maintains that the problem was not that Roman citizens were dying too much in war but rather that they were procreating too much in peace.[10] When their paltry plots were parceled out to their progeny, even more citizens became impoverished. At fifty years old, Ligustinus still lived on his one *iugerum* of property, which was the only land he had to will to his six sons. How would Ligustinus' sons eke out a living for themselves? In what way could they acquire land? From whom they might expect to receive a special reward?

Marius' Mules

As the Romans fought more wars, poorer citizens like Ligustinus that could be rewarded with booty and grants of land were increasingly enlisted. Ligustinus may have been an anomaly at the beginning of the century, but by its end some argue he was becoming the norm. Later Roman historians found their villain for these nefarious reforms in Gaius Marius, a political outsider who obtained the consulship an unprecedented seven times (107, 104–100, 86). In order to raise armies for wars against Jugurtha of Numidia and barbarians rampaging in the north, he recruited from Rome's propertyless poorer classes. In the eyes of the ancients, the virtuous farmer was suddenly replaced with men dedicated more to their commanders than to the good of the republic. Plutarch condemns Marius' practices, lamenting that "contrary to law and custom he enlisted many a poor and insignificant man, although former commanders had not accepted such persons, but bestowed arms, just as they would any other honour, only on those whose property assessment made them worthy to receive these, each soldier being supposed to put his substance in pledge to the state" (*Gaius Marius*, 9). In this analysis no longer would it be necessary for men to meet a reasonable property qualification and no longer would soldiers fight on behalf of the republic. If an imperator—and not the republic—could bestow honor, then it would be the imperator—and not the republic—who would receive allegiance.

Marius was definitely the central figure in the last major restructuring of the republican army. After gaining fame for conquering the crafty Numidian king Jugurtha, grateful Romans elected him to his unprecedented consulships in the hope that he would be able to defeat Rome's greatest threat since Hannibal: the Germanic Teutones and Cimbri. Marius did not disappoint them and soundly defeated the Germans in a cautious but decisive campaign.

His successes against Jugurtha and the Germans were due in no small part to his emphasis on training and military discipline for his newly levied troops. Marius needed to upgrade Roman campaign logistics. His conscription of poor volunteers meant the state now had to furnish weapons, which in turn meant he could standardize equipment for every heavy infantryman. He also reduced the baggage train by forcing each legionary to carry much of his own equipment, including his mess kit, entrenching tools, and several days' worth of rations. Soldiers were burdened with up to a hundred pounds in supplies, and every squad was allowed a mule for its tent. Roman soldiers were so laden with their equipment that they marched while bent over, earning the nickname "Marius' Mules." Nevertheless, the simplification of the supply train made individual units and entire armies more agile.

The tactical structure of the army was also overhauled at this time. Smaller army units like maniples were already functioning with tactical independence under commanders like Scipio Africanus in the Punic Wars and Titus Flamininus in the Second Macedonian War, but the old checkerboard maniple formation was still the norm. This was scrapped, and legions were divided into independent tactical units called cohorts. Legionary strength remained around five thousand, but each individual legion was formed by ten cohorts, each with six centuries of eighty men. The cohort was small enough for tactical agility and large enough for independent action. By the time of the Pompeian-Caesarian civil war in the 40s, commanders could arrange these remarkably flexible units in any number of ways, from three lines in a three-four-three formation, to two lines in a five-five formation, to single lines used obliquely, in circles, and so on.[11] The most brilliant general of the era, Julius Caesar, perfected his use of the cohortal army while in Gaul, and the result was that his tactical genius and well-disciplined veterans could outmatch any of his fellow commanders. He was also known for his operational swiftness, which was made possible by Marius' logistical reforms.

Professional Armies or Professionalized Soldiers?

Despite the importance of these tactical and logistical alterations, the ancient authors overemphasized Marius' role in changing conscription rules. His "reform," which he probably introduced in 107 or 104, was to open up enrollment to volunteers from among the poorest Romans. This was not a radical alteration of conscription standards; in fact, the change was only of "marginal significance."[12] Poor citizens had always been liable to service in their own manner: as colonists defending the frontiers, marines and sailors, or replacements for well-equipped men that had died on campaign. Even slaves could be conscripted in times of emergencies.[13]

Although Marius was later villainized for opening up enrollment to the poorest Romans, his reforms were only one, albeit important, step on the path toward recruiting more volunteers and poorer citizens.[14] Property qualifications had already dropped, probably once between 214 and 212 and again sometime between the Gracchi brothers' reforms in 129 or 122. Based on evidence from Livy, Polybius, and Cicero, Brunt reasons that the pre-second-century property qualifications were eleven hundred denarii. This was then reduced to 400 denarii in the second century and to 150 denarii by the first. Rome was thus adapting its constitutional requirements for service, and the trajectory indicated an increasing reliance on poor volunteers and poorer smallholders.[15]

For some soldiers the financial rewards of military service served as more than compensation for lost income or boosts to income. Rather, these rewards provided a steady stream of revenue. The seeds of this system were planted long before. Scipio's veterans, for example, were given plots of land after the Second Punic War, and the colonies founded in northern Italy in the first decades of the second century included land set aside for veterans. Furthermore, booty had always provided a powerful incentive, prompting citizens to authorize wars or volunteer for service.[16] Ligustinus could have previously been an *assiduus* liable to conscription whose military service abroad reduced him to the status of a poorer *proletarius*. His professionalism made him a desirable asset for commanders, and his poverty made war a desirable endeavor for him. Volunteers such as Ligustinus were not unheard of in the late third and second centuries. Scipio Africanus, Publius Sulpicius Galba, and possibly Flamininus raised them as Rome began to pursue distant campaigns in places such as Greece and Asia. Aemilianus' reputation, promise of spoils, and base of clients enabled him to enlist four thousand volunteers for Spain in the 130s.[17]

Still, volunteers were not the norm in the second century, and conscription continued to be forced on Romans and Italians. This caused many men to protest their service. In 193 the urban legions complained about the fact that the nature of their service had not earned them exceptions, and in 191 maritime colonists claimed a standing exception from service (recall that poor citizens or colonists could still be enlisted as marines, sailors, replacements, and technical specialists). Failures or delayed victories also resulted in protests, as had occurred in a Spanish campaign in 184 and the early years of the war against Perseus. Yet commanders were reluctant to conscript another levy and therefore did not release them from service.[18] One can only wonder what was happening to their farms at home. If the Gracchi had accurately assessed the situation, their absence was devastating. Farms were failing and their land was being consolidated by wealthier citizens.

Polybius claims that the length of service could be as high as sixteen to twenty years, although other evidence indicates that this number was significantly lower. Debate on this question continues, but the norm was probably six years, which was still long enough to threaten family farms.[19]

Careerists such as Ligustinus were thus a great boost to commanders, especially in unpopular wars. Already in the third century wars had become "lengthy, distant, and difficult," requiring "a revision of earlier presuppositions" about the nature of service, including the idea that military service should no longer be thought of in terms of annual cycles but instead in terms of life cycles. An increasing reliance on experienced personnel ready and willing to serve for extended periods was another. Men like Ligustinus represented a small but important minority. They provided expertise, could train new recruits, and steeled the legions for the rigors of campaigns, especially difficult ones abroad. In return they could expect promotion and increased rewards for their service. These men were known as *homines militares*. Another *homo militaris*, Marcus Petreius, had already seen thirty years of service in 63. Nonetheless, he still fought for Pompey in Spain in the 50s and then again for him during the civil wars of the 40s, when he was in his sixties. This last conflict claimed his death in battle. Yet even a professionalized soldier still sought participation in civic life; Petreius, for example, earned his way into the senate and even the praetorship by 64. He was an ardent republican, comparable to Cato the Younger in his opposition to Caesar.[20] The republican armies of the second and first centuries were filled with the same dedicated yet independent soldiers as previous centuries, but this made them that much more dangerous when their commanders vied with one another for legitimacy.

So when did the Roman armies become "professional"? There were the few careerists, men whose primary vocation was war, but what about the rest of the soldiers, whose time in the army averaged out to about six years? A quick survey indicates that there is no precise consensus on this question today. The literature tends to date the transition vaguely to the time between the Marian and Augustan military reforms.[21] From a purely military standpoint, it is not unreasonable to locate the break early in the first century, and perhaps even sometime in the second. However, a more holistic view that takes into account republican institutions, motives for service, war authorization, soldiers' independence, degrees of unit permanence, and larger strategic goals, should place that decisive break after the Battle of Philippi.

Until that time Romans still saw themselves as operating under a system that stretched back to earlier epochs of the republic. Julius Caesar, the man most responsible in the 50s for professionalizing specific units, concentrating Roman military authority in himself, and diverting troop loyalty away from the republic, did not ultimately succeed. His death, however, did create a very volatile situation and left to others the task of managing these troops. Some commanders did so with republican ends in mind. Others did not.

Republican Armies in the Coming Civil Strife

Throughout this period, continuity, rather than discontinuity, characterized Roman conscription and warfighting. Just as in the previous centuries of the republic, citizens in the second and first centuries would be called away from their farms for annual campaigns or to serve for certain periods of their lives. Changes were occurring in the Roman Empire, but the decisive break in conscription methods would not come in the late second century with Marius, but in the late first century after the republic ceased to exist. Before that time, the republic was continuing to adapt its armies to meet new threats. Rome had learned how to fight long-term, distant wars in the fourth and third centuries, and in the second and first centuries it was training its citizen armies to make them more adept at fighting new foes to the north and throughout the entire Mediterranean.

As we have seen, Rome may have fielded citizen-soldiers, but these citizens were part of a militarized society—a "martial republic"—that habituated its citizens to kill.[22] Part 2 demonstrates how the early republic's soldiers could be politicized, and, as I note in part 3, Roman republican soldiers would sometimes demonstrate a remarkable independence, manifested most particularly in Rome's dueling culture and the occasional mutiny. The ancient authors emphasize how the political violence that surfaced in the age of the Gracchi did not dissipate and was fully transferred to the army in the age of Marius and Sulla. The tendency toward independent, violent action by the soldiers had been a part of Rome from the beginning, but civil war now inspired more outbreaks of soldiers' independence in the pursuit of internal—and destructive—political ends.[23]

Marius' removal of "the last legal obstacles" to volunteers was not without consequence, but it did not change the fact that Roman, and eventually Italian, farming citizens continued to fill the ranks and fight its wars. Army pay, intended for subsistence, remained the same until Caesar. Increasing citizenship throughout Italy and recruiting volunteers also reduced the possibility for revolution, for it allowed those with political and economic grievances an elevated status and another means of income. Nor did this suddenly create a vast manpower base for client armies wielded by competing warlords. In fact, the opposite was true. Troops were not loyal to commanders, but like Greek and Roman republican citizens had always been, they proved loyal to themselves.[24] This made them particularly perilous for commanders who in some way violated what the troops felt was right or just. Sometimes this worked to the advantage of republican principles, and sometimes it worked against it. Ideally citizen-soldiers and their commanders would prosecute foreign wars as harmoniously as Cicero indicates they should under a wise and competent republican like Aemilianus. But what if such commanders were in short supply?

Conscription continued to the very end of the republic. Pompey, Caesar, Antony, Octavian, and the last true consuls, Hirtius and Pansa, had seasoned veterans at their disposal, but they also found it necessary to levy fresh troops. The last republicans, and their Caesarian opponents, all needed levies. From 49 to 30, an "average of 23,000 men were enrolled in the army each year." Down to the very end, the republic was able to stock their killing machines. It was only under the emperors Augustus and Tiberius that this kind of conscription was abandoned for good, and by this time it was probably for the better.[25]

When civil war erupted in the first century, armies suffered from divided loyalties. In the end, the strongest motivators for troops' support proved to be what they had always been: a successful commander who inspired allegiance and the promise of glory and economic reward. After all, when there were equal claims to republican legitimacy, who wants to fight for a loser? However, civil war corrupted civic militarism because it created competing internal claims to legitimacy, justice, and the focus for a citizen's martial virtue. Cicero believed this was the worst kind of war because "even when good men achieve victory in a civil war, they have often behaved with less restraint and more violence than they otherwise would have done. In some ways civil wars create no victors, with the survivors as defeated as those that perished."[26] If the state ceased to exist in a legitimate form, where would armies ultimately place their loyalty? In this kind of peril, Cicero had insisted that there was only one remedy: an ideal statesman that could reunite the state and provide a focal point for its citizen armies.

THE BATTLEGROUND IN ROME

The statesmen who dominated the scene in the years after Aemilianus' death were far from ideal. Republican politics and factions persisted into the late second and first centuries, producing the usual crop of *nobiles*, but the ancient historians emphasize the activities of the few dynamic figures that stirred civil strife, first by inciting mob violence among the growing urban population of Rome and then by wielding armies against each other in a struggle for legitimacy and personal prestige.

The first of these were the Gracchi brothers. Their reforms were reasonable in many ways, but they still faced opposition. At first Tiberius, a tribune of the plebs, played by the rules, securing powerful backers in the senate, presenting his legislation to the senate for debate, and then seeking a compromise when resistance was met. However, another tribune, Octavius, vetoed the bill, putting the personal prestige of both men at stake. The issue did not need to escalate, and if the senate had intervened it might have been possible to arrive at a suitable conclusion. When the senate did nothing and Octavius maintained his position, Tiberius took radical measures. On the flimsiest of precedents, he went directly to the assembly, passed a bill deposing Octavius, and then passed his legislation. Now it was the senate's turn to become radicalized. When Tiberius tried to break precedent again by seeking another term as tribune, the elections turned into a brawl. Tiberius used a mob of his followers to seize the voting place on the Capitoline, and his cousin, the pretentious senator Scipio Nasica, led a band of senators to expel Tiberius' mob. In the ensuing struggle, Tiberius was struck with a bench and killed.[27]

The ancient authors remark on this incident as an unprecedented use of violence and a tragic departure from the peaceful functioning of the constitution. Unfortunately, it helped violence gain ground as a way of doing politics in Rome. Gaius' more comprehensive reforms a decade later led to the same result, except this time makeshift weapons like benches were unnecessary. Gaius' followers seized the Aventine using Gallic weapons that had been decorations in a former commander's house. The consul Opimius responded with troops that happened to be waiting outside the city and prepared for an assault on the Aventine. Gracchus and his supporters tried to escape and perished in a bloodbath of three thousand citizens. Political violence had been a feature of Roman politics from the earliest days of the republic (recall Cassius, Maelius, and Manlius), but previous incidents "had been comparatively harmless to the state." The Gracchi were simply applying ancient precedents in novel ways to achieve political dominance, but they regularized it in a manner that was unpredictable at the time.[28]

Two decades later the tribune Saturninus, who had made a political alliance with Marius, precipitated another outbreak of political violence. Saturninus was reported to have already assassinated two political rivals, Nunnius in 101 and Memmius in 100, but he got his comeuppance when Marius was forced to abandon him. Marius detained Saturninus in the senate house under the promise of protection, but this did not prevent a mob from taking the tiles from the roof and stoning him and his supporters to death. As these events demonstrate, at the height of its imperial successes, the city of Rome itself periodically turned into miniaturized war zones, with the Capitoline, the Aventine, and the Forum serving as mob battlefields. Levies of citizen-soldiers had already been used to suppress the mobs, and it would only take a spark to bring the armies into a general conflagration.

That spark came in 91 with another significant act of political violence, the murder of yet another tribune, Marcus Livius Drusus. As part of a larger reform package that included a grain law that would please the urban poor and a land law that would garner support from the rural poor, Drusus resurrected the notion of broadening Roman citizenship, proposing that all non-Roman Italians should receive citizenship. As with the efforts of the Gracchi and Saturninus to push legislation through, Drusus' attempts to pass his reforms were accompanied by escalating tensions, which only ended when he was assassinated in his own home. This was the third time an attempt at Italian citizenship had failed (the other two attempts had been made in 125 and 122), and the Italians responded by rebelling against Rome and setting up their own rival state named Italia.[29]

The demand for citizenship was part of a broader set of grievances that resulted from Rome's imperial expansion. Rome had introduced necessary changes to the administration of its dominions after the First Punic War. The system of alliances in Italy could not be extended beyond the peninsula, so the typical Mediterranean methods of taxation, tribute, and provincial governors were established in the islands of Corsica, Sardinia, and Sicily. When Rome acquired territory in Spain, Greece, Gaul, and northern Africa, this trend expanded. There were other changes as well. In the year of Pydna, Roman citizens were no longer required to pay taxes because the revenues from foreign theaters exceeded the needs of the state. Abroad, Rome began to treat with allies and enemies from an increasingly dominant position. Meanwhile booty and slaves flowed in from Roman conquests in the Mediterranean, and the distribution of those spoils became problematic. In Italy, allies received an inequitable allotment of spoils after the Istrian War in 177, and that trend continued. It was becoming difficult for the allies to understand the growing number of wars abroad that did not threaten Italian soil. Without the incentives for conquest, the Italian federation felt old strains that had lain dormant for some time.[30]

As Rome acquired its empire, foreigners increasingly viewed Italians as the equals of Romans. Back home in Italy, however, Rome treated them more and more like subjects. The allies complained that they supplied a disproportionate number of troops, suffered under the whim of sometimes capricious Roman magistrates, and yet received less than an equal share of the spoils of empire. The individual soldier felt this in particular. A shared culture and physical resemblance made him appear as the equal to his Roman counterpart when he was fighting in Spain, Gaul, Greece, or Africa. Romans and Italians, like distant kinsmen, also experienced a shared affinity abroad. Yet the Italian ally did not have the same rights and privileges as his Roman counterpart. As these points indicate, the Italians' motives for rebellion were primarily political, not economic, and despite military defeat, the war ended with the satisfaction of their chief demand. They were granted citizenship.[31]

The Social War—Rome's war with its allies (socii) from 91 to 88— was a crisis of the first order for the Roman system. On the one hand, it illustrated the enormous value of Roman citizenship. Its extension over the past centuries had gradually enabled Rome to increase manpower as no other state in the Mediterranean. Yet citizenship was more than a practical means of gaining more troops. It carried privileges and embodied ideas of law, order, security, and identity that contributed to the creation of a unique and powerful community. The governing elite in Rome severely blundered in being stingy with the citizenship at this stage. In the desire of some to protect their own status, they compromised what had made Rome so appealing to allies against a Pyrrhus or a Hannibal and abandoned the mercy Rome had famously shown to its defeated enemies.

Thus far Rome had skillfully combined Cicero's idea of the two patrias—one's homeland and the larger republic—but the Social War saw these two turned against one another (*On the Laws*, 2.2.5). Italian coinage captured the fratricidal fury. The allies created their own federation and issued coins defiantly tweaking existing Roman models, with those in the north using Latin, and in the south Oscan. They used classic images like the Dioscuri, Mars, and a bust of Italia (instead of

Roma). These icons had bound Rome and its allies together, but now they were invoked against Rome. What the coins lacked in originality they made up for in vitriol. Images of the oath hearkened back to the sanctity of the old alliance, but now the oath bound the allies together against Rome. One featured an Italian bull trampling and goring the Roman wolf.[32] These coins simultaneously illustrated how the allies now hated Rome but still wanted to be Roman.

The war was so vicious and brutal because the allies and citizens were similar, especially in the manner of their fighting. With their early successes in the war, the Italians demonstrated that they deserved citizenship, at least with respect to the manner of how they fought. And even when the war was concluded and the cherished citizenship finally granted, the fact that Italian manpower had to be used against Roman manpower remained a bitter reminder that the Roman constitution was in need of reform. The most disturbing aspect of the war was that Rome had once again been unable to achieve a constitutional compromise. This time, however, armies were used to secure a political settlement. Citizen fought ally. The next logical step was for the legions to begin devouring one another.

The rebel Italian state had been an odd creation, similar to Rome with its magistrates, senate, federation, and armies, but it missed a crucial element—the capital of Rome itself—leading many to see the Italian rebellion as a failed political experiment from its inception. The Italians were also denied Rome's most important allies, the Latins, almost all of whom remained loyal to Rome. Nonetheless, the Italians initially inflicted a number of military defeats on the Romans. These disasters helped recall Marius from retirement and also afforded one of his former lieutenants from the Jugurthine War, Sulla, the chance for military achievement. Marius was successful in the north and Sulla in the south. With the aristocracy still leery of Marius, he was abruptly shunted back to retirement even after he reversed a humiliating defeat. But Marius had tasted power once more and was determined to get it back.

Marius' main rival was his former subordinate. Sulla drew the ire of the old general by erecting a monument on the Capitol emphasizing that he, Sulla, had personally captured Jugurtha and concluded the war back in 105 (Plutarch, *Sulla*, 6). This stirred the rivalry between the two men, and Marius was already hankering for revenge over being snubbed twice now by the senatorial aristocracy. In 88 Sulla had been elected consul, and he was clamoring for the command of a potentially glorious and lucrative war against Mithridates of Pontus. He was awarded the command by lot. Marius once again relied on the efforts of a tribune, this time Publius Sulpicius Rufus, and had the command transferred to himself. Like Marius' old ally Saturninus, Sulpicius used violence to get his legislation passed. Sulla responded by marching his troops on Rome to regain the command. It was an event unprecedented in the history of the republic. Even the legendary Coriolanus had turned back from marching on his country.

Once Sulla had broken that taboo, it was open season. After he departed for the First Mithridatic War, Marius and his allies in turn marched on the city and purged Sulla's supporters. Marius died days after being elected to his seventh consulship in 86. Marius' death precluded him from witnessing Sulla's second march on Rome in 82. This time Sulla had a hard fight regaining the city, but afterward he massacred Marius' former supporters using an official posting called a proscription, wherein a bounty was placed on those deemed to be enemies of the state. An estimated two thousand leading citizens were put to death. Sulla had twice relied on the rank-and-file citizen-soldiers to seize Rome, and now he was using opportunistic citizens to hunt down his political opponents. Although most of his officers had refused to march on Rome, the common soldiers themselves were willing to follow his vices in their own official and private deeds.[33]

Something was clearly wrong with the Roman Republic. Normal political rivalries had begun harnessing mob violence and then escalated into the political use of the army. The constitution was incentivizing some of the leading political figures to pursue their prestige and ambitions in the most destructive ways, destroying their colleagues, themselves, and republican legitimacy. Even if the system itself was in need of reforms, one should never forget that the individual choices of these men were morally and constitutionally abominable. The worst of men were determining the fate of the republic in the worst of ways.

Throughout all of this, the soldiers stayed true to their independent nature. They were citizen-soldiers with agency. But a lack of legitimate authorities made these soldiers a threat to any who dared take command. Many commanders who participated in the Sullan-Marian civil war of the 80s got more than they bargained for. Sulla's proconsul for Italy, Quintus Pompeius, was murdered by his troops, who preferred their former commander, the proconsul Pompeius Strabo (the father of Pompey). This did not stop a Roman mob from dragging Strabo's body through the streets after he had died of a pestilence. The consul Octavius was killed along with several other consulars, earning him the distinction of being the first magistrate to have his head hung up on the rostra. The suffect consul Lucius Valerius Flaccus, sent to fight the First Mithridatic War by the Marians, was betrayed by his subordinate Gaius Flavius Fimbria and murdered. Fimbria got his just deserts when his troops later abandoned him, prompting his suicide. Marius' fellow consul Cinna was stoned to death in the middle of a mutiny by his troops.[34] Far from controlling the legions as client armies, Roman commanders were at their mercy.

At a time when republican soldiers were being given conflicting information about who was legitimate, any commander became fair game for desertion, betrayal, or assassination if he behaved incompetently or failed to look out for their interests. In order for Rome's civic militarism to avoid hastening the republic's demise, the constitution and its political authorities needed to restore concord and resume normal operations. Could the republic be saved? Or was it doomed for more disaster?

THE NONIDEAL OF POMPEY, CRASSUS, AND CAESAR

The constitutional tweaking came from an unlikely source: Sulla. Sulla managed to survive the chaos of his civil war through a felicitous combination of diplomacy, military success, well-placed bribes, and lavish rewards for his troops. Nonetheless, he saw in his own position something to be avoided and seemed to justify his own actions on the grounds that the circumstances warranted it. After forcing his appointment as dictator, he was able to establish a broad spectrum of measures that adjusted the constitution for Rome's empire. The cursus honorum was standardized. The senate was enlarged and restored as the preeminent deliberative, diplomatic, judicial, and foreign policy arm of the state. Tribunes, so often the spark for constitutional crisis, had their powers greatly curbed. Most importantly, Sulla sought to remedy the growing problem of provincial administration. More magistrates were created to regularize provincial governors and their subordinates. The military and diplomatic activities of these provincial governors were also heavily regulated. Old governors were to depart their province within thirty days, and new governors could not "leave their province, wage war, or enter an allied kingdom" without authorization.[35] The question, as it had been with the Gracchi, was whether his reasonable reforms would outweigh his unreasonable violation of Roman customs. Commanders had repeatedly used military force to gain control of the city, and that broken precedent did not bode well for the republic's future.[36]

Despite all expectations, the years following Sulla saw a return to normalcy. It was a new normalcy, but it held. At Sulla's death in 78, an insurrection involving the consul Lepidus and a rebel state in Spain led by the commander Sertorius suggested that the constitution was doomed and chaos would resume. Instead, Rome's varied political factions banded together and both rebellions were trounced. By the end of the 70s, Romans had begun tweaking Sulla's constitutional reforms as confidence grew in the system. The senatorial aristocracy and new senators elevated to power by Sulla worked hard to maintain the republic, and politics began to resume. Factions developed, alliances were forged and broken, individuals (often called *populares*) once again took up popular causes like grain and land laws and were resisted by others preferring senatorial dominance (often referred to as *optimates*). A new generation of political leaders rose to fame in a world that seemed relatively secure.[37]

Pompey (anglicized from Gnaeus Pompeius), the son of Pompeius Strabo, earned prestige in the traditional manner: through conquest. Pompey and Cicero were born in the same year, and the two probably met while serving under the former's father during the Social War. Unlike Cicero, Pompey thirsted for a quick rise to power and was not squeamish about violence. After Strabo's death Pompey raised legions from among his father's veterans to help Sulla win the civil war. His brutality in these early wars earned him the title *adulescens carnifex*, the young butcher. The term came from a vivid anecdote recounted by Valerius Maximus in which a man imagined he had visited the underworld where the bloodstained and distinguished victims of Pompey cursed his illegal and immoral savagery in the civil war (6.2.8).

Sulla humorously gave him another title: *magnus*, "the great" (Plutarch, *Pompey*, 13). By the time of Cicero's consulship in 63, he had earned it. Over the course of twenty years he put down the revolt of Lepidus, defeated Sertorius in Spain, mopped up slaves defeated by Crassus in the Third Servile War, cleared the Mediterranean of pirates, defeated Mithridates in the Third Mithridatic War, and ended two dynasties, the Seleucids and the Hasmoneans. To be sure, others played an important role in all of these endeavors, but Pompey proved himself to be a capable and ruthless general. More importantly, he was an administrative genius with few, if any, parallels. Pompey had been given a number of exceptional commands to achieve these victories, several of which were passed through the popular assemblies instead of the senate. The Lex Gabinia and Lex Manilia, for example, allowed him to delegate imperium and bestowed enormous provincial jurisdiction and resources on him.[38] Despite Sulla's legislative precautions, Pompey had burst out of constitutional constraints, and he might have the opportunity to seize Rome when he returned.

This opportunity presented itself during Cicero's consulship in 63 when another conspiracy was mounted by the senator Catilina, who threatened to kill the senators and seize the state. Using his oratory, Cicero acted decisively to unite his allies and crush the conspiracy in the city. True to form, he left it to others to defeat Catilina in the field. In the wake of the conspiracy, it was understandable that Cicero and Cato, another conservative, did not want Pompey returning to a destabilized Rome at the head of an enormous and triumphant army. Swift action prevented this. Catilina had been defeated and the conspirators done away with. Pompey returned to a peaceful Rome and disbanded most of his army so that he could celebrate a triumph. His third tri-

umph was a magnificent two-day affair that celebrated fifteen countries pacified, thirty-nine cities founded, a thousand strongholds captured, and the doubling of the Roman treasury (Plutarch, *Pompey*, 45).[39]
It seemed that Pompey was far more interested in making his way to
the head of the senatorial aristocracy, albeit in an unconventional manner, than grasping control of the state.

As dangerous as Pompey was, there were other individuals even
less concerned about following the rules. Crassus and Caesar, two
men who had possibly been behind Catilina's plot in its early stages,
sought to dominate the senatorial aristocracy rather than lead it. Crassus and Pompey had been old enemies, but Caesar convinced the two
men that it was in their best interests to join forces. Like other political
factions of the day, the three men brought their resources together.
The power of this alliance, however, outweighed all the other factions
in Roman politics, at least temporarily. Their alliance has been fan-
cifully labeled the "first triumvirate," a term that is problematic but
entrenched.[40]

In early 59, Caesar, who had been elected consul, tried to bring Cicero into the alliance. Cicero seriously considered the matter, remarking to his friend Atticus that joining it would bring an "intimate association with Pompey, with Caesar too[,] . . . reconciliation with my
enemies, peace with the populace, tranquility in my old age." However,
Cicero recalled his own belief in the leadership of a virtuous aristocracy as opposed to one composed of ambitious and vicious men. He
resolved to decline the offer and "fight for fatherland" (*Atticus*, 23). The
three did not take the rejection well, and Cicero was punished shortly
thereafter with exile on the grounds that he should not have executed
the Catilinarian conspirators.[41] Cato and his allies also needed to be
dealt a blow, so the gang of three engineered for Cato to be given an
assignment in Cyprus. Other factions, of course, remained powerful
forces in Roman politics, but in the first years of their alliance, Caesar,
Pompey, and Crassus brushed opponents aside and successfully pushed
through most of their agenda.[42]

The formation of such an alliance, which was a normal feature in
Rome, was no threat to republican politics. However, Caesar's and his

allies' continued use of mob violence to achieve their ends demonstrated two things: normal politics alone was not enough to achieve the aims of the gang of three, and the three men, and especially Caesar, were willing to imperil the republic for their own personal gain. Cicero had been right to see their actions as a threat to the republic and the ideals it was supposed to represent.

Military command was at the top of the gang of three's list. During Caesar's consulship, political violence resurfaced, cowing his fellow consul Marcus Calpurnius Bibulus, who was attacked with a bucket of dung when he tried to obstruct Caesar. Caesar used a tribunician law passed through violence to award himself a five-year command in Cisalpine Gaul and Illyricum. In April of 56 Caesar, Crassus, and Pompey renewed their alliance in a meeting at Luca. In attendance were no less than 120 senators that were their supporters and clients, a testament to how the political factions of the three men managed to control the republican system. In 55 Pompey and Crassus held the consulship. Once again, they had resorted to violence to win the elections. A supporter of Cato was killed, and Cato himself was wounded. When a similar incident occurred the next year, even Pompey returned home with blood on his toga. With their offices secured, the three arranged for their own commands. Pompey was assigned Spain, and Crassus was assigned Syria. Whereas Pompey saw no need for further military glories and governed Spain through legates, Crassus needed victories to rival his partners, so he unjustifiably launched a campaign against Parthia. It ended in disaster, with Crassus and his son getting killed in 53.

THE SOLDIERS OF CAESAR

Meanwhile, Caesar was establishing his own reputation in Gaul as a great conqueror. When Caesar entered his assigned province in 58, he opened up a series of campaigns in modern-day France that became known as the greatest and quickest conquest in Roman history. Caesar recounted his own adventures there in a seven-book commentary that is still widely read today.[43] Despite his tendency to justify and romanticize his actions with his disarming, simple style, Caesar's Gallic campaigns were an atrocity that had few, if any, parallels in Roman history.

Caesar accumulated a remarkable amount of plunder and prestige during his nine-year conquest of Gaul. More importantly, he spent a decade amassing an enormous army that slowly became the most disciplined and capable fighting machine in the Mediterranean world. In 59, he was in control of four legions: the Seventh, Eighth, Ninth, and Tenth. The Eleventh and Twelfth were added in 58, the Thirteenth and Fourteenth in 57, Fifteenth and First in 53, and then the Fifth and Sixth by 51, raising his total number to twelve legions.[44] Even taking into account battle casualties and other losses, the acquisition of these legions represented an enormous growth in power. And unlike Pompey in the 60s, he had no intention of laying down this army and returning to the status of an ordinary citizen.

Caesar was in command of the most technically and tactically proficient force Rome had ever fielded, whose legions were becoming more and more permanent, some having served under him for nearly a decade. These legions began developing their own identities and the unremitting loyalty of their soldiers. Not only did Caesar field the finest infantrymen in the Mediterranean, but many of them had become specialists in siegeworks, engineering, sapping, artillery, the manipulation of terrain, and psychological warfare. The details of Caesar's extraordinary use of these talented troops at the two great sieges at Avaricum and Alesia in 52, for example, still fill military textbooks to this day. They showcased his ability to defeat an enemy deep within foreign territory despite being outnumbered by as much as four to one.

Caesar has earned a sterling reputation among many students of military history for his daring, camaraderie with the troops, ability to inspire confidence and loyalty, tactical genius, and strategic foresight. There is no question that Caesar was one of the finest generals Rome ever produced, but he was no republican. Instead, he is better compared to Philip, Pyrrhus, Hannibal, and other conquerors in the Hellenistic mold. He deserves his place in history alongside other great generals like Cyrus, Alexander, Attila, Genghis Khan, Cortés, and Napoleon, but like them, he was nothing short of a monster.

Caesar's conquests added two hundred thousand square miles to Roman territory, but the cost was a staggering 1,192,000 Gauls he claimed to have killed.[45] His military policy was genocidal, a fact even noted in the ancient world. After hearing how Caesar had massacred 430,000 Germans in 55, which included fleeing women and children that he sent his cavalry to hunt down, Cato recommended that Caesar ought to be ritually delivered to the Germans to atone for his crimes (*Gallic War*, 4.14–15; Plutarch, *Caesar*, 22). Those scholars who see Caesar's methods and his accumulation of prestige, loyal soldiers, and wealth in this decade as the doom of the republic are not without warrant.[46]

As Caesar was achieving greatness in Gaul, Cicero was languishing in exile and exclusion. His exile devastated him, and he returned in 57 to a radically altered set of alignments. Cicero initially attempted to oppose some of their efforts and drive a wedge in the alliance, but eventually he gave in to his sense of obligation to Pompey, to whom he believed he was bound by *amicitia*, the Roman notion of friendship. His ties to Caesar would also increase during this period, with Caesar loaning him eight hundred thousand sesterces and his brother Quintus serving under Caesar in Gaul. He took up the causes of the gang of three and defended several of their allies. Despite his personal disagreement and previous opposition, in 56 he publicly supported Caesar's renewal of command in Gaul in his speech *On the Consular Provinces*. The speech is an early formulation of Cicero's just war theory, arguing that Roman intervention in Gaul was warranted because it served to protect a perennially dangerous frontier and finally bring peace to a wild and lawless land. All the same Cicero was twisting the facts and whitewashing Caesar's moral and constitutional improprieties.[47]

This was Cicero at his most pathetic, and he occasionally indulged in bouts of self-loathing. In a letter to Atticus, the ever-humorous Cicero quipped that he had been "a complete ass." "But now it's time for me to love myself since they won't love me whatever I do" (*Atticus*, 80). Even his oratory failed him. In 52 his defense of his friend Milo collapsed in public. He was so intimidated by Pompey and the Roman mob that he scurried off after a sorry performance.[48] If Caesar could use his resources and prestige to guide the behavior of republican idealists such as Cicero, consider how easy it must have been for him to sway the average citizen, especially those bearing arms under his command. Caesar had already secured land for Pompey's veterans against senatorial opposition, and now he asked those men that had fought alongside him for years in Gaul to remain loyal as he rescued his personal vision of the republic. These men were not the republic's to command. They were Caesar's.[49]

As for Cicero, his descent into ignominy forced him to write more. It was during this time that he started crafting many of his greatest works on republican philosophy, starting with *On the Republic* and *On the Laws*. Ever the pragmatist, Cicero used philosophy to figure out what to do with his life and what to do with Roman politics. Through his writings he came to the conclusion that the leader Rome needed was one whose chief virtues were *sapientia, prudentia*, and *auctoritas*. *Sapientia*, or wisdom, was earned through the study of philosophy and a proper reflection on one's experience. *Prudentia* was achieved through a "traditional Roman education" and by focusing on the great exemplars of Roman history: men such as Fabius Maximus, Scipio Africanus, and Aemilianus. *Auctoritas* resulted from the inherently moral man behaving in accordance with accepted norms. In politics, this meant a man was only good if he behaved justly and constitutionally.[50] Armed with these things, a man could rise above petty politics, determine what the common good required, and then unify his fellow citizens in achieving it.

Cicero was desperately seeking to discover what contemporary leader held these qualities or could at least be shaped by them. Caesar and Pompey were great conquerors and shrewd political operators, but their lives were hardly manifestations of these virtues. Yet circumstances were about to force Cicero to choose between them.

In 51 Cicero was pulled out of retirement and forced to serve as governor of Cilicia. Pompey, who was celebrating his third consulship, had passed a new law mandating a delay between holding office and assuming provincial governorships. The law, Lex Pompeia de magistratibus, was a very good one, and it testified to a genuine attempt to continue adapting the constitution in order to rein in the abuses of provincial governors.[51] Whether intended to or not, the law also sparked a challenge to Caesar and threatened to sever the alliance between the two surviving members of their pact. In the late 50s Pompey had attempted a delicate balancing act of working his way back into the good graces of the senatorial aristocracy while still maintaining his alliance with Caesar. Caesar, however, continued to demand exceptions in his attempt to maintain imperium. Their alliance held together until late 50, when Pompey finally sided with the hardliners in the senate. Caesar was isolated and thus forced to choose between following law and precedence or pursuing his own prestige regardless of the damage it inflicted on his fellow citizens and the republic. Prestige and ambition won out, of course.[52]

From the start Cicero had boxed himself into an impossible position. Neither Pompey nor Caesar fit the man of his musings. They were not a contemporary Africanus or Aemilianus who could unite the citizens of Rome, lead its citizen-soldiers in battle, and rescue the republic. Cicero first leaned toward Pompey, but when Pompey abandoned Italy and fled to the East, Cicero could not forgive him. He lingered in Italy and watched Caesar seize the state by force. In a strong testament to how different the loyalties of Caesar's junior officers were from Sulla's, only one of them, Titus Labienus, refused to march on Rome. By contrast, all but one of Sulla's officers had deserted him when he did the deed in 88.[53]

Cicero wrestled with Caesar's temporary subjugation of Italy, which he foresaw would lead to an unquestioned dominance of the empire. In March he wrote to Atticus as he considered a course of action:

Ought a man to remain in his country under a despotism? Ought he strive for the overthrow of a despotism by every means, even if the existence of the state is going to be endangered thereby? Ought he to beware of the overthrower lest *he* be set up as a despot? Ought he to try to help his country under a despotism by taking opportunity as it comes and by words rather than by war? Ought a man to enroll himself on the side of the best citizens even if he does not approve of overthrowing the despotism by war? (*Atticus*, 173)

Cicero did not approve of any of the commanders in the civil war, and the letter's last question to Atticus hints at a desire to avoid the whole conflict: "May he be allowed to begin to think of himself and his family, giving up political opposition to those in power?"

This struggle intensified in the coming months. Pompey and Caesar both requested that Cicero join their side. Caesar even paid him a visit, asking for oratorical support so the senate would grant him funds to prosecute the war. Cicero refused, and Caesar seized the treasury in the Temple of Saturn anyway. Eventually Cicero earned the ire of Caesar and his two most valued officers, Lepidus and Antony, when he finally opted for Pompey and made his way to Greece. When he arrived, the Pompeians were annoyed as well. What good was an old man with no military prowess, drifting around making cracks about the indecisiveness and unpreparedness of Pompey's forces?

Cicero was right to mock, for Caesar crossed to Greece and soundly defeated Pompey at the Battle of Pharsalus, despite the fact that Pompey enjoyed an overwhelming numerical superiority. Diehards like Cato pledged to keep fighting, which they did until they were all defeated or dead. Cicero and Marcus Junius Brutus, on the other hand, sought Caesar's mercy, which was granted. Brutus' motives in doing so are obscure to this day. Cicero, on the other hand, simply gave up hope for the republic and sailed back home to enjoy retirement in the coming autocracy's new "peace." Pompey himself sailed for Egypt but was assassinated there by his former allies, who hoped to ingratiate themselves to Caesar. In this they misjudged, for Caesar had the assassins executed for murdering his old friend.[54]

After Pompey's death Caesar campaigned in Egypt and the East in 48–47, before crushing the final republican resistance in Africa in 46 and Spain in 45. His soldiers and officers were the best in the empire, fighting under the most talented commander. They proved to be an unstoppable force in deciding who would be accorded legitimacy in what was left of the republic.

Caesar's armies from 59 to 45 demonstrated a critical flaw that had developed in the constitution. The Roman state and the senatorial aristocracy in particular were not looking after its citizen-soldiers. This was particularly dangerous at the beginning and end of the 50s, when well-trained, battle-tested veterans returned home behind exceptionally capable generals. In 59 Caesar had pushed through legislation granting land for Pompey's veterans in Italy. The gang of three never would have been able to form if the republic had taken care of Pompey's veterans immediately. In 50 the tribune Curio, ostensibly in agreement with Caesar, was working to pass another agrarian law for Caesar's veterans. Throughout his campaigns in Gaul, Caesar made sure to enrich his troops with booty, and as the conflict loomed in 50, he rewarded them with even more and then increased their pay.

When the civil war opened, Pompey and the republicans were able to muster large armies of citizen-soldiers, far more than Caesar, in fact. But they did not have the best soldiers. Caesar's veterans from the Gallic Wars, including many *homines militares*, had received little support from the state, and it suited them to follow him more than the republic. This was a colossal error the republic had obstinately refused to remedy, even though events since the Gracchi taught that lesson time and again. The best fighting men in the Mediterranean required more of the republic than it was offering them. It was not enough to levy citizens. They needed to be equipped, trained, and disciplined before they fought. And when they fought, they expected to be led by competent, inspiring commanders. What followed battle was just as important. They needed to be rewarded with spoils and guaranteed a future when they returned. Only then would they be fully incorporated back into the state and only then could they function as good citizens. In this the republic had failed them. Since the Gracchi it had too often been apparent that the strongest advocates for veterans were politicians operating on the fringe of acceptable political norms. To Caesar's men, he may not have been the ideal statesman, but that was for philosophers to worry about. All that mattered to them was that he was *their* ideal commander.

Still, not all of Caesar's soldiers felt this way. Take, for example,

Titus Labienus. Hailing from Picenum, he very likely enjoyed the early patronage of Pompey. He served in Cilicia in the 70s, where he might have met Caesar briefly, but he probably earned his illustrious military background under Pompey in the 60s, after which he worked with Pompey's agents in Rome as a tribune of the plebs. He then served as a legate with Caesar in Gaul in the 50s, earning further distinctions and possibly even intending to run with Caesar for the consulship in 48. This, of course, never occurred because Caesar decided to attack the republic, which prompted Labienus to leave Caesar and support Pompey. This earned him the enmity of Caesar, who characterized him as a hotheaded warmonger in his *Civil War*. This characterization may not be far off given that Dio cites Labienus' motives as envy, ambition, and wounded pride, and Plutarch marks him as a violator of friendship. On the other hand, Cicero describes him as a model for others, one who preferred justice to Caesar. Cicero also appreciated that Labienus inspired a flagging cause.[55]

All are agreed that Labienus was a *homo militaris*, but scholars disagree on his motives for parting with Caesar. Some follow the meager hints of the ancient historians, citing personal flaws and grievances that caused him to desert his friend. The opposite view, following Cicero, sees Labienus as a defender of the legitimate government. A moderate stance argues that his loyalties lay with that other great conqueror and member of the gang, Pompey. This view sees Labienus as a client of Pompey and primarily motivated by the old traditional mores of "*fides* and *amicitia*." He died for the republic, but only because he was personally allied to Pompey, whose cause in the civil war happened to be the republic. Any of these views could be true, and perhaps all of them to a degree.[56]

Labienus can be seen as representing a crucial portion of the fighting men whose allegiance was up for grabs and motives were hard to pin down. They had their own backgrounds, ambitions, interpersonal alliances, and ideas of what was right and wrong, legitimate and illegitimate. Citizen-soldiers of the empire were critical to success but often unpredictable; they did not engage in as much strategic forethought as is often imagined today. Pompey himself waited until the final hour to abandon Caesar, and vice versa. Cicero lingered in indecision between Caesar and Pompey for months. In the same way, many—including possibly Caesar—were surprised by Labienus' "desertion." It could be difficult to predict how far a military man like Labienus, "with no delusions about war and apparently without thought for the aftermath of victory," could be pushed.[57] As individuals, such men would not decide the republic's fate, but they would follow and be used by stronger personalities with clearer and broader objectives.

In the final battle of the Pompeian civil war, Labienus faced off against Caesar at Munda. Caesar was nearing defeat and had been forced to shame his soldiers by rushing into the fray, shouting "This shall be the end of my life and of your military service," as if the two were of equal value (Appian, *Civil Wars*, 2.104). Ironically, Caesar might have lost the battle had not a maneuver by Labienus been misinterpreted by his troops as a retreat, which caused the Pompeian forces to crack. The battle was finally ended with the slaughter of tens of thousands of soldiers loyal to the republic, including Labienus.

Even after the civil war, this republican manpower base was still vast. Many potential threats had been eliminated, but the suicides of Cato, Metellus Scipio, and Marcus Petreius—who preferred death over Caesar's clemency—galvanized those who survived under Caesar's domination. One was Brutus. Another was Gaius Cassius Longinus. Unlike the case of Labienus, the motives animating their decisions were known and would be preserved in historical texts.

Caesar miscalculated if he believed republican sentiment had been totally quashed and the citizen body as a whole was ready for one-man rule. He had killed or cowed most of the old senatorial elite, but many committed republicans simmered beneath the surface. And what about "the people"? Caesar assiduously cultivated his image among them, surpassing all of his rivals in an age when widespread gift giving (or bribery?) and championing popular causes could not be avoided by anyone. From the proverbial "bread and circuses" to settling veterans, restoring the rights of estranged citizens, showing mercy to his enemies, building public works, and reforming the calendar, Caesar benefited and manipulated the people. Some scholars see his actions, especially from 49 onward, as angling toward monarchy. Others see him as merely outdoing all previous Roman statesmen. Either way it would have been impossible for the old senators who had survived, the new senators he had appointed, or even the people not to have noticed that Caesar was making Rome something different than it had been.[58]

In fact it is not entirely certain what Caesar thought would happen when he emerged as the victor. His true vision for the future—impossible for us to understand today—eluded his contemporaries, creating an opportunity for others to manipulate public opinion. Enter Cassius and Brutus. Many of Caesar's former officers—now magistrates such as praetors and provincial governors—grew leery of the assumption of republican powers into his own autocratic hands. "His officers and legates were drawn from lesser senatorial families, the municipal aristocracy, and the equestrian class." Even before the civil war, they "were not men eager to destroy the existing order."[59] On the Ides of March, several days before his departure for a grand campaign against Parthia, Cassius and Brutus convinced a group of these men to assassinate him.

THE STRUGGLE FOR LEGITIMACY

For the period between the assassination of Caesar in March 44 and the aftermath of the Battle of Mutina in the late summer of 43, there is an enormous amount of information available that allows us to understand the motives, maneuvers, and machinations of those involved in the flurry of activity following Caesar's assassination. Not only do we have historical writings about this period from Appian, Dio, and Plutarch, but we also have several volumes of correspondence to and from Cicero. From these sources taken together, it is possible to get a very well-rounded picture of the events and remarkably acute insights about the personal feelings and decisions of a number of the key men involved.[60]

The months following the assassination could have immediately launched another round of civil wars, but, despite some initial rioting stirred up in part by Lepidus on 16 and 17 March, an uneasy peace was established between the liberators and those devoted to Caesar. Many scholars see this peace as inevitably transitory, but it is also reasonable to see the following years as one final bid to restore the republic, if not through constitutional means, then at least through force of arms.[61] Perhaps peace was indeed transitory, but the efforts of the republicans in 44 and 43 indicate that the fall of the republic was far from inevitable when the new consuls took office in 43.

As in the Sullan-Marian civil war, and to a certain extent, the Pompeian-Caesarian civil war, legitimacy was again in question. Scholars have been divided over whether the troops determined the commanders' decisions or the leaders coerced the troops, but it went both ways, and as I have demonstrated, this was in keeping with the long-standing traditions of commanding magistrates and empowering citizen-soldiers. An additional fact is clear: among Caesar's veterans and any troops that were yet unpaid or unsettled based on his pledges, his legacy loomed large. His Gallic War veterans—including many of his officers (of which Sulla could not boast)—were especially devoted to him. For these men, Caesar *and his acts* were legitimate. He must be avenged, and his deeds must be upheld.[62]

It is possible, however, to overemphasize the decisions of the troops. Rome was a republic, constitutionally until 43 and with military structures lingering in the East into 42. Even after his death, Caesar represented an idea: this republic was no longer necessary. When he perished, there were those eager to assume his autocratic mantle. But they would have to fight for it. The letters, orations, and tracts Cicero wrote and the speeches we have been provided for Brutus and Cassius give us the republican alternative. They were the last great lyrics of the republic, singing the praises of the republican way of life and beckoning men to once again lay down their lives for more than money, land, or power. These last three years forced all the important men of the republic to be "great" in the mold of Caesar or "good" in the mold of Cicero's ideal statesman. This final civil war thus became a titanic struggle, and only one side would survive because the other side would perish in a bloodbath of those important men who resisted. And, in a last great testament to the republic, there would be tens of thousands of citizen-soldiers more willing to die for a republic than live for an autocrat.

The Commanders and Their Loyalties

After Caesar was assassinated, there were essentially three factions in Rome.[63] First, there were the supporters of the "liberators" who had assassinated Caesar and desired a return to republican politics. They were opposed by radical Caesarians that sought the liberators' immediate destruction and stood to gain little with the return to a functioning republic. Chief among these were Caesar's aides, but certain powerful lieutenants of the dead dictator were also among the radical Caesarians. Moderate Caesarians lay somewhere in between these two.

These factions were by no means fixed but could shift based on the circumstances and the relationships between the men who composed them. They developed over the course of 44, and two crucial questions emerged. First was whether the moderates would support the memory of Caesar by seeking revenge on the assassins and renewing the dominance of an individual or whether they would support a return to the republican constitution. The second question was where the numerous legions dotted throughout the empire stood. These armies needed commanders, but who would lead them, and where would their loyalties lie? Would the citizen-soldiers in the ranks follow those loyalties or act independently? Cicero considered these questions as he surveyed the political scene from the sidelines.

A description of the commanders of importance surrounding the Battle of Mutina allows us to understand who the men were in these factions and what motivated them. It also enlightens us as to how Cicero assessed his political battleground and formed his strategy for a last grand alliance that, in his mind at least, would save the republic or perish in the attempt.

Many of the liberators had supported Caesar at some point during the civil wars, which is why so many of them were well placed after his death. Brutus and Cassius were the most famous assassins, but Decimus Brutus and Trebonius were also important commanders in 44. Brutus was the *praetor urbanus* and Cassius was *praetor peregrinus*. Cassius spearheaded the conspiracy to assassinate Caesar, but Brutus' greater reputation made him the leader. The two held the most prestigious

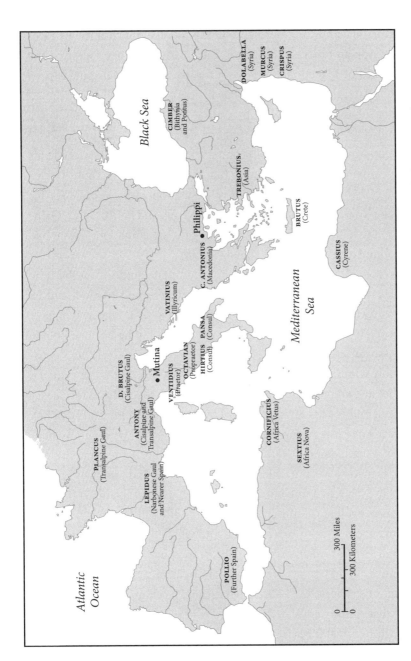

Key commanders in the Roman Empire during the Mutina campaign and its aftermath (late 44–42 BC)

Atlantic Ocean

Black Sea

Mediterranean Sea

DOLABELLA (Syria)
MURCUS (Syria)
CRISPUS (Syria)
CIMBER (Bithynia and Pontus)
TREBONIUS (Asia)
BRUTUS (Crete)
CASSIUS (Cyrene)
C. ANTONIUS (Macedonia)
● Philippi
VATINIUS (Illyricum)
PANSA (Consul)
HIRTIUS (Consul)
OCTAVIAN (Propraetor)
VENTIDIUS (Praetor)
● Mutina
D. BRUTUS (Cisalpine Gaul)
ANTONY (Cisalpine and Transalpine Gaul)
PLANCUS (Transalpine Gaul)
LEPIDUS (Narbonese Gaul and Nearer Spain)
CORNIFICIUS (Africa Vetus)
SEXTIUS (Africa Nova)
POLLIO (Further Spain)

300 Miles
0
300 Kilometers
0

praetorships and thus were among the more significant magistrates in 44. Appian reports that Brutus and Cassius had been allotted the provinces of Macedonia and Syria for 43, but this is disputed (*Civil Wars*, 3.8, 12, 16).[64] Decimus Junius Brutus Albinus had been assigned proconsul of Cisalpine Gaul by Caesar for 44 and had been given a consulship for 42. Brutus had fought for Caesar in Gaul, and his close relationship with Caesar, being named one of Caesar's heirs, made his involvement in the assassination that much more remarkable. Lucius Tillius Cimber initiated Caesar's assassination with a request for his brother's pardon and was governor of Bithynia and Pontus in 44. Gaius Trebonius had lured Antony away during the assassination. Caesar had appointed him as proconsul in Asia for 44.

As consul, Antony was the leading legitimate authority at the time of Caesar's death. Antony inherited a very delicate situation, and he was lucky that Brutus prevented him from being assassinated alongside Caesar. He descended from a consular family, but he became known for associating with Roman lowlifes, drinking excessively, and occasionally vomiting in public (Plutarch, *Antony*, 4.9). He was a soldier's soldier and enjoyed a fine military reputation, especially under Caesar in Gaul and for his famous victory over Pompey in Pharsalus. When Caesar was prosecuting the second half of the civil war, Antony bungled the management of Italy when he was left in charge. Nonetheless, he was made Caesar's consular colleague in 44 and famously offered Caesar a diadem at the Lupercalia festival, which galvanized the conspirators against Caesar and Antony. It is difficult to ascertain which claims about Antony are accurate and which are mere slander. The overall picture is of an exceptionally competent military man who, like a number of aristocrats of his generation, disregarded certain Roman mores and proprieties. Politically, he could be clumsy, but it cannot be said that Antony consistently angled for the republic's overthrow, although circumstances might push him in that direction.

Marcus Aemilius Lepidus was Caesar's master of horse until the latter's dictatorship was ended with his assassination. Like Antony he descended from a consular family, but his father had fallen into disrepute when he militated against Sulla's reforms, even unsuccessfully leading an army against Rome in 78. Lepidus nonetheless secured the praetorship by 49. He supported Caesar during the civil war and then served as consul with Caesar in 46. Lepidus had entertained Caesar the night before his assassination, and immediately afterward, he used his troops to restore order and buttress Antony's authority. After reaching an equilibrium with the assassins, he was sent to deal with Pompey's son, who was still causing trouble in Spain. In 43 Lepidus commanded legions as a proconsul in Narbonese Gaul and Hither Spain.

Antony and Lepidus, like Caesar, were born into the senatorial club, making it easier for them to earn distinction there than outsiders like Marius, Cicero, and, to a certain extent, even Pompey. Like Caesar, their actions before the Mutina campaign can be interpreted as manifesting a general disdain or disregard for the old order and an ambitious desire to follow the kind of example Caesar had set. Throughout 44, opinion shifted as to whether they supported a return to republican government or the establishment of a tyrant in its place. Their objectives are unclear to us for much of 44. On the one hand, they may have initially been interested in a compromise with the liberators. On the other hand, they could have simply been biding their time until either or both of them could make their own bid to seize autocratic power. Antony's activities in 44, spurred on in no small part by Octavian, increasingly hinted that he intended to marshal the political, military, and financial resources of Caesar against the liberators. At least that's what the liberators believed.

Publius Ventidius Bassus was a Roman *homo militaris* from Picenum. Like Marius and Cicero, he came from a distinguished local family that was otherwise unknown to Roman politics. As a boy he had walked as a prisoner in the triumph of Pompey's father. The experience was probably one of the formative events that prompted his career as a military man. Ventidius fought under Caesar in Gaul and was raised to the Roman senate in 47. Praetor in 43, Ventidius was devoted to Caesar's memory and would prove to be a valuable asset to Marc Antony.

Two other men who made a name for themselves under Caesar were Quintus Cornificius and Titus Sextius. Cornificius had served under Caesar in the Pompeian civil war, receiving several important assignments in the eastern Mediterranean. Caesar probably appointed him as governor of Africa Vetus, where he remained in command in 43. Sextius governed Africa Nova at this time and had a similar background as Cornificius, except that Sextius had also served under Caesar in the Gallic Wars. This difference was probably what motivated them to pick different sides in the coming conflict.

The incoming consuls for 43, Gaius Vibius Pansa and Aulus Hirtius, had served under Caesar in Gaul and throughout the civil wars. As the consuls for 43, their loyalties represented the best hope for the survival of the republic. If they kept peace with the liberators and placated Caesar's most devoted partisans, it could reasonably be assumed that the republic had a chance. If, on the other hand, they sought punishment for the assassins or estranged too many in Caesar's old following, civil war would likely follow. Gaius Asinius Pollio and Lucius Munatius Plancus served with Caesar during the civil wars and would emerge as important, moderate Caesarians during the Mutina campaign. Pollio had been appointed governor of Farther Spain for 44, a position he held at the beginning of 43. Plancus was appointed proconsul of Transalpine Gaul by Caesar for 44, a position he held into 43. These four men had earned their military reputations and political standing under Caesar. However, it could be in their interest to see their positions maintained in a restored republican order. They found themselves caught between the liberators and those that believed the liberators should be handed the same fate they had dealt Caesar. Many of them cherished his memory but had little desire to see the republic thrown into another civil war so that he could be replaced by a warlord in his mold.[65]

Tyranny or Liberty, Peace or War?

The liberators took no decisive action after killing Caesar, prompting Antony to call in Caesar's master of horse, Lepidus, to occupy the Forum with troops. Antony then went to Caesar's widow Calpurnia and took charge of his personal papers and finances. This was a shrewd maneuver that could have been thwarted if he had been dispatched with Caesar or if the liberators had acted more comprehensively. At first, however, delicate negotiations on the part of Antony and the liberators seem to grant a glimmer of hope for peace. Cicero was one of the leading consulars still alive in Rome, and he helped patch together a legislative compromise between the two sides. Antony formally accommodated this in the senate meeting on 17 March. Publius Cornelius Dolabella, already slated to replace Caesar when he departed for Parthia, was immediately raised to the consulship. Caesar's assassins were to be pardoned, but Caesar's acts were to remain in place. Dolabella was later assigned Syria as his province and Antony Macedonia.

The funeral of Caesar threatened to fracture this fragile state of affairs. Brutus had already given a tepid speech after the assassination, and the Roman mob, who greatly loved Caesar with his lavish gifts and games that benefited the populace, forced the liberators to retreat to the Capitoline. On the day of the funeral, 20 March, after a number of stirring speeches and the reading of Caesar's will, in which Caesar bequeathed benefits to the Roman poor, a riot erupted. Still, the peace held. Brutus and Cassius had to flee Rome, but Antony made several crucial gestures on their behalf. Brutus' flight was granted legality, despite the fact that he was the urban praetor. A law was also passed abolishing the dictatorship.

Nonetheless, some of the key Caesarians hankered for an all-out fight. Cicero wrote to Atticus that Gaius Matius and Lepidus were in this camp. They rattled their sabers and opined that "no one could find a way out" and "Rome was finished." They seemed determined to escalate the dispute into armed conflict or at least to seek punishment for the assassins, believing that it could not "all just pass quietly off" (*Atticus*, 355). Yet Antony did not seem disposed to a conflict. Cicero joked that he was "more concerned about the composition of his menus than about planning any mischief" (*Atticus*, 357). He was even on good terms with Brutus (*Atticus*, 362).

Up to this point, everything seemed to indicate that the truce would be maintained. If it could hold, the constitution would hold up with it and the republic had a chance for normality. Cicero's letters attest to this much. He vacillated between begrudging acknowledgment that

Antony was behaving himself and wishing that more could be done to smear or erase Caesar's legacy. He thought the liberators should have taken more decisive action after the Ides, but he also dedicated time to writing philosophy, handling his finances, and planning a trip to Greece. It seemed like the republic would make it.

But then Octavian entered the picture. Octavian was the son of Gaius Octavius and Caesar's niece Atia, making him the great-nephew of Julius Caesar. For reasons that are unclear, Caesar bequeathed him the majority of his estate and formally adopted him on his death, whereupon his name became Gaius Julius Caesar Octavianus (Octavian being the anglicized version of his name). In mid-44, when Octavian entered the scene in which this delicate state of affairs prevailed, a series of at times farcical events took place that reshaped the political scene.[66]

Octavian arrived at Brundisium, where he attracted a number of Caesar's veterans to his support. He had collected more soldiers by the time he reached Rome in May. A meeting between Antony and Octavian went very badly, causing many to fear that war would descend on Rome. Appian remarks how most Romans were alarmed because they were uncertain of the obscure Octavian and fearful that Antony would co-opt the young heir "and grasp the sovereignty held by the elder Caesar." Others—and surely Appian is thinking of the liberators—"were delighted with the present state of affairs, believing that the two men would come into conflict with one another" (*Civil Wars*, 3.21). The fears and hopes of all seemed confirmed by upcoming events.

Cicero documented Octavian's entrance onto the scene in April. Octavian immediately began to court his support, but Cicero was wary of Caesar's heir, remarking that "he cannot be a good citizen. There are too many around him. They threaten death to our friends and call the present state of things intolerable" (*Atticus*, 359, 364, 365, 366). Despite Octavian's overtures, Cicero remained skeptical. By June he still doubted Octavian's motives: "But how much faith to put in one of his years and name and heredity and education—that's a great question" (*Atticus*, 390).

The liberators' chief problem in 44 was that, unlike Antony and Octavian, they did not have ready access to the citizen-soldiers of Rome.

Cicero quipped, "What remains to do needs men and money, and we have none" (*Atticus*, 358). The Caesarians, on the other hand, controlled the armies, as Cicero also observed: "You see the tyrant's lieutenants in their commands, you see his armies, you see the veterans on our flank" (*Atticus,* 359, 368). There was also a dearth of leadership. So many of the "good men," whether they leaned toward the moderates or the liberators, desired to stay out of the conflict (*Atticus*, 360, 364). Cicero did not know how to proceed, saying "if there is to be civil war[,] . . . I cannot tell what we ought to do. Neutrality, which was possible in Caesar's war, will not be possible now." Departure seemed the only suitable option. He would travel to Greece as a commissioner and visit his son (*Atticus*, 367).

As Cicero indicates, thus far, the republicans had remained passive or defensive, watching Antony and Octavian's competition for Caesar's resources from the sidelines. Appian held that Antony's behavior had become tyrannical immediately after Caesar's death. He puts an inflammatory speech into Antony's mouth at Caesar's funeral, which is not found in Suetonius, the earlier source.[67] He also portrays him as not only using Caesar's finances to fund his own armies but also forging documents for all manner of schemes. When Brutus and Cassius left the city, Antony became even worse, according to Appian, who remarks that "being in possession of something like monarchical power, he cast about for the government of a province and an army for himself" (*Civil Wars*, 3.6–7).

The contemporary correspondence does not confirm this assessment until later in the year. In his letters Cicero gloomily repeats that "we are free of the despot, but not of the despotism" (*Atticus*, 368; *Friends*, 327, 375). He was particularly leery of Antony's control over Caesar's papers, which were being used to formulate policies. "Laws are posted up, exemptions granted, large sums of money assigned, exiles brought home, decrees of the Senate forged" (*Friends*, 327; *Atticus*, 367). This only intensified as the months passed. "All manner of forged decrees were registered at that time" (*Friends*, 433). Still, Cicero was determined to remain aloof, especially regarding Antony. At the end of May, he wrote "I certainly want to keep my old-established friendship with Antony—we have never had a quarrel" (*Friends*, 330). The two had even corresponded cordially (*Atticus*, 367, 367B, 377).[68] Cicero also mocked his old age. What were men such as Cicero and Atticus to do? "Soldiering, especially in a civil war, is not for people of our age." "Am I then to come into the open and go to the wars? Better a thousand deaths, especially at my age" (*Atticus*, 372, 376). The fight now belonged to other men.

With the liberators remaining on the sidelines, Antony had a free hand to take drastic measures against Octavian in the summer of 44. In a move criticized by Brutus and Cassius, he gathered an enormous bodyguard of Caesar's veterans around himself in order to push through his legislation (Cicero, *Friends*, 329; *Atticus*, 375, 376, 381). Antony's use of military force was alarming. But aside from writing letters and keeping away from the city, the liberators let Antony have his way (*Atticus*, 383). By the end of May, Cicero began to give up hope on Antony remaining neutral between the hardline Caesarians and the liberators. Octavian had forced Antony's hand, and now Antony's "whole policy" seemed to Cicero "to point to war" (*Atticus*, 380, 381).

A trepidation settled on the liberators, who had not only taken flight from Rome but had now decided to depart Italy altogether by taking commissions abroad. Brutus and Cassius were running away from the struggle and leaving the "good men" around Rome in a perilous position (*Atticus*, 372, 373, 374). The state, especially "country towns and the honest men," needed a leader that could bind the good men of the republic. Without this, its defenders would drift away, and moderates like Hirtius would be lured into the hardline Caesarian camp that was "scared of peace" (*Atticus*, 374, 376).

Antony's June legislation was comprehensive. First, he increased his control over Caesar's papers. Initially Antony, Dolabella, and a commission would review them. A new law removed the commission and kept only the two consuls in charge. He also needed to command a large military force. He used a tribunician law to grant himself a five-year command for both Cisalpine and Transalpine Gaul; at the same time, he maintained control of his Macedonian legions. This alienated the senate and set the stage for a confrontation with Decimus Brutus, who currently held Cisalpine Gaul. The laws Antony pushed through between June and November would come under scrutiny, with many claiming constitutional irregularities and arguing that the use of violence negated them. Whether these laws were legitimate or not, it was hard to escape the conclusion that Antony was taking the same steps as Caesar to consolidate power. He was setting himself up as the natural leader of the Caesarians, especially Caesar's veterans. Antony had personally overseen the settling of Caesar's veterans in April, but Octavian's arrival forced him to take stronger measures in his bid for these men.

By June it became apparent that the liberators' safety was in danger, and Cicero recommended Brutus do whatever was best to ensure his safety. But he was still frustrated with their lack of decisiveness: "I found the ship going to pieces, or rather its scattered fragments. No plan, no thought, no method" (*Atticus*, 389). With great foreboding, Cicero saw that armed conflict was looming, as Antony's behavior was increasingly reminiscent of Caesar's. Unfortunately, the liberators were hardly inspiring. "Which camp then?" he asks himself. "For Antony is putting middle courses out of the question. Weakness on one side, villainy on the other." He recalled his indecision regarding Pompey and Caesar. This time it was different because he knew where his loyalties lay, but he doubted his own courage and his ability to influence events (*Friends*, 335). So in late June he decided it was best to leave for his scheduled trip to Greece, where he would stay until the new consuls took office on 1 January (*Atticus*, 389, 396, 397, 403). Fate intervened.

Antony and Octavian's War

In July Octavian entertained the Roman crowds and ingratiated himself with Caesar's veterans and supporters in the city by hosting games in his honor. From the beginning, Octavian exhibited a mastery for propaganda. The games he hosted had been scheduled by Caesar and pushed through over the opposition of senators. This itself was a marvelous coup, and a comet that appeared in the sky seemed a good omen. Octavian interpreted it as a sign of Caesar and would later use it as a symbol of his adoptive father, whom he had publicly deified in 42. After this time, Octavian could officially call himself the "son of the deified Caesar."[69] Antony may have been an agile maneuverer on the battlefield, but in the political arena Octavian had few equals. Antony and Cicero would both underestimate him, and the consequences would be fateful.

Despite the fact that Octavian and Antony had been openly at odds, the veterans demanded a reconciliation, which the two publicly demonstrated. However, it was obviously staged, as the two men were still vying for dominance of the dead dictator's legacy. Rome was merely in the eye of the storm.

The same month Cicero set sail, but guilt began to plague him, and he asked himself "What am I running away from? Danger? . . . I would rather be frightened at home than secure in your Athens" (*Atticus*, 414). Adverse winds turned his ship back to Italy, and he was greeted back on shore with a bout of news. Antony was attempting a reconciliation with the liberators so that they could return, and people were criticizing Cicero for leaving Italy when he was needed most. A timely letter from Atticus then fell into his hands, in which his old friend admonished him for leaving. Cicero was halted. "On hearing all of this I unhesitatingly threw aside my plan to go abroad, about which to tell the truth I had already been feeling none too happy." Then Cicero met with Brutus and learned that far from effecting a reconciliation, the breach between Antony and the liberators had grown wider. Cicero determined to stay, for good or for ill (*Friends*, 336; *Atticus*, 415).

On 1 September, Cicero had returned to Rome, only to be greeted by a verbal tirade from Antony. He viciously attacked Cicero for not attending the senate meeting for the day, when he had planned to heap more honors on Caesar. Enraged, Antony even threatened to employ slaves to tear down Cicero's house. Antony had just thrown down the gauntlet. But Cicero was ready. He attended the next day with a counterattack in hand. He praised Antony's disposition after the Ides but then carefully detailed how he had abandoned good sense and the republic by aiming to install a tyranny. He criticized Antony's theft of Caesar's finances, his forging of Caesar's papers, his use of military force instead of legitimate politics, and his fomenting of a civil war that threatened to destroy the fragile peace (*Philippics*, 1).[70]

Cicero had thus far been relatively restrained with his rhetoric. His response to Antony's attack was only one of several that were now targeting the consul. Lucius Cornelius Piso and Publius Servilius were among others, who, with Cicero were now denied a safe entrance to the senate (*Friends*, 344). Antony remained on the offensive. He "gets crazier every day," Cicero wrote to Cassius. "Their whole plan is to avenge Caesar's death." Antony raised the stakes by blaming Cicero for Caesar's assassination (*Friends*, 345). Writing to Plancus, Cicero wrote "Antony has not left me a quiet moment. . . . [H]e cannot bear anybody to look like a free man, let alone speak like one" (*Friends*, 340). In this Cicero was surely recalling how Caesar had cowed free oratory during his domination. Politics had once again been reduced to "an armed camp" (*Friends*, 347). Cicero found it exasperating, and his own indignation was dragging him back into the fray.

Antony soon had other things to worry about. Throughout the latter half of 44, he and Octavian had been appealing to Caesar's veterans, both those still in arms and those recently settled. To fuel their contest, they "were hurrying about Italy trying to bring into the field by large pay that part of the soldiery which was already settled in their colonies, and to get the start of one another in winning the support of that part which was still arrayed in arms" (Plutarch, *Antony*, 16).

The rivalry escalated into absurdity when Octavian marched on Rome with his troops in mid-November. Octavian had been sending out men bearing money and promises to Caesar's veterans. He took great care to target Antony's troops, who were awaiting the latter's arrival in Brundisium. Meanwhile, Octavian's ally, the tribune Tiberius Cannutius, had opened an oratorical attack on Antony on 2 October (Dio, 45.12). There was even one report that Octavian attempted to engineer Antony's assassination (Cicero, *Friends*, 347). However, it became clear when Octavian marched on Rome that he had misjudged the situation. The senate, several of whose members had been in negotiations with him, abandoned the young upstart. His troops also failed to act, not wanting to fight against Antony. When Antony responded with his own military force, Octavian turned tail and retreated into Etruria.

Things were not going well for Antony either. Appian describes how Antony's troops mustered from Macedonia used the two rivals, getting them to bid against each other as a way to raise their pay. Antony's initial offer was too low, but when they agitated "he reduced them to submission by ordering centurions as well as others to be slain before the eyes of himself and his wife. So for the time being the soldiers were quiet." Surely once he calmed down, he realized that this was only a temporary fix. When he himself marched on Rome a few days after Octavian, many troops deserted, including two entire legions. These two, the fourth and the Martian legion, would play a crucial role in the upcoming battles. Octavian then "won their attachment by giving money to them likewise—an act which added many more to his cause" (Dio, 45.13). Thus far, the Caesarian veterans of both Antony and Octavian had not allowed the two to fight, proving themselves more loyal to Caesar's memory than either of his attempted successors.

Antony's march on Rome was equally embarrassing, so he attempted to remedy his failure with legislation. On 28 November, Antony resorted to coercion yet again, barring the participation of his opponents and then reassigning a number of provinces. These moves were designed to eliminate the liberators' control of military forces in favor of his allies. Brutus and Cassius, for example, were stripped of their commands, and his brother Gaius Antonius was given Macedonia. Several magistrates, however, refused to legitimize or participate in the reassignments.[71] After this tactless display of authoritarianism, Antony marched to Gaul to take his province, by force if necessary.

In this fiasco, the citizen-soldiers of the republic were, as before, up for grabs in a contest for legitimacy. There were also two different ideological models claiming legitimacy. One was the autocratic model set by Caesar. Another was the republican model initiated and then squandered by the assassins. The deciding vote between these two positions would be cast by the moderate Caesarians, who could sway the majority of the troops still loyal to Caesar's memory, conscript new soldiers according to the established procedures, and maintain the normal functioning of the state. But in which direction would moderates like Hirtius, Pansa, Plancus, and Pollio lean?

Once again, the state had plunged into a destructive conflict over legitimacy, and Rome's citizen armies were the pawns. Octavian was the spark for war, in Cicero's view: "His object is plain: war with Antony and himself as commander in chief" (*Atticus*, 418). Octavian's intentions were to use Caesar's veterans as well as distinguished senators such as Cicero. Cicero was no fool and saw him for what he was: an opportunist using the state's greatest resource—its citizen-soldiers—for his own ambitions. But who was worse, Antony or Octavian? Cicero remained undecided and uncommitted (*Atticus*, 418, 419, 420). On 10 November, he wrote Atticus, "You go on to ask what I think you should do. It's difficult to advise, not being on the spot, but if they are evenly matched I think you should lie low" (*Atticus*, 423).

The historian Dio agreed with Cicero, seeing the next civil war as beginning with this rivalry between Antony and Octavian. This time the citizen-soldiers had demonstrated a reluctance to follow the course of the two chief rivals. Dio characterizes the urban masses and the rural veterans as vacillating back and forth: "For in their irritation against the men successively in power they regularly took up with the weaker side and attempted with its help to overthrow the others; afterwards they would become estranged from this side also. Thus exposing both of them to envy in turn, they alternately loved and hated, elevated and humbled, the same persons" (Dio, 45.11). Many veterans still loyal to Caesar were eager for a chance to eradicate the liberators, but their supposed champions were more interested in fighting one another.[72]

Once again there was no clear republican to heal the wounds of the state, only competing warlords. Thus far the armies in Italy had avoided an open conflict, but Antony was about to force a battle by marching against Decimus Brutus in Cisalpine Gaul. The republic needed an ideal statesman.

By mid-November Cicero was considering a course of action. He was going to take a calculated risk and back Octavian and his "band of veterans" provided that they backed the tyrannicides. Antony was too recalcitrant, too strong, and too far gone. Octavian might yet be moldable (*Atticus*, 426). A month later he explained to Decimus Brutus how he would bring Octavian, "the young man, or rather boy," who had already gained the loyalty of so many troops, to their cause (*Friends*, 354). Nevertheless, Octavian would not be the war's leader. Cicero would use the strife between Antony and Octavian to unify the moderate Caesarians in favor of the republic.

Cicero would also take another gamble. He encouraged Decimus Brutus to hold Cisalpine Gaul against Antony, regardless of the legal technicalities: "In safeguarding the liberty and welfare of the Roman People you must not wait to be authorized by a Senate which is not yet free" (*Friends*, 354). It was a delicate matter to push Decimus Brutus to hold his ground. On the one hand, Antony was the outgoing consul legally en route to assume his proconsular command. On the other hand, many saw Antony's use of violence as negating these reassignments.

These were great risks that depended on a stout rhetorical effort by Cicero. He would need to find a way to legitimize those aspects of his plan that were not yet so. Those troops loyal to Octavian would have to be brought into the republican order, and the quickest way to do this would be to grant Octavian titles and power despite his youth and inexperience. Decimus Brutus' defense of Gaul would need to be given legal sanction. Cicero would also have to unify the already legitimate Caesarian commanders in the field.

Cicero's strategy has been unfairly criticized over the centuries in various ways.[73] Cicero stirred up the war. Cicero was duped by Octavian. Cicero should have backed Antony. Cicero opened the attack against Antony. None of these claims is borne out by the evidence. First, as the foregoing has demonstrated, Cicero stayed out of the brouhaha until it became an all-out battle, a fact confirmed by other correspondence from the period and the interpretation of Dio. The peace obtained between the liberators and the Caesarians was broken by Octavian's entrance. Second, Cicero's letters clearly demonstrate that he saw Octavian as a threat from the beginning. Both Cicero and Octavian would cooperate as long as their ends remained the same, and outside circumstances could affect this rapprochement regardless of the shrewd maneuvering of either. Third, Antony was the imminent threat, not Octavian, for Antony had taken armies to attack one of the

liberators. If Antony should succeed, their cause would suffer a catastrophic blow in terms of legitimacy. Finally, it was Antony who opened
the attack on Cicero, not vice versa. That Cicero's attack was more
damning merely means that he was the more gifted orator.

This time Cicero would attempt to be the ideal statesman himself in
one last bid for freedom.[74] But Cicero was nothing like the men who
controlled the armies in the past: Marius, Sulla, Pompey, and Caesar.
They had been soldiers' soldiers, savvy strategists, and great conquerors. Could the decidedly unmilitary Cicero marshal Rome's citizen-
soldiers and then lead them to victory for the republic?

"But it is no fair match," he wrote to a friend back in October,
"words against weapons" ("contra arma verbis"). "The whole country
is under heel. The honest men have no leader, our tyrannicides are at
the other end of the earth." The incoming consuls Hirtius and Pansa
were solid, but they lacked the charisma to inspire unity against a returning tyranny. Something had to happen so "that the People of Rome
will at last show themselves like their ancestors. I at any rate shall not
fail the commonwealth and shall bear with courage whatever may be-
fall" (*Friends*, 346). Cicero would not give in to despair. He would be
their leader. And words would be his weapons.

THE WAR OF WORDS

Throughout 44, Cicero had been writing philosophy, penning no fewer
than eight philosophical works, including several of his most influential like *On Friendship* and *On Duties*. With his writing Cicero found a
new courage that helped him overcome his "scares in the old days." He
was now protected by his "proof armor of philosophy" (*Friends*, 330).[75]
In *On Duties* Cicero describes how in previous decades civil war had
broken out among men motivated by selfish ambitions and factional
divisiveness. The ideal statesman or citizen, he notes, should reject this
approach to civic life:

All this the citizen who is patriotic, brave, and worthy of a leading
place in the state will shun with abhorrence; he will dedicate himself
unreservedly to his country, without aiming at influence or power for

himself; and he will devote himself to the state in its entirety in such a way as to further the interest of all. Besides, he will not expose anyone to hatred or disrepute by groundless charges, but he will surely cleave to justice and honour so closely that he will submit to any loss, however heavy, rather than be untrue to them, and will face death itself rather than renounce them. (*On Duties*, 1.25.86)

Cicero also stresses the importance of free oratory. "We should regard only those as adversaries who take up arms against the state, not those who strive to have the government administered according to their convictions" (*On Duties*, 1.25.87). The republic would only survive if it fought in the manner that it always had. Persuasion needed to unite the people of Rome. The senate needed to lead according to the republican norms of justice and truth. Citizen-soldiers must defend the state under the leadership of legal authorities who were dedicated to the republic more than their own ambitions, even at the cost of their own lives.

The Oratorical Campaign

Cicero's rhetorical strategy was twofold. He would use oratory at home and correspondence abroad. His oratory took the form of speeches that by 43 had gained such repute they were called "philippics," after Demosthenes' famous orations against Philip II of Macedon back in the fourth century. The *Philippics* were politically charged speeches in which Cicero used, exaggerated, or ignored facts depending on his objectives.[76] True to his career as an advocate, he used all his lawyer's tricks to prosecute a case against Antony at the same time that he defended the life of the republic.

On 20 December, Cicero publicly committed himself by opening up a verbal barrage against Antony (*Friends*, 364). He had originally intended to stay out of politics until 1 January, but the question of who was the legitimate commander of Cisalpine Gaul was up for discussion, so he came prepared to defend Decimus Brutus (*Friends*, 356). He addressed the senate and the people with two separate speeches, the

Third Philippic and the *Fourth Philippic*. He exhorted the senate to resist Antony by rescinding his provincial reassignments. The senate must also support those who opposed Antony with armies, in this case, Brutus and Octavian. He raised them up as bulwarks against Antony's aggressions. The praise of Brutus was hardly surprising, but he also commended Octavian's "incredible and superhuman spirit and energy" that was being used for "the salvation of the Republic" (*Philippics*, 2.3). In these speeches, Cicero committed himself by vouching for Octavian, a gesture even more pronounced in his *Fifth Philippic*. If Octavian left the republican camp, Cicero would be culpable.

As in previous civil wars, there were competing claims of legitimacy. Cicero's first task was to establish as quickly as possible that the republicans were on the side of law and order. Unlike Caesar, who secured legitimacy by defeating enemy armies on the battlefield, or Antony, who derived his legitimacy from laws achieved through violence, Cicero intended to use persuasion to convince the senate and the people of Rome to bestow legal authority on whomever would preserve the republic. In his vision of republican politics, statesmen would use persuasion instead of coercion to unify the good citizens in concord.

True to republican oratory, Cicero was not without opposition, which he faced most often from Quintus Fufius Calenus, Lucius Cornelius Piso, and Lucius Varius Cotyla, respectively, the senior consular, the father-in-law of Caesar, and the uncle of Antony. These voices defended Antony and sought to reach a peace and prevent his being declared an enemy. In this they were successful until April. Cicero faced a particularly difficult challenge from Calenus, who, as the senior consular, was always the first invited to speak, meaning that Cicero would have to respond in a way that enabled him to turn the discussion to his objective.[77] Yet he maintained the offensive, arguing that peace with Antony would only facilitate a return to autocracy. In his *Seventh Philippic*, he responded to their claims that he was a warmonger. "Why then, am I against peace? Because it is dishonorable, because it is dangerous, because it is impossible" (*Philippics*, 7.3.9). He was arguing that they would no longer be able to have debates such as this if autocracy returned. And he was right. This would be the last time that republican politics and free oratory would function as they had for centuries.

Cicero used the *Philippics* to condemn the domination of Caesar and Antony without offending dedicated Caesarians. Instead of directly naming Caesar to condemn tyranny, he appealed to that classic foe of Roman *libertas*, Rome's last king, Tarquin Superbus. Cicero warned the senate and the people that if Antony were to win the struggle, or even if he were granted peace, Roman liberty would be forever quashed under a renewed kingship.[78]

He delivered the *Fifth Philippic* and *Sixth Philippic* on 1 January when the new consuls took office, during which he insisted unsuccessfully that war be declared on Antony. The senate did, however, grant honors to Antony's enemies. Cicero's speeches were meaningless if they were not followed by action. In this he was mostly successful. Senatorial actions from 20 December to 20 March annulled most of Antony's legislation, including the provincial reassignments from June and November, on the grounds that they had been passed through violence. The senate also praised the quaestor Lucius Egnatuleius for turning over the fourth legion to Octavian and legitimized Decimus Brutus' resistance in Gaul. Octavian was also honored for resisting Antony throughout 44, and he was given the rank of an ex-praetor, allowing him to serve in the senate.

For the time being, Octavian was granted formal power, which meant he was no longer wandering throughout Italy with unauthorized armies of Caesar's veterans. Some have seen this elevation of Octavian as a sign of Cicero's and the senate's willingness to behave in an unprecedented manner. This may be a just criticism, but it should be remembered that Octavian was only one Caesarian Cicero was trying to lure into the republican defensive against Antony.

Cicero sets up others as foils to Antony in the *Philippics*, including Hirtius, Pansa, Decimus Brutus, Lepidus, Marcus Brutus, and Cassius.[79] Cicero must have known there was a risk some of these men might not accept his invitation or that they might later betray the coalition. A letter to Brutus near the end of the war makes it clear that he was seeking to persuade the senate to bestow legitimacy and honors or inflict punishments on all the key figures in a manner that would give the best chance for success (*Letters to Brutus*, 24).

By early January Antony had reached Decimus Brutus, who had moved his forces into Mutina. He was now in an odd position. Although Antony had not yet been declared a formal enemy, the senate had removed his legal right to take over the province. An embassy from the senate reached Antony in January and another in February, but both failed to reach a negotiated settlement. Meanwhile, the senate was maintaining its own balancing act. Negotiations continued in the city, with Calenus leading the supporters of Antony and Cicero leading the opposition. At the same time, the republic was put on a war footing. Hirtius, who had overall command, and Octavian took their troops north. They would encamp in winter quarters and assist Decimus Brutus in whatever way possible. Meanwhile, Pansa, the other consul, would levy troops in Italy.

Cicero continued his rhetorical war until reports of the real battles finally reached Rome. He delivered the *Eighth Philippic* through the *Eleventh Philippic* in February, the *Twelfth* and *Thirteenth* in March, and the *Fourteenth* and final one on 21 April. He did more than speak, however. In some remarkable displays of populism, he regularly addressed assemblies, raised funds, and even convinced craftsmen to begin producing arms for the republican armies without pay.[80] As a sign of solidarity, the Romans laid aside their everyday wear and "donned military cloaks" (Livy, *Periochae*, 118). Cicero also reached out to Caesar's veterans. As conscription was under way, one of Pansa's tasks was to settle some of them, which a law of the Centuriate Assembly authorized, a point Cicero stressed in his *Thirteenth Philippic* (13.31).

Cicero's transformation of words into weapons was an astonishing achievement. Even those who see him as a warmonger must acknowledge this, for his warmongering had successfully brought on the war. Cicero, as we have seen, did not believe he was starting a war but rather saw himself as trying to win one that was already under way against the republic. And his relentless campaign had brought back the republican constitution he cherished. Once again deliberation was determining the course of events under the leadership of a reinvigorated senate in concert with the will of the assemblies of the people. Cicero had done more than fight for the republic; he had helped restore its constitution.[81]

The Correspondence Campaign

Cicero's oratorical campaign in front of the Romans was only one prong of his attack on Antony. The *Philippics* had mustered Rome's citizens and stirred republican sentiment, but he also had to win over the field commanders. It was one thing to unify the decision-making bodies in the capital, but—as the last century had demonstrated—that was pointless if those who exercised imperium and commanded Rome's citizen-soldiers were not loyal to these republican institutions. The commanders with citizens currently under arms must be converted to the cause.

His external correspondence strategy was already well under way by December. The position of the moderates was unclear. Hirtius, for example, had not taken part in the assassination, but he met with Decimus Brutus shortly after, and during that meeting, they discussed the disposition of Antony and the predicament of the liberators (Cicero, *Friends*, 325). It would be Cicero's job to win over moderates like Hirtius. Throughout the spring and summer of 44, he had been regularly meeting with many of the magistrates and magistrates-designate, from Brutus and Cassius to Hirtius and Pansa (*Atticus*, 365). Cicero had taken it on himself as early as May to "make a better republican out of Hirtius" (*Atticus*, 374, 383). In late June of 44 he was still communicating with both consuls-elect, even giving rhetoric lessons to Hirtius (*Atticus*, 399).

Cicero had followed up his 2 September speech against Antony with a canvassing of current and future commanders. He developed a particularly close relationship with Plancus, the commander of Transalpine Gaul. The two had shared family connections since before Plancus was born, and Cicero spoke of his long affection for Plancus, who responded in kind. In December Plancus wrote that "I have invested you, and only you, with the sacred character of a father." With Cicero's encouragement, Plancus pledged that "I shall assuredly not disappoint you, whom I am most especially anxious to content, or the whole body of honest men [*omnibus viris bonis*]" (*Friends*, 340, 355).

Here Cicero was playing out his ideal statesman in an extremely personal way, binding the good men (*boni*) together in close ties of friendship under a common cause. The cause he was espousing was a free republic. "For what hope can there be in a commonwealth," he wrote to Plancus, "where all lies crushed by the armed force of a violent, licentious individual, where neither Senate nor People has any power, where neither laws nor law courts exist, nor any semblance or trace whatsoever of a free community" (*Friends*, 340, 355). Mentoring Plancus, he exhorted him to "consecrate all your thoughts and care to the commonwealth." With Plancus commanding in the field, Cicero would lead the political fight at home through the concord of the good men: "I shall most easily render what is due both to the commonwealth, which is most dear to me, and to our friendship, which I hold us bound religiously to maintain" (*Friends*, 340; see also 371). Among the moderates, Plancus would be Cicero's greatest and closest correspondent (see, e.g., *Friends*, 359, 370, 372, 375, 377, 379), but there were others. He used the same tools—an appeal to friendship and virtue—as he attempted to bind Matius to the common cause (*Friends*, 348, 349).

Republicanism was expressed once more as it had been for centuries. Roman citizens should look to their own advancement and glory, but only as long as it accorded with their friends' honor and the common good. Virtuous defenders of the republic should not be joined by "bonds forged by circumstances." No, they must choose an honorable course that saw peace "not in the mere laying down of weapons, but in the banishment of the fear of weapons and servitude" (*Friends*, 370).

When Cicero opened his defense of Decimus Brutus on 20 December, he dutifully reported the events in a letter to Brutus the same day. He noted that there were "many fellow labourers" working with him on Brutus' behalf (*Friends*, 356). The next day he wrote a similar letter to Cornificius in Africa, exhorting him to "allow no person any jurisdiction in your province" and to "be sure to keep your province in the control of the commonwealth" (*Friends*, 357). Cicero saw himself as the unofficial champion of the republican cause. Republicanism was the antithesis of autocratic rule because it depended on admiring the qualities of other men and persuading them to partake in a common effort, not as subordinates but as equals.

He was also exchanging news, advice, and encouragement with the liberators, especially Decimus Brutus, Marcus Brutus, and Cassius. He was deeply prescient about the coming struggle. Throughout 44 he had beseeched Brutus and Cassius to act aggressively. Their tyrannicide had given the republic another chance, but it did not magically spring back into being. Their leadership was critical, and its absence created the present circumstances. First they fled Rome and then Italy, but even after they had finally departed for the East, he still believed "all our hope lies in yourselves" (*Friends*, 344).[82]

Throughout the spring campaign, Cicero maintained his correspondence and his sense of humor. Writing to Papirius Paetus, he chided him for starting a new diet, which Cicero joked was detrimental to the republic. Then, with characteristic subtlety, Cicero turned the letter to higher things, arguing that Papirius needed to return to feasting because it was only through communal dining that one enjoys the "community of life and habit and of mental recreation." This distinctly Roman habit of "coliving" unified the good men into a common purpose because in communal feasts "more than anywhere else life is lived in company" (*Friends*, 362).

Cicero also exchanged letters with Pollio, the commander stationed in Further Spain. Like Plancus, Pollio promised support. He "crave[d] for peace and freedom" and was devoted to the memory of Caesar, but the past year had taught him "how pleasant a thing is freedom and how miserable life under despotic rule." "I shall not stir a yard from your side," he promised Cicero on 16 March. Cicero's exchange with Lepidus was more terse; Cicero doubted his loyalty from the beginning, but he nonetheless sought to win him over, earning a response from Lepidus that promised support (*Friends*, 368, 369).

By the spring of 43 Decimus Brutus had become the most important of his correspondents because he was besieged in Mutina by Antony. As the forces arrayed themselves, Cicero foresaw the importance of the upcoming battles there, writing to Cassius that "the decision of the whole war depends entirely" on its outcome (*Friends*, 365). He was right.

THE VICTORY AT MUTINA?

Over the course of 43, commanders would rely on veteran units and volunteers as well as new levies conscripted in the traditional manner. Antony had six legions, three to four of which included newly levied soldiers. Hirtius and Pansa had levied five legions, one of which remained behind in Rome when they departed for Mutina. Cicero noted this ongoing task throughout the spring as Pansa actively conscripted an army "raised by levy throughout Italy" (*Friends*, 365; see also Appian, *Civil Wars*, 3.65). Octavian combined with the consuls his four to five legions that had been reconstituted from Caesar's veterans or deserted to him from Antony. At one point Decimus Brutus had four legions in Mutina, but then he had as many as seven. It seems he started with a core of two veteran legions, meaning five of his had been levied.[83]

So what motivated the citizens in these armies, especially those that had previously refused to fight each other under Antony and Octavian? Why would they fight now? The key difference between mid-44 and early 43 was the decisive stand of the senate under Cicero's leadership. He had succeeded in raising the stakes and isolating Antony. The senate had regained its own voice, conferred legitimacy on Octavian, and by April denied it to Antony. The scales had tipped, with the people of Rome and many in Italy now seeing Antony as the threat to peace and the republic. Many of the citizens that had just been conscripted had not fought under Caesar. The consular armies and at least one of Decimus Brutus' legions were "new recruits as yet inexperienced" (*Civil Wars*, 3.49). They would fight for the republic as citizen-soldiers had for centuries, and they had a clear rallying point: legitimate consuls with a legitimate assignment under a legitimate republican order.

As for those loyal to Caesar, Octavian momentarily represented the best hope for the preservation of his memory and deeds. Decimus

Brutus also had two legions of veterans that were loyal to his fight for the republic. And there were many soldiers who would fight for other reasons. Brutus' numbers included a host of gladiators, and Antony would reinforce his legions with slaves (*Civil Wars*, 3.49). Many of Caesar's veterans were uncommitted ideologically. Appian notes that in the coming battles some units were motivated by pride, some by revenge, and others by shame (3.67). Comrades who had become increasingly professionalized relished the opportunity to demonstrate their superiority. The traditional competition among nobles for political power would be acted out at the lower levels among men eager to demonstrate who was the most proficient warrior, not against foreign enemies but among themselves. Those who felt betrayed by the vacillations of their fellows engaged in battle with the scorn of jilted lovers.

In March Antony sent a damaging dispatch to Hirtius and Octavian, who had already encamped near his position. He outlined Cicero's strategy of dividing the Caesarians in his attempts to support the assassins. Antony called for unity among Caesar's former officers so they could exact revenge, especially on Cicero, whom Antony had already portrayed as the architect of the conspiracy. Antony also claimed he had already won the support of Lepidus and Plancus. These two had just recently petitioned for peace in separate letters, so it was possible that negotiations between them and Antony were already under way. When these letters reached the senate, Cicero replied to Antony's dispatch with his *Thirteenth Philippic* on 20 March. This was also when he fired off letters to Plancus and Lepidus to gauge their support (*Friends*, 369, 370). Antony's dispatch exposed Cicero's tactics and hinted at the possible dissolution of his coalition.[84] The republican initiative stood on the precipice, and if they did not crush Antony quickly, it could tip into the abyss.

Fortunately, Hirtius and Octavian were already preparing to lift Antony's siege when Pansa arrived. Pansa had departed in late March with the legions levied throughout the spring. In order to make themselves known to the beleaguered Brutus, Hirtius and Octavian had already skirmished with Antony, but they tried to avoid a full engagement because of his heavy superiority in cavalry (Appian, *Civil Wars*,

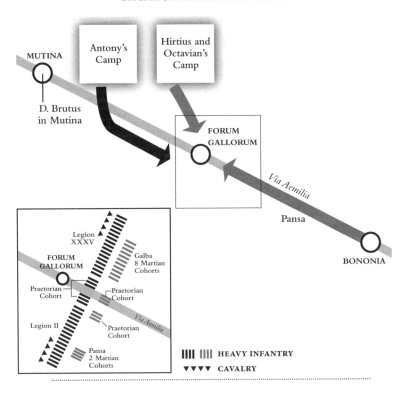

Positions around Mutina and movements to Forum Gallorum, spring 43 BC

3.65). In a move indicative of troop loyalty during the civil wars, a band of German auxiliaries switched sides twice during the skirmishing (Dio, 46.37).

When Antony learned that Pansa was en route, he left his brother in charge of the siege, opened another skirmish at Hirtius' and Octavian's camp, and then secretly traveled down the Via Aemilia to set a trap for the oncoming Pansa on 14 April. Antony was unaware that on 13 April, Hirtius had already sent "Octavian's praetorian cohorts and the Martian legion" under the command of Carsuleius to assist Pansa as he approached a defile south of Forum Gallorum (Appian, *Civil Wars*, 3.66).

Antony shrewdly took advantage of the terrain past the town, using the wooded areas to conceal his troops as they waited to pounce on Pansa's advancing columns. Frontinus would later praise Antony's maneuvering as a textbook example of an ambush (2.5.39). Antony set up his second and thirty-fifth legions on either side of the road in the marshy terrain. Two praetorian cohorts lay astride the road itself. He would use his cavalry and light infantry to lure in the attackers, where he planned to then crush Pansa's unseasoned recruits with his legions.

Antony's plan went well from the beginning, despite the fact that the veteran reinforcements sent by Hirtius engaged in the action. Galba, one of the commanders on the scene, described the engagement in a letter to Cicero the next day (*Friends*, 378). Hirtius' and Octavian's praetorian cohorts and the Martian legion were immediately drawn in, spoiling for a quick victory that would demonstrate their prowess to the fresh recruits. Appian writes that they even forbade the new levies from joining in, lest their inexperience cause disorder. Pansa, who was dismayed at this typical display of the citizen-soldiers' initiative, nonetheless ordered two legions of recruits to follow behind them. The Martians and praetorians divided themselves into twelve cohorts and approached in a line up to Antony's forces, with the legions of recruits some distance behind.

When the Martians and praetorians reached the position, Antony sprung his trap, throwing in his legions against them. Three separate battles developed. Antony's thirty-fifth legion engaged with Carsuleius, Galba, and eight Martian cohorts in the marshes on the right. His second legion confronted Hirtius' praetorian cohort and two Martian cohorts in the marshes on the left. Meanwhile, the road was bitterly disputed by Antony's praetorian cohorts against Octavian's.

The republican sense of independence, rivalry, and bloodthirstiness, seen in so many battles over the course of so many centuries, manifested itself again at Mutina as Romans killed each another with the same relish they had killed foreign foes in the past. Antony's forces sought to punish the Martians for deserting to Octavian, and the Martians sought to punish his legions "for condoning the slaughter of their comrades at Brundisium." The praetorians fought for the dignity of each of their commanders. Each side was motivated by the "animosity and ambition" they found in their fellow citizens, "considering this their own affair rather than that of their generals" (Appian, *Civil Wars*, 3.67–68).

With Antony's legions engaged, Pansa's first battle line was heavily outnumbered. This was irrelevant to the Martians, if Appian is to be believed. He depicts a grim expertise as the soldiers clashed:

> They raised no battle-cry, since they could not expect to terrify each other, nor in the engagement did they utter a sound, either as victors or vanquished. . . . No blow missed its mark. There were wounds and slaughter but no cries, only groans; and when one fell he was instantly borne away and another took his place. They needed neither admonition nor encouragement, since experience made each one his own general. (3.68)

The battle raged for some time with neither side gaining a clear advantage. Galba and the right wing then began to push back Antony's thirty-fifth, and Antony responded by sending his cavalry around their flanks. Galba used some light-armed troops to break a path to their rear so he could reach the reinforcements of recruits. He even gained sight of Antony amid the cavalry attacking their flank and rear as he attempted to make an orderly retreat. The situation on the left began to deteriorate. Pansa put up a stiff defense, but he was surrounded by Antony's cavalry and forced to effect a retreat back to their camp. In the midst of the fighting, Pansa himself was badly wounded by a javelin and rushed back to Bononia. His departure crumpled their resistance. When the levies saw the retreat, they took flight as well. There was no need for Octavian's cohort on the road to retreat. Appian reports that they all "perished to the last man" (3.69).

Antony followed the rout, eager to seize the enemy camp and destroy Pansa's forces. However, it was late in the day and he only managed to inflict losses—perhaps among the levied legions if we follow Appian—before attrition caused him to withdraw to his own camp (3.69). Flushed with success, he was then ambushed himself. Reports had reached Hirtius that battle was joined, so the consul raced his forces down the Via Aemilia to join his colleague. His fresh armies crashed into Antony's and inflicted a devastating reverse on him. Galba gladly reported the complete loss or rout of Antony's army. Antony's scattered forces made it back to his camp, protected from Hirtius' pursuit by the darkness of night. It had been a bloody affair for both sides. Antony and Pansa lost half their forces engaged, and Octavian's praetorians were wiped out (Appian, *Civil Wars*, 3.70). Galba triumphantly closed his letter with the report that "two eagles and sixty standards of Antony's have been brought in. It is a victory" (*Friends*, 378).

Hirtius refused to let the republican initiative slip. Over the next week he probed Antony's position in an attempt to bring him into another engagement. Antony wisely refrained from any action except for the occasional cavalry sortie. Hirtius and Octavian then began to move their forces to the other side of Mutina, planning to relieve the city from the side where the siege lines were not fortified by Antony's camp. Understanding their intentions, Antony was forced to bring out his legions with his cavalry. A second general engagement ensued, and a second crushing defeat was inflicted on him. Hirtius even managed to break into Antony's camp before the latter narrowly averted a complete destruction of his forces. This second engagement decided the siege. Antony's losses had been too great, and he was forced to abandon Mutina and withdraw (Appian, *Civil Wars*, 3.71; Dio, 16).

Despite the glowing terms the *Res gestae* (1.1), Florus (2.15), and Vellius Paterculus (2.61) use to describe him, Octavian's performance does not seem to have been very distinguished. He had merely guarded the camp when Hirtius fought at Forum Gallorum. There was even a rumor that he ran away at the first sign of combat. "He took to flight and was not seen again until the next day, when he returned without his cloak and his horse." This was contrasted by another story that he gallantly lifted a standard when an eagle bearer had been wounded in the second battle. Future authors under the emperor would ensure that the second tale was the one preserved (Suetonius, *Augustus*, 10). Earlier accounts of the battle either ignore or minimize his influence, so we'll never know how bravely he behaved. Unlike the consuls, however, Octavian had emerged unscathed from the brutal fighting. One gets the sense that perhaps this ultimate survivor was not so willing to enter the thick of combat to rescue standards. Many doubted both his sincerity and his bravery, which boded ill for the future.

As for the man who had orchestrated the entire campaign and its victory, the republic's esteem for Cicero could not have been higher. When the news reached Rome, Cicero recorded a triumphant mood that captivated the city. Romans swarmed his house, took him to the Capitol, and seated him on the rostra, showering him with applause (*Letters to Brutus*, 7). Cicero saw this as his second rescue of the state. Just as with Catilina, he had unified the various orders. They all now responded by thanking him for saving them yet again. The news of the two victories at Mutina was supplemented by the incoming reports of successes among the liberators in the East. Throughout the early months of 43, Brutus and Cassius had started consolidating control of the key eastern provinces in a series of moves quickly legitimized by the senate. Now Antony was defeated in the West. The republican armies had won. With the prospects so bright and the celebrations so jubilant, few at the moment would have predicted that this would be its last victory.

What about the soldiers themselves? They had been as brave, ferocious, and dedicated as ever, but to what end? Throughout the last century republican citizen-soldiers had continued killing for what they believed was the republic, and at times this changed from month to month or even day to day. The civil wars had turned that killing instinct against the republic itself. This was vividly put on display at Forum Gallorum, where Roman citizen-soldiers fought the way they always had, but this time their enemies were themselves. The men described in the battle were just as vicious as any barbarian tribal chieftain, Samnite warrior, Carthaginian mercenary, or Macedonian phalangite. If Appian's picture of the battle has any veracity, those men had been so hardened by the recent civil wars that they were the most proficient soldiers the Mediterranean world had ever seen. But the cold rage of these killing machines had lost a proper outlet. Civic militarism had become its most proficient at the moment that it devoured itself. These citizen-soldiers were no longer killing *for* the republic. They were killing *it*.

9 · Suicidal Finish

LAST STAND OF THE
CITIZEN-SOLDIER AT PHILIPPI

On Friday night 16 June 2017 two individuals unexpectedly participated in the assassination of Julius Caesar, but they weren't Brutus
and Cassius. They were Laura Loomer and Jack Posobiec, two political
activists alarmed by the fact that Caesar in Shakespeare's eponymous
play had been styled as Donald Trump. When the Trump-like Caesar
was assassinated according to the script, the interlopers erupted in
protest. Loomer even charged the stage before she was removed by
security guards. The actor playing Brutus, Corey Stoll, was later inter-
viewed about this and other protests, which continued to escalate as
the show ran to its final night. As the days passed, he became increasingly "scared" and "paranoid" that some modern-day supporters of
the Caesar-like Trump might try to do him in. The play's final days, of
course, drew national attention and scores of opinions, most of which
were trite at the time and will be forgotten in the future. Stoll remarked
that the play had become far more than a simple performance of a
great work. It revivified the last days of the republic and provided am-
biguous insights into our own modern political problems.[1]

Shakespeare would no doubt have appreciated the attention the
2017 performance—or a similar 2012 performance starring an Obama-
like Caesar—garnered. Shakespeare's tragedy accurately captures how
the tyrannicide of Brutus, Cassius, and the other conspirators has lingered as one of the most controversial acts in history. This was true
among ancient authors as well. Appian, Dio, and Plutarch all uphold

Brutus' principles yet criticize his willingness to betray and murder a friend (Appian, *Civil Wars*, 4.134; Dio, 48.1–2; Plutarch, *Comparison of Dion and Brutus*, 3). Republican purists throughout history see no ambiguity in Brutus' tyrannicide, but this has not cleared Brutus' character. Sane republicans, like the Brutus-loving American founders that threw off the "tyranny" of King George III, and insane tyrannicides, like the Brutus-quoting John Wilkes Booth, reveal the same American ambivalence over whether Brutus was a hero or a villain.

An even stronger contrast comes from the Republic of Florence, which boasts a much closer link to the Roman Republic. Its most famous author, Dante, placed Brutus and Cassius in the ninth circle of hell with Judas Iscariot. All three are continually devoured by Lucifer. And yet Florence's most famous artist, Michelangelo, sculpted a heroic bust of Brutus. The bust rivaled Michelangelo's other great heroes preserved in stone, David and Moses. David stood in front of the Palazzo. Michelangelo sculpted him at the moment he decides to fight Goliath, and his blazing eyes are those of Florence, threatening all tyrants that would challenge the republic. Moses' posture is no less fierce. Tyrants, both internal and external, have done their worst, yet the old man is not wizened but muscular and intimidating.

Michelangelo, who was ironically patronized by both the Florentine Republic and the Medici family, creates a Brutus that is equally powerful. The bust was inspired by his patron, Donato Giannotti, a Florentine secretary of state whose dedication to republicanism prompted him to condemn Dante and uplift Brutus and Cassius as civic heroes. Michelangelo and his patron were schooled in humanism and inspired by the ancient accounts of Brutus and the writings of Cicero. Cicero's *Dream of Scipio*, for example, saw ten printings in Italy from 1471 to 1521. The Brutus bust is modeled on Roman coinage and has a symmetrical form, with each side of his face showing different expressions. While one side is tense and stern, the other nears haughtiness with a bitter yet "heroic disdain" for those opposing his righteous fight for liberty. Michelangelo's Brutus has an "iron will and a resigned consciousness." The bust reflects the artist himself, his patron, and diehard republicans of any age.[2]

Opinion will remain divided over the wisdom and legality of the last republicans' decisions, but on one matter, at least, the ancient sources are agreed. Cicero, Brutus, and Cassius were fighting for a system of government and a way of life they knew was in mortal peril. They may have pushed the constitutional boundaries as far as they could, but they still believed in the idea of a republican constitution, which cannot be said of their opponents. As Caesar, Antony, and Octavian had proven, citizen-soldiers could be corrupted, used to concentrate power, and harnessed to usurp the state, making them less like Machiavelli's independent citizens in a republic and more like Montesquieu's subservient soldiers of a king.

But in April 43, the game in Rome was not yet up. There were still tens of thousands of men willing and ready to fight, kill, and die for the Roman Republic. Brutus, Cassius, and Cicero had good reason to believe that their heroic efforts had just barely succeeded. The tyrant Caesar was dead, his political successor Antony was defeated, and his adoptive heir Octavian had been co-opted. But fate was about to catch up, and Rome's citizen-soldiers would be its deadliest weapon.

OUTMANEUVERING THE STATESMAN

How republican were the armies in April 43? Who were the real men with the real power? Cicero's tireless oratorical and correspondence campaigns had been designed to win over and unite as many senators and magistrates as possible, but he made sure to target Hirtius, Pansa, Decimus Brutus, Octavian, Pollio, Lepidus, Cornificius, and Plancus. Why these individuals? Because they were the men currently in command of the legions, and the legions were especially impressionable at that moment. Throughout 44 and 43, Octavian had been competing with Antony for Caesar's veterans, both those already levied and those volunteer units that had rallied to Caesar's heir. Most of the other commanders had served under Caesar and were leading men whose loyalty was in question. If push came to shove, would the commanders and the troops support the legacy of Caesar or the constitution of the republic? The next eighteen months showed that Rome's soldiers and resources were divided on this question, and the answer would once again be decided by a battle.

Two unanticipated blows struck the republican forces in the moment of their glory in April 43. Both consuls were dead. Hirtius had been killed in the intense fighting in Antony's camp, and shortly thereafter Pansa succumbed to his wounds from the engagement at Forum Gallorum. The power vacuum was fatal to Cicero's efforts. In a radical change of fortune, Antony's forces slowly rematerialized and Cicero's allies slowly abandoned him.

Immediately after the battle the praetor Ventidius mustered three legions from his hometown and Caesar's colonies. Most were personally dedicated to Antony. Ventidius then rushed to a rendezvous with Antony on the coast. Antony's numbers were also boosted by slaves that he was liberating along his path of retreat (*Friends*, 385). He now controlled a total of four legions. Antony's opponent Decimus Brutus had ten legions, but these had suffered from the siege and battles. Others were dotted in the surrounding provinces. Lepidus had seven, Plancus five, and Pollio three. Octavian retained control of at least six legions from the combined armies sent to defeat Antony. In the next several months, he would recruit two more and then assume command of the *legio urbana* and two African legions transferred to Rome.[3]

The allied armies were not in the best shape after the battles. They were leaderless, low on supplies, out of funds, and—despite their victory—suffering from low morale. In late April Plancus and Brutus expressed their growing concern regarding Lepidus' disposition. Would he prevent Plancus joining forces with Brutus? Would he oppose Antony? Brutus had his doubts. "Lepidus will never behave well," he remarked. Plancus saw Lepidus and his army of Caesar's veterans as Antony's chief hopes. Octavian was also a problem. Not only was he not cooperating with Brutus, but he could not maintain control of his army either. Brutus angrily cracked, "There is no giving orders to Caesar, nor by Caesar to his army—both very bad things." Brutus also hinted ominously that Octavian's motives were in question. Far from mourning the deaths of the two consuls, it seemed a "greedy spirit" was impelling him to seek the office as one of their successors. How would he behave if this request was denied (*Friends*, 379, 380, 385)?

Brutus tried to pursue and destroy Antony's army, but he only returned with more gloomy news. An understanding had supposedly been reached between Antony and Lepidus, and Brutus believed this understanding was the product of Antony's own correspondence campaign, which he had been waging with the moderate Caesarians. He now had doubts about Pollio and Plancus as well (*Friends*, 386, 388). Cicero's offensive had been halted on the brink of success. The fact that the war had not ended had put a strain on him. He remarked to Cornificius in May that "I shall fight the good fight as ever, though I am now very tired" (*Friends*, 383). Nonetheless, he kept up his correspondence with the moderates, encouraging Plancus with the promise of glory, saying "the man who crushes Mark Antony will have won the war. It was Ulysses whom Homer called sacker of cities, not Ajax or Achilles" (*Friends*, 389).

But the news that trickled in over the coming months continued to be bad. Decimus Brutus, despite his numbers, was not seizing the initiative. Cicero rebuked him for being "apprehensive to a degree unworthy of your and the Roman People's victory" (*Friends*, 397). Word also reached Cicero that Octavian had heard a rumor that once Antony had been defeated, Cicero planned on casting him aside. Cicero dismissed it as idle chatter, but it did not bode well for their temporary alliance. Octavian was the one ally Cicero had not genuinely intended to bind himself to by *amicitia* and a common cause. Here Cicero had not followed his own advice and instead allied with Octavian because of the "circumstances" of the moment. Octavian must have known this from the beginning, as his intentions toward Cicero were little different (*Friends*, 401).

In late May Lepidus renewed his promise of loyalty, saying it was only some of his troops that were stirring up trouble, a situation confirmed by Plancus (*Friends*, 390, 395, 396, 400, 404). But he had obviously been negotiating with Antony. On 29 May their forces joined, and Lepidus kept up the charade, pleading in a letter the next day that "Fortune wrested my decision out of my hands. My entire army, faithful to its inveterate tendency to conserve Roman lives and the general peace, has mutinied" (*Friends*, 408). Regardless of who betrayed the republic—his troops or himself—the absence of any duly-elected consuls had created a void of legitimate command that was paralyzing the republican government and strengthening its enemies.

The senate responded in late July by impotently declaring Lepidus a *hostis*, but this infused neither energy nor reinforcements into the war. In the final two months of his correspondence, Cicero would reiterate that "there is general amazement at the revival of the war in the north" (*Friends*, 413, 421; *Letters to Brutus*, 21, 22). While Plancus and Brutus maneuvered unsuccessfully against the armies of Lepidus and Antony, Pollio suffered a disaster in Spain. His quaestor Balbus fled with the treasury, leaving Pollio in charge of unpaid, mutinous troops. He gave a colorful description of Balbus' flight and adventures abroad, but Cicero must have concluded that it was only a matter of time before Pollio's resolution would collapse (*Friends*, 415). Lepidus' and Antony's forces now cut him off from Italy. Pollio had already been pessimistic about raising more forces for the republic. He could "see little hope in a levy" (*Friends*, 410). Caesar's veterans were far more experienced, and if they all joined the same side, any hastily mustered forces on the part of republicans would suffer defeat.

On 9 June Cicero wrote to Cornificius that the war effort had reached a new low. Meanwhile, the republicans in Rome were in despair: "The Senate is bereaved, both Consuls lost; and the Treasury is in terribly low water" (*Friends*, 417). This was followed by a sullen letter, with Cicero grumbling that "the fact is, Brutus, we are made a mockery by the caprices of the soldiers and the insolence of their generals. Everybody demands as much political power as he has force behind him" (*Letters to Brutus*, 17). Late June and July were filled with Cicero's repeated requests to Cassius and Brutus to rush to their aid in Italy. "You are expected" he wrote, "indeed from day to day." But they never came. In his final letters, Cicero even admitted his failure in picking Octavian, who had failed to finish the war when Antony was already defeated. Cicero "went bail to the commonwealth" for Octavian, but the boy had been "quite happy to leave his backer to pay." In the end all he could do was complain that "every imaginable evil chance has dogged us in this war" (*Friends*, 425; *Letters to Brutus*, 18, 21, 23, 24).

Plagued by a failure to seize the initiative, in late July Brutus and

Plancus desperately pleaded for reinforcements from Africa's veteran legions. They believed that Brutus' army, being filled with fresh recruits, would be no match for the veterans of Ventidius, Lepidus, and Antony. And why was Octavian not assisting them? Despite repeated appeals, the young heir of Caesar was now sitting out the war, with his attention "shifted to other projects." Brutus complained, to no avail, saying "If he had chosen to come, the war would by now have been either quashed altogether or thrust back into Spain (a province thoroughly unfriendly to them) with heavy loss on their side. What he can be thinking of . . . is more than I can fathom" (*Friends*, 428).

The "other project" on Octavian's mind was the consulship, which he expected to gain from a senate grateful that he had merely survived the battles without betraying them thus far. Cicero attempted to dissuade Octavian from this course, knowing his ambitions, like those of his adoptive father, would only threaten the constitution. But Octavian's desires could not be pushed aside, not by the senate and not by the old senator.

Meanwhile, the senate steeled itself to finish off any who styled themselves as a new Caesar. Appian writes of Octavian's concerns at the outset of the campaign: "The changing of commands of Brutus and Cassius to the largest provinces, the granting of great armies and large sums of money to them and putting them in command of all the governors beyond the Adriatic Sea—all pointed plainly to the building up of the party of Pompey and the pulling down of that of Caesar" (*Civil Wars*, 4.64). Appian's bias for autocratic rule cannot disguise the fact that the senate was attempting to reclaim its constitutional prerogatives and safeguard the republic from potential tyrants. However, now that the campaign had ended in success and Octavian was the commander with the most troops, he intended to enforce his will, with the senate or without it.

The senate did not fully understand its danger until an embassy of no less than four hundred soldiers arrived. Dio stresses that it was unclear whether the soldiers were sent by Octavian or if they sent themselves. Octavian had shrewdly bound his soldiers in a mutual-defense pact wherein they pledged not to fight their former comrades that had served under Caesar. The soldiers were so enthusiastic about it that they believed they had taken the oath of their own accord. Having taken such an oath, it was obvious that the soldiers were no longer republican. The oath made it clear that it was not the republic that was worth fighting or dying for. They were a band of brothers bound to no cause but themselves.

When the soldiers arrived in Rome, they engaged in sword-point diplomacy, demanding payment for themselves and the consulship for Octavian. One of them pointed to his sword, asserting "If you do not grant the consulship to Caesar, this shall grant it." Cicero glumly responded, "If you exhort in this way he will get it" (Dio, 46.42–43).

Crossing the Rubicon in imitation of his adoptive father, Octavian then marched on Rome for a second time in July to secure the consulship by force. En route, they ravaged the countryside and murdered potential enemies and spies. The city was in a panic, with the senators paling in comparison to their forebearers, who stubbornly stayed in their homes as a *devotio* to be killed when the Gauls sacked the city in 390. Such bravery was wanting in August of 43, a fact the senators themselves recognized, as Appian records:

> They felt that they ought not to be so weakly terror-stricken, or accept a new tyranny without bloodshed, or accustom those seeking office to gain it by violence, or the soldiers to govern the country by the word of command. Rather should they arm themselves as best they could and confront the invaders with the laws. . . . They recounted the high spirit and endurance in behalf of freedom of the Romans of old, who never yielded to anything when their liberty was at stake. (*Civil Wars*, 13.90)

When the two reinforcement legions from Africa arrived, it seemed that they might find their courage. They even conducted a hasty levy of all who could bear arms and began to fortify the city. But as Octavian's army neared, the senate flinched first, sending money to the troops and appointing Octavian consul. The soldiers were only galvanized by the weakness of their enemies; they were "not at all grateful to them for what they had done not willingly but under compulsion" (Dio, 46.44). With no moral or military ground to stand on, the senate was a sorry cause to die for, so, in another display of legionary independence, the city's defending legions defected to Octavian. Dismayed by the loss of his men, the *praetor urbanus*, Marcus Caecilius Cornutus, committed suicide. At this point there was nothing left but a humiliating capitulation. The leading citizens were the first to rush out of the city with welcoming arms. They were in turn followed by the commoners (Appian, *Civil Wars*, 3.91–92).

Octavian was now merely playing the part that so many tyrants from the previous century had played, from Sulla and Marius to Pompey and Caesar. On 19 August he was made the youngest consul in Roman history, but in time he would make this position much less than it had once been. One of his first acts mimicked Caesar's. He seized the treasury and distributed it to his troops.[4] Cicero was eventually granted an audience with Octavian, during which he tried to influence the young Caesar once again. Octavian's coldness hinted that their duplicitous, diplomatic dance was over. The old statesman had been outmaneuvered.

Octavian then marched north, ostensibly to resume the war. Instead, by 27 November he had made a pact with Lepidus and Mark Antony, known today as the second triumvirate. Unbeknownst to the senate, negotiations between the three had been under way for months (Dio, 46.43). Antony and Lepidus had already won over Pollio, who then won over Plancus. When Plancus deserted Decimus Brutus, Brutus attempted to escape, journeying east to join Marcus Brutus and Cassius. The hapless proconsul, the center of all the strife for the last several months, was caught by a Gallic chieftain and executed on Antony's orders. And what of Pollio and Plancus? These last two would be known as survivors, living through the next rounds of civil wars and into the sole rule of Octavian. We will never know if they regretted their promises to a man that Plancus once described as his father or if their betrayal of Cicero was dismissed as just another moral expedient of the republic's final days.

PROSCRIBING THE REPUBLIC

Before making his rendezvous with Antony, Octavian focused his energies in Rome on two objectives: money for his troops and the legal rearrangement of enemies and allies. Octavian shared the consulship with Quintus Pedius, another relative of Caesar's, but in reality he "dominated the Senate" and "arranged affairs in general in the city to suit his taste" (Dio, 46.46, 48). His first order of business was paying the troops out of the public funds and his private resources. Then he took the war coffers stored up for the campaign against Antony and Lepidus and lavished it on the populace. With the political wheels greased, he used Pedius to push through legislation condemning the assassins of Caesar and then coaxed the senate to lift the condemnation of Antony and Lepidus (Appian, *Civil Wars*, 3.96).

With no small amount of political acumen, Octavian had pulled off an exceptional legal coup, turning the heroes of the civil war into villains and vice versa. None of this would have been possible without the power of Caesar's name or the money he assiduously doled out. Both were necessary to convince the citizen-soldiers in the western half of the empire that Octavian was worth fighting for. With no military charisma, command ability, or strategic savvy, Octavian would continue to rely on fame and money to manipulate them.

Cicero was right to see the war in the north as a do-or-die affair. When Octavian joined Lepidus and Antony, the three immediately behaved as capriciously as the republicans had feared they would. They set their term of office for five years, divided the empire between them, created a list of lackeys to fill the old republican magistracies, and began planning how to prosecute the war against Caesar's assassins in the East.

A telling event occurred after the private negotiations. The triumvirs gathered the soldiers together as "hearers and witnesses" of the pact. The triumvirs however, divulged only as much information as they thought was necessary to make them feel included. They also employed theft and bribery, promising the soldiers eighteen cities in Italy as colonies, "cities which excelled in wealth, in the splendor of their estates and houses" (Dio, 46.54–56; Appian, *Civil Wars*, 4.3). Dio lays bare the cutthroat agendas of the three men after the pact was sealed: "After forming this compact and taking oaths they hastened to Rome, giving the impression that they were all going to rule on equal terms, but each having the intention of getting the entire power himself" (47.1).

The assassins of Caesar were now all marked men. Gaius Trebonius, who had diverted Marc Antony immediately before the assassination, was the first to die in early 43 when he was betrayed and beheaded by P. Cornelius Dolabella, a corrupt opportunist who had switched sides in the civil wars four times already. Decimus Brutus had been killed in Gaul, and to this list was added Minucius Basilus, who was killed by his slaves (Appian, *Civil Wars*, 3.98; Dio, 47.29).

Killing the assassins, however, was not enough. The triumvirs also needed money and a playing field cleared of any opponents that could muster military opposition. They turned to Sulla's example and proscribed an estimated three hundred to twenty-three hundred men. They famously proscribed their own family members and wealthy equites to fund the continuation of the war. Dio and Appian record all the gory details and the chaos such massacres prompted throughout Italy. Children were murdered for their inheritances, and soldiers were permitted to plunder wantonly. Beneath all the drama was the simple fact that with the proscriptions the triumvirs had managed to seize the wealth and extinguish the lives of the remaining republicans of note in Italy. If salvation were to come, it would not be from the West.

They proscribed the moderate Cornificius, the friend and correspondent of Cicero that was proconsul of Africa Vetus. From late 43 into 42 he raised several legions on behalf of the senate and attempted to resist the invading Sextius, who had sided with the triumvirs. Cornificius was defeated and killed. His soldiers and junior officers, many of whom were still loyal to the republic, were forced to flee (Appian, *Civil Wars*, 4.56). Plancus' brother, the praetor Plotius Plancus, was proscribed and killed as well.[5] Antony made sure that Cicero, his brother, and their sons were on the list.

When Cicero and his brother found out they had been sentenced to death, they fled to the coast. His brother and nephew, however, turned back to get more funds for their journey. They were then overtaken and killed by bounty hunters. Soldiers continued their pursuit of Cicero. Two men in particular, "Herennius a centurion, and Popillius a tribune, who had once been prosecuted for parricide and defended by Cicero," were determined to bring back Cicero's remains as a prize for

Antony. It seems in his final despair Cicero began vacillating once again. He tried to board ship but was turned back. In one account, he considers whether he should find Octavian, either to plead for mercy or commit some sort of *devotio*, although this is not likely true.[6] Livy records the least fanciful and probably the most reliable tale. After failing to take ship, he returned to his country house at Formiae, once again resolved on a course of action. "Let me die in the fatherland I have so often saved," he said. He was out in his litter being carried by servants when he was found by the assassins. His servants insisted on fending them off, but Cicero forbade them. He extended his neck and offered his final words to the killers: "There is nothing proper about what you are doing, but at least make sure you cut off my head properly."[7]

Herennius and Popillius proudly returned the head and hands of Cicero to Antony, where they were nailed to the rostra. Livy wrote that "people could hardly raise their eyes for their tears, in order to look at his butchered parts." Perhaps some of them remembered how they had carried Cicero there with thunderous applause only eight months before. Livy's own assessment is fair, praising his achievements and criticizing him for not bearing his trials better. "However, if one balances his faults against his virtues," Livy concludes, "he was a man of greatness, energy, and distinction—a man, the complete exposition of whose merits would demand a Cicero as eulogist" (*Fragments*, 120).

Cicero's death represented the end of free oratory, the end of republican politics, and the final usurpation of the constitution. The triumvirate was a blatant overthrow of the republican constitution. As one scholar sums it up, "Nobody, then or since, could dispute that the Triumviral period was profoundly marked by violence, illegality, and the arbitrary exercise of power."[8] The triumvirs would not lay down their powers and could not countenance those who fought them, even with their words. They controlled the majority of Caesar's veterans and the newly levied troops from the war in the north. They had ruthlessly eliminated their rivals in the West, creating legitimacy by the process of elimination. Roman soldiers like Herennius and Popillius would continue to do their bidding. Perhaps they would not behave properly, but they could still kill properly.

WARLORDING IN THE EAST

By December 43 constitutional and legal legitimacy were no more. Roman politics was now in the hands of warlords with competing visions for the future, and the end was in doubt.[9] Would it be the autocratic heirs of Caesar who had seized power in the West, or would it be the republican assassins of Caesar who had seized power in the East?

With an irony that the ancient historians use to maximum effect, the situation of 49–48 had been repeated in 43–42. Originally, Brutus' and Cassius' praetorships of 44 would transition in 43 to their governorships of Macedonia and Syria, respectively. However, after their popularity plummeted, they fled Rome in April 44. Antony's increasing authoritarianism later that month seemed like it might be neutralized by the Caesarian cannibalism between Antony and Octavian. The troops prevented this, however, and Brutus and Cassius were given insignificant responsibilities, first the grain supply, and then the governing of Crete and Cyrene. The same month that Cicero returned to Rome, Brutus departed for Athens, and Cassius left for the East shortly thereafter. The senate changed the appointments several more times in 44 and 43, first, when it was strong-armed by Antony in November, then in early 43 under the leadership of Cicero, and then again in late 43 when it was dominated by the triumvirs. When the western war ended in an unexpected victory for Caesar's heirs, Brutus and Cassius found themselves in a similar position as Pompey. Once again, Italy was no longer in republican hands.

Like Pompey, they could be blamed for abandoning the West. Unlike in 49, or even in 44, however, the tyrants themselves were not the most dangerous enemy. Throughout 44 and 43, it had been Antony, Octavian, and Lepidus' troops that inspired unity by refusing to fight one another. Only when Cicero united the consuls, most of the field commanders, the Roman populace, and the senate had Caesarian veterans been convinced of the justness of a fight. But now Cicero, Hirtius, Pansa, and the others were dead. The senate was cowed, and all the major western field commanders, except for the rogue son of Pompey, were united under the triumvirs. To win, the liberators would have to erase the memory of Caesar, and to do this they would need to kill more than the triumvirs. They needed to slaughter as many of their troops as possible.

The Liberators and Their Strategy

Perhaps Brutus and Cassius did not deserve all the blame Cicero heaped on them in 43. Antony should have been eliminated along with Caesar, but it is hard to fault the moral and constitutional scruples of Brutus. The days following the assassination were volatile and difficult to navigate for all involved, but Cicero was right that a comprehensive plan should have accompanied the tyrannicide. On the other hand, their consolidation of the East into republican hands had earlier precedents. It had worked for Sulla in the 80s and nearly worked for Pompey. A similar strategy saved Rome during the Second Punic War, when Spain and Africa were invaded and subdued before Italy was reclaimed.

Cassius and Brutus were the undisputed leaders of Caesar's assassination, and their differences in experience and approach made them a solid command team in a final bid for republican victory. Cassius was the elder of the two. He had served under Crassus during the latter's catastrophic Parthian invasion. Like Scipio Africanus after Cannae, he was the hero of that dark hour. Not only did he gather Crassus' shattered legions after Carrhae, but he kept a cool head and prepared a defensive line in Syria. He then subdued a rebellion in Judea in 52 and thwarted a Parthian invasion force the next year. Cassius thus earned a reputation as a seasoned and disciplined commander who made up for any lack of genius with a staying power that could inspire troops in the worst of situations.

Brutus had a complicated background. On the one hand, he was supposedly descended from the Junius Brutus that expelled the last Roman king and from Servilius Ahala who had killed the attempted tyrant Spurius Maelius, and he was the nephew and son-in-law of Cato, whom Brutus held "in higher esteem" than "any other Roman." This ultra-conservative and republican background was complicated by the fact that his mother (and Cato's half sister) Servilia had been Caesar's mistress, a circumstance that led some to believe he was actually the son of Caesar. Plutarch contrasts his temperament with that of Cassius and with his namesake Junius Brutus. He did not have the making of a resolute tyrannicide, but was more suited for teaching and academic debate. Like Cicero, he had been steeped in philosophy, and "there was practically no Greek philosopher with whom Brutus was unacquainted or unfamiliar" (*Brutus*, 1-2).

Cassius' and Brutus' fates were intertwined despite their difference in temperament. They were brothers-in-law and both supported Pompey in the civil war, despite the fact that Brutus' father had been murdered by Pompey's henchman. Cassius was given a naval command, and Brutus accompanied Pompey on land, spending much of his time reading books and compiling a collection of Polybius' works. With Servilia in mind, Caesar supposedly took care to ensure Brutus was not killed at Pharsalus, instructing his men to capture him alive (Plutarch, *Brutus*, 3-4). In any case, Brutus surrendered, and a year later Cassius followed suit. True to Caesar's clemency, the two were given assignments and eventually the two praetorships that put them in such a good position to organize and carry out the conspiracy against him.

Cinema, Shakespeare, and even, to a certain extent, the ancient authors, play up the exigencies that drove Cassius and Brutus to kill Caesar. Regardless of the role that Brutus' parentage, Caesar's pitting of them against one another, the guile of Cassius, the righteousness of Brutus, Caesar's stealing of Cassius' lions, or even their skinniness ("the pale and lean ones" were more likely to conspire) played in their thinking, their fundamental motive was an ardent belief in the republic (Plutarch, *Brutus*, 8). The two made mistakes in their last two and a half years of life, but they never misunderstood the cause they were fighting for. This point is stressed repeatedly by the sources, and their commitment to the end is the reason why the republic still had a fighting chance when it was constitutionally terminated by the triumvirate.

The assassination of Caesar had imperiled the legitimacy of Cassius and Brutus. Unlike Cicero, who relied on his ability to guide and shape republican politics to achieve a victory, the assassins preferred armed coercion. Cassius was the undisputed leader of the conspiracy, and—despite the reputation he has derived from modern drama—

appears as the more devoted republican in the ancient sources. Plutarch argues that Cassius had been born with "a great hostility and bitterness towards the whole race of tyrants," recording an incident of him as a child thrashing the son of Sulla for boasting about his tyrannical father. Cassius' desire to kill Caesar had been instinctual. Brutus, on the other hand, had to be convinced with philosophical arguments and the memory of his own lineage back to the original Brutus (9). Once the latter had been convinced, the two were a powerful force, able to win over other disaffected leaders.

Brutus' reputation was a great boon for the conspiracy, but it had its drawbacks. Against Cassius' better judgment, Brutus prohibited Antony's assassination, and then he allowed for a public funeral and reading of the will. When Antony capitalized on Brutus' punctiliousness, he and Cassius discovered the major flaw in their plan: they had neglected to consider the military element behind the political power of Caesar. Thus, when Antony experienced a "change of heart" and began to consolidate power, he earned the support of Caesar's veterans, who had just received land and cities under their tyrannical benefactor. On learning that these men not only would support Antony but also desired the assassins' deaths, Brutus and Cassius fled Rome and then Italy (Plutarch, *Brutus*, 21).

Having learned their lesson, the two would not make the same mistake again. As the Antony-Octavian war and then the Mutina campaign unfolded in the West, they embarked on a consolidation of republican power in the East. Once again, they cast aside technical legitimacy, and over the next several months they cajoled, coerced, and killed to amass as many legions as possible to their side. By the time the three tyrannical warlords had taken control of the West, Brutus and Cassius had set themselves up as the republican warlords of the East. The final confrontation over Rome's regime would not be determined by who behaved with the most constitutional scruples.

Men and Money

The manner in which Cassius and Brutus arrived in the East in mid-44 reflected their varying temperaments. Brutus landed in Athens to great acclaim. The Athenians celebrated his arrival with public decrees and references to the famous Athenian tyrannicides, Harmodius and Aristogeiton. He immediately busied himself with the tasks of a professor, attending lectures and engaging in philosophical debate with Athens' leading luminaries. Secretly, however, Brutus was plotting, "getting ready for war." He began targeting the same kind of men in the East that Cicero was in the West, using emissaries and letters to win over the "commanders of the armies." He also collected young Romans loyal to Rome, including Cicero's son and the poet Horace (Dio, 47.20–21; Plutarch, *Brutus*, 24). At the same time that Cicero was thundering away with pen and voice in an attempt to secure the West through legal means, Cassius and Brutus were surpassing all legal boundaries. The liberators had two immediate objectives: men and money. Once acquired, they planned to consolidate the Roman East with a speed and guile reminiscent of Caesar.

Brutus made his intentions public when he seized Roman treasure transports en route from Asia. He then secured additional funds from the quaestor of Trebonius, a fellow liberator and the current governor of Asia, and from Antistius Vetus, a quaestor from Syria. Acting swiftly Brutus then took possession of five hundred cavalry destined for Dolabella and made his way to Demetrias in Thessaly, where he confiscated the arms stored up for Caesar's intended Parthian campaign. The outgoing governor had declared for Brutus by the time that Gaius Antonius, the brother of Antony, arrived in early 43. Meanwhile, Vatinius, the governor of Illyricum, supported Antonius and blocked Brutus by seizing Dyrrachium on the coast of modern-day Albania, but his efforts were in vain. Antonius' tactical abilities paled in comparison to those of his brother, and he was soundly defeated in several small engagements by Brutus, who dared bad weather and illness to outmaneuver his enemies. Brutus defeated and captured him at Dyrrachium. Over the next several months he secured Macedonia, Illyria, Greece, and Thrace.

Throughout Brutus' early successes, the disposition of Roman citizens and allies in the region had been critical. Republican veterans of the Caesarian civil war still lingered there after the defeat at Pharsalus, and these men immediately rallied to his name. Many cities and most of the troops currently under arms welcomed him as well. Epidamnus quickly surrendered and then happily took in the sick commander and his hungry troops. Vatinius' three legions, dissatisfied and unpaid, deserted to Brutus, after which they were ironically used against Antonius. The soldiers in the vicinity of Apollonia, despite being summoned by Antonius, elected to join Brutus instead, taking the citizens of the city along with them. Brutus sagely encouraged this behavior by consistently honoring Antonius and his troops after they had been defeated. The strategy worked, with Antonius' troops eventually surrendering and agreeing to serve Brutus instead (Appian, *Civil Wars*, 4.75; Dio, 47.21; Plutarch, *Brutus*, 24–26).

Brutus had secured eight legions and an enormous war chest from Macedonia and Asia. He had proven himself as a commander and even been hailed as imperator by his troops after a campaign in Thrace. A finishing touch to his success was the issuing of coins, which have remained to this day. They summarize the motives and focus of republican efforts in the East, with his portrait and the title "Imperator" on one side and two daggers, a liberty cap, and the words "Ides of March" on the reverse.

Cassius enjoyed even more success in the south. When he arrived in Asia, he wasted no time in academic disputation. While Brutus relied on his fame as a virtuous philosopher, Cassius used his reputation as a warrior. Like Brutus', his name was attached to the spirit of the republic, but others remembered him as the savior of the East that had defeated the Parthian counteroffensive after the disaster at Carrhae (Dio, 47.21). Working with his fellow liberator Trebonius, he set about undermining Dolabella, the incoming governor of Syria and an erstwhile ally who had switched sides to join Antony. Trebonius was to hold on to Asia while Cassius moved south to win Syria using money from Trebonius, Asiatic and Cilician allies, and an advance force of cavalry he commandeered that was originally sent by Dolabella.

The legions east of Greece were ripe for the picking in early 43. Caecilius Bassus, one of the Pompeians lingering in the region, had already begun to win over many of the soldiers under the command of the Caesarian governor of Syria, Sextus Julius. Bassus was defeated in battle by Sextus, but afterward, in a testimony to republican sentiment in the East, the soldiers of Sextus then murdered their governor and transferred their loyalty to Bassus. Bassus then began raising revenue and actively enlisting all military-aged men, both slave and free, throughout the province. When the Caesarian Gaius Antistius fought him to a draw, Bassus again used guile to secure victory. He walked outside his base at Apamea, called for a bidding war for allies and troops, and then won the contest. Before Bassus could consolidate any of his gains, two more commanders, Lucius Staius Murcus, given command of Syria for 44, and Quintus Marcius Crispus, besieged him. It seems Crispus originally departed from Bithynia and Pontus, where the liberator Cimber became governor in 44, to aid Murcus against Bassus (Dio, 47.26–31).

It was onto this volatile scene of new commanders and shifting loyalties that Cassius arrived. Dio remarks that his fame alone immediately led all the cities and troops to support him. Apamea surrendered to him, as did the seven legions of Murcus, Crispus, and Bassus. Like Brutus he was tactful in his treatment of those Romans unwilling to fight for him. Bassus and Crispus were left unharmed, but Murcus he retained as commander of the fleet (Dio, 47.28). Once again, it had been the will of the troops that determined the course of events. Cassius reported to Cicero that Bassus' troops passed over to him against the will of their commander (*Letters to Friends*, 387). These men, like those that had gravitated to Brutus, were loyal to the republic and eager to serve under a commander whose republican credentials were as sterling as his tactical record.

A new development in Asia threatened the gains Brutus and Cassius were making when Dolabella arrived. Trebonius rebuffed him outside Smyrna, but Dolabella gained the upper hand when he feigned a retreat to Ephesus, doubled back and ambushed a force Trebonius sent to shadow him, and then stormed Smyrna at night. Dolabella captured Trebonius in his sleep and decapitated him. Despite the fact that the fickle Dolabella had praised Caesar's death to the skies in the spring of 44, he now ostentatiously cast the head of Trebonius at the feet of a statue to Caesar. His soldiers then kicked the head around for sport

(Appian, *Civil Wars*, 3.26). Cassius had moved down to secure Judea when he received the news that Asia was held by Dolabella, which meant his lines to Brutus were severed. Dolabella took advantage of Cassius' distance and moved through Cilicia into Syria. He had overplayed his hand, however, for Cassius marched north and defeated him in battle. After Murcus crushed Dolabella's fleet from Asia, the latter realized his situation was hopeless. Dolabella and his lieutenant committed suicide at Laodicea before Cassius' besieging armies occupied the city. The loss of Trebonius was tragic, but Cassius had avenged his death, eliminated the most shameless opportunist of the war, and acquired the legion currently under Dolabella's command as well as four more of his legions en route from Egypt.[10]

Cassius now commanded "twelve first-rate legions," which, according to Appian, "had been enlisted and trained by Gaius Caesar long before" (*Civil Wars*, 4.58–59).[11] These legions were disciplined and ready for action, having originally been intended to avenge the defeat at Carrhae. Any loyalty they retained for Caesar's memory would have logically been transferred to the man who best represented the hopes for their intended assignment. The arrival of the commander that had kept a cool head in the face of a Parthian onslaught was surely more inspiring than the pathetic jockeying for power of Sextus, Bassus, Crispus, or Murcus. Cassius himself was confident in their loyalty, and after he persuaded them to join him in countering the triumvirs, he fastidiously reassured them with payment and purpose. They were already inspired by his charisma as a commander. They would learn to trust his promises of money. And they would share his belief that the republic was still worth killing and dying for.

There is another side to Brutus' and Cassius' campaigns, which were hardly all virtue and justice. Some went over to the republicans unwillingly. Brutus' famous coinage was derived from a confiscated Thracian treasure. He also thoroughly plundered those cities he conquered in Lycia in 42. He had to obliterate Xanthus, much to his own chagrin. The upside was that this prompted the surrender of Patara, where he confiscated "whatever gold and silver the city possessed," including the citizens' "private holdings" (4.75, 80–81).

Cassius behaved even more ruthlessly. He fleeced Judea, exacting seven hundred talents of silver and selling those towns that resisted into slavery to raise additional war funds. At Laodicea he "plundered the temples and the treasury . . . punished the chief citizens, and exacted very heavy contributions from the rest, so that the city was reduced to the extremist misery." Dio wrote that the Tarsians, who had been so devoted to Caesar's memory that they renamed their city Juliopolis, were brought in "against their will." Cassius then levied so much money that the people were forced to sell all the public property and then coin money from sacred articles and temple offerings. He did the same to Rhodes the following year, and for good measure he levied an additional ten years tribute from Asia. Livy baldly states that the purpose of these campaigns was "plundering the allies" in preparation for the coming campaign (Appian, *Civil Wars*, 4.62–64, 73–74; Dio, 47.26; Livy, *Julius Obsequens*, 69).[12] Such was the course of ancient warfare, but the questionable legitimacy under which Brutus and Cassius operated made them at times seem like little more than warlords dedicated to a republican regime rather than a monarchic one.

As the republican war effort in the West was crumbling in the autumn of 43, Brutus and Cassius commanded an enormous army poised for action. Their commands had been legitimized in early 43 by a free senate, but this, of course, was undone when the triumvirs took control of Italy later that year. When the two met in Smyrna to discuss the next year's objectives, they were aware that the fate of the republic now rested on the men under their command. Their individual successes had given rise to rumors that they were nothing more than freewheelers. The two reassured each other that despite such accusations and their admittedly dubious methods, they would not themselves become tyrants in Caesar's mold. Their campaigns shared one goal: "to defend the freedom of the people" and "overthrow these men . . . engaged in such evil undertakings" (Dio, 47.32; Plutarch, *Brutus*, 28–29).

The Road to Philippi

As the fighting season commenced the following year, once again, Cassius and Brutus did not tarry. Two states, Rhodes and the Lycian

Confederacy, hoped to remain neutral in the upcoming struggle, but the liberators forced their submission through conquest. Brutus struck at Lycia and Cassius at Rhodes, with both securing victories and more resources. In mid-July they rendezvoused in Sardis, which was the starting point for a joint march into Macedonia.

The strategic situation in 42 was evenly matched. On the one hand the triumvirs held Italy, the government, and tens of thousands of troops. On the other hand they were stymied by an inability to use these armies because the republicans or their allies held the seas. The eastern fleets and those blocking the passage to the East were under the control of Cassius and Brutus. The western Mediterranean was in the hands of Sextus Pompeius (Pompey's son). Like the liberators across the empire, the remnants of the republicans in the West had flocked to his standard. All "those who had served with his father and his brother, and who were leading a vagabond life, drifted to him as their natural leader" (Appian, *Civil Wars*, 4.83). Italians in particular flooded his growing numbers.

The proscriptions did not cover the triumvirs' war costs, so they levied new taxes and then ejected the wealthy inhabitants of certain Italian cities so they could hand the cities over to their troops as "prizes of victory." This policy of murder and theft seemed unending and was a harbinger of what would follow in the new order. Those Italians that lost their property, escaped the proscriptions, or wanted to fight for the republican cause were right to see Pompeius as the last hope in that theater (Appian, *Civil Wars*, 4.83–84). The senate had regularized him in early 43, and then he had been condemned along with the assassins of Caesar (despite his playing no role in the conspiracy). These changes of heart did not seem to dint Pompeius' sense of purpose. He had always been a maverick operating against Caesar and his heirs, first in Africa, and then in Sicily. By 42 he held the largest navy in the West and was loosely allied with the liberators.

Antony attempted in vain to slip past Murcus' fleet, getting bested in repeated naval skirmishes. It was only after Octavian abandoned his efforts against Pompeius to join Antony that they were able to make progress. Octavian's arrival afforded their forces some breathing space at Brundisium because Murcus had to avoid being caught between them. Favorable winds then prompted them to risk several crossings en masse.

An advance force led by their lieutenants Saxa and Norbanus reached Thrace in late summer, but they were outmaneuvered by the republicans in September. Cassius and Brutus secured control of Philippi and began fortifying their position. When Antony and Octavian finally eluded the republican naval gauntlet, they crossed the Adriatic and approached their opponents. Octavian was supposedly ill, so Antony advanced without him. He dashed to the rescue of Norbanus, who was surrounded and about to be overrun. The move reminded the liberators that regardless of his personal and political shortcomings, Antony was a daring field commander that was not to be underestimated (Plutarch, *Brutus*, 38). From his first entrance onto the scene, it was apparent that the real contest would be with Antony.

Because contingents throughout Macedonia, Greece, Asia Minor, Syria, Arabia, and Parthia joined the republicans in their struggle, the republican armies fielded a greater percentage of allies. Plutarch remarks that the Greeks and Macedonians saw this as an ideological struggle. They hoped the liberators would perform "a similar service to their country" as when they freed Rome from the tyranny of Caesar (*Brutus*, 47). Brutus took particular pride in his Macedonian soldiers that he "drilled . . . in the Roman way" (Appian, *Civil Wars*, 4.75). Still, the majority of the men who fought for the republic at Philippi "were certainly Italians, enlisted before Caesar's death."[13]

The Romans and allies mustered in 42 were the largest in republican history. As the campaign season unfolded, the triumvirs had forty-three legions and the republicans twenty-one. Over three hundred thousand Italians were under arms. The ratio of legionaries to junior citizens was one to two and a half, and "the ratio of legionaries to citizens 1:11.6, meaning more than one of every 12 adult Roman males was in uniform."[14] Octavian arrived ten days after Antony. When these four commanders met outside Philippi, seventeen republican legions, some only partially full, would face nineteen complete triumviral legions. Ninety thousand republican and 110,000 triumviral citizen-soldiers had been gathered from around the Mediterranean to kill each other, and this enormous figure doesn't include the numbers of allied contingents. Plutarch remarks that "Roman forces of such size had never before encountered one another" (*Brutus*, 38; see also Appian, 4.137).[15]

DECIDING VIA BATTLE

The republican disadvantage in numbers was compensated for by the strength of their position. The ancient historians stress the similarities with Pompey: the liberators were not only well provisioned and occupied carefully fortified positions but also controlled access to the sea and the resources beyond. Brutus' camp was at the foot of the heights behind Philippi, and Cassius' camp was on the other side of the Via Egnatia. He also occupied the strategic hillock Kutchuk-tepe further down the plain. Their line stretched from the heights to the marshes, with the Gangites River providing a natural moat against their enemies. The fortification line has been archaeologically attested and was an impressive feat. The one major flaw was the separation of their camps by twenty-seven hundred meters, which would be a serious detriment to their cooperation and communication. Otherwise, it was an excellent position, and, as long as they maintained access to the sea, their morale and provisions would remain strong while their opponents' dwindled.[16]

This placed the burden of action on Antony, whose greater experience compared to his young counterpart ensured that only his initiative would force a decision in their favor. Indecision guaranteed failure, but this was precisely the scenario in which Antony usually surpassed all expectations.

Another War of Words

Both sides performed the usual lustration (ritual cleansing) of their armies before the anticipated battle. The republicans did so at the Gulf of Melas, which is the setting for their most important prebattle exhortation in Appian. The triumvirs completed a lustration at Philippi, but

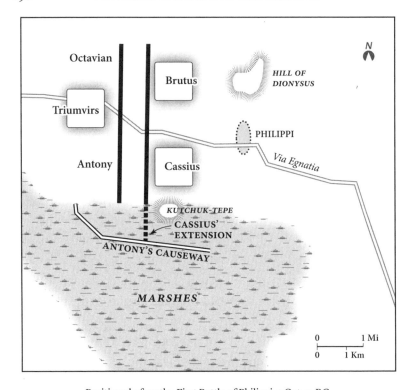

Positions before the First Battle of Philippi, 3 Oct 42 BC

we only have speeches from later in the campaign. The words put in the mouths of the commanders summarize their motives and objectives, and the differences between the two sides are telling.

Brutus may have been better in academic disputation, but Cassius was more suited to motivating men on the eve of combat. Cassius had already deftly handled a rhetorical exchange with representatives from Rhodes. When they accused him of violating the letter of their treaty, he retorted that such quibbles were meaningless when the republic itself was at stake. The Rhodians would put their own freedom in jeopardy in a "war of the republic against monarchy" if they abandoned the fight for the freedom of the republic (Appian, *Civil Wars*, 4.69).

This is not to say that the republicans were above offering financial incentives. Troops always expected some form of compensation, and the enormous war chest gained from throughout the East was immediately put to use. Cassius and Brutus had "provided themselves with an abundant supply of money in order to propitiate them with gifts" (Appian, *Civil Wars,* 4.89). Plutarch has Brutus make up for his inferior numbers with the lavishing of gold and silver on the armor of his troops, providing them constant reminders even in the midst of battle that they had much to lose and a commander whose promises would be honored (*Brutus*, 38).

Nonetheless, the similarities between the opposing commanders end here. Appian puts a fine speech in the mouth of Cassius as the republicans are reviewing the armies. As with most ancient speeches, the details are difficult to account for, but its sentiments are verified across the historical accounts and in the correspondence of Cicero. Cassius sometimes commanded out of fear, but this was due to a fiery temperament governed by a devotion to republican ideals. To his closest companions, he was known for his laughter and banter. He was also as loyal to his colleague as he was to the republic. Unlike the triumvirs whose ambition constantly pitted themselves against one another, Cassius shared a third of the wealth his campaigns had yielded with Brutus and ensured that their status as colleagues was maintained (Plutarch, *Brutus*, 29–30).

Before Cassius uttered a word, the troops were already inspired. Regular payment and additional rewards before the speeches proved that their commanders honored their pledges. The soldiers constructed an enormous speaker's platform, in a sense creating a copy of the rostra back in Rome, from which speakers had attempted to sway citizen-soldiers for centuries. The men were mustered for the speech and had already raised a great din of approval before trumpeters quieted them. Cassius mounted the platform with Brutus and all of the other senators present. Stepping in front of this impressive body of republican leaders, he opened his speech (Appian, *Civil Wars*, 4.89–97; Plutarch, *Brutus*, 39).

Cassius began by reminding them of their common peril and the fulfilled promises of payment. Commanders and citizen-soldiers were bound by shared goods and a shared threat. The future of the republic—their "common purpose and common interests"—rested on them and them alone. He acknowledged the slanders of their enemies and then pleaded that they all needed reminding about what they were fighting for. Their cause had begun when Caesar usurped power "against the laws, against the order of the commonwealth." His death had been necessary to return sovereignty to the "law," the "people," and the "Senate." Cassius acknowledged that the common man may not have understood this at the time, but as leaders he and the other assassins were bound to perform their civic duty on behalf of the republic and on behalf of its citizen-soldiers. Caesar had inspired them with his martial courage, but he was a tyrant, and no man's abilities outweighed the good of the republic.

Cassius then reassured the men of their purpose. He reminded those who served with and respected Caesar that they "were not his soldiers, then, but our country's." This tradition was long-standing, and the men before Cassius were the only ones that could save it. "The institutions our fathers established when they expelled the kings and swore never to tolerate royal government again" would perish if they did not succeed. They now must fight to save their way of life and their republic, with its offices, elections, and "balance of powers." This constitution was worthy of preservation because it had given them an empire that had no historical parallels. The republic was now the prisoner of evil men, who dominated Italy and had neutralized the senate. Such men had been seen before, both internal tyrants such as Tarquin and external invaders such as the Gauls. As the tyrants had been defeated before, the soldiers before him would do so again.

His closing remarks in this part of the speech draw clear ideological battle lines. The enemy aims at "monarchy and despotism . . . while we seek nothing but the mere privilege of living as private citizens under the laws of our country made once more free." They have no reason to despair because "in war the greatest hope lies in the justice of one's cause." Cassius then references the commanders and senators on the stage. The common citizen-soldier will defend this cause alongside leaders who do not wish to master them, as did the triumvirs, but who only saw themselves as "your fellow-soldiers . . . fighting only for the freedom of the Senate and people of Rome."

When Antony arrived outside Philippi, he had no time for fine speeches. His situation was dire. Before him was an impregnable position, defended by ninety thousand men. Behind him was a lackluster colleague, a youngster that was either ill or feigning illness because he was too terrified to act. All that Antony had was with him, troops dedicated to his generalship who believed in his ability to secure victory, regardless of the odds. These men did not expect victory as much as they demanded it, so Antony needed to deliver. He immediately set to work, fortifying his position down in the plains and sending out his cavalry to skirmish with Cassius. By the time Octavian finally arrived it was clear that Antony intended to target Cassius' vital position between the Via Egnatia and the marshes on the republican left, leaving Octavian to manage Brutus on the right.

The triumvirs formed up for battle, but the republicans wisely kept to their fortified line, intending to wear down the triumvirs with hunger and low morale. Their strategy was to force desertion or a dangerous retreat back toward the republican-controlled sea, where they would be hemmed in and forced to surrender. Nonetheless, to keep up morale, the republicans mustered out to face the triumvirs, keeping to the high ground and daring them to make an ill-advised charge. As at Forum Gallorum, the men mustered for battle with an eerie iciness. They advanced "leisurely, as though they were competitors in a game, and then quietly drew themselves up in battle order." The silence was then broken by commanders, then tribunes, and then centurions offering more prebattle exhortations. Only smatterings of these speeches remain, but we know they reminded the troops why they fought. On the side of the republicans, "the prizes of liberty and democracy, of freedom from tyrants and freedom from masters" and "the benefits of equality and the excesses of monarchy" were cited. On the side of the triumvirs were mentioned "vengeance," gaining the "property of their antagonists," and financial reward—specifically "twenty thousand sesterces apiece" (Dio, 47.42).

The First Battle

Antony knew his supplies from the nearby terrain were scarce and that the republicans had the resources of the East within reach via local ports and supply cities, so he decided on a bold gamble. He secretly began hacking a passage through the marshes to the south of Cassius' fortifications. His men worked tirelessly. At night they used the cover of darkness. During the day, he mustered his men out for battle, keeping Cassius preoccupied with the potential for an assault on his positions. The reeds prevented the republicans from seeing the extension of Antony's line, and within ten days he had made a great deal of progress making a fortified causeway that threatened the republican left flank.

By the time Cassius finally discovered Antony's project, the causeway was already protected by manned redoubts. Cassius immediately began extending his own lines in an attempt to sever Antony's troops. He too was successful and now a portion of Antony's men were cut off from their comrades, making them easy targets from a republican line that was just as strong as before. Antony had apparently lost this positional game of chess, but instead of conceding defeat, he changed the game and launched an attack. Gathering tools and ladders, Antony pounced on Cassius' lines in a brazen assault on his counterworks. No one on the republican lines was expecting this after nearly two weeks of cat-and-mouse maneuvers for terrain. Antony's own men were almost as surprised, but they had learned to expect such things of their general. At noon on 3 October, his "audacious charge . . . obliquely and up hill" defied all expectations and overwhelmed Cassius' left flank (Appian, *Civil Wars*, 4.108–10).

The conflict at the counterfortifications brought on a general engagement, much to Antony's delight. None of the other commanders were prepared for such an event. Brutus characteristically dithered, but his troops took immediate action. "Provoked at the insolence of the enemy . . . they charged on their account, without any orders from their officers, and killed with much slaughter." Here once again was that famous independent initiative of the citizen-soldier. Their tepid commander should have either reinforced Cassius or ordered the assault, but when he failed in his duty, his men did not. They rushed downhill into the triumviral lines and killed with the same relish as the citizen-soldiers had at Pydna, New Carthage, and Sentinum. Octavian's men on the triumviral left were as bewildered as Cassius' men on the other side of the battle. They shattered and fled. Meanwhile, Brutus' men seized and then plundered the triumvirs' camp.

Events on the republican left followed the opposite course. Antony saw that his men were not only gaining ground but that their enthusiasm at finally bringing on an engagement would be difficult to direct. Instead of turning them, he "continued his charge as he had begun it, on the run, and advanced under a shower of missiles." Cassius' men appeared to be fixed in their previously assigned positions, amazed at the audacity of Antony's troops. Antony's men then kept moving diagonally, slaughtering the republican advance guard, breaking through the fortifications, filling in the ditch to keep their comrades flowing across, and then overwhelming the gates of Cassius' fortifications. At the same time the gates were taken, others broke through the walls, and still more ascended them to get inside. The speed at which they accomplished all of this made Cassius' workers from the swamps easy targets when the latter mustered a counterattack from that direction. Antony's soldiers swatted them back into the marsh and then "wheeled against the camp of Cassius itself." The camp was wholly unprepared for an assault because all of the men were standing in battle lines or working the transverse wall. It fell with very little effort, and Antony's troops immediately set about spoiling Cassius' camp.

As Cassius was desperately trying to rally his men in the face of Antony's attack, Brutus was being carried to success by his. And what of Octavian? He had scurried out of his camp, with the ancient sources claiming that a divine dream had warned him of impending doom. Divine inspiration or not, Octavian had abandoned his men to save his own skin. Pliny reports that he hid out in the marshes for three days (7.46). His consistency in surviving battles was almost certainly the result of a penchant for avoiding their most dangerous moments.

The first Battle of Philippi was thus started by the initiative of Antony, who deserves all the glory for the triumvirs' successes that day. But once the battle had begun, the commanders were no longer in control. Far from leading his troops, Brutus was led by them (Plutarch, *Brutus*, 42). Octavian had absconded. Cassius was so thoroughly stunned that his men were defeated before he could direct them. It had been the citizen-soldiers that determined to decide the question of what regime Rome would have once and for all. A grim determination seized each of them, with Dio capturing the drama of the contest:

> Some cast away their shields and seizing hold of the foes facing them choked them by means of their helmets while they struck them in the back or else tore away their armour and smote them on the breast. Others seized hold of the swords of their opponents . . . and then ran their own into their own bodies. . . . Some clutched their opponents in an embrace that prevented either one from striking and perished through the commingling of their swords and bodies. (Dio, 42.44)

Human determination was thus transformed into animalistic instinct. Dio has the Roman citizen-soldiers abandon the weapons that had won them the Mediterranean so that they can engage in a fratricidal frenzy of strangulation and suicide.

The results of this macabre descent into barbarism were republican casualties numbering eight thousand and triumviral casualties at sixteen thousand. Deadliness alone never decides a battle, however. Only accomplishing objectives can do this, and both sides lost sight of these in the looting. Because commanders had yet again lost control of their armies, neither side crushed the other. Instead, as Plutarch states, "Brutus was completely victorious as Cassius was completely defeated" (*Brutus*, 42). If Antony had swung his men around and taken Brutus' camp or struck Brutus' lines, his victory would have been complete. Or if Brutus had exercised any control over his men, he could have wheeled them to Antony's rear or come to the aid of Cassius in the center. Instead, no commander demonstrated the same discipline that Fabius Rullianus had at Sentinum or Scipio at New Carthage. The troops fought only as long as they wanted to, after which they set about pillaging. This continued until darkness, when the men were finally recalled. In an absurd situation only real life can invent, they passed each other in the night, arms brimming with loot, looking more like "porters rather than soldiers," not knowing whether they glimpsed the shadowy shapes of friend or foe (Plutarch, *Brutus*, 42; Appian, *Civil Wars*, 4.112).

The most decisive moment of the first Battle of Philippi had occurred in the aftermath of the fighting, but few realized it until after the troops had slunk back to their respective sides. While Brutus was attempting to restore order among his men, he learned that Cassius was in trouble and then that he had perished. The fiery republican died as a result of ill fortune and momentary weakness. When Antony's men overwhelmed his lines and then his camp, Cassius tried to rally them, uplifting the standards himself. Nonetheless, his cavalry and then his infantry gave way, and he was forced to flee. Cassius retreated to the hill of Philippi, where he surveyed the situation. Despite his vantage point, the dust and noise of the melee below obscured Brutus' success, and he wrongly concluded that Brutus had suffered a defeat as bad as his own. Thinking all was lost, he killed himself.

That Cassius died in this manner is clear in all the sources, but the specifics leave a conflicting set of options for the reader. According to Plutarch, Cassius had premonitions of his death before the battle. These were boosted by a lengthy discussion between Brutus and him about the merits of suicide. When his army was routed by Antony in the battle that followed, he sent a troop led by Titinius out into the plain to get information, but they were delayed and assumed to be overtaken, or, as they were returning, were confused with the enemy. In ignorance, he then hastily succumbed to despair and bid Pindarus, his freedman, to slay him. Titinius finally arrived only to find Cassius dead. Realizing his delay caused the misunderstanding, Titinius then committed suicide as well. Appian simplifies the situation, having Cassius discover Brutus' success and then commit suicide out of shame for his own defeat. Another tradition has it that Pindarus murdered him (Appian, *Civil Wars*, 4.113–14; Dio, 47.46; Plutarch, *Brutus*, 39–44). However Cassius died, the simple fact was that the most experienced republican commander left alive had perished. The fate of the republic now rested on Brutus.

The Second Battle

Brutus mourned the death of his friend privately. Once again he consoled himself with philosophical musings, debating whether Cassius should be condemned for hastily abandoning hope or blessed because he had lived a virtuous life and was now freed from its "cares and troubles." His conclusion that Cassius was beckoning him to his side was not merely dramatic license on the part of the ancient historians. Brutus had become increasingly convinced that the Stoic ethic of suicide in the face of utter shame, defeat and capture, or life under a tyranny was an honorable decision (Appian, *Civil Wars*, 4.114; Plutarch, *Brutus*, 40). This left little doubt what course he would take in the event of a defeat.

Still, Brutus had some fighting spirit left. Not wanting to discourage his troops with a public funeral, he sent Cassius' body to Thasos. As a sign of republican strength, he marshaled his forces out for battle the next day when Antony did the same, but both sides were merely testing one another. Brutus would continue to rely on his superior position and supplies. To a certain extent, this could still be a valuable plan. Autumn rains had inundated the triumviral camps, adding low morale and the fear of famine and disease to their already poor situation. Another disaster had struck the triumvirs on the day of the first battle when Murcus' fleet destroyed triumviral transports bearing men and supplies across the Adriatic.

Nonetheless, Brutus must have realized that the situation had also changed in other ways of equal importance. After the first battle he unwisely abandoned the Kutchuk-tepe, which Antony and Octavian wasted no time in occupying. They then extended their lines southeast toward the sea, meaning they were now poised to surround Brutus or cut off his lines of supply and retreat. Appian makes it very clear that the new position of Antony and Octavian meant they had the opportunity of severing his logistical link along the Via Egnatia (*Civil Wars*, 4.121). If he waited too long, he might find himself cut off from his base of support.[17]

The next two and a half weeks became a waiting game, with each side looking for the other to start what would inevitably be the decisive moment of the war. This delay proved fatal to the vacillating Brutus. His troops were already frustrated, preferring an outright fight to a war of attrition. Dio plays up their clamoring, depicting them as itching for

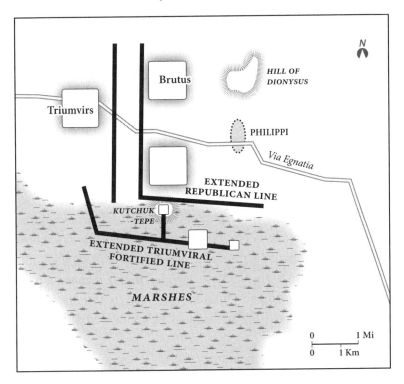

Positions before the Second Battle of Philippi, 23 Oct 42 BC

battle as soon as the triumvirs arrived (42.38). This certainly conforms with their behavior in the first battle. Plutarch, stressing the similarity with Pompey who fought Caesar when he should have waited him out, has Brutus' soldiers again demanding a fight after the first engagement. Now, however, Brutus was bereft of Cassius, who had previously kept the men in line and the officers focused on a sound strategy.

Appian has Brutus deliver his major battlefield speech immediately after the first battle, but it was hardly worth noting. Brutus stresses that they just killed twice as many soldiers as their opponents. He re-emphasizes the strength of their position. He also remarks on how they seized the initiative in the first battle but failed to follow through by defeating the enemy. He pleads with them not to act independently in the future, because all they need do is wait for hunger and a swampy camp to finish off their enemies. He hopes that none will think his "generalship has become sloth rather than action," but the only assurance he offers them is to give "each soldier 1000 drachmas" (Appian, *Civil Wars*, 4.118).

Brutus' speech to the troops was as lame as his performance in the first battle. Here we have a commander who lost control of troops that could have finished the war. Had he properly exercised command on 3 October, he could have rescued Cassius and crushed Antony. His lack of control the day of the battle was exacerbated by his rewarding men that should have been punished or at least chastised. Brutus' men were not merely demonstrating initiative but insubordination. His first duty was to restore discipline and retain command, but in this he failed and would continue to do so. Where was the legendary republican discipline that prompted fathers to execute their own sons when they disobeyed orders? Cassius had commanded in this manner, a point emphasized by Appian and Plutarch (*Civil Wars*, 4.123; *Brutus*, 46), but Brutus did not have the stomach or the courage to do what was necessary.

Brutus also makes no mention of the cause Cassius so eloquently articulated. Repeatedly mentioning this cause was critical, especially because Cassius had died in a manner that suggested he had despaired of the republic. Plutarch remarks that Cassius' troops desperately needed to be reminded what they were fighting for. Men who had fought and won under Caesar had just lost under Cassius. All of this was made worse by Antony's psychological warfare. His men had begun casting pamphlets into the Roman line, petitioning them to either wise up and join the winning side or act like men and take the field. Prisoners from the first battle joined in the jeering, mocking Cassius' suicide and prompting Casca, another of the assassins, to goad Brutus into killing all of his POWs (Dio, 47.48; Plutarch, *Brutus*, 45).

The morale of the republicans was teetering. This was especially so among Cassius' troops and any that understood what his suicide meant for the cause. Why would these men keep fighting? Why would they follow Brutus? What promised victory, and how would they be led? Brutus answers none of these questions, merely repeating their strategic plan and offering more money. The last citizen army of the republic was thus left with a lax and insipid commander stymied by his frequent philosophical flights and a desire to please his subordinates.[18]

Compare Brutus' speech with that given by Antony on the same day. Appian has Antony deride the republican fortifications, which are merely covers for their cowardice. Instead of fighting like men, the republicans build walls. Once again, he reminds them why they fight: for conquest and plunder. The loss of their own camp would be reversed because his troops cared most of all about "conquering with might." Once they defeated the enemy, the plunder would come. Not only would they take the goods of the citizen-soldiers that they killed, but they would also have access to the wealth of Asia. As a deposit, he then pledges a reward of five thousand drachmas for the soldiers and more for the centurions and tribunes (*Civil Wars*, 4.119–20). Antony's speech may not be republican, but it correctly gauged the motives of his men and reassured them he would lead them where they wanted to go.

Brutus held to his strategy of attrition, but his troops grew tired of waiting. For one last time, the independence of republican citizens manifested itself as the men pushed for action. As the days trickled by, more men became restive. A few defectors left the lines. Murmurings turned to grumblings. Grumblings turned to outcries. Why was Brutus not seizing the initiative? Why was a victorious army now refusing battle to those they had just defeated? Where was the honor in waiting for an army to retreat and then pouncing on them from the rear? The criticism was egged on by Brutus' own disposition, being "gentle and kindly" with a "mildness of temper." Cassius or Antony would never have tolerated this insubordination; they expected their orders to be followed, not questioned. Brutus' good sense was thus worn down by psychological weakness. Instead of reassuring the veterans of Caesar that they fought for a nobler cause, he remained silent, fearing their treachery. Instead of reminding all of his troops that waiting for a sure victory was better than risking a possible defeat, he gave in to their logic. Instead of rebuking his officers for questioning his orders, he allowed them to command him (Plutarch, *Brutus*, 45; Appian, *Civil Wars*, 4.123).

It is possible that Brutus also feared the cutting off of his supply lines, but the ancient sources all agree that the desires of his men over-whelmed his better judgment. Once again the speech provided by Appian after he musters his men reflects his troops' destructive independence and his own lack of *auctoritas*. "You have chosen to fight[;] . . . you have forced me to battle when I could conquer otherwise" were pathetic words from a battlefield commander. When the triumvirs gathered they offered speeches as well, naming the same incentives as before. Hunger would finish them if they did not fight, but they could "gain in one day and by one blow provisions, money, ships, and camps, and the prizes of victory." They also appealed to their warrior's spirit to finish the job this time and not allow the cowards to hide behind fortifications again. This must be a fight of annihilation (*Civil Wars*, 4.127).

Plutarch has the battle open as Brutus again dithers while inspecting the troops. Inspired by treachery or disgusted with Brutus' weakness, Camulatus, one of his bravest men walked out between the two lines and then deserted to Antony. Finally stirred to action by anger and the fear of further treachery, Brutus launched a general attack. This time both sides were prepared and all the generals stayed with their troops, rallying the men and making sure they focused on killing and not merely plundering (Plutarch, *Brutus*, 49).

When the lines clashed Appian has the men once more abandon tested tactics for raw, up-close killing. Avoiding the usual exchange of missile weapons, even the famous pila, they rushed on one another to engage in the hacking and thrusting of close sword work. Both Roman armies fought as they had for centuries. When the first ranks had fallen "the others stepped into their places from the reserves." The Roman preference for gladius wielding made every death face-to-face, creating an unusually gruesome scene: the "slaughter and the groans were terrible." The fight was no easy one because both sides, "being of like discipline and power of endurance," were "mutually invincible" (*Civil Wars*, 4.128, 137).

At first it seemed as though victory might go to the republicans. Their cavalry on the right flank drove off their opponents and then wheeled to the triumvir's left. Brutus led the infantry to success as well, and it looked like the left flank of the triumviral army would collapse.

Unfortunately, the maneuver weakened a republican center already thinned out by overextension. Finally, the triumvirs' numerical superiority paid off. Appian has Octavian's men begin to exploit this. Not wanting to be outshined again by Antony's troops, they cracked Brutus' lines, progressively pushing back the republican ranks until they broke. Then they turned and enveloped Brutus. A fierce fight broke out around the republican commander. All of the officers and his friends swarmed to his side (*Civil Wars*, 4.128). The site became the killing zone for many of the last republican officers and their sons. They "fell . . . risking their lives in defence of Brutus." With these horrifying final moments of the battle fixed in his mind, Brutus fled the field (Plutarch, *Brutus*, 49).

The rout of the republican forces was thorough. Although Octavian, supposedly still sick, had "no great achievements," his troops maintained their focus (Plutarch, *Antony*, 22). They attacked and seized the gates of Brutus' camp, not to plunder it but to cut off their enemies' escape. Seeing they could not reach safety in that direction, the republican soldiers fled toward the sea. Safety was equally elusive there, for Antony's cavalry rode them down as they fled. Antony desired to exterminate the enemy. He had been fighting republicans for eight years, and this was his chance to avenge his misfortunes and cleanse the empire of their opposition:

> Antony was everything and attacked everywhere, falling upon the fugitives and those who still held together, and upon their other camping-places, crushing all alike with vehement impetuosity. Fearing lest the leaders should escape him and collect another army, he despatched cavalry upon the roads and outlets of the field of battle to capture those who were trying to escape. (Appian, *Civil Wars*, 4.129)

The fortunate ones made it to the sea and the mountains, but they were few and scattered. The battle was over. There would not be another.

The reality of his situation slowly dawned on Brutus as he escaped up to the heights behind Philippi. Those who followed him were confronted with a haunting scene as Brutus began calling out the names of all his friends and fellow noblemen he had just seen slaughtered at his side (Plutarch, *Brutus*, 51). Once he regained his composure, he observed that he had men enough to fill less than four legions, enough possibly for another desperate fight. Perhaps suicide did not sound so appealing after all. Yet again the men under his command made his decision for him. Despite the fact that they had forced him to fight in the first place, they would not fight for him again. With an uncharacteristic coldness, they dismissed him, saying that "he should look out for himself." As for themselves, they would pursue "the last remaining hope of accommodation" (Appian, *Civil Wars*, 4.131).

It is hard to feel sorry for Brutus at this point. He had lost the respect of his men and should not have expected their support after he surrendered his authority. In the beginning, Cassius and Brutus' virtue had won these men over, even the supporters of Caesar and his memory. They lured them away from Caesar's heirs and united them together under the "cause of democracy." These last citizen-soldiers were not perfect, but they had performed admirably and stayed true to the cause articulated eloquently at times by Cassius and Brutus. No, the men had not abandoned the commanders. It was the other way around. Cassius, the general who was said to have fought with the ferocity of a gladiator, abandoned them when he turned this ferocity against himself. Brutus did it when he refused to lead (Appian, *Civil Wars*, 4.133).

Brutus' last request was denied by the men as well. As night fell, he asked his servant, his shield bearer, an old philosophy colleague, and then anyone nearby to help him kill himself. None could bring themselves to do it. Determined on his next course of action, he then walked around the circle of men and shook each of their hands. Seeing what he was about to do, the men recovered their respect for him and for his "reputation for virtue." They bid farewell. Brutus withdrew from the circle, tightly grasped his inward-pointing sword, and fell on it to his death (Plutarch, *Brutus*, 52). The last two republican commanders thus perished in the most ironic of ways; having "never received any hurt in battle[,] . . . both became the slayers of themselves, as they had been of Caesar" (Appian, *Civil Wars*, 4.134).

KILLING THEMSELVES

In a sense Cassius, Brutus, and the other leaders reflected the citizen-soldiers as a whole, who had spent more time slaughtering themselves than the enemy. The casualties at Philippi were substantial. Statistics from the ancient sources are confusing, but it seems that the battles were as catastrophic as the disaster at Cannae, with more than forty thousand dead. Most importantly, the battled had killed off all of the last republican leaders. Philippi finished off in the East what the Mutina campaign and the proscriptions had already accomplished in the West. The outspoken conservatives, the liberators, and many of their sons were now all dead, meaning that "never again would military force be used overtly in the name of the Republican form of government."[19]

This last generation of republican statesmen had not been without flaws. Cicero's rhetorical campaign against Antony was the last great expression of the republican orator. Indeed, Cicero was the last great expression of republicanism in the ancient world. Yet the republic's greatest exponent lacked the command abilities of his predecessors, from Romulus and Camillus to the Fabii and the Cornelii.

The republic needed competent commanders like Caesar and Antony. Scipio Africanus played that role in the Second Punic War. The republic also needed ardent republicans like Fabius Cunctator, who were not brilliant tacticians but represented the aristocratic values that held the republic together, especially in times of crisis. There were the rare great commanders that had both qualities, like Cincinnatus, Camillus, and Aemilianus, but the republic did not require individuals like that to survive. Caesar did not need to have all the qualities of Cicero, nor did Cicero need to have all the qualities of Caesar. They just needed to be on the same side. In the final years of the republic, the finest tacticians and the finest republican peacemakers were not, so a choice had to be made. If statesmen had worked in harmony like the *nobilitas* of old, or if, like Camillus, one of them had been "foremost in peace and war," such a choice would never have been necessary.

Cicero is thus a foil for all of the commanders of his day, especially his opponent Antony. He could sing the song of the republic, but he failed to embody it. When Hirtius and Pansa died, he could not take command. He often pleaded old age, but this did not prevent Fabius Maximus from fighting Hannibal when he was in his seventies or Aemilius Paullus from fighting Perseus when he was in his sixties. No, Cicero was deficient in temperament, and in this he was not the ideal statesman he so often wrote about. Perhaps we may forgive the prolific author who described so poignantly what it meant and how it felt to be a Roman republican. Nonetheless Cicero's execution eight months after the victory he engineered—but did not fight and did not command—showed that his dream of the ideal republican statesman and commander died with him, partly because he could not fully defend it.

A Cult of Suicide

And what about the liberators? Why did Cassius give up? Where was the man that turned a crushing defeat at Carrhae into a successful defense of Syria? Is it more reasonable to assume that Pindarus killed Cassius? This is unlikely for three reasons. First, the sources generally favor the suicide angle, either because he was misinformed or because he felt humiliated. Second, Cassius was almost certainly infected with the paralyzing despair that was spreading among the Roman elite. He was inspired by what was already becoming known as the most legendary suicide in Roman history, that of Cato the Younger. This had occurred after Caesar's victory at Thapsus in 46. When the inveterate foe of Caesar realized his only way to survive would be to surrender to Caesar and earn his clemency, he opted instead to commit suicide as a Stoic martyr of the republic. Gathering all of his available companions, Cato discussed philosophy late into the night, and then retired into his room where he attempted to kill himself. He was prevented by a wound in his hand. Despite the desperate efforts of his friends, he finally finished the deed by gorily pulling apart his bandages fashioned after his first attempt, spilling his innards out onto the floor, and slowly bleeding to death. The manner of the deed was important as it embodied all the hallmarks of Stoic suicide. It was communal, theatrical, carried out by one determined to control his own destiny, and seen as a last resort in the face of tyranny or utter shame.

Whence Cato's preference for such an end? A tidal wave of Greek philosophy had inundated Rome since its third-century conquests, and after conquering Greece at the Battle of Pydna, Romans became familiar with the "cult of suicide" developed by the various philosophical traditions. Cassius and Brutus had explored the philosophy of the Skeptics and the Epicureans, but like many Romans, they had a particular affinity for Stoic ethics, and Cato's suicide was stoical to perfection.[20]

There is a third reason to accept the suicide account for Cassius. It is surely no coincidence that Cassius killed himself after his ignominious failure on 3 October. This was a particularly auspicious day for him, being his birthday (Appian, *Civil Wars*, 4.113). Not only did he adopt a gloomy interpretation of contemporary omens, but in his own mind fate had ordained that he suffer defeat on the same day that he was born and the same day that he would die. He and Brutus had discussed how suicide was only permissible if the gods ordained it, and there could be no clearer sign that they did in his case.

There was another, more ancient tradition of suicide independent of the Greeks, traceable back through the *devotiones* of the Decii, the senators during the Gallic invasion, and the foundational act of the republic itself, the rape and suicide of Lucretia. In a dismal irony, Cassius' philosophy-inspired suicide bore little resemblance to the older Roman traditions. Lucretia's suicide brought the republic into existence. Those of the Decii saved it in moments of crises. Cassius' death, however, sounded the republic's doom. Like Cato, he had despaired too early and thrown his life away before the end of the war had actually come. If he had not, he and Brutus would have stood an excellent chance of winning at Philippi. Instead, in killing himself, he eliminated the best republican commander and provided fodder for Antony's propaganda. The tipping point of the campaign, then, was the moment that Cassius, in his confusion and despair, turned to a misguided ideology and disregarded the real needs of the moment.

The leadership of the republic had enmeshed itself in this culture of suicide. Cato, Metellus Scipio, Cassius, and Brutus were only the most famous that perished at their own hands. Readers may recall Marcus Petreius, Caecilius Cornutus, and Titinius as well. After the battle, many of the young officers "killed themselves as the two generals had done." Some did so with panache. Cassius' nephew and Cato's son both charged the enemy without armor. Others did so in utter calmness. Labeo, whose philosophical disposition matched Brutus, returned to his tent where he settled all his affairs, arranged for his wife and children, sent letters to his domestic slaves, and then had another slave slit his throat (Appian, *Civil Wars*, 4.135). Even after the battle, the suicide contagion claimed more victims. "Most of the prominent men who had held offices or still survived of the number of Caesar's assassins or of those who had been proscribed straightway killed themselves, or . . . were captured and put to death" (Dio, 42.49).

The End of Civic Virtue

Another casualty on the battlefield at Philippi was civic virtue. But how long had its carcass been rotting? For Polybius, greed, bribery, dishonor, dishonesty, impiety, pederasty, and other forms of sexual immorality began to prevail after the conquest of Greece. Polybius also cites the growing intellectual predilection for cynicism and nihilism, which, as we have already seen, was linked to the cult of suicide (6.56, 18.34, 31.25). Sallust lived through the fall of the republic and mentions a similar list of vices, although he is able to specify more egregious examples of a culture becoming rife with lawlessness and injustice (*The War with Catiline*, 2). A generation later Livy opens his monumental *From the Founding of the City* with a reflection on how the traditions of austerity, discipline, incorruptibility, and civic sacrifice had suffered a long decline (preface). Polybius predicted, Sallust experienced, and Livy recounted the same story. Civic virtue—the traditions and customs that habituated citizens and bound their republic together—had undergone a nearly crippling assault.

The chief offenders in the growing pandemic of civic vice were the men whose names are most commonly associated with the republic's final years. Personal immorality, intoxicating ambition, and a general disdain for tradition and order had crippled the republic, especially among the commanders. In the days of Marius and Sulla, those who followed the more traditional path were suborned or assassinated by the gangs of two men that history has recognized as the definers of an age. By all accounts, these two—the men who became, for better or worse, the "leading statesmen"—were anything but virtuous. In the 80s Rome had been militarily occupied by its opposing factions three times. Opponents had been hunted down and assassinated. Taboos had been shattered, and new precedents set. There seemed to be a brief recovery after Sulla, but that then dissolved in another round of machinating chiefs, first Crassus, Pompey, and Caesar, and then Lepidus, Antony, and Octavian. These decisions at the top provided poor examples, offered no unity, and represented civic vice for the men under their command.

Even those traditional upholders of civic virtue, the conservative elite, were not blameless. In its last century, the republic had created remarkably capable veterans, yet the conservative elite had failed to assimilate them into Roman society. Even the ultratraditional Livy paints hardline conservative senators of early Roman history as lacking two of the most crucial elements of a statesman: prudence and moderation. The result was that many veterans turned to the commanders most willing to reward them, regardless of their regime preferences. The republic could still raise loyal levies, as the statistics for its final years bear out, and these levies fought as levies had always fought for the republic. But at Philippi, they were momentarily in the minority.

It must be assumed that many of the men of the forty-three legions mustered by the triumvirs simply swayed with the prevailing winds. We rarely hear their voices except through the occasional spokesman. Significant bodies of these men had fought for Caesar, and then for his lieutenants and heirs, three of whom became the triumvirs. These soldiers had learned to follow a warrior ethos. They had no conception of civic virtue, having served with Caesar, first to slaughter Gauls and then their fellow citizens in the Pompeian civil war. These men had been difficult to control by all the commanders after Caesar's assassination and were assiduously petitioned and manipulated by Antony, Octavian, and Lepidus even before the formation of the triumvirate.

During the escalation between Antony and Octavian in 44, these soldiers were guided by their devotion to the memory of Caesar. They insisted that they would follow Antony, but only insofar as he himself was loyal to Caesar. In some ways they still negotiated like republican soldiers, saying, for example, that only if he granted them security would they grant him power. But they had different objectives from citizen-soldiers of the past. The government they would "establish" and "maintain" had to be in the mold of Caesar. They were the "faithful supporters" of Caesar. Their piety would be devoted to Caesar's memory. Their objectives and motives had little to do with the republic. They also had a different target: the enemies of Caesar, and most especially the senate itself (Appian, *Civil Wars*, 3.31). In his description of these soldiers, Appian surely has the armies of the emperors in mind.

From 44 to 41 these men were reluctant to fight their fellow Caesarian veterans, but they had no compunctions about killing unarmed citizens. Their reign of terror in Italy was the surest sign that these soldiers were as vicious toward the republic as they were independent of it. When Octavian announced the wholesale theft of land and the upcoming slaughter of the proscriptions, "they applauded and embraced each other in token of mutual reconciliation." The soldiers would execute the orders with relish, bringing Italy to heel in a manner Tarquinius Superbus could have only dreamed of. Terrified by this, the senate called in a soothsayer, who said it was nothing less than the return of the kingship, and only suicide would free them from the coming enslavement. To make his point, the soothsayer then killed himself (Appian, *Civil Wars*, 4.3–4).

In the final battles there were others who knew they were still fighting for the republic. They believed the words and promises of Cicero, Cassius, and Brutus. The republic did not go quietly, and its last words— the letters and speeches of Cicero and Cassius—were powerful. But the republic was certainly dead when the dust settled on the battlefield of Philippi. The last generation of republican leaders and most of their sons were dead. The last citizen-soldiers died alongside them. They had been killed by men that were not really citizen-soldiers any longer.

The victors at Philippi had been habituated to kill the enemy just like Roman citizen-soldiers had been for centuries, but they misidentified who that enemy was. In the process, they began altering their own identity. The moment they starting killing their fellow citizens, they transitioned into a different kind of soldier. At the start of the last rounds of civil war, whether they were Caesar's troops in 49, Antony's in 43, or the triumvirs' in 42, these men knew they were fighting for autocrats and the rewards they offered.

The triumvirs took possession of the old republican legions after Philippi. These men realized that "there was no one in command," and did the triumvirs' bidding. With no leadership, the "latter wars were sporadic." Pompey's son was grafted into the triumvirs' new order in 39, but Octavian renewed their conflict two years later. He finally defeated him in 36 and executed him the next year. In the process, he found an excuse to accuse Lepidus of treachery and stripped him of power (Appian, *Civil Wars*, 5.1–3).

Octavian always kept a close eye on the soldiers and their demands. Immediately after Philippi, he and Antony took up the task of doling out the promised rewards. Antony fleeced the eastern provinces in another round of collections. Octavian had the far more difficult task of settling the men in the promised Italian colonies. He faced no small amount of protest. Eighteen of the best cities and numerous parcels of land were to be delivered to forty thousand veterans.[21] The Italians from the assigned cities flooded him with petitions:

> They came to Rome in crowds, young and old, women and children to the forum and the temples, uttering lamentations, saying that they had done no wrong for which they, Italians, should be driven from their fields and their hearthstones, like people conquered in war. The Romans mourned and wept with them, especially when they reflected that the war had been waged and the rewards of victory given, not in behalf of the commonwealth, but against themselves and for a change of the form of government. (Appian, *Civil Wars*, 5.12)

Protests meant nothing in this new form of government. What mattered was who controlled the troops and what the troops were willing to do. They descended on Italy, "seizing more than had been given." The soldiers supported Octavian, even after his pathetic performance at Philippi, because only he could legitimize their theft. Appian sums it up nicely: "The chiefs depended on the soldiers for the continuance of their government, while, for the possession of what they had received, the soldiers depended on the permanence of the government of those who had given it" (*Civil Wars*, 5.13). By forcing through the settlement, Octavian had just secured the loyalty of the soldiers that served under him and pledged it to those that would do so in the future. From now on, the soldiers would work for men like Octavian, and he would work for them. There was no longer a republic and no need for republican soldiers. The men who would now serve the emperors had not merely killed their fellow Romans; they had killed their own nature as citizen-soldiers.

EPILOGUE
War Stories for the Emperor

Horace was studying in Athens when Brutus and Cassius began raising armies for the Philippi campaign.[1] Like so many soldiers in the last days of the republic, Horace was imbued with republican sentimentality. He enrolled in the republican army and was made an officer. As a participant of the Battle of Philippi in 42, he witnessed the republic's demise. Fortunately for Horace he was pardoned and later earned a place in the elite literary circle surrounding Octavian, now called Augustus. Horace had fought for the enemies of Augustus, but he used his position in the Augustan court to idealize imperial warfare with a patriotism that no longer existed.

Horace sums up the republican ethos in Ode 3.2, where he uplifts the citizen dedicated to martial pursuits. He is battle hardened and ruthless compared to a royal prince who has never tasted combat. Moreover, the republican's civic militarism will prompt him to sacrifice everything for the state. For him, "it is sweet and right to die for his country." Horace's phrase would later be drummed into the minds of patriotic schoolboys in the lead-up to World War I, prompting the British soldier and poet Wilfred Owen to call it "the old Lie."

Horace himself had seen this lie at Philippi. In Ode 2.7 he praises the valor of the republican soldiers, but he also describes how the survivors prostrated themselves like humiliated beasts before the victors. War, even for a noble cause, mocked the dead and the living. Horace's friend on the battlefield, Pompeius, had kept fighting at Philippi and would continue fighting in the last scattered bouts of resistance. Pompeius' republican valor was nothing laudable, however. He had simply been "swallowed up again" into a futile struggle for the republic's corpse, whereas Horace had been spirited away to a prosperous peace. The glorious moment came when Augustus freed Pompeius and restored his citizenship. The war-ending Augustus is the hero, not the die-hard republican Pompeius.

Ode 2.7 also recalls Horace's own cowardice when he abandoned his shield in order to hastily flee the field. Keeping your shield until death in battle was the mantra of the citizen-soldier. Horace's decision to flee and then make the earliest peace possible demonstrated his willingness to abandon civic virtue for the possibility of a posh life as a poet in the imperial court. He may have eulogized the old republic and its virtues, but Horace did not seriously wish their return. Instead, he applied the old values to a regime that would never truly accommodate them.

Titus Livy offers a contrasting view. Livy was born in Patavium, probably in 59. He was ten years old when Caesar crossed northern Italy after his conquests in Gaul en route to the Rubicon. As a teenager Livy may have even witnessed operations in the Mutina campaign. The battles were 130 kilometers away from Patavium, and Patavium itself was harassed by Antony's subordinates that same year.

Unlike Horace, Livy always longed for the civic militarism shared among citizens willing to kill and die for the idea of a republic. Livy avoided the elite circle of Augustus and became known for his "Patavinity," which referred to his preference for the moralizing culture of his conservative hometown as opposed to the urbanity of Rome. Livy sought inspiration from the past and retreated into the consolation of history. But Livy does more than tell us *what* the Romans did. His work describes *who* a Roman republican was and *how* he dedicated his life to the common good. Most often in Livy, this is manifested in the heroic leadership of republican statesmen in war: characters this work has explored like Brutus, Cincinnatus, Camillus, the Decii, Fabius Maximus, Scipio Africanus, and Aemilius Paullus.[2]

His history of Rome's republican wars subtly challenged the new regime by hearkening back to the republicanism of a previous age. In Livy's day, inspiring leaders like Camillus and Fabius contrasted with those of recent history—grasping, ambitious, and amoral men such as Caesar, Antony, and even Augustus himself. Livy's overarching moral theme is as much a damnation of the Augustan peace as it is approbation for the peace having finally been achieved. Augustus may have brought decades of violence and civil war to an end, but the soul of the republic—its freedoms, civic culture, and virtues—was destroyed in the process he completed.

A few Romans under the newly fashioned empire still dreamed of restoring the republic, but they were naive to dream. By 27 the new constitutional order, the charisma of unfolded history, and the culture of the people were all now perfectly suited to autocracy. The empire would become stable, mild in its injustices, and look very much like what had been the republic in some important ways. The world was still a good one for average Romans. The difference was that what sovereignty remained in the old assemblies, senate, and consuls was concentrated in an emperor, who was originally simply called princeps. The title had long represented the leading man of the senate, but, in a culture that still despised the word "rex," it was now employed for the emperor. The euphemistic name did not change the fact that liberty in the Roman Empire meant something much less and required much less of those who earned it.

THE EMPEROR'S MEN

The Roman Republic did not decline so much as shipwreck after veering wildly out of control. The events surrounding its final years illustrate how, with the stakes of a Mediterranean empire being higher than those of an Italian federation, the typical demands of soldiers and veterans made the situation even more volatile. Still, the army had not failed. Nor was the ship—the constitution—unfit for service.[3] The constitution had taken some hits, especially after Sulla and again after Caesar, but it recovered in the 70s, and there were signs that it could have recovered again after the Ides of March. And what of the soldiers? If anything, the constitutionally conscripted Roman legions at the end of the republic demonstrated that men were still willing to die in droves for the republic and republican commanders. The army was part of the problem from 49 to 42, but it was a tool that could be reshaped. With enough time, the ship could have been patched and the tool refashioned. In the end, it was the captains. And the most powerful captains of the hour—Caesar, Antony, Lepidus, and Octavian—were determined on the ship's destruction.

But it needn't have happened that way. What if Fortune had not smiled on Caesar and he had been killed in any of the numerous battles he won? Or what if Fortune had smiled on the republic? As I have demonstrated, the argument that the republic's fall was not inevitable is convincing, and I add to that argument the observation that the "last generation of the Roman Republic" was not finished off in 49 but in 43 or 42. The republic almost won in 43 and again in 42. In April 43, Antony had been crushed. Lepidus, Pollio, and Plancus had pledged loyalty to the republic and were not moving against it. Octavian was cowed, for although he had a reputation as Caesar's heir, he had no experience and no credibility. And the armies that created this situation had fought, killed, and died for the republic. Cicero had identified the republic's enemy and brought about concord against that foe. The republic had won.

Even after the surprising resurrection of Antony and his reconciliation with the other Caesarian commanders and Octavian, the republic had stood a good chance of winning again. The forces were evenly matched at Philippi. The republicans had the superior position. They had control of the Mediterranean. They overran Octavian's army and his camp in the first battle. History could have gone very differently, with the ambitions of Caesar and his heirs being condemned alongside those of Tarquin, Coriolanus, Spurius Maelius, and other famous traitors and tyrants the republic had historically crushed. Loyalty to Caesar would eventually have been seen as the worst sort of treason, and that core of veterans so devoted to him would have given up and slowly died off. The other soldiers that had been so wildly independent would have been leaderless and could have been tamed under a republic that learned its lesson.

Could civic virtue have recovered? What about the memory of escalating, unprecedented violent acts? Could these be forgotten? It is possible they could have been overwritten with newer and stronger memories. Cicero, Cassius, and Brutus could have steered the ship back into safe waters. These men were republican down to the bone. They could not have survived under a monarchy. It would have been difficult to overcome the culture of warlordism and selfish ambition, but the fact that it was a possibility was attested to by Cicero's, Cassius', and Brutus' final actions. People in every age have choices, and sometimes they choose to do the most remarkable and unexpected things. Roman history is filled with Romans who had the exceptional ability to create, improve, protect, and expand their republic. The unexpected almost happened in 43 and again in 42, but perhaps Polybius was right to believe that fate had finally caught up.

Neither did Fortune smile on the republic like it had on Caesar and Octavian. Hirtius and Pansa were killed. Antony and Octavian survived. Dust and noise confused Cassius, causing him to abandon reality. Brutus lost his nerve. If these things had not happened, it does not seem unreasonable to believe that the triumvirate never would have been, moderates and liberators would have maintained peace like the republic had seen in the 70s, statues of Brutus and Cassius would have littered the forum, and Cicero would have died peacefully, after writing more philosophy and singing more of his own praises about how he had saved the republic as its greatest orator in the moment of its greatest peril.

Instead, the republic lost. And once personalities such as Octavian had achieved control, one of their principal objectives would be to replace civic militarism with the ethos of a warrior class. Under the principate's military autocracy, standing, professional legions replaced the conscriptions of citizen-soldiers. The republican veneer was maintained in many ways, but all things republican—especially soldiers— were tamed and brought under the control of the princeps.

With the republic dead, the republican armies had to be killed off too. After his victory over Antony in 31, Octavian began reducing the overall number of legions by half, resettling thousands of veterans, and standardizing service in the empire. Legions that were increasingly regularized were given official names and positioned in semipermanent locations along the frontiers in camps that eventually became walls and forts. With over three hundred thousand permanent soldiers on the payroll, the Roman army became the most important item in the budget. Eventually the empire fielded a standard thirty legions, whose troops were paid in hard coin. By the time Octavian died in AD 14, for the first time "the Roman army had become a fully professional and permanent institution."[4] The republic had been replaced with an imperial, military autocracy.

The republican armies, especially in the late republic, could behave with notorious independence, so Augustus needed to ensure loyalty. Soldiers' ties to family and home were curtailed or severed. Volunteers made up the bulk of the army. Soldiers were forbidden to marry and previous marriages were annulled before they entered service. The legion was the soldier's new family, and devotion to the emperor replaced devotion to the republic. The emperor's personal image— vividly captured in a special standard bearing the image of the emperor and carried by an *imaginifer*—became more important than ancestors' busts.[5]

As legionary tombstones illustrate, especially in contrast to the Tomb of the Scipios or the inscription for Appius Claudius Caecus, the citizen-commander and citizen-soldier were no more. Many legionaries make no mention of families, farms, or other civic communities in death, instead emphasizing their units: legions if they were citizens and cohorts if they were auxiliaries. The titles that mattered to them were not agricultural or civic but purely military. They mention their decorations, their functions (e.g., *aquilifer*, *signifer*, *medicus ordinarius*, etc.), important battles they fought or died in like Actium or the Teutoberger Wald, and the units that were the only families some of them ever knew. Some men were released from service to take up different lives as civilians, but others made the army a way of life, living on the frontier and dying as soldiers past the age of fifty. Titus Calidius

Severus, for example, started at the bottom before working his way up to become a centurion, a cavalryman, and an auxiliary cavalry officer. He died at the age of fifty-eight after thirty-four years of service.[6]

These were the emperor's men, and it was fitting that Augustus could triumphantly state in his propaganda piece *Res gestae divi Augusti*: "Wars, both civil and foreign, I undertook throughout the world, on sea and land, and when victorious I spared all citizens who sued for pardon. The number of Roman citizens who bound themselves to me by military oath was about 500,000" (1.3). This description indicates the new nature of the military. Soldiers no longer belonged to themselves, the senate, the people of Rome, or the republic. They were the personal possession of an autocrat. Throughout the *Res gestae*, "the adjectives *meus*, *mea*, and *mei* dominate: *milites mei* (my soldiers), *exercitus meus* (my army), *classis mea* (my fleet)."[7] Legitimacy would no longer be a question as it had been in the final years of the republic. The emperor controlled the armies. They were loyal to him alone.

Civic virtue received an overhaul as well. Rome's "cultural identity" had been lost in the upheavals of the first century. Augustus found it necessary to rebuild public and private morality with an expansive reform program. To literary masterpieces created by the likes of Livy, Horace, and Virgil were added "'works of art,' buildings, . . . poetic imagery, . . . religious ritual, clothing, state ceremony, the emperors conduct, and forms of social intercourse." This "tapestry of images" revived some of the old mores, but it was impossible to disguise the fact that the "new ritual of power" sought to direct all aspects of life upward to the emperor. Virtue was never the highest aim because it flowed from the imperial office. The scheming, bloodthirsty Octavian was forgotten, and he was refashioned into Augustus, a paragon that emanated morality. Like a god Augustus' position slowly became a new focal point for the army, the state, and virtue itself.[8]

WESTERN WAYS OF WAR

Modern representative democracies are different in so many ways from ancient, martial republics. Modern citizens are not used to animal or human carnage, and they are less accustomed to death as well, with lower birth and mortality rates separating them from the higher birth and mortality rates of the premodern world. Roman citizens, especially in the early years, were bound together as a face-to-face society; they expected to move infrequently, if ever, and to see and know their countrymen and leaders. Today, bureaucratic institutions, celebrities, TV shows, sporting events, and national news outlets bind together citizens who can take nearly any job in nearly any part of the country. Political allegiances in the Roman Republic were determined by close, personal and familial bonds that were constantly shifting and competing with one another. Current democratic politics is determined by party or parliamentary procedures that have entrenched positions, overarching principles, and stable platforms. Modern citizenship and society is more inclusive and unstratified compared to the Roman world that emphasized distinctions based on birth, sex, and wealth. These are only a few of the more obvious differences that make any modern democracy different from any ancient republic. However, there are still continuities between premodern and modern republics, raising some questions about what modern republics expect of their citizens and how they defend what they value.

This study has used Rome to explore how ancient citizen armies came into being, the way they fought, and the ideas and customs they fought for. After the fall of its republican constitutions, citizens and subjects were habituated to new lifestyles with new demands and new expectations. Rome traded its citizen armies for a professional corps of soldier-citizens and mercenary allies. War was the same on the surface, but it was different underneath. If a republic is defined as it often is today—as a government that belongs to the people and where the people participate of their own free will—then things were very different indeed. War might be forced on people, like an earthquake or an erupting volcano, but it was no longer something in which the people participated. Militarism still remained, but it was not the civic kind. It was defined by the professional code of the warrior. Soldiers no longer killed or died for the state or their local communities as much as they killed or died for their code, their commander, their emperor, and their pay. For the individual soldier, war went from duty to opportunity. Some might argue that things were better this way, but there is no doubt that they were different.

I do question if the professional model is better than the participatory. Civilians in most Western nations still exercise ultimate control over the war authorization process, but an increasing minority of those who vote for wars fight them. In the Roman federation, half citizens and allies had to fight even if they had not participated in the process of authorizing it. During the first several centuries of their existence, Romans were also simply fighting to survive. Citizens were habituated to kill so that peace for farming and fathering would be possible. When they had pacified enough of their neighbors, they found themselves creating an empire out of instinct.

Gone is this sort of killing instinct among modern republics, and it is probably for the better. How comfortable would moderns be with average citizens willing to rob their enemies' food supplies, hack up people and animals in the streets, pillage their houses, and then obliterate their towns? Even if we replace the up-close killing with ancient sword and javelin with the modern trigger and button, like Sherman said, war is still nasty and shouldn't be idealized in and of itself. So it is perhaps better that war is rarely experienced and rarely touches most people in modern representative democracies.

However, there is something inconsistent about a republic where citizens are willing to authorize a war but not willing to fight it. Historical republics such as Carthage and Venice hired out their fighters, but these seem to have been the exception. This prompts some questions about modern republics. Would citizens still support a conflict if they had to go through the process of fighting it? Would they separate themselves from their families in order to complete several months of training? Would they spend months in barracks and tents without amenities in a truly pluralistic setting where they would be forced to live with people they might otherwise not choose to live with? Would all of these citizens be willing to deploy to a foreign country, point a rifle at a person about whom they know next to nothing, pull the trigger, and end that person's existence? War is easy to authorize when it involves a biannual trip to the ballot box. What if everyone in the United States knew authorization guaranteed personal fighting? Americans at least have demonstrated that they are not willing to pay for wars they choose (unless accumulating more debt counts as paying); if they were expected to actually fight them, is there any doubt how interventionist American national policy would be? And would the world be better or worse for this lack of intervention?

Some might dismiss these questions as irrelevant and focus on the continuity in Western fighting. They argue that there is such a thing as a "Western way of war." In some ways, they may be right, but I have attempted to explain how we should instead see Western *ways* of war. Rome relied on a different civic ethos to fight its wars on the other side of the divide that separated the republic from the principate. In the same way, modern nations change from one way of war to another. When, for example, horrified, enraged, dishonored, and fearful Americans made the 2001 and 2003 decisions to fight wars in Afghanistan and Iraq, the overwhelming majority of military-aged citizens who were polled or who wrote letters to their congressmen encouraging war knew they would not don armor and shoot the enemy. They would make other people do it, their professional soldier-citizens. Is this not remarkably different from the mindset of the colonists of the American War of Independence and the citizens of the American Civil War, world wars, and Vietnam?

Several important breaks in Western history make the ancient world very different from the modern. But the dark and the light remain in human nature, and modern societies still cater to both. War primarily brings out the dark, but it can also reveal some of the light. The civic cultures of ancient republics like Rome were different in what they expected of their citizens, and they had different ideas about how their citizens should navigate the light and the dark of war. This should give us pause when we think of the price we are willing to pay for our definitions of peace and liberty.

A citizenry's preference for participatory or professional soldiery says more about its willingness to participate than its desire for proficient killers. So when the modern republic engages in warfare, our increasing preference for professional over participatory armies reveals an ethos entirely different from that of the Roman Republic and from that of our own past. If the way we fight wars has changed, if the price of civic participation is so much cheaper, and if life and death are no longer on the line, then the way we understand peace has changed as well. Does the citizen of a modern republic who authorizes war but is unwilling to fight it have more respect for peace or less?

Acknowledgments

Livy, Polybius, and Cicero inspired this book. I never would have known about them—at least the way I came to know them—had it not been for the two professors who still inspire every moment I spend in my own classroom today, Cary Nederman and Christoph Konrad. Once they introduced me to Titus Livy, Polybius, and Marcus Tullius Cicero, fate determined that this would be my first book.

Fortune took me on a much longer journey than intended because of these three men who have been dead for over two thousand years. Livy sang the song of the world's greatest republic with a tune that has been etched into my conscience. I began to hum along the more I read. Polybius, like me, was not a Roman but marveled at the Roman constitution. He bullied me into the army by insisting that any historian who wishes to write about war and politics needs to have experienced real command in real wars. Cicero—and his heir Augustine—counseled me back into academia by reminding me that the intellectual should always have the peace of his own republic in mind. Not doing so means abandoning one's forebearers and giving up on the divine dream.

As is the case for all junior scholars, my greatest support on the path from dissertation to publication came from those who were much wiser and more knowledgeable. My intellectual mentors—Arthur Eckstein, Doyne Dawson, Antonio Santosuosso, Paul Rahe, Barry Strauss, and, most importantly, Victor Davis Hanson—set my feet upon the ground. I could not have asked for a better personal mentor than Bruce Thornton, whose encouragement and counsel demonstrated true *amicitia*, particularly when obstacles obscured my vision. I am also indebted to the patronage of Will Inboden and the Clements Center, who provided me the opportunity to return to academia after my military detour. They gave me the restful space to complete the book. I am grateful to the Johns Hopkins University Press editorial team, especially Matt McAdam, who brought this decade-long journey to its final destination.

The book has been expanded and sharpened by several hardworking readers of the manuscript, some of whom are unknown to me. Their critiques and encouragements honed my arguments and kept me close to the primary sources and the spirit in which they were written. The most brutal and beneficial of them at the end was MJ Devaney, who attacked my writing imperfections like a dentist who scraped, cleaned, and polished my textual teeth while pointing out all the flaws in my brushing.

Most importantly, I must thank Megan, Arien, Elinor, Katharina, Margaret, and Aethelflaed. You have endured living in different continents and six different states, a deployment on the other side of the world, holidays dedicated to writing, and having to tolerate my obsession, first as a citizen-soldier and then as a professor. I felt the burdens of the Roman husband and father who becomes the Roman citizen-soldier at your expense. Perhaps an apology is more in order.

And to Colonel John Hixson, who is in Afghanistan as I write, I hope I fulfilled my pledge to you from our last conversation. I have endeavored to speak only the truth and to do so with the mindset of a farmer-citizen-soldier.

Notes

Preface. Why Care about Long-Dead Fighting Farmers?

1. Unless otherwise noted, all translations from classical sources in the text come from the editions that make up the Loeb Classical Library.

2. For recent approaches to Roman civic militarism, both at the popular and academic levels, see, for example, Arthur M. Eckstein, *Mediterranean Anarchy, Interstate War, and the Rise of Rome* (Berkeley: University of California Press, 2006); Adrian Keith Goldsworthy, *The Complete Roman Army* (New York: Thames and Hudson, 2003); Adrian Keith Goldsworthy and John Keegan, *Roman Warfare* (New York: Collins, 2005); Chris McNab, *The Roman Army: The Greatest War Machine of the Ancient World* (Botley, UK: Osprey Publishing, 2010); and Nathan Rosenstein, *Rome at War: Farms, Families, and Death in the Middle Republic* (Chapel Hill: University of North Carolina Press, 2004). On civic militarism, see Doyne Dawson, *The Origins of Western Warfare* (Boulder, CO: Westview Press, 1996); Victor Davis Hanson, *Carnage and Culture* (New York: Doubleday, 2001); Victor Davis Hanson, *The Western Way of War* (Berkeley: University of California Press, 2000); and Antonio Santosuosso, *Soldiers, Citizens, and the Symbols of War* (Boulder, CO: Westview Press, 1997).

3. John Keegan, *A History of Warfare* (New York: Knopf, 1993), 12.

4. There is a vast literature on early Roman warfare, both popular and scholarly. A few examples from recent years include Lee L. Brice, *Warfare in the Roman Republic* (Santa Barbara, CA: ABC-CLIO, 2014); Brian Campbell, *Greek and Roman Military Writers* (New York: Routledge, 2004); Paul Chrystal, *Wars and Battles of the Roman Republic* (Stroud, UK: Fonthill, 2015); Dexter Hoyos, *Mastering the West* (Oxford: Oxford University Press, 2015); McNab, *The Roman Army*; Michael M. Sage, *The Republican Roman Army* (New York: Routledge, 2008); Patricia Southern, *The Roman Army* (Gloucestershire, UK: Amberley, 2014); Robin Waterfield, *Taken at the Flood* (Oxford: Oxford University Press, 2014); and Sheila Dillon and Katherine E. Welch, *Representations of War in Ancient Rome* (Cambridge: Cambridge University Press, 2006).

5. Eric H. Cline, *1177 B.C.: The Year Civilization Collapsed* (Princeton, NJ: Princeton

University Press, 2014); Eckstein, *Mediterranean Anarchy, Interstate War, and the Rise of Rome*; Josiah Ober, *Democracy and Knowledge* (Princeton, NJ: Princeton University Press, 2010). Other works draw on ancient history for modern diplomatic, political, and strategic insights, including Amy Chua, *Day of Empire* (New York: Doubleday, 2007); Eric H. Cline, *The Battles of Armageddon* (Ann Arbor: University of Michigan Press, 2002); Lawrence Freedman, *Strategy* (Oxford: Oxford University Press, 2013); David Edward Tabachnick and Toivo Koivukoski, eds., *Enduring Empire* (Toronto: University of Toronto Press, 2009); Victor Davis Hanson, *Makers of Ancient Strategy* (Princeton, NJ: Princeton University Press, 2010); Victor Davis Hanson, *The Father of Us All* (New York: Bloomsbury, 2010); and Barry S. Strauss and Josiah Ober, *The Anatomy of Error* (New York: St. Martin's Press, 1990).

Prologue. The Roman and American Republics

1. Portions of this chapter appear in an earlier version in Steele Brand, "Sources of American Republicanism: Ancient Models in the U.S. Capitol," *Humanitas* 29, nos. 1–2 (2017).

2. Donald R. Kennon and Thomas P. Somma, eds., *American Pantheon* (Athens: Ohio University Press, 2004).

3. On the classical and neoclassical influences on the founding generation, see Bernard Bailyn, *The Ideological Origins of the American Revolution* (Cambridge, MA: Harvard University Press, 1967), 23–26; David J. Bederman, *The Classical Foundations of the American Constitution* (Cambridge: Cambridge University Press, 2008), 1–49; Barbara Borngasser, "Neoclassical and Romantic Architecture in the United States of America," in *Neoclassicism and Romanticism*, ed. Rolf Toman (Cologne: H. F. Ullmann, 2006), 124–147; and Carl J. Richard, *The Founders and the Classics* (Cambridge, MA: Harvard University Press, 1994), 12–38.

4. On the numerous historical models, take, for example, John Adams' massive *A Defence of the Constitutions of Government of the United States of America*, which explores the modern historical constitutions of San Marino, Biscay, Switzerland, United Provinces of the Low Countries, Lucca, Genoa, Venice, England, Poland, Neuchatel, Florence, Siena, Bologna, Pistoia, Cremona, Padua, Mantua, and Montepulciano and the ancient republics of Carthage, Athens, Achaea, Crete, Corinth, Argos, Elis, Thebes, Sybaris, Locris, Rome, Lacedaemon, Crotona, the "Ancient Germans," Phaeacia, and Ithaca.

5. Jennifer Tolbert Roberts, *Athens on Trial* (Princeton, NJ: Princeton University Press, 1994), 177.

6. Alexis de Tocqueville, *Democracy in America* (Indianapolis, IN: Liberty Fund, 2012), 490–91.

7. Roberts, *Athens on Trial*, 177–78.

8. Tocqueville, *Democracy in America*, 815–17.

9. Charles Francis Adams, ed., *The Works of John Adams* (Cambridge, MA: Cambridge University Press, 2011), 4.521, 42.

10. For a summary of Plutarch's "Heroes and Villains," see Robert Lamberton, *Plutarch* (New Haven, CT: Yale University Press, 2001), 115–42.

11. Adams, *The Works of John Adams*, 4.434, 540–41.

12. Richard, *The Founders and the Classics*, 158.

13. Richard, *The Founders and the Classics*, 214.

14. Bederman, *The Classical Foundations of the American Constitution*, 31.

15. Richard, *The Founders and the Classics*, 94–95, 116–17. Richard also provides a survey of classical antimodels (87–94).

16. See the discussion in Bederman, *The Classical Foundations of the American Constitution*, 52–59.

17. Fisher Ames, *Works of Fisher Ames*, ed. W. B. Allen (Indianapolis, IN: Liberty Fund, 1983), 498, 421, 424, 132–33, 63–64, 223–27, 384–85.

18. Ames, *Works of Fisher Ames*, 97–103.

19. Richard examines the founders' discussion on the Greek leagues (*The Founders and the Classics*, 104–15).

20. Robert Scigliano, *The Federalist* (New York: Modern Library, 2000), 21.

21. Scigliano, *The Federalist*, 111.

22. Roberts, *Athens on Trial*, 178.

23. Scigliano, *The Federalist*, 80, 47, 356.

24. Scigliano, *The Federalist*, 404.

25. Roberts, *Athens on Trial*, 176, 175, 185, 184; see also 179.

26. These constitutional features are explored in depth in Bederman, *The Classical Foundations of the American Constitution*, 95–175.

27. Richard offers an overview of the founders' penchant for classical models (*The Founders and the Classics*, 53–84).

28. Henry Hope Reed, *The United States Capitol* (New York: Norton, 2005), 162.

Chapter 1. The Soldier's Farm

1. For more on Addison's *Cato*, see Mark Evans Bryan, "'Sliding into monarchical extravagance': Cato at Valley Forge and the Testimony of William Bradford Jr.," *William and Mary Quarterly* 67, no. 1 (2010): 123–44; Randall Fuller, "Theaters of the American Revolution: The Valley Forge 'Cato' and the Meschianza in Their Transcultural Contexts," *Early American Literature* 34, no. 2 (1999): 126–46; and Fredric M. Litto, "Addison's Cato in the Colonies," *William and Mary Quarterly* 23, no. 3 (1966): 431–49.

2. The following remarks are based primarily on my role as a participant-observer in the US Army between 2008 and 2013.

3. Dalia Sussman and Megan Thee-Brenan, "For Midterm Voters, War Is Off the Radar," *New York Times*, 15 October 2010.

4. Arthur A. Ekirch Jr., "The Idea of a Citizen Army," *Military Affairs* 17, no. 1 (1953): 30–36; Victor Davis Hanson, "Soldier-Citizens to the Rescue?," *Real Clear Politics*, 6 May 2010, www.realclearpolitics.com/articles/2010/05/06/soldier-citizens_to_the_rescue_105470.html. Barry S. Strauss, another ancient historian, also stresses the strides that

can be made in academia to close the civil-military gap; see his "Reflections on the Citizen-Soldier," *Parameters* (Summer 2003): 66-77.

5. William Tecumseh Sherman, "The Veterans of the War," *New York Times*, August 12, 1880.

6. For more on the modern technocratic ethical dilemma, see the contributions to *Killing by Remote*, ed. Bradley Jay Strawser (Oxford: Oxford University Press).

7. Iseult Honohan, *Civic Republicanism* (London: Routledge, 2002), 33-35.

8. Jock Haswell, *Citizen Armies* (London: Peter Davies, 1973), 15.

9. Thomas Jefferson, *Notes on the State of Virginia*, 9th ed. (Boston: Sprague, 1802), 225-27.

10. Jefferson later clarified that his insistence on the independent farmer-citizen did not preclude cities and industry, but he maintained that there must be "a due balance between agriculture, manufactures, and commerce"; see Garrett Ward Sheldon, *The Political Philosophy of Thomas Jefferson* (Baltimore, MD: Johns Hopkins University Press, 1991), 77.

11. On Jefferson's view of an agrarian republic, see Carl J. Richard, *The Founders and the Classics* (Cambridge, MA: Harvard University Press, 1994), 158-66; and Sheldon, *The Political Philosophy of Thomas Jefferson*, 76-78.

12. Quoted in Richard, *The Founders and the Classics*, 161-62.

13. See, for example, the fragments from his *Annals*, 475; *Satires*, 1.14-19; and *Rules of Conduct*, 1-3.

14. For a brief survey of the Italian farmer's agricultural setting and methods, see Lionel Casson, *Everyday Life in Ancient Rome* (Baltimore, MD: Johns Hopkins University Press, 1998), 28-29.

15. On early Roman education, see Mark Joyal, Iain McDougall, and J. C. Yardley, *Greek and Roman Education* (New York: Routledge, 2009), 151-65; H. I. Marrou, *A History of Education in Antiquity* (Madison: University of Wisconsin Press, 1956), 229-41; and A. S. Wilkins, *Roman Education* (Cambridge: Cambridge University Press, 1914), 5-17.

16. See the discussion in Joyal, McDougall, and Yardley, *Greek and Roman Education*, 152-59.

17. Preston Bannard, "Military Training," in *A Companion to Ancient Education*, ed. W. Martin Bloomer (Hoboken, NJ: Wiley, 2015), 487-88.

18. On this idealization, see Suzanne Dixon, *The Roman Family* (Baltimore, MD: Johns Hopkins University Press, 1992), 21; and Marrou, *A History of Education in Antiquity*, 234-36. Keith R. Bradley offers an analysis of the late republican and imperial Roman family in his *Discovering the Roman Family* (Oxford: Oxford University Press, 1991).

19. T. J. Cornell, ed., *Fragments of the Roman Historians*, vol. 2 (Oxford: Oxford University Press, 2013), 222-23.

20. Cornell, *Fragments of the Roman Historians*, 206-7.

21. Flavius Vegetius Renatus, *The Military Institutions of the Romans*, trans. John Clark (Harrisburg, PA: Military Service Publishing Company, 1944).

22. I address these matters in greater detail in part 2. The best studies on the life cycles of Roman military and family life are Nathan Rosenstein, *Rome at War: Farms, Families, and Death in the Middle Republic* (Chapel Hill: University of North Carolina Press, 2004); and Richard Saller, *Patriarchy, Property, and Death in the Roman Family* (New York: Cambridge University Press, 1994).

23. Matthew Melko and Richard D. Weigel, *Peace in the Ancient World* (Jefferson, NC: McFarland, 1981), 131.

24. This perspective on the classical world before the Roman Empire has been recently argued by Arthur M. Eckstein, *Mediterranean Anarchy, Interstate War, and the Rise of Rome* (Berkeley: University of California Press, 2006).

25. Kathleen Freeman, *Ancilla to the Pre-Socratic Philosophers* (Cambridge, MA: Harvard University Press, 1983), 28.

26. Mary Beard, John North, and Simon Price, *Religions of Rome*, vol. 1 (Cambridge: Cambridge University Press, 1998), 47–48.

27. Niccolo Machiavelli, *The Art of War* (Cambridge, MA: Da Capo Press, 2001), 14–15.

28. Machiavelli, *The Art of War*, 18.

29. Montesquieu, *Considerations on the Causes and the Greatness of the Romans and Their Decline*, trans. David Lowenthal (Indianapolis, IN: Hackett, 1965), 39–42.

Chapter 2. The Citizen's Republic

1. Hagen Schulze, *States, Nations, and Nationalism* (Oxford, UK: Blackwell, 1996), xii.

2. Dick Howard, *The Primacy of the Political* (New York: Columbia University Press, 2010), 4; Yvon Garlan, *War in the Ancient World* (New York: Norton, 1975), 23.

3. David J. Bederman, *International Law in Antiquity* (Cambridge: Cambridge University Press, 2001), 1, 17–19. For a more pessimistic view of states and state systems from the realist perspective, see Arthur M. Eckstein, *Mediterranean Anarchy, Interstate War, and the Rise of Rome* (Berkeley: University of California Press, 2006). Bederman's use of 358 is curious because 348, the year Rome concluded its second treaty with Carthage, or 338, when Rome altered its federal arrangement with the Latins, are better dates.

4. Charles Howard McIlwain, *Constitutionalism, Ancient and Modern* (Ithaca, NY: Cornell University Press, 1947), 22–23. For similar conclusions regarding medieval political thought see, for example, McIlwain, *Constitutionalism, Ancient and Modern*, 67–92; and Cary J. Nederman, "Conciliarism and Constitutionalism: Jean Gerson and Medieval Political Thought," *History of European Ideas* 12, no. 2 (1990): 189–209.

5. Scott Gordon, *Controlling the State* (Cambridge, MA: Harvard University Press, 1999), 5, 16.

6. There are several recent studies on the constitutional features of Rome. See, for example, Andrew W. Lintott, *The Constitution of the Roman Republic* (Oxford: Oxford University Press, 1999); Gordon, *Controlling the State*, 86–115; Hans Julius Wolff, *Roman*

Law (Norman: University of Oklahoma Press, 1951), 22-44; Kurt Von Fritz, *The Theory of the Mixed Constitution in Antiquity* (New York: Arno Press, 1975); and William R. Everdell, *The End of Kings* (Chicago: University of Chicago Press, 2000), 44-67.

7. Daniel E. Fleming, *Democracy's Ancient Ancestors* (Cambridge: Cambridge University Press, 2004); Thorkild Jacobsen, "Primitive Democracy in Ancient Mesopotamia," *Journal of Near Eastern Studies* 2, no. 3 (1943): 159-72; Robert Gordis, "Democratic Origins in Ancient Israel—the Biblical Edah," in *Alexander Marx Jubilee Volume* (New York: Jewish Theological Seminary of America, 1950); Geoffrey Evans, "Ancient Mesopotamian Assemblies," *Journal of the American Oriental Society* 78, no. 1 (1958): 1-11; Abraham Malamat, "Kingship and Council in Israel and Sumer," *Journal of Near Eastern Studies* 22, no. 4 (1963): 247-53; C. Umhau Wolf, "Traces of Primitive Democracy in Ancient Israel," *Journal of Near Eastern Studies* 6, no. 2 (1947): 98-108; Jacob Milgrom, "Priestly Terminology and the Political and Social Structure of Pre-Monarchic Israel," *Jewish Quarterly Review* 49, no. 2 (1978): 65-81.

8. A sample of contemporary surveys of constitutionalism and republicanism includes Gordon, *Controlling the State*; Iseult Honohan, *Civic Republicanism* (London: Routledge, 2002); Alan Ryan, *On Politics* (New York: Liveright, 2012); Richard Dagger, *Civic Virtues* (Oxford: Oxford University Press, 1997); Paul Anthony Rahe, *Republics Ancient and Modern*, 3 vols. (Chapel Hill: University of North Carolina Press, 1994); Everdell, *The End of Kings*; Quentin Skinner, *Liberty before Liberalism* (Cambridge: Cambridge University Press, 1998); Maurizio Viroli, *Republicanism* (New York: Hill and Wang, 2002); Patricia Springborg, "The Primacy of Politics: Rahe and the Myth of the Polis," *Political Studies* 38 (1990): 83-104; Philip Pettit, *Republicanism* (Oxford: Oxford University Press, 1997).

9. Charles Francis Adams, ed., *The Works of John Adams* (Cambridge: Cambridge University Press, 2011), 6.415-16.

10. Adams, *The Works of John Adam*, 6.416.

11. Honohan, *Civic Republicanism*, 5-6; Everdell, *The End of Kings*, viii-xiii; Martin Van Gelderen and Quentin Skinner, introduction to *Republicanism: A Shared European Heritage*, vol. 1 of *Republicanism and Constitutionalism in Early Modern Europe*, ed. Martin Van Gelderen and Quentin Skinner (Cambridge: Cambridge University Press, 2002), 1-6.

12. Daniel J. Kapust, *Republicanism, Rhetoric, and Roman Political Thought* (Cambridge: Cambridge University Press, 2011), 9-11; Pettit, *Republicanism*, 4-13; Chaim Wirszubski, *Libertas as a Political Idea at Rome during the Late Republic and Early Principate* (Cambridge: Cambridge University Press, 1968), 1-3; Daniel Judah Elazar and Stuart A. Cohen, *The Jewish Polity* (Bloomington: Indiana University Press, 1985), 11-13.

13. On voting procedures and the organization of the assemblies, see Lintott, *The Constitution of the Roman Republic*, 44-61.

14. On definitions of federalism, see Mikhail Filippov, Peter C. Ordeshook, and Olga Shvetsova, *Designing Federalism* (Cambridge: Cambridge University Press, 2004), 5; and Dimitrios Karmis and Wayne Norman, eds., *Theories of Federalism* (New York: Palgrave Macmillan, 2005), 14-15.

15. For an introduction to the debate over popular sovereignty in Rome, see, for example, Allen M. Ward, "How Democratic Was the Roman Republic," *New England Classical Journal* 31, no. 2 (2004): 101-19; Karl-J. Hölkeskamp, *Reconstructing the Roman Republic* (Princeton, NJ: Princeton University Press, 2010); and Fergus Millar, *The Roman Republic and the Augustan Revolution* (Chapel Hill: University of North Carolina Press, 2002).

16. Honohan, *Civic Republicanism*, 21; Viroli, *Republicanism*, 71.

17. Shelley Burtt holds that political, or civic, virtue is *"the* distinguishing feature" of Aristotelian and Roman conceptions of the polity; see "The Good Citizen's Psyche: On the Psychology of Civic Virtue," *Polity* 23, no. 1 (1990): 23. See also Mark J. Lutz, "Civic Virtue and Socratic Virtue," *Polity* 29, no. 4 (1997): 565-92.

18. Kurt A. Raaflaub, "Searching for Peace in the Ancient World," in *War and Peace in the Ancient World*, ed. Kurt A. Raaflaub (Oxford, UK: Blackwell, 2007), 9.

19. See also V. G. Kiernan, "Foreign Mercenaries and Absolute Monarchy," *Past and Present*, no. 11 (1957): 66-86.

20. Jeri Blair DeBrohun, "The Gates of War (and Peace): Roman Literary Perspectives," in *War and Peace in the Ancient World*, 256-78; Karl-J. Hölkeskamp, "Conquest, Competition, and Consensus: Roman Expansion in Italy and the Rise of the 'Nobilitas,'" *Historia: Zeitschrift für alte Geschichte* 42, no. 1 (1993): 12-39; Kurt A. Raaflaub, "Born to Be Wolves: Origins of Roman Imperialism," in *Transitions to Empire: Essays in Greco-Roman History, 360-146 BC, in honor of E. Badian*, ed. Robert W. Wallace and Edward M. Harris (Norman: University of Oklahoma Press, 1996), 273-314.

21. T. P. Wiseman, *Clio's Cosmetics* (Leicester, UK: Leicester University Press, 1979), 3.

22. Arnaldo Momigliano, "Biblical Studies and Classical Studies: Simple Reflections about Historical Method," *Biblical Archaeologist* 45, no. 4 (1982): 224.

23. For a discussion of these events in greater detail, I refer the reader to Gary Forsythe, *A Critical History of Early Rome* (Berkeley: University of California Press, 2005); Kurt A. Raaflaub, ed., *Social Struggles in Archaic Rome* (Malden, MA: Blackwell, 2005); Christopher John Smith, *Early Rome and Latium* (Oxford, UK: Clarendon Press, 1996); Don Nardo, ed., *The Rise of the Roman Empire* (San Diego, CA: Greenhaven Press, 2002), 29-54; Stephen P. Oakley, "The Early Republic," in *The Cambridge Companion to the Roman Republic*, ed. Harriet I. Flower (Cambridge: Cambridge University Press, 2004), 15-30; and T. J. Cornell, *The Beginnings of Rome* (London: Routledge, 1995).

24. Wiseman, *Clio's Cosmetics*, 9-26; Elizabeth Rawson, "The First Latin Annalists," *Latomus* 35, no. 4 (1976): 689-717.

25. F. W. Walbank, *A Historical Commentary on Polybius*, 3 vols. (Oxford: Oxford University Press, 1957-79), 1:16. See also Brian McGing, *Polybius' Histories* (Oxford: Oxford University Press, 2010), 129-68; and Craige B. Champion, *Cultural Politics in Polybius's Histories* (Berkeley: University of California Press, 2004).

26. Peter Green, ed., *Diodorus Siculus, Books 11-12.37.1: Greek History 480-431 B.C., the Alternative Version* (Austin: University of Texas Press, 2006), 1-34.

27. Emilio Gabba, *Dionysius and the History of Archaic Rome* (Berkeley: University of California Press, 1991), 8-9, 20-22.

28. P. G. Walsh, *Livy* (Cambridge: Cambridge University Press, 1961), 18.

29. Alain M. Gowing, *Empire and Memory* (Cambridge: Cambridge University Press, 2005), 22–23, 35.

30. Gary B. Miles argues for a greater degree of embellishment in *Livy* (Ithaca, NY: Cornell University Press, 1995). See also Kapust, *Republicanism, Rhetoric, and Roman Political Thought*, 81–110, Jason P. Davies, *Rome's Religious History* (Cambridge: Cambridge University Press, 2004), 21–142; John Briscoe, ed., *A Commentary on Livy: Books XXXI–XXXIII* (Oxford: Clarendon Press, 2009), 1–22; and Stephen P. Oakley, *A Commentary on Livy: Books VI-X* (Oxford: Clarendon Press, 2005), 3–34.

31. Regarding the available manuscripts, I refer the reader to the Loeb Classical Library introductions for each of the historians.

32. Ronald Mellor, *The Roman Historians* (London: Routledge, 1999), 6–29.

33. The traditional models have been the standard representation and are ubiquitous. A representative sample could include H. H. Scullard, *A History of the Roman World* (London: Routledge, 1980); H. H. Scullard, *From the Gracchi to Nero* (London: Routledge, 1988); Wolff, *Roman Law*; Nardo, *The Rise of the Roman Empire*; Andrew W. Lintott, *The Roman Republic* (Gloucestershire, UK: Sutton Publishing, 2000); Gian Biagio Conte, *Latin Literature* (Baltimore, MD: Johns Hopkins University Press, 1999); Michael M. Sage, *The Republican Roman Army* (New York: Routledge, 2008); P. A. Brunt, *Social Conflicts in the Roman Republic* (New York: Norton, 1972); E. Badian, *Roman Imperialism in the Late Republic* (Ithaca, NY: Cornell University Press, 1968); Nathan Rosenstein, *Rome at War: Farms, Families, and Death in the Middle Republic* (Chapel Hill: University of North Carolina Press, 2004); and John Rich, "Fear, Greed, and Glory: The Causes of Roman War-making in the Middle Republic," in *War and Society in the Roman World*, ed. John Rich and Graham Shipley (London: Routledge, 1993), 38–68.

34. Harriet I. Flower, *Roman Republics* (Princeton, NJ: Princeton University Press, 2010), esp. 33.

35. Flower, *Roman Republics*, 138. Flower argues against the view articulated by Eric S. Gruen in *The Last Generation of the Roman Republic* (Berkeley: University of California Press, 1974).

36. Flower, *Roman Republics*, 33, 53, 152–54.

Chapter 3. Origins: Kingly Armies of the Roman Hills

1. Charles Francis Adams, ed., *The Works of John Adams* (Cambridge: Cambridge University Press, 2011), 4.542–49.

2. For a review of these ordinances, see Naphtali Lewis and Meyer Reinhold, eds., *Roman Civilization* (New York: Columbia University Press, 1990), 64–68.

3. On the Capitoline wolf, see T. J. Cornell, *The Beginnings of Rome (c. 1000-264 BC)* (London: Routledge, 1995), 60–63. On the discussion surrounding the Regia, see Cornell, *The Beginnings of Rome*, 239–41; and R. Ross Holloway, *The Archaeology of Early Rome and Latium* (New York: Routledge, 1994), 60–66. On early Roman statuary, see J. J. Pollitt, *The Art of Rome* (Cambridge: Cambridge University Press, 1983), 12–14. On

the Bolsena mirror, see Andrea Carandini, *Rome: Day One* (Princeton, NJ: Princeton University Press, 2011), 38–40.

4. On Greek colonization, see the collection of literary data in Matthew Dillon and Lynda Garland, *Ancient Greece* (London: Routledge, 1994), 1–28. See also the map, chart, and discussion in Robin Osborne, *Greece in the Making* (London: Routledge, 1996), 119–29. On Phoenician colonization, see William Culican, *The First Merchant Venturers* (London: Thames and Hudson, 1966), 103–18; and Glenn E. Markoe, *Phoenicians* (Berkeley: University of California Press, 2000), 170–89.

5. Bruno D'Agostino, "Military Organization and Social Structure in Archaic Etruria," in *The Greek City from Homer to Alexander*, ed. Oswyn Murray and Simon Price (Oxford, UK: Clarendon Press, 1990), 60–61, 75.

6. D'Agostino, "Military Organization and Social Structure in Archaic Etruria," 62; Michael Grant, *The Etruscans* (New York: History Book Club, 1980), 117; Timothy W. Potter, *Roman Italy* (Berkeley: University of California Press, 1987), 30; H. H. Scullard, *The Etruscan Cities and Rome* (London: Thames and Hudson, 1967), 236–37.

7. Jacques Heurgon, *Daily Life of the Etruscans* (London: Phoenix Press, 1961), 40–43; Scullard, *The Etruscan Cities and Rome*, 221–23.

8. Grant, *The Etruscans*, 119–22; Scullard, *The Etruscan Cities and Rome*, 231–36.

9. For more on Etruscan aggression, see Arthur M. Eckstein, *Mediterranean Anarchy, Interstate War, and the Rise of Rome* (Berkeley: University of California Press, 2006), 122–31.

10. Grant, *The Etruscans*, 18; Potter, *Roman Italy*, 31.

11. The archaeological evidence for this interpretation is detailed in D'Agostino, "Military Organization and Social Structure in Archaic Etruria," 63, 67–81. See also Grant, *The Etruscans*, 118; Heurgon, *Daily Life of the Etruscans*, 45–49; Michael M. Sage, *The Republican Roman Army* (New York: Routledge, 2008), 15–16; Scullard, *The Etruscan Cities and Rome*, 238–40; and Nigel Spivey, *Etruscan Art* (London: Thames and Hudson, 1997), 54.

12. Sage, *The Republican Roman Army*, 43. For a review of the mountain peoples, see Potter, *Roman Italy*, 33–40.

13. Stephen P. Oakley, *The Hill-forts of the Samnites* (London: British School at Rome, 1995), 139–48.

14. E. T. Salmon, *Samnium and the Samnites* (Cambridge: Cambridge University Press, 1967), 78–100. On other Italian republics, see Cornell, *The Beginnings of Rome*, 230–32.

15. On the Sacred Spring, see Sage, *The Republican Roman Army*, 43–50; and Salmon, *Samnium and the Samnites*, 35–39.

16. Michael T. Burns, "The Homogenisation of Military Equipment under the Roman Republic," *Digressus* supp. 1 (2003): 62–70, 77–85; Sage, *The Republican Roman Army*, 43–44; Salmon, *Samnium and the Samnites*, 102–10. See also the depictions and archaeological evidence presented in John Gibson Warry, *Warfare in the Classical World* (Norman: University of Oklahoma Press, 1995), 102–7.

17. For more on Samnite aggression, see Eckstein, *Mediterranean Anarchy, Interstate War, and the Rise of Rome*, 138–47.

18. Potter, *Roman Italy*, 29–30; Christopher John Smith, *Early Rome and Latium* (Oxford, UK: Clarendon Press, 1996), 186; "Early and Archaic Rome," in *Ancient Rome: The*

Archaeology of the Eternal City, ed. Jon Coulston and Hazel Dodge (Oxford: Oxford University School of Archaeology, 2011), 18-23.

19. *Early Rome and Latium, 186-94.*

20. Sage, *The Republican Roman Army*, 29-30; A. N. Sherwin-White, *The Roman Citizenship* (Oxford, UK: Clarendon Press, 1973), 6-9.

21. Rex Stem, "The Exemplary Lessons of Livy's Romulus," *Transactions of the American Philological Association* 137, no. 2 (2007): 435-71.

22. Cornell, *The Beginnings of Rome*, 114-18; Gary Forsythe, *A Critical History of Early Rome* (Berkeley: University of California Press, 2005), 108-10; Andrew W. Lintott, *The Constitution of the Roman Republic* (Oxford: Oxford University Press, 1999), 27-30.

23. Adrian Keith Goldsworthy, *The Complete Roman Army* (New York: Thames and Hudson, 2003), 20-21; Sage, *The Republican Roman Army*, 10-14. On the Lapis Satricanus, see Cornell, *The Beginnings of Rome*; and Forsythe, *A Critical History of Early Rome*, 198-200.

24. The Stoic determinism of Livy, which sees the guiding hand of providence behind Roman war and peace, is described in P. G. Walsh, "Livy and Stoicism," *American Journal of Philology* 79, no. 4 (1958): 373.

25. M. D. Goodman and A. J. Holladay, "Religious Scruples in Ancient Warfare," *Classical Quarterly* 36, no. 1 (1986): 160-65; Patrick Kragelund, "Dreams, Religion and Politics in Republican Rome," *Historia: Zeitschrift für alte Geschichte* 50, no. 1 (2001).

26. Mary Beard, *SPQR* (New York: Liveright, 2015), 102.

27. Russell T. Scott, "The Contribution of Archaeology to Early Roman History," in *Social Struggles in Archaic Rome: New Perspectives on the Conflicts of Order*, ed. Kurt A. Raaflaub (Malden, MA: Blackwell, 2005), 102-3; Frank Sear, *Roman Architecture* (Ithaca, NY: Cornell University Press, 1982), 7-14; Smith, "Early and Archaic Rome," 24-29. Holloway takes a more minimalist view of these sites and their relation to the tradition in *The Archaeology of Early Rome and Latium*, 7-10, 86-88. See also L. F. Janssen, "The Chronology of Early Rome," *Mnemosyne* 23, no. 1 (1970): 316-29. Carandini argues for the traditional date of Rome's founding in the mid-eighth century in *Rome: Day One*.

28. Forsythe, *A Critical History of Early Rome*, 117; Smith, "Early and Archaic Rome," 27.

29. Quoted in Sage, *The Republican Roman Army*, 17-18.

30. Sage, *The Republican Roman Army*, 15-18. The archaeological evidence includes the Etruscan data reviewed here and items such as the fourth-century bone plaques of hoplite warriors from Praeneste, which date later but clearly illustrate the adoption of hoplite armor. Helpful reviews that discuss the tactics and cover helmets, shields, cuirasses, and weapons can be found in Burns, "The Homogenisation of Military Equipment under the Roman Republic"; Goldsworthy, *The Complete Roman Army*, 20-25; Nathan Rosenstein, "Armies of the Roman Republic," in *The Ancient World at War*, ed. Philip de Souza (London: Thames and Hudson, 2008), 138-39; and Warry, *Warfare in the Classical World*, 109. Data from Greek artists includes notable items that show hoplites in battle such as the (Etruscan) seventh-century Chigi vase, a late seventh-century Corinthian vase, and the late sixth-century bronze Dodona statuette, as discussed in Hans van Wees, "War in Archaic and Classical Greece," in *The Ancient World at War*, 101-18.

31. Sage, *The Republican Roman Army*, 24. For further discussion, see, for example, Cornell, *The Beginnings of Rome*, 183-86; Goldsworthy, *The Complete Roman Army*, 24-25; Forsythe, *A Critical History of Early Rome*, 108-17; Sage, *The Republican Roman Army*, 18-27; Yvon Garlan, *War in the Ancient World* (New York: Norton, 1975), 86-89; and Smith, *Early Rome and Latium*, 203-10. A review of the literature illustrates how difficult it is to find consensus on many aspects of the Servian reforms.

32. G. V. Sumner, "The Legion and the Centuriate Organization," *Journal of Roman Studies* 60 (1970): 77-78.

33. On the first Carthage-Rome treaty, see John Serrati, "Neptune's Altars: The Treaties between Rome and Carthage (509-226 B.C.)," *Classical Quarterly* 56, no. 1 (2006): 114-18.

Chapter 4. Proving Ground: Surviving in Central Italy

1. Carl J. Richard, *The Founders and the Classics* (Cambridge, MA: Harvard University Press, 1994), 143-44, 144.

2. For more on republican exemplarity, see, for example, Alain M. Gowing, *Empire and Memory* (Cambridge: Cambridge University Press, 2005), 55; Matthew B. Roller, "Exemplarity in Roman Culture: The Cases of Horatius Cocles and Cloelia," *Classical Philology* 99, no. 1 (2004): 1-56; and S. E. Smethurst, "Women in Livy's 'History,'" *Greece and Rome* 19, no. 56 (1950): 80-87.

3. J. J. Pollitt, *The Art of Rome* (Cambridge: Cambridge University Press, 1983), 12-13; Roller, "Exemplarity in Roman Culture." On the Capitoline Brutus statue, see the discussion and depiction in T. J. Cornell, *The Beginnings of Rome (c. 1000-264 BC)* (London: Routledge, 1995), 390-92. On the circulation of the legends, Polybius, for example, cites the ancient legend of Horatius in 6.55.

4. For surveys of the events, see, for example, Cornell, *The Beginnings of Rome*, 304-13; Gary Forsythe, *A Critical History of Early Rome* (Berkeley: University of California Press, 2005), 238-39; Naphtali Lewis and Meyer Reinhold, eds., *Roman Civilization* (New York: Columbia University Press, 1990), 94-132; Andrew W. Lintott, *The Constitution of the Roman Republic* (Oxford: Oxford University Press, 1999), 31-39; and Stephen P. Oakley, "The Early Republic," in *The Cambridge Companion to the Roman Republic*, ed. Harriet I. Flower (Cambridge: Cambridge University Press, 2004), 17-19, 23-24.

5. One possible layout is diagrammed and described in Frank Sear, *Roman Architecture* (Ithaca, NY: Cornell University Press, 1982), 14-15. See also T. J. Cornell, "The City of Rome in the Middle Republic," in *Ancient Rome: The Archaeology of the Eternal City*, ed. Jon Coulston and Hazel Dodge (Oxford: Oxford University School of Archaeology, 2011), 43; and R. Ross Holloway, *The Archaeology of Early Rome and Latium* (New York: Routledge, 1994), 81-88.

6. As I have noted, the debate over popular sovereignty in Rome is represented, for example, in Karl-J. Hölkeskamp, *Reconstructing the Roman Republic* (Princeton, NJ: Princeton University Press, 2010); and Fergus Millar, *The Roman Republic and the Augustan Revolution* (Chapel Hill: University of North Carolina Press, 2002). The classic argument for Rome as an oligarchy is found in Ronald Syme, "Oligarchy at Rome: a Paradigm for

Political Science," *Diogenes* 36, no. 141 (1988): 56-75. A measured defense of the republican nature of Rome is found in Lintott, *The Constitution of the Roman Republic*. On the early political structure of the republic, see, for instance, T. Corey Brennan, "Power and Process under the Republican 'Constitution,'" in *The Cambridge Companion to the Roman Republic*, 31-65; and Oakley, "The Early Republic," 15-30. See also Cornell, *The Beginnings of Rome*, 215-30; Forsythe, *A Critical History of Early Rome*, 147-83; and H. H. Scullard, *A History of the Roman World* (London: Routledge, 1980), 78-91.

7. See, for example, Kurt Von Fritz, *The Theory of the Mixed Constitution in Antiquity* (New York: Arno Press, 1975); and F. W. Walbank, "Polybius on the Roman Constitution," *Classical Quarterly* 37, nos. 3-4 (1943): 73-89.

8. Andreas Kalyvas, "The Tyranny of Dictatorship: When the Greek Tyrant Met the Roman Dictator," *Political Theory* 35, no. 4 (2007): 412-42.

9. The existence of these secessions is a matter of debate. The first *secessio* supposedly occurred in 494 (Dionysius, 5.63ff.; Titus Livy, 2.23ff.), a second in 449 (Livy, 3.49ff.), and a definite third in 287. There were perhaps two more, one in 445, recorded by Florus (1.17.25), and one in 342 (Livy, 7.40ff.). For a measured view of the Twelve Tables that sees its benefits to the elite as well, see Walter Eder, "The Political Significance of the Codification of Law in Archaic Societies: An Unconventional Hypothesis," in *Social Struggles in Archaic Rome: New Perspectives on the Conflicts of Order*, ed. Kurt A. Raaflaub (Malden, MA: Blackwell, 2005), 239-67.

10. Clifford Ando, "Was Rome a Polis?," *Classical Antiquity* 18, no. 1 (1999) : 5-34.

11. Cornell, "The City of Rome in the Middle Republic," 42-43; Russell T. Scott, "The Contribution of Archaeology to Early Roman History," in *Social Struggles in Archaic Rome*, 104.

12. Cornell, *The Beginnings of Rome*, 308.

13. Stephen P. Oakley, "The Roman Conquest of Italy," in *War and Society in the Roman World*, ed. John Rich and Graham Shipley (London: Routledge, 1993), 14-16. For later centuries, see William V. Harris, *War and Imperialism in Republican Rome* (Oxford: Oxford University Press, 1979), esp. 256-63.

14. On multipolar anarchy in early Rome see especially Arthur M. Eckstein, *Mediterranean Anarchy, Interstate War, and the Rise of Rome* (Berkeley: University of California Press, 2006), 118-58.

15. Nathan Rosenstein, *Rome at War: Farms, Families, and Death in the Middle Republic* (Chapel Hill: University of North Carolina Press, 2004), 26-28.

16. Rosenstein, *Rome at War*, 28-29.

17. Cornell, *The Beginnings of Rome*, 308-9.

18. Yvon Garlan, *War in the Ancient World* (New York: Norton, 1975), 41, 42. See also Lewis and Reinhold, *Roman Civilization*, 68-71; and Nathan Rosenstein, "War and Peace, Fear and Reconciliation at Rome," in *War and Peace in the Ancient World*, ed. Kurt A. Raaflaub (Oxford, UK: Blackwell, 2007), 229-30.

19. Garlan, *War in the Ancient World*, 42. See also M. D. Goodman and A. J. Holladay, "Religious Scruples in Ancient Warfare," *Classical Quarterly* 36, no. 1 (1986): 160-65.

20. K. W. Meiklejohn, "Roman Strategy and Tactics from 509 to 202 B.C.," *Greece*

and Rome 7, no. 21 (1938): 170-78. Adcock likens the Roman territorial expansion to "a kind of expanding circle" based on a continuing series of defensive efforts during the early republic; see *The Roman Art of War under the Republic* (Cambridge, MA: Harvard University Press, 1940), 51. On Caere, see Cornell, *The Beginnings of Rome*, 320-21.

21. Andrew B. Gallia, "Reassessing the 'Cumaean Chronicle': Greek Chronology and Roman History in Dionyisus of Halicarnassus," *Journal of Roman Studies* 97 (2007): 50-67. For more on the Battle of Lake Regillus, the Latin League, and the Treaty of Cassius, see Cornell, "The City of Rome in the Middle Republic," 293-301; Forsythe, *A Critical History of Early Rome*, 183-88; Michael M. Sage, *The Republican Roman Army* (New York: Routledge, 2008), 29-34; A. N. Sherwin-White, *The Roman Citizenship* (Oxford, UK: Clarendon Press, 1973), 15-32; and Christopher John Smith, *Early Rome and Latium* (Oxford, UK: Clarendon Press, 1996), 210-23.

22. Forsythe, *A Critical History of Early Rome*, 184. The table is principally derived from Cornell, *The Beginnings of Rome*, 302-4; Forsythe, *A Critical History of Early Rome*, 190-91; and E. T. Salmon, *Roman Colonization under the Republic* (Ithaca, NY: Cornell University Press, 1970), 40-44. It offers the traditional founding dates of the colonies, but recent archaeological evidence has challenged certain aspects of this tradition, particularly with regard to their dates. A second date in the year column indicates its refounding, or at least a second recorded founding. The strategic notices are primarily drawn from Salmon. Termeer challenges aspects of the traditional founding of these colonies, especially their dating in M. K. Termeer, "Early Colonies in Latium (ca 534-338 BC): A Reconsideration of Current Images and the Archaeological Evidence," *Bulletin Antieke Beschavingen* 85 (2010): 43-58. The strategic outlook associated with the approach of scholars such as Salmon has also been discussed in depth in Jeremia Pelgrom and Tesse D. Stek, "Roman Colonization under the Republic: Historiographical Contextualisation of a Paradigm," in *Roman Republican Colonization: New Perspectives from Archaeology and Ancient History*, ed. Jeremia Pelgrom and Tesse D. Stek (Rome: Palombi, 2014), 11-41.

23. Salmon, *Roman Colonization under the Republic*, 43.

24. On this debate, see *Roman Republican Colonization*.

25. On the later Roman colonies, see the list, maps, and discussion in Callie Williamson, *The Laws of the Roman People* (Ann Arbor: University of Michigan Press, 2005), 146-66.

26. It is possible that these changes completed or reformed the Servian constitution. See Cornell, *The Beginnings of Rome*, 187, 313; and Sage, *The Republican Roman Army*, 51-52, 64, 141-42.

27. On the nature and extent of the Gallic sack, see, for example, the competing views of Eckstein, who views the raid as having caused extensive damage (*Mediterranean Anarchy, Interstate War, and the Rise of Rome*, 132-34), and Cornell (*The Beginnings of Rome*, 313-22), who sees it as not having been that destructive. On the Roman wall from this time, see Cornell, "The City of Rome in the Middle Republic," 45-46; and Sear, *Roman Architecture*, 15-16.

28. On the historicity, see Arnaldo Momigliano, "Camillus and Concord," *Classical Quarterly* 36, nos. 3-4 (1942): 111-20.

29. Jan Felix Gaertner, "Livy's Camillus and the Political Discourse of the Late Re-

public," *Journal of Roman Studies* 98 (2008): 27–52. See also Cornell, "The City of Rome in the Middle Republic," 43–44.

30. Karl-J. Hölkeskamp, "Conquest, Competition, and Consensus: Roman Expansion in Italy and the Rise of the 'Nobilitas,'" *Historia: Zeitschrift fur alte Geschichte* 42, no. 1 (1993): 26, 33; Hölkeskamp, *Reconstructing the Roman Republic*, 78.

31. Hölkeskamp, "Conquest, Competition, and Consensus," 21–26.

32. Pollitt, *The Art of Rome*, 22, 27–29, 56–57.

33. Hölkeskamp, "Conquest, Competition, and Consensus," 28–30. On temple building, see Cornell, "The City of Rome in the Middle Republic," 46–50; Eric M. Orlin, *Temples, Religion, and Politics in the Roman Republic* (Boston: Brill, 2002), 45–75; and Scott, "The Contribution of Archaeology to Early Roman History," 104–5.

34. Hölkeskamp, "Conquest, Competition, and Consensus," 32–33.

35. Salmon, *Roman Colonization under the Republic*, 44–45.

36. In his review of premodern federal systems, Judah Elazar includes Israelite and Greek forms, but Rome is noticeably absent (*Exploring Federalism* [Tuscaloosa: University of Alabama Press, 1987], 118). See also S. Rufus Davis, *The Federal Principle* (Berkeley: University of California Press, 1978), 1–34.

37. Iseult Honohan, *Civic Republicanism* (London: Routledge, 2002), 25–26, 36.

38. Ando, "Was Rome a Polis?," 14.

39. Emma Dench argues that these local traditions carried down beyond the late republic. See, "Roman Identities and Italian Voices," *Papers of the British School at Rome* 66 (1998): 248.

40. Scullard, *A History of the Roman World*, 146–48; Sherwin-White, *The Roman Citizenship*, 39–58, 58–94; Salmon, *Roman Colonization under the Republic*, 47–50. There is some confusion over whether Capua and other Campanian polities were allies or half citizens. See the discussion in Sherwin-White, *The Roman Citizenship*, 39–47. Sherwin-White's analysis includes details and nuances of the Roman citizenship that provide an excellent ground for further study.

41. Scullard, *A History of the Roman World*, 148–49; Sherwin-White, *The Roman Citizenship*, 96–118, 19–33; Salmon, *Roman Colonization under the Republic*, 50–54, 55–69.

42. Saskia T. Roselaar, "Assidui or Proletarii? Property in Roman Citizen Colonies and the *Vacatio Militiae*," *Mnemosyne* 62 (2008): 609–23; Salmon, *Roman Colonization under the Republic*, 46–47; Sherwin-White, *The Roman Citizenship*, 77; Salmon, *Roman Colonization under the Republic*, 70–81. See also the discussion in Richard E. Mitchell, "Ager Publicus: Public Property and Private Wealth during the Roman Republic," in *Privatization in the Ancient Near East and Classical World*, ed. Michael Hudson and Baruch A. Levine (Cambridge, MA: Harvard University, 1996), 253–91.

43. Cornell, *The Beginnings of Rome*, 365.

44. Antonio Santosuosso, *Soldiers, Citizens, and the Symbols of War* (Boulder, CO: Westview Press, 1997), 158–59, 204.

45. Rosenstein, "War and Peace, Fear and Reconciliation at Rome," 231–39.

46. Oakley, "The Early Republic," 21; David Potter, "The Roman Army and Navy," in *The Cambridge Companion to the Roman Republic*, 69; Sage, *The Republican Roman Army*, 65.

47. This argument is concisely introduced with regard to the Samnite Wars in Rosenstein, *Rome at War*, 29-32. Rosenstein exhaustively describes the life cycle argument and the effects it had on Rome, especially in the third and second centuries.

48. Cited in Cornell, *The Beginnings of Rome*, 170. For others, see, for example, Arrian, *Tactica*, 30.1; and Polybius, 6.25.

49. On the alae, see Sage, *The Republican Roman Army*, 127-32.

50. For depictions and discussion of Roman tactics, see Adrian Keith Goldsworthy, *The Complete Roman Army* (New York: Thames and Hudson, 2003), 26-33; Nathan Rosenstein, "Armies of the Roman Republic," in *The Ancient World at War*, ed. Philip de Souza (London: Thames and Hudson, 2008), 141-46; John Gibson Warry, *Warfare in the Classical World* (Norman: University of Oklahoma Press, 1995), 110-13; and Lawrence Keppie, *The Making of the Roman Army* (New York: Barnes and Noble Books, 1994), 33-36. For an explanation on the specific movements and equipment, as well as the centuries-long evolution of the manipular legion, see the lengthy treatment in Sage, *The Republican Roman Army*, 42-198. The Centuriate Assembly itself underwent a reform in the middle of the third century. For more, see Stephen P. Oakley, *A Commentary on Livy: Books VI-X* (Oxford: Clarendon Press, 2005), 5-6; and Lily Ross Taylor, "The Centuriate Assembly before and after the Reform," *American Journal of Philology* 78, no. 4 (1957): 337-543. See also the Ahenobarbus relief, now located in the Louvre, which depicts Roman soldiers from the end of the second century.

51. See the depiction and discussion in Keppie, *The Making of the Roman Army*, 19-23.

52. Michael T. Burns, "The Homogenisation of Military Equipment under the Roman Republic," *Digressus*, supp. 1 (2003): 75-76; Meiklejohn, "Roman Strategy and Tactics from 509 to 202 B.C.," 170-74; Sage, *The Republican Roman Army*, 80-81; E. T. Salmon, *Samnium and the Samnites* (Cambridge: Cambridge University Press, 1967), 107.

53. The *xiphos* was usually no longer than two feet, and the legionary sword was between half a foot to a foot longer. See Sage, *The Republican Roman Army*, 84-87.

54. Potter, "The Roman Army and Navy," 70-72.

55. Alexander Zhmodikov, "Roman Republican Heavy Infantrymen in Battle (IV-II Centuries B.C.)," *Historia: Zeitschrift für alte Geschichte* 49, no. 1 (2000): 76-77. Zhmodikov includes a listing of Livy's battle lengths as follows: "The battles of about two hours: 25.19.15; 36.38.3; the battles of about three hours: 22.6.1; 42.7.5; the battles of about four hours: 23.40.9; 24.15.3; 24.42.2; the battles of more than four hours: 8.38.10; 9.44.11; 10.12.5; 10.29.8; 27.2.7; 35.1.5; 40.50.2; the long battles of unknown duration: Liv. 7.33.13; 25.15.14; 27.12.10; 27.14.6; 28.15.2; 34.28.11; 40.32.6" (71). See also, Sage, *The Republican Roman Army*, 81-84.

56. Salmon, *Samnium and the Samnites*, 110.

Chapter 5. Breakout: Competition and Discipline at Sentinum

1. Thomas P. Somma, "The Problem with Public Art," in *American Pantheon: Sculptural and Artistic Decoration of the United States Capitol*, ed. Donald R. Kennon and Thomas P. Somma (Athens: Ohio University Press, 2004), 116-17.

2. On the sources and historicity of the campaign, see Stephen P. Oakley, *A Commentary on Livy: Books VI–X* (Oxford: Clarendon Press, 2005), 268ff.

3. See Oakley, *A Commentary on Livy*, 290, for an explanation of why Sentinum should be viewed as historical.

4. Daniel J. Kapust, *Republicanism, Rhetoric, and Roman Political Thought* (Cambridge: Cambridge University Press, 2011), 26.

5. For a survey of their accomplishments during these years, see T. Robert S. Broughton, *The Magistrates of the Roman Republic*, 3 vols. (Atlanta: Scholars Press, 1984–86), 1:164, 67, 75, 77–78.

6. On the discussion of these factors, see T. J. Cornell, *The Beginnings of Rome (c. 1000–264 BC)* (London: Routledge, 1995), 360–61, 71–72; Callie Williamson, *The Laws of the Roman People* (Ann Arbor: University of Michigan Press, 2005), 452; and Oakley, *A Commentary on Livy*, 214.

7. John Patterson, "Living and Dying in the City of Rome: Houses and Tombs," in *Ancient Rome: The Archaeology of the Eternal City*, ed. Jon Coulston and Hazel Dodge (Oxford: Oxford University School of Archaeology, 2011), 265. On the debate, see Oakley, *A Commentary on Livy*, 272–74, 83–84.

8. Gary Forsythe, *A Critical History of Early Rome* (Berkeley: University of California Press, 2005), 340–41; Penelope J. E Davies, *Death and the Emperor* (Austin: University of Texas Press, 2004), 67–68.

9. A description, with a picture of the tomb and its Old Latin inscription, can be found in Karl-J. Hölkeskamp, *Reconstructing the Roman Republic* (Princeton, NJ: Princeton University Press, 2010), 91–92. See also Patterson, "Living and Dying in the City of Rome," 265–67. On the tomb's possible discrepancies with Livy's account of the Third Samnite War, see Forsythe, *A Critical History of Early Rome*, 328–29.

10. Forsythe, *A Critical History of Early Rome*, 341.

11. Hölkeskamp, *Reconstructing the Roman Republic*, 87.

12. Livy includes the disputes about Scipio Barbatus' defeat in 10.26. See also Broughton, *The Magistrates of the Roman Republic*, 1:178; and Oakley, *A Commentary on Livy*, 274–75, 85–88.

13. Cornell, *The Beginnings of Rome*, 361; Stephen P. Oakley, "The Roman Conquest of Italy," in *War and Society in the Roman World*, ed. John Rich and Graham Shipley (London: Routledge, 1993), 28–29. See also *A Commentary on Livy*, 213–14.

14. Ross Cowan, *For the Glory of Rome* (London: Greenhill Books, 2007), 90. Oakley offers a more measured take in *A Commentary on Livy* (289).

15. Presumably, the Samnites fought using a similar formation as the Romans and their allies. The breakdown of Roman forces is based on the standard arrangement of a legion, with an additional one thousand Campanian cavalry (Livy, 10.26).

16. On the Gallic chariot, see Michael M. Sage, *The Republican Roman Army* (New York: Routledge, 2008), 60.

17. Alexander Zhmodikov, "Roman Republican Heavy Infantrymen in Battle (IV–II Centuries B.C.)," *Historia: Zeitschrift für alte Geschichte* 49, no. 1 (2000): 70.

18. See Oakley, *A Commentary on Livy*, 278–79, 90–91, on the event itself as well as a discussion of those who doubt that it occurred at all.

19. The Loeb edition preserves its fragments in *Remains of Old Latin*, vol. 2, 553-59.

20. For an in-depth analysis of the *devotio deciana* and its relationship to other Roman offerings, see L. F. Janssen, "Some Unexplored Aspects of *Devotio Deciana*," *Mnemosyne* 34, nos. 3-4 (1981): 357-81; and H. S. Versnel, "Two Types of Roman *Devotio*," *Mnemosyne* 29, no. 4 (1976): 365-410.

21. Janssen, "Some Unexplored Aspects of *Devotio Deciana*," 376.

22. Oakley makes the same observation in Oakley, *A Commentary on Livy: Books VI-X*, 291.

23. Versnel, "Two Types of Roman *Devotio*," 390, 401.

24. Some see the types of Fabius the disciplined and Decius the impetuous as reason enough to discount the details of the battle. For discussion, see Oakley, *A Commentary on Livy*, 290.

25. It is possible that Fabius' "reserve" was a separate force already set aside. However, it is far more likely that Fabius had only employed his *hastati* up to this point, and the *principes* and/or *triarii* were still fresh. Fabius' intention had been to delay a decision and keep as many of his forces as fresh as possible. In the middle of the battle, several maniples of his *triarii* reinforced Decius' forces. At the end of the battle, he used his allied cavalry and *principes* (possibly with the remaining *triarii* as well) to drive the fighting to a conclusion. The Latin here is not describing his forces "held in reserve," as Loeb translates, but rather any forces that he "had saved" or "reserved" up to this point. They were not in a separate force but had to be collected from his battle lines and then directed to a new purpose. Livy is merely describing the way he believed the third-century army fought, namely, without the dedicated reserves more common in first-century warfare.

26. Livy acknowledges as much in 10.27, stating that "at the first shock the strength put forth on both sides was so equal that if the Etruscans and Umbrians had been present either in the battle or at the camp, in whichever quarter they had thrown their weight the Romans must have suffered a disaster." See also, for example, E. T. Salmon, *Samnium and the Samnites* (Cambridge: Cambridge University Press, 1967), 267.

27. On the funeral, see also Harriet I. Flower, "Spectacle and Political Culture in the Roman Republic," in *The Cambridge Companion to the Roman Republic*, ed. Harriet I. Flower (Cambridge: Cambridge University Press, 2004), 331, 34-36.

28. Oakley, "The Roman Conquest of Italy," 29.

29. Valerie M. Hope, "Trophies and Tombstones: Commemorating the Roman Soldier," *World Archaeology* 35, no. 1 (2003): 82.

30. On the temple to Jupiter Victor, see Oakley, *A Commentary on Livy*, 327-28; and Oakley, "The Roman Conquest of Italy," 29-30.

31. On the Gallic threat during these years, see J. H. Corbett, "Rome and the Gauls 285-280 B.C.," *Historia: Zeitschrift für alte Geschichte* 20, no. 5 (1971): 656-64.

32. For strategic concerns of the period, I refer the reader to K. W. Meiklejohn, "Roman Strategy and Tactics from 509 to 202 B.C.," *Greece and Rome* 7, no. 21 (1938): 175-78; and Salmon, *Samnium and the Samnites*, 280-92.

33. On the militarism of Tarentum, see Arthur M. Eckstein, *Mediterranean Anarchy, Interstate War, and the Rise of Rome* (Berkeley: University of California Press, 2006),

147–58. For its relations with the Italiote League and Syracuse, see John W. Wonder, "The Italiote League: South Italian Alliances of the Fifth and Fourth Centuries BC," *Classical Antiquity* 31, no. 1 (2012): 128–51, esp. 147.

34. Dexter Hoyos, *Mastering the West* (Oxford: Oxford University Press, 2015), 21; Matthew Trundle, "Ancient Greek Mercenaries (664–250 BCE)," *History Compass* 3, no. 1 (2005).

35. H. H. Scullard, who views Rome as a defensively imperial power, similarly observes that Pyrrhus' campaign "demonstrated the rock-like solidarity of the Roman confederacy, against which Pyrrhus had flung his professional soldiers in vain, and it showed the whole Hellenistic world that the unknown barbarians of central Italy were in fact a great military and imperial state, with which Ptolemy II of Egypt now established diplomatic relations and *amicitia* (273)" (*A History of the Roman World* [London: Routledge, 1980], 144; see also 249–50). Some take a more cynical view of the Roman federation. See, for example, Henrik Mouritsen, *Italian Unification* (London: BICS Supplement 70, 1998).

36. Appian, *The Samnite History*, 8–12; Cassius Dio, 9.39–41; Diodorus Siculus, 22.1–10; Plutarch, *Pyrrhus*, 13–25; and Zonaras, 8.2–6 provide sources for Pyrrhus' Italian campaigns.

37. Interestingly, one line of reasoning that does not seem to play a role in Rome's accumulation of empire is interstate kinship as described in Sue Elwyn, "Interstate Kinship and Roman Foreign Policy," *Transactions of the American Philological Association* 123, no. 1 (1933): 261–86. The Roman apathy toward ethnic purity that manifested in the early years expanded as Rome accumulated its empire.

38. For an extended discussion of the Carthaginian constitution, see Serge Lancel, *Carthage* (Oxford: Blackwell, 1995), 114–21. See also Nigel Bagnall, *The Punic Wars* (New York: Thomas Dunne Books, 1990), 12–18; J. F. Lazenby, *The First Punic War* (Stanford, CA: Stanford University Press, 1996), 20–25; and J. F. Lazenby, *Hannibal's War* (Norman: University of Oklahoma Press, 1998), 4–6.

39. On the Carthaginian military, see Bagnall, *The Punic Wars*, 8–11; Adrian Keith Goldsworthy, *The Punic Wars* (London: Cassell, 2000), 30–36; Lazenby, *The First Punic War*, 26–30; and Lazenby, *Hannibal's War*, 14–17. The Gauls may have only fought naked or half naked during rituals, which makes sense given some Gallic warriors' use of chain mail. See Sage, *The Republican Roman Army*, 58–59.

40. Quoted in Cornell, *The Beginnings of Rome*, 170.

41. Richard Glover, "The Elephant in Ancient War," *Classical Journal* 39, no. 5 (1944): 255–56. Notable battles where Romans encountered elephants were Heraclea in 280 (Plutarch, *Pyrrhus*, 16; Zonaras, 8.3; Livy, epitome 13), Asculum in 279 (Plutarch, *Pyrrhus*, 21; Dionysius of Halicarnassus, 20.1–3; Zonaras, 8.5; Livy, epitome 13), Beneventum in 275 (Plutarch, *Pyrrhus*, 24; Dionysius of Halicarnassus, 20.10–11; Livy, epitome 14), Trebia in 218 (Polybius, 3.71–74; Livy, 21.54–56), Metaurus in 207 (Livy, 27.43–49; Polybius, 11.1–3), Zama in 202 (Polybius, 15.9–14; Livy, 30.32–35), and Magnesia in 190 (Livy, 37.37–44; Appian, *Syrian Wars*, 30–36).

Chapter 6. The Greatest Trial: Beating Your Betters at New Carthage

1. Fisher Ames, *Works of Fisher Ames* (Indianapolis, IN: Liberty Fund, 1983), 401.

2. Calvin Coolidge, *The Autobiography of Calvin Coolidge* (Plymouth, VT: Calvin Coolidge Memorial Foundation, 1989), 46.

3. John Peddie, *Hannibal's War* (Thrupp, UK: Sutton Publishing, 1997), 217-18.

4. On the bellicose nature of Carthage and its generals, see Arthur M. Eckstein, *Mediterranean Anarchy, Interstate War, and the Rise of Rome* (Berkeley: University of California Press, 2006), 158-80.

5. On the treaties between Rome and Carthage and who was responsible for violating them, see Dexter Hoyos, *Mastering the West* (Oxford: Oxford University Press, 2015), 19-20, 84-94; and John Serrati, "Neptune's Altars: The Treaties between Rome and Carthage (509-226 B.C.)," *Classical Quarterly* 56, no. 1 (2006): 113-34. Serrati takes a more critical stance against Rome, and Hoyos spreads the blame a little more evenly. On the brutality and belligerence of Carthage compared to Rome, see Eckstein, *Mediterranean Anarchy, Interstate War, and the Rise of Rome*, 158-76.

6. Hoyos calculates that Hannibal kept 12,600 infantry and cavalry and 160 elephants in Spain under his brother's command. He began with ninety thousand men and thirty-seven elephants as an expeditionary force. Meanwhile, Carthage itself had a force of twenty thousand and a fleet of fifty-five warships defending North Africa (*Mastering the West*, 97-107).

7. Despite many modern criticisms of the Carthaginian home government for not sending reinforcements, Hannibal did not need men. He was able to secure enough men from his new Italian allies. From Carthage, he needed money, which it did on occasion supply. See Hoyos, *Mastering the West*, 132.

8. Meiklejohn calls Publius Scipio's decision to continue the war in Spain, thereby isolating Hannibal, "the most decisive move of the war" ("Roman Strategy and Tactics from 509 to 202 B.C. (Cont.)," *Greece and Rome* 8, no. 22 [1938]: 10).

9. On the context of the human carnage of Cannae in relation to the burial and memorialization of the troops, see Valerie M. Hope, "Trophies and Tombstones: Commemorating the Roman Soldier," *World Archaeology* 35, no. 1 (2003): 87-88.

10. Hannibal's obstacles with relation to loyal allies are surveyed in Hoyos, *Mastering the West*, 79, 131.

11. Victor Davis Hanson, *Carnage and Culture* (New York: Doubleday, 2001), 10, 11, 131.

12. For a comprehensive discussion of Roman manpower during the Hannibalic war, see P. A. Brunt, *Italian Manpower* (Oxford: Clarendon Press, 1987), 416-22. See also, Peddie, *Hannibal's War*, 122; and H. H. Scullard, *A History of the Roman World* (London: Routledge, 1980), 207.

13. For more, see Andreola Rossi, "Parallel Lives: Hannibal and Scipio in Livy's Third Decade," *Transactions of the American Philological Association* 134, no. 2 (2004): 359-81.

14. On the funeral mound, see John Patterson, "Living and Dying in the City of Rome: Houses and Tombs," in *Ancient Rome: The Archaeology of the Eternal City*, ed. Jon

Coulston and Hazel Dodge (Oxford: Oxford University School of Archaeology, 2011), 264-65; and G. K. Tipps, "The Rogum Scipionis and Gnaeus Scipio's Last Stand," *Classical World* 85, no. 2 (1991): 81-90. On the Scipio brothers' generalship and independence in Spain, see Arthur M. Eckstein, *Senate and General: Individual Decision Making and Roman Foreign Relations, 264-194 B.C.* (Berkeley: University of California Press, 1987), 187-207.

15. Hasdrubal Barca eventually did cross the Alps in the manner of his brother, but he was decisively defeated by the surprise combination of the consular armies of Claudius Nero and M. Livius Salinator at the Metaurus River (Livy, 27.43-49; Polybius, 11.1-3; Zonaras, 9.9). On the success of the Scipios, see Eckstein, *Senate and General*, 207.

16. On the Roman masks, I refer the reader to J. C. Rolfe, *The War with Jugurtha*, in *Sallust* (Cambridge, MA: Harvard University Press, 2002), 138-39n1: "A Roman had the right to make waxen masks of those of his ancestors who had held a curule office (consul, praetor, censor, or curule aedile) and keep them in the atrium of his house. They were worn in funerals of members of the family by actors who impersonated the dead, and were exhibited on other solemn occasions." The Barberini statue in the Capitoline Museum, Rome, of a Roman patrician carrying two waxen busts of his ancestors gives evidence of this practice. For their use in funerals, see Harriet I. Flower, "Spectacle and Political Culture in the Roman Republic," in *The Cambridge Companion to the Roman Republic*, ed. Harriet I. Flower (Cambridge: Cambridge University Press, 2004), 331, 334-37.

17. Flower, "Spectacle and Political Culture in the Roman Republic," 336-37.

18. Robert Turcan, *The Gods of Ancient Rome* (Edinburgh: Edinburgh University Press, 2000), 15-18. See also the older description of the ancestral hearth in Numa Denil Fustel De Coulanges, *The Ancient City* (Mineola, NY: Dover, 2006), 25-27, 94-100.

19. Whether this religious conviction on the part of Scipio was genuine or not is a debate even in the histories of Polybius and Livy. For a discussion, see Patrick Kragelund, "Dreams, Religion and Politics in Republican Rome," *Historia: Zeitschrift für alte Geschichte* 50, no. 1 (2001): 81-86.

20. On the general nature of classical prebattle orations and the like, see Edward Anson, "The General's Pre-Battle Exhortation in Graeco-Roman Warfare," *Greece and Rome* 57, no. 2 (Oct. 2010): 304-18.

21. See, for example, Polybius' subsection on the generalship and character of Scipio, which follows that of Hannibal (9.22-26, 10.2-5). Livy's speech for Scipio includes more than the speech Polybius provides. For more on Livy's practice of inserting rhetorical flourishes, see P. G. Walsh, *Livy* (Cambridge: University Press, 1961), 219-44.

22. Edward E. Best Jr., "The Literate Roman Soldier," *Classical Journal* 62, no. 3 (1966): 122-27; William Stuart Messer, "Mutiny in the Roman Army," *Classical Philology* 15, no. 2 (1920): 158-75; Stephen P. Oakley, "Single Combat in the Roman Republic," *Classical Quarterly* 35, no. 2 (1985): 392-410.

23. For descriptions and depictions of the bay, see Adrian Keith Goldsworthy, *The Punic Wars* (London: Cassell, 2000), 272; Benedict J. Lowe, "Polybius 10.10.12 and the Existence of Salt-Flats at Carthago Nova," *Phoenix* 54, nos. 1-2 (2000): 42; and F. W. Wal-

bank, *A Historical Commentary on Polybius*, 3 vols. (Oxford: Oxford University Press, 1957-79), 2:206.

24. For an analysis of the varying scientific positions, see Lowe, "Polybius 10.10.12 and the Existence of Salt-Flats at Carthago Nova"; Dexter Hoyos, "Sluice-Gates or Neptune at New Carthage, 209 B.C.?," *Historia: Zeitschrift fur alte Geschichte* 41, no. 1 (1992), 124-28; and M. J. Walker et al., "On Polybius X.10.12 f.: The Capture of New Carthage," *Historia: Zeitschrift fur alte Geschichte* 37, no. 4 (1988): 477-80.

25. Patrick Kragelund, "Dreams, Religion and Politics in Republican Rome," *Historia: Zeitschrift fur alte Geschichte* 50, no. 1 (2001): 81-86.

26. On the positioning of the men in the citadel, which lay to the west, see Walbank, *A Historical Commentary on Polybius*, 2: 213-14.

27. Adam Ziolkowski, "Urbs Direpta: or How the Romans Sacked Cities," in *War and Society in the Roman World*, ed. John Rich and Graham Shipley (London: Routledge, 1993), 69-91. On the brutality of sacking among other ancient states, see Eckstein, *Mediterranean Anarchy, Interstate War, and the Rise of Rome*, 202-5.

28. Polybius likewise discusses such ceremonies in his treatment on the Roman army (6.39).

29. Oakley, "Single Combat in the Roman Republic," 397.

30. Oakley, "Single Combat in the Roman Republic," 404; Messer, "Mutiny in the Roman Army," 162.

31. Meiklejohn, "Roman Strategy and Tactics from 509 to 202 B. C. (Cont.)," 12.

32. For Scipio's victories in Spain, see the Battle of Baecula in 208 (Polybius, 10.38-39; Livy, 27.18), the Battle of Carmone in 207—which may be identical to Ilipa—(Appian, *Spanish Wars*, 25-27), the Battle of Ilipa in 207 (Polybius 11.20-24; Livy, 28.12), the Battle of Astapa in 206 (Livy, 28.28), and the Battle of Carteia in 206, won by Laelius (Livy, 28.30). On Scipio's campaigns and freedom of action in Spain and Africa, see Eckstein, *Senate and General*, 209-67.

33. Livy's account is confusing and has been brought into question. A thorough review of the evidence is found in Brunt, *Italian Manpower*, 393 and appendix 22, esp. 655-57. See also the recent discussion in Hoyos, *Mastering the West*, 198-99.

34. The story of Scipio's exile was debated even when Livy was writing his histories, but the story says a great deal about the successful republican. A member of the *nobiles* should not outpace his colleagues too far. For discussion of the exile, especially the view of Livy and Seneca, see Alain M. Gowing, *Empire and Memory* (Cambridge: Cambridge University Press, 2005), 80-81.

Chapter 7. Triumph: Phalanx Killers at Pydna

1. Francis Fukuyama, "The End of History?," *National Interest* 16 (1989): 3-18.

2. On the lead-up to Roman intervention in Greece, see the survey in Eric S. Gruen, "Rome and the Greek World," in *The Cambridge Companion to the Roman Republic*, ed. Harriet I. Flower (Cambridge: Cambridge University Press, 2004), 242-54. For a recent take on Rome's expansion abroad that is extremely critical of its intervention in Greece,

see Robin Waterfield, *Taken at the Flood* (Oxford: Oxford University Press, 2014). Mary Beard's and Anthony Everitt's recent works take a more balanced view; see *SPQR* (New York: Liveright, 2015) and *The Rise of Rome* (New York: Random House, 2012), respectively. Arthur Eckstein sufficiently neutralizes the notion that Macedon and the Greek city-states were innocent victims of Roman aggression. Instead, they were equally aggressive but less successful on offensive fronts than their Roman counterparts (*Mediterranean Anarchy, Interstate War, and the Rise of Rome* [Berkeley, CA: University of California Press, 2006], chaps. 4, 7).

3. The older view of a more peaceful, defensive imperialism is best articulated in Tenney Frank, *Roman Imperialism* (New York: Macmillan, 1914). William V. Harris' classic *War and Imperialism in Republican Rome* (Oxford: Oxford University Press, 1979) reshapes the debate. A good survey of the views can be found in Eckstein, *Mediterranean Anarchy, Interstate War, and the Rise of Rome*, 1–11, 181–243. See also, for example, E. Badian, *Roman Imperialism in the Late Republic* (Ithaca, NY: Cornell University Press, 1968); Kurt A. Raaflaub, "Born to Be Wolves: Origins of Roman Imperialism," in *Transitions to Empire: Essays in Greco-Roman History, 360–246 B.C., in Honor of E. Badian*, ed. Robert W. Wallace and Edward M. Harris (Norman: University of Oklahoma Press, 1996), 273–314; John Rich, "Fear, Greed, and Glory: The Causes of Roman War-making in the Middle Republic," in *War and Society in the Roman World*, ed. John Rich and Graham Shipley (London: Routledge, 1993), 38–68; and Nathan Rosenstein, "War and Peace, Fear and Reconciliation at Rome," in *War and Peace in the Ancient World*, ed. Kurt A. Raaflaub (Oxford, UK: Blackwell Publishing, 2007), 226–44. For the ancient authors on the subject, see Ryan Balot, "Polybius' Advice to the Imperial Republic," *Political Theory* 38, no. 4 (2010): 483–509; and Miriam T. Griffin, "Iure Plectimur: The Roman Critique of Roman Imperialism," in *East and West*, ed. T. Corey Brennan and Harriet I. Flower (Cambridge, MA: Harvard University Press, 2008), 85–111. For a specific examination of Roman imperialism related to the Greek East, see Craige B. Champion, "Empire by Invitation: Greek Political Strategies and Roman Imperial Interventions in the Second Century B.C.E.," *Transactions of the American Philological Association* 137, no. 2 (2007): 255–75; and Waterfield, *Taken at the Flood*.

4. Gruen, "Rome and the Greek World," 246.

5. For a summary of these events, see John Drogo Montagu, *Battles of the Greek and Roman Worlds* (London: Greenhill Books, 2000), 133–34.

6. Livy presents a normal election process and even records the continued use of the lot for Paullus (45.17). Plutarch may have invented the exception, but if so, the Romans were certainly enjoying a large measure of good fortune. Plutarch and Livy could also both be right if the lots were "fixed," which was not unheard of in Roman politics.

7. For a detailed examination of the geography involved in the battle, see N. G. L. Hammond, "The Battle of Pydna," *Journal of Hellenic Studies* 104, no. 1 (1984): 31–47; and F. W. Walbank, *A Historical Commentary on Polybius*, 3 vols. (Oxford: Oxford University Press, 1957–79), 3:382–85.

8. N. G. L. Hammond, *The Macedonian State* (Oxford, UK: Clarendon Press, 1989), 382–86; Waterfield, *Taken at the Flood*, 160. On the Macedonian army, see Duncan Head,

Armies of the Macedonian and Punic Wars (Goring-by-Sea, UK: WRG Publication, 1982), 11-12, 45-51; and Nicholas Sekunda, *Macedonian Armies after Alexander* (Botley, UK: Osprey, 2012).

9. Head, *Armies of the Macedonian and Punic Wars*, 11-12.

10. Hammond, *The Macedonian State*, 386.

11. We have knowledge of the precise date in this instance because of the eclipse mentioned. See P. J. Bicknell, "The Lunar Eclipse of 21 June 168 B. C.," *Classical Review* 18, no. 1 (1968): 22. For the identification of Paullus' lieutenants and the chronology associated with his campaign, see O. P. Dany, "Livy and the Chronology of the Years 168-167," *Classical Quarterly* 50, no. 2 (2000): 432-39; Jerzy Linderski, "Roman Officers in the Year of Pydna," *American Journal of Philology* 111, no. 1 (1990): 53-71; Stewart Irvin Oost, "The Roman Calendar in the Year of Pydna (168 B.C.)," *Classical Philology* 48, no. 4 (1953): 217-30; and Walbank, *A Historical Commentary on Polybius*, 3:381.

12. In Plutarch's description, the explanation for the eclipse stems from Paullus' own knowledge, and the commanders' account of it follows its occurrence (*Aemilius Paulus*, 18).

13. Like Hammond ("The Battle of Pydna," 44-45), I find Livy's portrayal of the beginning of the battle as accidental more convincing than Plutarch's version, where Paullus sets loose a horse in order to bring on the battle. On the final formations, see Walbank, *A Historical Commentary on Polybius*, 3:388.

14. See, for example, Polybius' comparison of the phalanx and the manipular legion in 13.28-32. For depiction and description, see John Gibson Warry, *Warfare in the Classical World* (Norman: University of Oklahoma Press, 1995), 72-97.

15. How many feet were between each man in the maniple is the subject of debate; some argue for three, but six seems much more likely. See Nathan Rosenstein, "Armies of the Roman Republic," in *The Ancient World at War*, ed. Philip de Souza (London: Thames and Hudson, 2008), 143; and Michael M. Sage, *The Republican Roman Army* (New York: Routledge, 2008), 85-87.

16. The Pelignian effort could have occurred during the escalating skirmishing before the battle fully commenced or during the early stages of the battle. The lacuna in Livy 44.40-41 surely described the event.

17. For details on Rome's complex management of its new eastern empire and its gradual incorporation of other eastern states, see the exhaustive treatment by A. N. Sherwin-White, *Roman Foreign Policy in the East* (Norman: University of Oklahoma Press, 1983).

18. The friezes also portray some (possibly) Ligurian infantry involved in the initial skirmish. The friezes are currently located in the Archaeological Museum of Delphi. A photograph of them is included in Harriet I. Flower, "Spectacle and Political Culture in the Roman Republic," in *The Cambridge Companion to the Roman Republic*, 332-33.

19. J. J. Pollitt, *The Art of Rome* (Cambridge: Cambridge University Press, 1983), 44-45.

20. The triumph has been covered in numerous works. See, for example, Flower, "Spectacle and Political Culture in the Roman Republic," 328-31; and Miriam R. Pelikan Pittenger, *Contested Triumphs* (Berkeley: University of California Press, 2008), 246-74.

21. Karl-J. Hölkeskamp, *Reconstructing the Roman Republic* (Princeton, NJ: Princeton University Press, 2010), 86.

22. Flower, "Spectacle and Political Culture in the Roman Republic," 331–34.

23. Flower, "Spectacle and Political Culture in the Roman Republic," 335.

Chapter 8. Questionable Legitimacy: The Ideal Statesman's Battle at Mutina

1. Thomas P. Govan, "Alexander Hamilton and Julius Caesar: A Note on the Use of Historical Evidence," *William and Mary Quarterly* 32, no. 3 (1975): 475–80.

2. I have argued this elsewhere; see "Republican Warfare: The Life and Thought of Cicero," in *Philosophers on War*, ed. Eric Patterson and Timothy J. Demy (Silverton, OR: Stone Tower Books, 2017), 63–80.

3. On the debate surrounding the Scipionic Circle, see A. E. Astin, *Scipio Aemilianus* (Oxford, UK: Clarendon Press, 1967), 298–306.

4. For the ancient and modern discussions about Aemilianus' death, see Astin, *Scipio Aemilianus*, 239–41.

5. As I note in chapter 2, an example of this contrast in opinion can be seen between Gruen and Flower. See Harriet I. Flower, *Roman Republics* (Princeton, NJ: Princeton University Press, 2010); and Eric S. Gruen, *The Last Generation of the Roman Republic* (Berkeley: University of California Press, 1974).

6. On *The Dream of Scipio*, see Jed W. Atkins, *Cicero on Politics and the Limits of Reason* (Cambridge: Cambridge University Press, 2013), 47–79; Dean Hammer, *Roman Political Thought* (Cambridge: Cambridge University Press, 2014), 76–79; J. G. F. Powell, "Cicero's *De Re Publica* and the Virtues of the Statesman," in *Cicero's Practical Philosophy*, ed. Walter Nicgorski (Notre Dame, IN: University of Notre Dame Press, 2012), 37–38; John A. Stevens, *M. Tulli Ciceronis somnium Scipionis* (Bryn Mawr, PA: Bryn Mawr Commentaries, 2002); and Neal Wood, *Cicero's Social and Political Thought* (Berkeley: University of California Press, 1991), 65–66.

7. This is a hotly debated topic. See P. A. Brunt, *Italian Manpower* (Oxford: Clarendon Press, 1987), 121–30; Nathan Rosenstein, *Rome at War: Farms, Families, and Death in the Middle Republic* (Chapel Hill: University of North Carolina Press, 2004), 171–73; and Walter Scheidel, "Human Mobility in Roman Italy: The Slave Population," pt. 2, *Journal of Roman Studies* 95 (2005).

8. For a recent survey of their reforms, see Klaus Bringmann, *A History of the Roman Republic* (Cambridge, UK: Polity, 2007), 136–67; and Christopher S. Mackay, *The Breakdown of the Roman Republic* (Cambridge: Cambridge University Press, 2009), 30–83.

9. For a discussion of the speech, see Lawrence Keppie, *The Making of the Roman Army* (New York: Barnes and Noble Books, 1994), 53–54; and Michael M. Sage, *The Republican Roman Army* (New York: Routledge, 2008), 108–9.

10. This argument is eloquently presented in Rosenstein, *Rome at War*. For an archaeological approach to the agrarian question, see D. W. Rathbone, "The Development of Agriculture in the 'Ager Cosanus' during the Roman Republic: Problems of Evidence and Interpretation," *Journal of Roman Studies* 71 (1981): 10–23.

11. For more on the Marian reforms, see, for example, Adrian Keith Goldsworthy, *The Complete Roman Army* (New York: Thames and Hudson, 2003), 46–49; Keppie, *The Making of the Roman Army*, 57–79; Chris McNab, ed., *The Roman Army: The Greatest War Machine of the Ancient World* (Botley, UK: Osprey, 2010), 85–96; Sage, *The Republican Roman Army*, 199–288; Antonio Santosuosso, *Storming the Heavens* (Boulder, CO: Westview Press, 2001), 1–21; and John Gibson Warry, *Warfare in the Classical World* (Norman: University of Oklahoma Press, 1995), 130–43.

12. Brunt, *Italian Manpower*, 406. Mackay, by contrast, argues that "the crisis of military recruitment would become intolerable, and this would lead to the adoption of new form[s] of conscription that had ominous consequences for the Republican form of government" (*The Breakdown of the Roman Republic*, 84; see also 97).

13. Brunt, *Italian Manpower*, 408.

14. For a discussion of the census reductions, see Emilio Gabba, *Republican Rome, the Army and the Allies* (Oxford, UK: Basil Blackwell, 1976), 1–19; and Keppie, *The Making of the Roman Army*, 61–63.

15. Brunt, *Italian Manpower*, 403.

16. See the discussion in Gruen, *The Last Generation of the Roman Republic*, 370–71.

17. Keppie, *The Making of the Roman Army*, 55; Brunt, *Italian Manpower*, 392. Brunt traces the financial incentives for campaigns and distributions from commanders (*Italian Manpower*, 392–96).

18. These and other numerous examples are discussed at length in Brunt, *Italian Manpower*, 396–99. See also Gruen, *The Last Generation of the Roman Republic*, 366–68.

19. Brunt, *Italian Manpower*, 399–402; Gruen, *The Last Generation of the Roman Republic*, 379. Recall that Rosenstein (*Rome at War*) holds the opposite view, that overpopulated rather than underpopulated farms caused the decline in smallholders.

20. Gruen provides Petreius' biography and that of other military men in *The Last Generation of the Roman Republic*, 379–83.

21. Goldsworthy and McNabb, for example, see the emergence of Roman professionalism sometime in the first century, with a truly "professional" army definitely established sometime in the principate in Goldsworthy, *The Complete Roman Army*, 440–41; and McNab, *The Roman Army*, 80–81. Keppie argues along the same lines as this study, that the late republican army was becoming professionalized, but the real break occurred with the institutional reforms of Augustus (Keppie, *The Making of the Roman Army*, 51–52).

22. This term, used by Rahe regarding Greece, applies to Rome as well. See Paul Anthony Rahe, "The Martial Republics of Classical Greece," *Wilson Quarterly* 17, no. 1 (1993): 58–71.

23. Gruen holds the same view; see *The Last Generation of the Roman Republic*, 366–73.

24. Gruen, *The Last Generation of the Roman Republic*, 368–69, 74–78.

25. Brunt, *Italian Manpower*, 409–15, 511–12.

26. This sentiment is found in *Friends*, 4.9.3. See my "Republican Warfare" and also Jonathan Zarecki, *Cicero's Ideal Statesman* (London: Bloomsbury, 2015), 105.

27. Andrew Lintott examines the place of the Gracchi in the broader role of violence

in Roman political and legal matters in *Violence in Republican Rome* (Oxford: Oxford University Press, 1999). Appian clearly places the beginning of Rome's internal destruction here; see the introduction to book 1 of *Civil Wars*.

28. Lintott, *Violence in Republican Rome*, 175-77.

29. For a discussion of these proposals within the broader context, see Bringmann, *A History of the Roman Republic*, 178-85; Mackay, *The Breakdown of the Roman Republic*, 122-23; and H. H. Scullard, *From the Gracchi to Nero* (London: Routledge, 1988), 62-65.

30. David J. Bederman, *International Law in Antiquity* (Cambridge: Cambridge University Press, 2001), 45; Scott Gordon, *Controlling the State* (Cambridge, MA: Harvard University Press, 1999), 90-94; H. H. Scullard, *A History of the Roman World* (London: Routledge, 1980), 322-23.

31. The argument that the Social War was primarily motivated by political aims is expounded by Arthur Keaveney, *Rome and the Unification of Italy* (Exeter, UK: Bristol Phoenix Press, 2005). See also Flower's take that this was essentially a political revolution in *Roman Republics*, 110-11.

32. For an extended discussion of the coins, see Keaveney, *Rome and the Unification of Italy*, 52, 57-58, 123-25.

33. Mackay discusses the numbers in *The Breakdown of the Roman Republic*, 188.

34. A good interpretation of these events in relation to changes in war and society can be found in Erik Hildinger, *Swords against the Senate* (Cambridge, MA: Da Capo Press, 2002). For a standard interpretation along the lines that the army was becoming increasingly rapacious, see Santosuosso, *Storming the Heavens*, 29-43.

35. Mackay, *The Breakdown of the Roman Republic*, 191.

36. Gruen, *The Last Generation of the Roman Republic*, 6-12; Flower, *Roman Republics*, 117-34; and Mackay, *The Breakdown of the Roman Republic*, 188-95, each offer very different takes of these reforms, along with an extensive overview. These three works give one a flavor of the scholarly disputes over Sulla's constitution, and over the question of whether it was doomed from the start. Flower holds that Sulla's constitution was part and parcel of "the shipwreck" of the last great republican phase of Rome; that is, the republic was already done for by the time Sulla enacted the reforms. Mackay argues that the constitution was a well-meaning attempt to salvage the republic but that it was doomed from the start by Sulla's methods. Gruen, who I find convincing on a number of points, believes that this constitution generally held together until Caesar crossed the Rubicon. Caesar's unintentional destruction of it was neither foreseeable nor inevitable.

37. An interpretation of these events in this light is found in Gruen, *The Last Generation of the Roman Republic*, 12-46. Again, Flower and Mackay represent those scholars that would disagree on many points.

38. For a discussion of the laws, see Mackay, *The Breakdown of the Roman Republic*, 215-16.

39. Pompey's triumphs are discussed in Mary Beard, *The Roman Triumph* (Cambridge, MA: Belknap Press of Harvard University Press, 2007), 7-41.

40. For more on this alliance as part of the broader political functioning of the republic, see Gruen, *The Last Generation of the Roman Republic*, 47-120.

41. The instigator of the exile was a political enemy of Cicero, the brilliant, unpredictable, and somewhat mad tribune Publius Clodius Pulcher. Clodius had wanted Cicero exiled earlier, but Caesar and Pompey restrained him until Cicero rejected them. For more on the exile, see Anthony Everitt, *Cicero* (New York: Random House, 2001), 113–45; and Kathryn Tempest, *Cicero* (London: Bloomsbury, 2014), 113–24.

42. These "alliances and alignments" are meticulously laid out in Gruen, *The Last Generation of the Roman Republic*, 47–120.

43. Caesar's Gallic Wars have drawn a great deal of attention from classicists and military historians. See, for example, Kate Gilliver, *Caesar's Gallic Wars* (Botley, UK: Osprey, 2002); McNab, *The Roman Army*, 97–121; John Sadler and Rosie Serdiville, *Caesar's Greatest Victory* (Havertown, PA: Casemate, 2016); Santosuosso, *Storming the Heavens*, 57–80; and Keppie, *The Making of the Roman Army*, 80–102.

44. This data is discussed in Keppie, *The Making of the Roman Army*, 96–100.

45. Mackay, *The Breakdown of the Roman Republic*, 261.

46. See, for instance, Mackay, *The Breakdown of the Roman Republic*, 250–51, 62, 89.

47. For a discussion of Cicero's shift, see Tempest, *Cicero*, 133–37.

48. Cicero's life from this period is colorfully depicted in his letters. It is also surveyed in Everitt, *Cicero*, 146–77; and Tempest, *Cicero*, 125–50.

49. See Jeffrey W. Tatum, "The Final Crisis (69–44)," in *A Companion to the Roman Republic*, ed. Nathan Rosenstein and Robert Morstein-Marx (Oxford: Wiley-Blackwell, 2010), 207. See also Paul Erdkamp, "Army and Society," in *A Companion to the Roman Republic*, 290–95.

50. Zarecki, *Cicero's Ideal Statesman*, 82.

51. On the law, see Gruen, *The Last Generation of the Roman Republic*, 456–60; and Mackay, *The Breakdown of the Roman Republic*, 278–79.

52. The legal arguments regarding the descent into civil war have filled many a page. They are summarized in Gruen, *The Last Generation of the Roman Republic*, 449–97; and Mackay, *The Breakdown of the Roman Republic*, 279–88.

53. Mackay, *The Breakdown of the Roman Republic*, 289–90.

54. These events are recounted in much greater detail in his letters. Helpful summaries of Cicero's involvement in them and of his thinking during this time can be found in Everitt, *Cicero*, 202–50; Tempest, *Cicero*, 161–78; and Zarecki, *Cicero's Ideal Statesman*, 102–12. Some argue that Pharsalus was the end of the republic; see, for example, Mackay, who argues that "the battle of Pharsalus can be taken as the deathblow of the Republic" (*The Breakdown of the Roman Republic*, 295).

55. True to his literary mannerisms, in his commentaries on the civil war, Caesar would malign Labienus for his treachery and double-dealing, despite the obvious inconsistency that in his commentaries on the Gallic Wars, he praises Labienus for his virtues. See Cicero, *Friends*, 146; Cicero, *Atticus*, 137; Dio, 41.4; and Plutarch, *Caesar*, 34.

56. On the debate, see Ronald Syme, "The Allegiance of Labienus," *Journal of Roman Studies* 28, no. 2 (1938): 113–25; and William Blake Tyrrell, "Labienus' Departure from Caesar in January 49 B.C.," *Historia: Zeitschrift für alte Geschichte* 21, no. 3 (1972): 424–40.

57. Tyrrell, "Labienus' Departure from Caesar in January 49 B.C.," 438.

58. Caesar's cultivation of his public image is explored in Zwi Yavetz, *Julius Caesar and His Public Image* (Ithaca, NY: Cornell University Press, 1983).

59. Gruen, *The Last Generation of the Roman Republic*, 491.

60. The unfortunate exception to this case is Antony, whose story was written by his two greatest enemies, first Cicero and then Octavian.

61. Mackay concludes as much, saying "the resumption of regular constitutional practice in Rome quickly proved to be impossible" (*The Breakdown of the Roman Republic*, 315).

62. Scholars had long taken measure of the years from 44 to 42 by focusing on the leaders. Helga Botermann was instrumental in refocusing attention on the troops. Her analysis only examines the period from Caesar's assassination to the formation of the second triumvirate, with her emphasizing the motives of the troops and the frequency of their influencing (or forcing) commanders' decisions. See *Die Soldaten und die römische Politik in der Zeit von Caesars Tod bis zur Begründung des Zweiten Triumvirats* (Munich: Beck, 1968).

63. These factions are described at greater length in Everitt, *Cicero*, 272–74; Mackay, *The Breakdown of the Roman Republic*, 315–27; and Tempest, *Cicero*, 183–84.

64. For the discussion of the provincial assignments, see T. Robert S. Broughton, *The Magistrates of the Roman Republic*, 3 vols. (Atlanta, GA: Scholars Press, 1984–86), 2:321.

65. For their activities as magistrates, see Broughton, *The Magistrates of the Roman Republic*, 2:315–57. Brief biographies of the commanders' lives can be found in *The Cambridge Dictionary of Classical Civilization* (2006) and *The Oxford Classical Dictionary* (1999).

66. These events and their sources are outlined in Broughton, *The Magistrates of the Roman Republic*, 2:315–34.

67. For a discussion of this, see Everitt, *Cicero*, 276–77.

68. Writing to Decimus Brutus, he later explained his break with Antony, saying, "I was always his friend until I saw him waging war upon the commonwealth not only without concealment but with relish" (*Friends*, 353).

69. On Octavian's manipulation of Caesar's assassination and deification, see Paul Zanker, *The Power of Images in the Age of Augustus* (Ann Arbor: University of Michigan Press, 1990), 34–35.

70. For more on the speech, see Tempest, *Cicero*, 186–90.

71. These included Gaius Cestus, Lucius Cornelius Cinna, Lucius Cornelius Lentulus, Lucius Marcius Philippus, and Marcus Vehilius.

72. Keppie, *The Making of the Roman Army*, 115.

73. This critical take begins with Plutarch's biography of Cicero, which, in standard Plutarch fashion, strips out the nuances of Cicero's story to provide lessons from his life. Much of Plutarch's interpretation of Cicero is drawn into question by his correspondence, which I have followed more closely.

74. This view is eloquently argued in Zarecki, *Cicero's Ideal Statesman*, 145–54.

75. For Cicero's philosophical maturation in 44, especially with relation to his pre-

paring to engage in the manner of the ideal statesman, see Zarecki, *Cicero's Ideal Statesman*, 135–45.

76. For a summary and outline of individual *Philippics*, see the introductions in the Loeb Classical Library's two-volume edition. See also Tempest, *Cicero*, 186–200; and Zarecki, *Cicero's Ideal Statesman*, 145–54.

77. Some of these speeches are described in Appian, *Civil Wars*, 3.50–60.

78. Zarecki, *Cicero's Ideal Statesman*, 148.

79. On the foils of Antony, see Zarecki, *Cicero's Ideal Statesman*, 148.

80. Appian puts a fanciful spin on these events in his *Civil Wars*, 3.66. See also Everitt, *Cicero*, 301.

81. On this view, see Zarecki, *Cicero's Ideal Statesman*, 154.

82. His correspondence with them would repeat these themes. See *Friends*, 363, 365, 366, 367, 376.

83. This is laid out in Brunt, *Italian Manpower*, 480–83.

84. The details of the dispatch are found in Cicero's *Thirteenth Philippic*. For a discussion, see Everitt, *Cicero*, 304–5.

Chapter 9. Suicidal Finish: Last Stand of the Citizen-Soldier at Philippi

1. Noah Millman, "Obama's Ides of March: The Acting Company Production of *Julius Caesar*," *American Conservative*, 21 May 2012, www.theamericanconservative.com /shakesblog/obamas-ides-of-march; Corey Stoll, "What It Was Like to Star in the Trump-Themed *Julius Caesar*," *Vulture*, 23 June 2017, www.vulture.com/2017/06/what-it-was -like-to-star-in-the-trump-themed-julius-caesar.html.

2. Edith Balas, *Michelangelo's Medici Chapel* (Philadelphia: American Philosophical Society, 1995), 270; Charles Tolnay, "Michaelangelo's Bust of Brutus," *Burlington Magazine for Connoisseurs* 67, no. 388 (1935): 23–29.

3. Helga Botermann, *Die Soldaten und die römische Politik in der Zeit von Caesars Tod bis zur Begründung des Zweiten Triumvirats* (Munich: Beck, 1968), 196–97; P. A. Brunt, *Italian Manpower* (Oxford, UK: Clarendon Press, 1987), 483–84.

4. Christopher S. Mackay, *The Breakdown of the Roman Republic* (Cambridge: Cambridge University Press, 2009), 328–30; Kathryn Tempest, *Cicero* (London: Bloomsbury, 2014), 204.

5. The exploits that accompanied the proscriptions, from harrowing murders and betrayals to the flight of the proscribed, are described vividly in Appian, *Civil Wars*, 4.8–51.

6. This account comes from Seneca's *Suasoriae*; see Anthony Everitt, *Cicero* (New York: Random House, 2001), 318.

7. On the death accounts see Appian, *Civil Wars*, 4.19–20; Livy, *Fragments*, 120; and Plutarch, *Cicero*, 47–49.

8. Fergus Millar, *The Roman Republic and the Augustan Revolution* (Chapel Hill: University of North Carolina Press, 2002), 242.

9. This period is described as a "descent into warlordism" in Nathan Rosenstein and

Robert Morstein-Marx, "The Transformation of the Republic," in *A Companion to the Roman Republic*, ed. Nathan Rosenstein and Robert Morstein-Marx (Oxford: Wiley-Blackwell, 2010), 635.

10. For detailed summaries of Cassius' and Brutus' campaigns, see John Drogo Montagu, *Battles of the Greek and Roman Worlds* (London: Greenhill Books, 2000), 237–38; and Si Sheppard, *Philippi 42 BC* (Botley: Osprey, 2008), 38–46.

11. On these numbers, see the primary sources cited in the text and the discussion in Brunt, *Italian Manpower*, 486.

12. Sheppard, *Philippi 42 BC*, 40, 45.

13. Many of these were the legions mustered for the Parthian campaign. Brunt (*Italian Manpower*, 487) correctly follows Appian here (*Civil Wars*, 4.98, 133, 137). Compare with Dio, 47.38.

14. Sheppard, *Philippi 42 BC*, 26. The figures are derived from Brunt in *Italian Manpower*, 480–88. See also the discussion in Mackay, *The Breakdown of the Roman Republic*, 335.

15. At the close of 43, Appian tallies the legions divided by the three triumvirs; three were left for Lepidus in Italy and forty were available for the eastern campaign (*Civil Wars*, 4.2–3). Sheppard puts the numbers of men at arms between 216,000 and 270,000 Italians and the number of provincials between 48,000 and 60,000 (*Philippi 42 BC*, 26). Appian gives Brutus eight and Cassius nine legions, not including allied cavalry and other contingents (*Civil Wars*, 4.88, 108).

16. An excellent description of the opposing positions and orders of battle can be found in Sheppard, *Philippi 42 BC*, 50–54.

17. Plutarch stresses that Brutus should have only fought a campaign of attrition, but he is probably too much a slave to his parallel of Pompey here. Sheppard also argues against this point (*Philippi 42 BC*, 65–66).

18. Plutarch claims that Brutus' words and rewards were reassuring to Cassius' troops, but immediately after he describes the general grumbling of the troops and how that swayed him, leading him to make poor decisions. Whether the initial speech was encouraging or not does not change Plutarch's overall depiction of Brutus' poor command.

19. Mackay, *The Breakdown of the Roman Republic*, 335.

20. Plutarch provides a full account of his death in his biography of Cato. On Roman suicide, see Miriam T. Griffin, "Philosophy, Cato, and Roman Suicide," pt. 1. *Greece and Rome* 33, no. 1 (1986): 64–77; Miriam T. Griffin, "Philosophy, Cato, and Roman Suicide," pt. 2, *Greece and Rome* 33, no. 2 (1986): 192–202; and Yolande Grisé, *Le suicide dans la Rome antique* (Montreal: Bellarmin, 1982).

21. Lawrence Keppie, *The Making of the Roman Army* (New York: Barnes and Noble Books, 1994), 122.

Epilogue. War Stories for the Emperor

1. Portions of this section appeared in a heavily edited op-ed of mine that ran several times on foreignpolicy.com in 2016.

2. A fitting summary of Livy and his conservative motives can be found in P. G. Walsh, *Livy* (Cambridge: Cambridge University Press, 1961), 1-19.

3. This argument is summarized in Eric S. Gruen, *The Last Generation of the Roman Republic* (Berkeley: University of California Press, 1974), 498-507.

4. Adrian Keith Goldsworthy, *The Complete Roman Army* (New York: Thames and Hudson, 2003), 50. For a list of the legions, their formation, and their names, see Goldsworthy, *The Complete Roman Army*, 51. Lawrence Keppie traces how some late republican armies, especially under Caesar, Antony, and Octavian became permanent units; see *The Making of the Roman Army* (New York: Barnes and Noble Books, 1994), 199-215.

5. For treatments on the military structure of the early principate, see Goldsworthy, *The Complete Roman Army*, 50-59; Keppie, *The Making of the Roman Army*, 132-98; Chris McNab, *The Roman Army: The Greatest War Machine of the Ancient World* (Botley, UK: Osprey, 2010), 140-69; H. M. D. Parker, *The Roman Legions* (New York: Dorset Press, 1992), 72-92; Patricia Southern, *The Roman Army* (Gloucestershire, UK: Amberley, 2014), 72-92; Chester G. Starr, *The Roman Empire* (Oxford: Oxford University Press, 1982), 16-24, 109-31; G. R. Watson, *The Roman Soldier* (Ithaca, NY: Roman Soldier, 1969); Christopher S. Mackay, *The Breakdown of the Roman Republic* (Cambridge: Cambridge University Press, 2009), 386-96; and Antonio Santosuosso, *Storming the Heavens* (Boulder, CO: Westview Press, 2001), 91-166.

6. See also, for example, S. Valerius Severus in Ross Cowan, *Roman Battle Tactics 109 BC-AD 313* (Botley, UK: Osprey, 2007), 26; Ti. Flavius Miccalus in Nic Fields, *The Roman Army* (Botley, UK: Osprey, 2008), 16, 18; Monimus in Samuel Rocca, *The Army of Herod the Great* (Botley, UK: Osprey, 2009), 21; T. Flavius Bassus in Michael Simkins, *Warriors of Rome* (London: Blandford, 1988), 24; T. Calidius Severus in Duncan B. Campbell, *The Rise of Imperial Rome* (Botley, UK: Osprey, 2013), 22; M. Caelius and Anicius Ingenuus in Southern, *The Roman Army*, 11, 234; and Cn. Musius, C. Romanius, P. Flavoleius, and M. Billienus in Keppie, *The Making of the Roman Army*, 130. See also Lawrence Keppie, *Understanding Roman Inscriptions* (Baltimore, MD: Johns Hopkins University Press, 1991), 80-90. Goldsworthy features legionary tombs and gravestones throughout in *The Complete Roman Army*.

7. Santosuosso, *Storming the Heavens*, 90.

8. Paul Zanker, *The Power of Images in the Age of Augustus* (Ann Arbor: University of Michigan Press, 1990), 3-4.

Index

Actium, Battle of, 62, 96, 318

Adams, John, 3, 5, 9, 12, 45–46, 67, 68, 201, 328n4, 329n11, 332n10. *See also* founders, American

Aemilianus, Scipio. *See* Cornelius Scipio Aemilianus, Publius

Aemilius Lepidus, Marcus (died 77), 222, 223

Aemilius Lepidus, Marcus (triumvir): background, 238–39; Cicero and Antony court support from, 260, 268, 269, 270; commander of legions, 269, 272, 274, 278, 309, 316, 356n15; declared *hostis*, 271; foil of Antony, 254; after Ides of March, 234, 237, 239, 240, 241; joins Antony, 270–71; member of "second" triumvirate, 274, 275; partisan of Caesar, 230; stripped of power by Octavian, 311. *See also* triumvirate, "second"

Aemilius Paullus, Lucius (died 216), 203

Aemilius Paullus, Lucius (died 160), 4; elected consul for Macedonian campaign, 180–81, 348n6; as exemplar, 306, 314; funeral, 196–97; leadership qualities, 181–82; in Pydna campaign, 182–83, 184, 186–87, 190–91, 349n11; searches for son, 195; settles Macedonia, 193–94; as speaker in Cicero's *The Dream of Scipio*, 203; triumph and speech, 195–96

Aeneas, 75

Aequi (mountain tribesmen), 73; raids into Latium, 90–91; Roman strategy against, 96, 98

Africanus, Scipio. *See* Cornelius Scipio Africanus, Publius

Alalia, Battle of, 72

Alba Longa, 75, 77, 80

Alexander I of Epirus, 140

Alexander (the Great) of Macedon: as antimodel for Americans, 6; builder of empire with father, 177, 183; initiator of Greek mercenary culture with father Philip, 141; Livy's Alexander digression, 54–55; as paradigmatic victorious conqueror, 33, 53, 139, 140, 150, 153, 176, 226; successor kingdoms, ix, x, xvii, xviii, 70, 174. *See also* Macedonia; Philip II of Macedon

Allia River, Battle of the, 91, 93, 99–100, 111

allies: agitations for citizenship, 207, 217–18; at Battle of Philippi, 288; and Hannibal's attempts to win in Italy, 149, 150, 152, 153, 155, 345n7, 345n10; Italian allies' similarity to Romans, 33,

Tarquinius (Tarquin) Superbus, Lucius, 82, 84, 86, 90, 98, 172, 254, 292

temple, 26, 37, 92, 101–2, 138, 158, 286, 311, 340n33; Aphaia in Aegina, 119; Bellona, 124; Concordia, 36, 101; Janus, 79, 95, 96; Juno, 101; Jupiter on the Capitoline, 80, 81; Jupiter Victor, 136, 139, 343n30; manubial, 102; Sant'Omobono, 81; Saturn, 230; Victoria, 139. *See also* gods; religion

Terentius Varro, Gaius, 151, 174

Terentius Varro, Marcus, 27–28, 29, 30, 32, 53

Thucydides, 52, 56, 75

Ticinus River, Battle of, 150, 155, 156, 159

Tocqueville, Alexis de, 3

tomb, 71, 76, 123–24, 158, 318, 342n9, 357n6. *See also* funeral; grave

Tomb of the Scipios, 124, 318

touto, 74

training, 18–19, 30, 31, 33–34, 52, 94, 145, 173, 209, 213

Trebia River, Battle of the, 150, 155, 159

triarii, 110, 111, 113, 114, 189, 343n25

trireme, 21, 107

triumph, 81, 93, 102, 349n20; of Camillus, 100; of Paullus, 194, 195–96; of Pompeius Strabo, 239; of Pompey, 352n39; triumphs of Fabius, 131, 138–39

triumvirate, "first." *See* gang of three

triumvirate, "second" (alliance of Antony, Octavian, and Lepidus), 61, 62, 317; administration of Rome, 309–12, 354n62; first Battle of Philippi, 293–97; formation, 274, 275–77; Philippi campaign, 286–93; second Battle of Philippi, 297–304; as warlords, 279, 280, 285. *See also* Aemilius Lepidus, Marcus (triumvir); Antonius, Marcus; Octavius, Gaius; proscription

Troy, 75

Tullius, Servius, 82, 83–84, 111

Tullius Cicero, Marcus, xix, 9, 24, 69–70, 223–24, 265, 276–77, 317; during Antony-Octavian war, 245–51; exile, 227–30, 270–71; letters, 234, 235, 241, 244, 245; political career, 223–25, 241;

proscription and death, 276–77; on republics, 44, 63, 243; rhetoric, 247, 252, 254, 256, 270, 305–6, 310; on statesmen, 206–7, 229, 230, 232, 236, 242–43, 249; and trial of Catilina, 223–24; on war, 202–3, 214–25

Twelve Tables, 57, 62, 63, 90, 338n9. *See also* law

Umbrians, 91, 98, 120, 121, 125–26, 135, 139, 343n26. *See also* Sentinum, Battle of

United States, xi, xvi, 13, 48, 175, 322; army, 18–20; Capitol, 1–2, 119; government, xvi, 11, 67; wars, 322. *See also* citizen-soldier; *The Federalist Papers*; founders, American; government; republic: American; soldier: professional; soldier: soldier-citizen

Valerio-Horatian Law, 62, 90

Valley Forge, 17–18

Varro (author). *See* Terentius Varro, Marcus

Varro (commander at Cannae). *See* Terentius Varro, Gaius

Veii, 58, 72, 78, 90–91, 93, 97, 99–101, 111, 172

velites, 110

Ventidius Bassus, Publius, 237, 239, 269, 272

Venusia, 152

Vibius Pansa, Gaius, 214, 237, 240, 251, 278, 306, 317; at Battle of Mutina, 254, 255, 256, 259, 260, 261, 262, 263, 264, 269. *See also* Mutina, Battle of

Virgil, 5, 26, 28, 29, 32, 70, 39

virtue: 24, 27, 28, 30, 36, 46, 122; agricultural, 26; military, 30; pastoral, 10–11, 13; patriotism, 4, 9, 24, 57, 138, 141, 206, 251, 313; piety, 4, 29, 32, 36, 55, 79, 125; public, 24. *See also* civic virtue; courage; justice

Volsci, 73, 90, 91, 93, 96, 98, 107

voting, 47–48, 105, 158, 185, 216, 321, 329n3. *See also* campaign: political; elections